Henry Beebee Carrington

Beacon Lights of Patriotism

Or, historic incentives to virtue and good citizenship. In prose and verse with notes.

Dedicated to American youth

Henry Beebee Carrington

Beacon Lights of Patriotism
Or, historic incentives to virtue and good citizenship. In prose and verse with notes. Dedicated to American youth

ISBN/EAN: 9783337308155

Printed in Europe, USA, Canada, Australia, Japan

Cover: Foto ©Suzi / pixelio.de

More available books at **www.hansebooks.com**

The pre-eminence of Washington suggests that his likeness, taken at different dates, be made central among "Beacon Lights." graphical Index for sketches of the artists above named.

BEACON LIGHTS

OF

PATRIOTISM;

OR,

HISTORIC INCENTIVES TO VIRTUE AND
GOOD CITIZENSHIP.

IN PROSE AND VERSE, WITH NOTES.

Dedicated to American Youth.

BY

HENRY B. CARRINGTON, U.S.A., LL.D.,

AUTHOR OF THE "BATTLES OF THE AMERICAN REVOLUTION," "INDIAN
OPERATIONS ON THE PLAINS," "CRISIS THOUGHTS," ETC., ETC.

"A nation's strength." — PSALM xxxiii.

SILVER, BURDETT AND COMPANY,
NEW YORK ... BOSTON ... CHICAGO.
1894.

PREFACE.

A SINCERE desire to contribute toward a higher grade of thought and sentiment among the youth of America has prompted the preparation of this volume.

Incentives to virtue and good citizenship have had expression in prose and verse, throughout human experience. The imagination and reason have been tasked to find words sufficiently terse, dramatic, and eloquent, by which to give to that expression a deep and abiding effect. Our own language has not failed to furnish the medium for a clear comprehension of all such literature and history. Themes so grand and inspiring find a quick response in the minds of youth. To re-fashion memorial utterances in simpler forms would only dishonor their source, and rob them of both beauty and value. Hence, a partial vocabulary of significant words has been added. Even this might seem needless, since even the News-boys on our streets announce, daily, the latest tidings from all foreign as well as domestic countries; and many youth know more of geography, current history, and political economy to-day than their fathers did at manhood's full maturity. Young America catches quickly the meaning even of "hard words," if inspired by motive. This volume seeks to minister to this real capacity and enterprise, and quicken the search after knowledge that will make him most useful and happy.

All passionate utterances of the periods when brethren were temporarily estranged, are excluded; but all material has been welcomed which breathes the spirit of genuine

American independence, intelligent liberty, right obligation, and the Union restored.

The theory of the compilation has rested upon three simple ideas.

First, — Human history is a Unit; and all events bear relations, B. C. or A. D., and illustrate corresponding thought and action. Hence, Hebrew, Roman, Grecian, and all other records are invited to testify of the universal trend of patriotic aspiration, and of one invariably constant factor, — that of the recognition of one Supreme Creator, Benefactor, and Guide.

Second, — Home must stand as the nursery of those pure emotions which expand into patriotic exercise; so that the domestic affections and true patriotism must develop exactly in proportion as home is honored, and responsibility to one Almighty Father enters into the mastery of individual life.

Third, — Peace is the essential condition of rational happiness; and permanent honors belong only to heroes, who, like Joshua, Gideon, and our own Washington, have made war tributary to peace, refusing all transitory rewards of personal aggrandizement and power.

Acknowledgments of hearty co-operative sympathy and endeavor are elsewhere tendered. A sense of responsibility for impressions sought to be made, inspires the hope that this contribution to the patriotic sentiment of the times will be accepted in the spirit of its preparation, and be attended with the divine blessing.

Henry B. Carrington

HYDE PARK, MASS., May 30, 1894.

CONTENTS.

PART I.

PATRIOTIC BEGINNINGS.

			PAGE
	INTRODUCTION	Editor	15
1.	SEEKING A COUNTRY	Editor	17
2.	THE EXILES IN EGYPT	Editor	19
3.	A PEOPLE DELIVERED	Cunningham Geikie	21
4.	THE FIRST CONSTITUTION	Book of Moses (chap. xx.)	24
5.	THE FIRST CIVIL CODE	Selections from Deuteronomy	25
6.	THE HEBREW CODES D...		
	...	New Testament Records	28
			28
7.	...	Horace Lorenzo Hastings	29
8.	BURIAL OF ...	Mrs. Cecil F. Alexander	30
9.	NO MAN KNOWETH HIS SE-CHRE	William Cullen Bryant	31
10.	JOSHUA, THE PATRIOT GEN...	Cunningham Geikie	32
11.	RUTH AND NAOMI	William B. O. Peabody	35
12.	DAVID, THE PATRIOT KING	Editor	36
13.	THE PATRIOT KING IN MO... ING	Nathaniel Parker Willis	38
14.	SAUL AND JONATHAN	Book II. Samuel (chap i.)	40
15.	SOLOMON, THE WISE KING	Book of Proverbs	41
16.	THE HEBREW CAPITAL ... FOILED	Bishop Reginald Heber	42
17.	THE DESPOILER DOOMED	...k of Isaiah (chap. xiii.–xiv.)	43
18.	THE HEBREW MINSTREL'S L... MENT	New England Magazine, 1832	45
19.	JERUSALEM AVENGED	Byron	46
20.	A NATION'S STRENGTH	Psalm xxxiii.	47
21.	THE PATRIOT'S CRY	Psalm cxxxvii. (a paraphrase)	48

PART II.

OLD ROME AND HER RIVALS.

1.	HORATIUS AT THE BRIDGE	Thomas Babington Macaulay	49
2.	REPRESENTATIVE GOVERNMENT	... Æmilius	51
3.	FABRICIUS REFUSES BRIBES		53
4.	VINDICATION OF VIRGINIUS	Kellogg	54
5.	REGULUS BEFORE THE ROMAN SENATE	Epes Sargent	56
6.	SEPARATION FROM TRAITORS	Marcus Tullius Cicero	58

CONTENTS.

	The Law of Virtue (Apothegm)	Cicero	59
7.	Roman Liberty in Peril.	Publius Scipio . . .	60
	Self-respect (Apothegm) .	Cato	61
8.	Carthage in Peril . .	Hannibal	62
9.	Hannibal pleads for Peace	Translation from Livy	64
10.	Scipio declines Hannibal's Overtures for Peace . .	Scipio Africanus . .	65
11.	Caesar's Death justified .	Caius Cassius . . .	67
12.	The Degeneracy of Athens	Demosthenes	69
13.	Virtue uncorrupted by Fortune.	Quintus Curtius . . .	71
14.	Merit before Birth . . .	Caius Marius	72
15.	Prince Adherbal before the Roman Senate . . .	Sallust	74
16.	The Wail of Jugurtha . .	Charles Wolfe	76

PART III.

OUR FATHERS AN[D ...]

1.	Old England	. . . .	79
2.	Erin and the Days of Old	. . . .	80
3.	Our Relations with England	[Edward] Everett . . .	81
4.	New England	[James G]ates Percival . .	82
5.	England's Relations to America	[James] Mackintosh . . .	84
6.	New England and Virginia	[Robert] Charles Winthrop .	85
7.	Pilgrims of New England	[Ruf]us Choate	86
8.	The Puritan	[Thom]as Babington Macaulay .	88
9.	Fatherland	[Ernst] Moritz Arndt . . .	90
10.	The Fatherland	[Jam]es Russell Lowell . .	91
11.	We were Boys together	[Geor]ge P. Morris . . .	92
	Jonathan's Love for David (Apothegm)	[2 Sam]uel xviii. 1	92
12.	Father-land and Mother tongue	[Sam]uel Lover	93
13.	The Land of my Birth	[Ele]za Cook	94
	Our Own the Best (Apothegm)	[B]erne	94
14.	Rocks of my Country . .	Felicia Dorothea Hemans . .	95
15.	The House where I was Born	Thomas Hood	96
16.	At the Old Home again .	William Cullen Bryant . .	97
	Ancient Landmarks (Apothegm)	Proverbs xxii.	97
17.	Wedding March of Grief	Charles Wesley Johnson . .	98
18.	The Old Oaken Bucket	Samuel Woodworth . . .	100
19.	Woodman spare that Tree	George P. Morris	101
20.	The Old Home and the New	Robert Bleakie	102
21.	Our Gardener's Burial	London Spectator	102
22.	My Fatherland . . .	Hoffmann von Fallersleben .	104
23.	Home	Bernard Barton	104
24.	Home, Home, Sweet Home	John Howard Payne . . .	106
25.	Love of Country . . .	Sir Walter Scott	106

PART IV.

AMERICAN INDEPENDENCE.

1. SEVENTY-SIX	*William Cullen Bryant*	107
2. INDEPENDENCE DAY	*James Gillespie Blaine*	108
AMERICA AN AGGREGATE OF NATIONS (Apothegm)	*Martin Farquhar Tupper*	108
3. CAROLINA AND MECKLENBURG	*James A. Delke*	109
4. THE FOURTH OF JULY	*Daniel Webster*	110
5. THE FIRST AMERICAN CONGRESS	*Jonathan Maxcy*	112
HONOR THE FATHERS (Apothegm)	*Richard Henry Lee*	113
6. THE PRINCIPLES OF THE REVOLUTION	*Josiah Quincy*	114
7. THE LESSONS OF THE REVOLUTION	*Jared Sparks*	115
8. THE AMERICAN CONSTITUTION	*Alexander Hamilton*	116
THE PATRIOT'S LONGING DESIRE (Apothegm)	*Samuel Adams*	117
9. THE CONSTITUTION TESTED	*John Adams*	118
10. THE CONSTITUTION NO EXPERIMENT	*Hugh Swinton Legare*	119
CENSUS OF THE UNITED STATES FROM 1790 TO 1890		120

PART V.

WASHINGTON.

1. WASHINGTON'S TRAINING	*Charles Wentworth Upham*	121
2. THE UNSELFISHNESS OF WASHINGTON	*Robert Treat Paine*	123
3. A STAR IN THE WEST	*Eliza Cook*	125
4. WASHINGTON A MODEL FOR YOUTH	*Timothy Dwight*	126
5. WASHINGTON AS A LEADER	*John Pierpont*	127
6. WASHINGTON AS A SOLDIER[1]	*Henry B. Carrington*	129
7. MOUNT VERNON, THE HOME OF WASHINGTON	*William Day*	133
8. CROWN OUR WASHINGTON	*Hezekiah Butterworth*	134
9. GENERAL WASHINGTON'S RESIGNATION		135

From "North American Review."

PART VI.

INCENTIVES TO PATRIOTISM.

1. The True Grandeur of Nations	Charles Sumner	137
2. The Cost of Liberty	Henry Giles	138
3. No Peace without Liberty	Louis Kossuth	139
4. The People Triumphant	Edward Everett	140
5. American Nationality	Rufus Choate	141
6. Our Nationality	Thomas Starr King	143
7. Individual Purity the Hope of the State	Charles Sprague	144
Sincerity and Truth (Apothegm)	Montaigne	145
8. Christianity as a Political Force	John A. Dix	146
9. Reverence for Law	Joseph Hopkinson	147
10. The Ideal Citizen (From "Civics")	John Habberton	148
11. Liberty of the Press	Edward D. Baker	151
12. Idleness a Crime (From "Civics")	Henry B. Carrington	151
Poverty of the Soul (Apothegm)	Montesquieu	154
13. National Injustice	Theodore Parker	155
14. A Republic Defined	Alphonse de Lamartine	156
15. The Torch of Liberty	Thomas Moore	157
True Liberty (Apothegm)	Bruyere	158
16. America, Fairest of Freedom's Daughters	Jeremiah E. Rankin	159
17. The Great American Republic a Christian State	Cardinal James Gibbons	160
18. The Flower of Liberty	Oliver Wendell Holmes	163
19. Our Country	William J. Peabody	165
20. Patriots and Martyrs	Anonymous	166
21. The Richest Prince	Andreas Justinus Korner	167
22. Patriotic Song	John Gottfried Kinkel	168
23. No Slave beneath the Flag	George Lansing Taylor	169
24. Laus Deo	John Greenleaf Whittier	170
25. Our Heritage	James Russell Lowell	171
26. The Roman Senate and the American Congress	Louis Kossuth	173
27. The Patriot President	Mark Lemon ("London Punch")	174
28. The Patriotic Prince	Henry B. Carrington	175
29. Tubal Cain	Charles Mackay	178
30. Song of the Union	Jeremiah W. Cummings	179
31. Our Flag is There	Naval Officer, 1812	180

PART VII.

MEMORABLE BATTLE-FIELDS AND INCIDENTS.

1.	The Battle-field	William Cullen Bryant	181
2.	The Honored Dead	Henry Ward Beecher	182
3.	The Bivouac of the Dead	Theodore O'Hara	184
4.	The Review of the Dead	Henry Jerome Stockard	186
5.	Our Martyred Dead	Rev. Mark Trafton	188
6.	The Mourning Hero's Vision	Louis Kossuth	189
7.	The Soldier's Widow	Nathaniel Parker Willis	191
8.	Dirge for the Soldier	George H. Boker	192
9.	The Brave at Home	Thomas Buchanan Read	193
	The Noise of Arms (Apothegm)	Montaigne	193
10.	The Scourge of War	William Henry Burleigh	194
11.	True Glory	John Milton (in "Paradise Regained")	195
12.	The Warrior's Wreath	From "National Preceptor," Anon., 1835	196
13.	Might makes Right	From "National Preceptor," Anon., 1835	197
14.	The Reign of Peace	Eliza Thornton	198
15.	Bannockburn	Robert Burns	199
16.	Marathon by Starlight	Richard Montgomery	200
17.	Joan of Arc's Farewell to Home	Schiller	201
18.	Leonidas	George Croly	203
19.	Fall of the Indian Heroes	Joaquin Miller	204
20.	The Dying Trumpeter	Julius Moser	206
21.	Alamance	Seymour W. Whiting	206
22.	The Death of Osceola	Alfred Billings Street	207
23.	The Boy of Ratisbon	Robert Browning	209
24.	The Burial of Sir John Moore	Charles Wolfe	210
25.	The Battle of Linden	Thomas Campbell	212
26.	The Battle of Waterloo	Byron	213
27.	The Battle of Lexington	Mason L. Weems	214
28.	Bunker Hill	John Pierpont	216
29.	Valley Forge	Henry Armitt Brown	217
30.	The Storming of Monterey	Charles Fenno Hoffman	218
31.	Hightide at Gettysburg	Will H. Thompson	219
32.	Once at Battle Eve	Mary Hannah Krout	222
33.	To Thee, O Country!	Anna Philipine Eichberg	224

PART VIII.

EMPHATIC APPEALS TO DUTY.

1. The National Ensign	Robert Charles Winthrop	225
2. The Bended Bow	Felicia Dorothea Hemans	226
3. The Boston Massacre	John Hancock	227
4. Scorn to be Slaves	Joseph Warren	229
5. Warren's Supposed Address at Bunker Hill	John Pierpont	230
6. Patriotism	Thomas Francis Meagher	231
7. The March of Freedom	Theodore Parker	232
8. General Wolfe before Quebec	Wolfe	233
9. Address of Caradoc the Bard	Edward George Lytton Bulwer	234
10. Boadicea	Cowper	235
11. Let there be Light	Horace Mann	237
12. Gustavus, King of Sweden, to his Soldiers	Pierre François Lefevre	238
13. The Defiant Seminole Chief	G. William Patten	240
14. Plea of the Pocomtuc Chief	Edward Everett	241
15. Bonaparte to his Army, 1796	Translation from the French	242
16. Grattan's Appeal for Ireland	Henry Grattan	244
17. Freedom	James Russell Lowell	245
18. Dead on the Field of Honor	Joshua L. Chamberlain	246
19. Be Just and Fear Not	William Shakespeare	248
20. A Burlesque Challenge to America	Mark Lemon, from "London Punch"	249
21. Death or Liberty	Theodore Dwight Weld	251
22. Press On	Park Benjamin	253

PART IX.

HINTS TO YOUNG AMERICA.

1. Our Country	Epes Sargent	255
2. The Young American	Alexander Hill Everett	256
3. Getting the Right Start	Joseph Gilbert Holland	257
4. The Supremacy of Conscience	Richard Salter Storrs	259
5. The True Aspiration of Youth	James Montgomery	261
6. To Whom Honor be Due	From the German	261
Haste Not, Rest Not (Extract)	Goethe	262
7. True Liberty	Frederick William Robertson	263

8.	THE AGE OF WORK	John Pendleton Kennedy	264
9.	SUCCESS IN LIFE	George W. Childs	265
10.	CRITICAL CONDITIONS OF LABOR	Benjamin Harrison	268
11.	NO EXCELLENCE WITHOUT LABOR	William Wirt	272
12.	LABOR HOURS HAVE LIMITS	Thomas Babington Macaulay	274
	THE LAW OF LABOR (Apothegm)	From "Civics"	275
13.	TRUE NOBILITY	Charles Swain	276
14.	DON'T GIVE TOO MUCH FOR THE WHISTLE	Benjamin Franklin	277
15.	WHITTLING TYPICAL OF YOUNG AMERICA	John Pierpont	276
16.	THE ROAD TO HAPPINESS OPEN	Alexander Pope	280
17.	NOT TO MYSELF ALONE	J. Russell Webb	282
18.	THE MIGHTY WORD "NO"	Theodore D. Cuyler	283
	A PREVENTIVE "NO"	Proverbs of Solomon	285
19.	BETTER THAN GOLD	Alexander Smart	286
20.	WISDOM AND WEALTH	Khnemnitzer (Ivan Ivanovich)	287
21.	THE WORLD WOULD BE BETTER FOR IT	H. M. Cobb	288
22.	THE WORTH OF FAME	Joanna Baillie	289
23.	THE THREE W'S, — WORK, WATCH, WAIT	Henry B. Carrington	290
24.	HOW TO HAVE WHAT WE LIKE	Horace Smith	291
25.	WHAT MIGHT BE DONE	Anonymous	292
26.	HOW WE TAKE IT	Theodore D. C. Miller	293
	HOW TO TAKE IT (Apothegm)	Racine	294
27.	AS THY DAY THY STRENGTH SHALL BE	From "New York Churchman"	295
	ALL-SUFFICIENT STRENGTH (Apothegm)	Racine	295
28.	IF I WERE A VOICE	Charles Mackay	296
29.	LOOK NOT UPON THE WINE	Nathaniel Parker Willis	297
30.	THE ALCOHOLIC AND THE TOBACCO HABIT	Neal Dow	298

PART X.

AMERICAN INDEPENDENCE CONSUMMATED.

1.	PRESIDENT LINCOLN'S ADDRESS AT GETTYSBURG		299
2.	THE PATRIOT DEAD	Samuel Francis Smith	300
3.	THE GREAT QUESTION SETTLED	George William Curtis	301
4.	GETTYSBURG: A MECCA FOR THE BLUE AND GRAY	John B. Gordon	302
5.	NO CONFLICT NOW	Charles Devens	303
6.	SEPARATE AS BILLOWS, BUT ONE AS THE SEA	Alexander Stephens	304
7.	THE NINETEENTH CENTURY ENDS SLAVERY	J. Q. C. Lamar	305

8.	Again Brethren and Equals	James W. Patterson	306
9.	Our Banner Unrent: its Stars Unobscured	Lawrence S. Ross	307
10.	Belligerent Non-combatants	William Tecumseh Sherman	308
11.	Immortal Memories	George A. Sheridan	309
12.	Benefits of the Civil War	Charles M. Busbee	310
13.	Our Heroes	John Albion Andrew	312
14.	The Eve of Decoration Day	Samuel Francis Smith	313
15.	Ode for Decoration Day	S. Dryden Phelps	314
16.	Decoration Day	Henry Wadsworth Longfellow	316
17.	Abraham Lincoln	Bishop John P. Newman	317
18.	Death the Peacemaker	Ellen H. Flagg	320
19.	The Dawning Future	William Preston Johnson	322

PART XI.

SCHOOL-ROOM ECHOES AND HINTS.

1.	American Education	Robert Charles Winthrop	323
	Contentment (Apothegm from "Fairie Queen")	Edmund Spenser	324
2.	The School-teacher	Henry (Lord) Brougham	325
3.	Desirable Objects of Attainment	John Stoughton	326
4.	Self-sacrificing Ambition	Horace Greeley	327
	Soul Culture (Apothegm)	James Thomson	328
5.	The Public School-teacher in the Republic	George T. Balch	329
6.	Souls, Not Stations	Anonymous	332
	Immortality (Apothegm)	Sarah F. Smith	333
7.	What is Ambition?	Nathaniel Parker Willis	334
8.	The Orator described	Richard Brinsley Sheridan	335
9.	Procrastination	Edward Young	336
10.	A Petition to Time	Bryan Waller Procter	337
11.	To-morrow	Nathaniel Cotton	338
12.	The Great Good Man	Samuel Taylor Coleridge	339
	Goodness and Greatness (Apothegm)	Francis (Lord) Bacon	339
13.	True Eloquence	Daniel Webster	340
14.	The Christian Orator	Abel François Villemain	341
15.	A Good Name	Joel Hawes	342
	My Good Name (Apothegm)	Shakespeare	343
16.	The Philosopher's Scales	Jane Taylor	344
17.	The Hill of Science	John Aiken	345
18.	The Serpent of the Still	Milford Bard (John Lofland)	348
19.	Courage	Bryan Waller Procter	349
20.	The Sanctuary within the Breast	Horace Smith	350
	Ye are the Temple	Bible	350
21.	Deeds of Kindness	Epes Sargent	351
22.	Military Training in the Schools	Henry B. Carrington	352

23. AIM HIGH	Benjamin Harrison	354
AIM AT PERFECTION (Apothegm)	Lord Chesterfield	356
24. CULTURE OF THE MORAL VIRTUES	Joseph Baldwin	357
25. PATRIOTIC WORDS FOR THE YOUNG	Edward Everett Hale	359

PART XII.

THE FIFTH CENTURY OF AMERICAN CIVILIZATION BEGUN.

1. A PROCLAMATION	President Harrison	361
2. A WELCOME TO THE NATIONS	Vice President Morton	363
3. DEDICATION ORATION	Henry Watterson	365
4. THE SCHOOLS TAKE PART	Henry Watterson	367
5. DEDICATION EXERCISES	Chauncey Mitchell Depew	368
6. COLUMBUS THE DISCOVERER	Chauncey Mitchell Depew	373
7. THE COLUMBIAN EXPOSITION OPENED	President Cleveland	377
CONTRIBUTING NATIONS SPECIFIED		378
8. THE CONGRESS OF NATIONS	Henry B. Carrington	379
PROLOGUE		379
I. THE EXPOSITION OPENED		380
II. THE PARLIAMENT OF RELIGIONS		381
III. THE NEW LIBERTY BELL		382
IV. THE ECHO		383
9. OUR FUTURE	Bishop John Ireland	383
10. DISCOVERY DAY	Hezekiah Butterworth	386
11. THE FUTURE OF THE UNITED STATES	Joseph Story	387
12. AMERICAN DESTINY	George Berkeley	389
13. OUR HISTORY	Julian Crommelin Verplanck	390
14. THE FUTURE OF OUR LANGUAGE	George W. Bethune	391
15. PROGRESS IS CONSTANT	Charles Sumner	392
16. AMERICA THE CHILD OF DESTINY	Cassius Marcellus Clay	394
17. THE PACIFIC SHORE	Anonymous	395
18. THE TWENTIETH CENTURY	Merrill Edward Gates	396
19. PATRIOT SONS OF PATRIOT SIRES	Samuel Francis Smith	399

MEMORABLE OBSERVANCES	401
SYMPOSIUM OF PATRIOTIC SONGS	405
ALPHABETICAL INDEX OF TITLES	409
BIBLIOGRAPHY AND ACKNOWLEDGMENTS	415
BIOGRAPHICAL INDEX OF AUTHORS	417
SPECIAL VOCABULARY	425

The Old and the New.

About the year 1490 B. C. a statute announced a Jubilee, or Liberty Day, in the following stately words: —

"**Proclaim liberty throughout all the land unto all the inhabitants thereof.**"

During the year 1753 A. D., a bell, brought from England for the old State House, Philadelphia, was found to be cracked. It was re-cast and placed in position, retaining the same gracious announcement, —

"**Proclaim liberty throughout all the land unto all the inhabitants thereof.**"

On the Fourth Day of July, 1776, that bell, ever since honored, saluted

AMERICAN INDEPENDENCE.

On the 11th day of September, A. D. 1893, at the opening of the Parliament of Religions, at the World's Exposition, the representatives of the chief religions there represented, in turn struck a new bell, as, after his own faith, each invoked the blessing of Almighty God upon the entire human family.

This New Bell had been cast from twenty-two thousand free-will offerings of gold, silver, national coins, personal jewelry, swords, and cannon, and whatever honored sacrifice and valor, and bore about its rim, —

"**Proclaim liberty throughout all the land unto all the inhabitants thereof.**"

Two additional mottoes, from the New Testament, as the first was from the earliest Hebrew Records, served to concenter all the elements that would ensure the purest liberty: —

"**Glory to God in the highest, on earth peace, good will to men,**"
and,

"**Another commandment give I unto you, that ye love one another.**"

The New Liberty Bell.

The above design of the New Liberty Bell, from the government photograph, is suggestive, as noticed on page 408, that at meridian on each Independence Day, and on Washington's Birthday, all bells throughout the land, which summon to labor, school, or divine worship, be rung together, at a signal from those in charge of the great Liberty Bell.

Its voice echoes the grand announcement of thirty-five centuries ago.

BEACON LIGHTS OF PATRIOTISM.

PART I.

PATRIOTIC BEGINNINGS.

INTRODUCTION.

EVERY boy and girl in America may well be proud of the bright flag which waves above so many school-houses to-day; and the youth of other countries also love their national flag and their native land, so that the patriotic spirit is not confined to any one people nor to any one period of human history.

Just because that spirit is sweetest where the people are most earnest to seek the happiness of all their countrymen, it is right that we study the history of other countries and peoples, to see if we can learn from them that which will make us more blessed and prosperous.

Sometimes we think that there never was a country where everybody had so much cause for being happy as in these United States. And sometimes we forget that nearly all the Laws, Maxims, and Incentives to Patriotism which move our own hearts and bless mankind had their real origin long before Greece and Rome were known to history.

The trials of our Forefathers when they first landed upon these shores, and during their gradual attainment of National Independence, never fail to awaken sympathy. And yet the most noteworthy adoption of a New Country by a wandering people was that of the Hebrew. Their national capital, Jerusalem, has been the most famous city of the world, and one of their descendants, Jesus of Nazareth, is the brightest " Model " character ever known. His birth and name fix all the dates and relations of human history.

The devotion of his Hebrew ancestors to their native land when they were captive exiles, far away from home, is a sublime type of the patriotic spirit in its noblest and best expression. That sad wail, " If I forget thee, O Jerusalem, let my right hand forget her cunning! If I do not remember thee, let my tongue cleave to the roof of my mouth!" is a sufficient incentive to begin a series of Patriotic Studies with a glance at the very beginning of a patriotic devotion never since surpassed.

1. SEEKING A COUNTRY.

(B. C. 1921.)

The beautiful country of Chaldea, with its hundred brazen gates, its miles of wall two hundred feet in height and fifty in breadth, its "hanging gardens" and magnificent palaces, is described by the Hebrew seer, Isaiah, as Babylon, "the glory of the kingdom, the beauty of Chaldea's excellency."

About two thousand years before the Christian era, Abram and his family left their old home in the city of Ur, — or City of Fire, as it was called, because its people worshipped the sun, — and took up their journey for the land of Canaan, which bordered on the Mediterranean, or Great Sea. According to ancient predictions, the people of that country, named after a grandson of Noah, were to be "servants of their brethren;" and Abram therefore sought a new home in the West, with the belief that he would realize a permanent home country, in which, as promised, all the families of the earth would be blessed. He had scarcely located his family, distributed his camps, and prepared for real settlement, when a famine arose. He at once made a journey to fertile Egypt, and the generous king amply supplied his wants. On his return, he extensively explored his new country, was victorious over all opposing enemies, and died at "a ripe old age." The inspiration of his life had been the acquisition of a "home country" for his people, so that they might realize his brightest conceptions of their future destiny.

His son Isaac, under a similar stress of famine, did not seek aid from Egypt, but so industriously developed the means at his command as to escape serious disaster, and finally became very rich and prosperous. Animated by the same patriotic aspirations which had guided his father's career, he transmitted to his children also the fullest confidence in the value and certainty of the inheritance of the entire country occupied as all their own. He even cautioned his son Jacob to go back to his ancient home in Chaldea, and marry among his kindred, rather than to marry one of the natives of Canaan. The eventful journey of the son to the fatherland of Abraham, where his uncle still lived, and the romantic courtship of his beautiful cousin Rachel, as well as the fourteen years of hard service under his mean and grasping father-in-law, were marked by indications that the patriotic yearnings of his father and grandfather had become the active principle of his vigorous young life. The death of his father introduced new responsibilities. He had taken a new name, that of Israel, under impressive circumstances, in the conviction, as given by the only reliable history of his times, that "a nation and a company of nations should come out of his loins," and that the realized "Land of Promise" would be even more fully enjoyed by his own posterity in the years to come.

And now, the waste places of Mesopotamia, the early home of Abraham, surrender to the most patient research only shattered fragments of the once magnificent Babylon, but the origin of the people who made home and country the inspiration of their literature, their prowess, and their development, is ever fresh in mind, through the historic record which Hebrew valor and devotion preserved through all the centuries, up to the present hour.

And now, the great American republic, itself "a nation and a company of nations," asserts as the crown of its maturing glory the very principles, patriotism, and sublime precepts which made the early Hebrew commonwealth the type of national prosperity and blessing.

NOTE.— The name Abram was changed to Abraham. See Index.

2. THE EXILES IN EGYPT.

(B. C. 1491 — 1406.)

After many years of domestic trouble, although very rich in herds and flocks, Jacob, the "farmer shepherd," was compelled during a period of short crops to seek aid from Egypt, as his grandfather had done many years before. Unknown to him, his favorite son Joseph, long mourned as dead, was living in that country. The memory of home and country had protected him from the vices of Egyptian life, and he had become so prized for temperance, integrity, and wisdom that the proud Pharaoh had made him his prime minister and guardian of the national charities and treasure.

At one time the king had strange dreams, and his shrewdest advisers could give them no sensible meaning. In those days, all dreams were supposed to have some prophetic meaning. An officer whom Joseph had befriended under similar circumstances brought him to the king, and he at once proved himself to be "the most wise and discreet of all;" for he so accurately foretold a future failure of the river Nile to supply sufficient water for a crop, that ample supplies were secured in advance to meet the famine which the dream predicted. And so it happened that Joseph, at the age of thirty, after an exile of thirteen years, was loved and honored second only to the king himself. Meanwhile, his cruel brothers who had sold him into slavery were actually at the point of starvation, and were sent by their aged father to beg help of Pharaoh.

The boy of seventeen had become a mighty prince, and held the keys of the vast grain warehouses whose ruins have recently been unearthed and fully recognized.

Without avenging his wrongs upon his dependent brothers, and ever mindful of the cherished traditions of his people that they were to have a country of their own, and one which should exceed all others in richness and beauty, he invited the family to make a temporary home with him. The aged father promptly emigrated to Egypt; and, because of their pastoral tastes, the entire family were located in one of the best agricultural tracts of land in the valley of the Nile.

As the venerable patriarch declined in years, he adopted the two sons of Joseph as his own, and died with the parting blessing which foretold the future greatness and power of his people.

"A procession of more than ordinary pomp," says Geikie, "accompanied his remains to the old home.

"Three generations were brought up on Joseph's knees, until his life also drew to its close. But princely surroundings and the luxury of a brilliant court had not abated his patriotic fervor, nor weakened his faith in a future national existence of his people. He solemnly bound his countrymen by an oath that when they should be brought out of Egypt, 'into the land promised to Abraham, Isaac, and Jacob,' his own bones should be borne thither, to rest with those of his fathers."

Long years passed away. The prosperous shepherds, located in a fertile valley, and for a long time favored as the kinsmen of the mighty Joseph, became content with their easy lot. It was not until his memory had faded out, and jealousy of their prosperity and growth had aroused Egyptian jealousy and hate, that they felt the burden of an increasing oppression which despoiled life of all that made it restful and blessed. Then they began to realize something of the inspiration, energy, and faith of their fathers, and found a deliverer able to lead them to the new country of their promised destiny.

3. A PEOPLE DELIVERED.

(B. C. 1491.)

A vast host started from Rameses under Moses, the earliest proclaimer of the essential equality of all ranks and races. He was virtually king, but disdained the ambition of the name. His office brought with it immeasurable difficulties. Out of a horde, he had to form a nation, conquering a home for it, giving it social and religious laws, and making it a people fit for a noble, religious life.

Yet, at first, all went well. Intense anxiety to escape from the hated oppressor, joyful trust in their leader, and bright hopes of the future, had aroused the long-enslaved masses to a wondrous energy; and the sight of thousands on every side must have awakened a new sense of power. They still had fresh water and fodder for their cattle, and the way was still open before them. The one thought in every bosom was, "Canaan, the land flowing with milk and honey," and their one tacit demand was, that they should be led thither at once.

At the close of a march of about fifteen miles they encamped at Succoth, "place of tents," perhaps already the settlement of some shepherd tribes. Camping the next day near the bastions of Etham, a fortress at the edge of the wilderness of the same name, voices were heard regretting that they had not remained slaves. Their great leader, however, knew not only the character of his countrymen, but also the relations of the kings of Egypt with the kings of Palestine, and had foreseen exactly what had now happened. The people had set out, full of hope that they would soon reach, and if necessary conquer, the promised land. He had led them to the frontier fortresses; and now that they stormily clamored for their old life rather than face the dangers that threatened them, he was ready to cheer them by the intimation that they would not have to fight, but might take another, less dangerous, road towards the sea. He had first to lead them out of Egypt, and then to train them to discipline, order, and worthy aims in life.

Turning, therefore, to the south, at some distance from the frontier-wall, the multitude hastened on. Their retreat from before Etham had the effect of deceiving the Egyptians, by leading them to suppose that Moses had lost his way, or had given up the design of breaking through to the east, and was wandering in the desert.

Ordering his own war-chariots and six hundred selected chariots besides, as his immediate escort, supported by all the chariot force of Egypt, with fighting men in each, Pharaoh started in hot haste after the Hebrews. Launching his magnificent squadrons upon the prey, the horses, to use the words of an old papyrus, "swift as jackals, their eyes like fire, their fury like that of a hurricane when it burst," the doom of the Hebrew seemed sealed.

The fugitives had broken up their encampment. Marching slowly towards the sea, the murmur of the waves on the beach was already heard, when the clouds of dust on the horizon told them that they were pursued. Terror once more seized the host at the sight, and fierce accusations of Moses were mingled with loud cries of despair of escape. And still their great leader, ever calm in the midst of danger, kept the alarm from degenerating into a ruinous panic, by words which, after the fine figure of Ebers, "shone out over the wailing multitude like the sun rising in his majesty on the lost and almost spent traveller." The order was given, "Go forward!" though the water apparently barred their way. The pursuing Egyptians reached the strand when most of the Hebrews, with their cattle, had crossed in safety. It was a question whether the pursuers should at once dash in after them, or seek to overtake them by a circuit along the shore. Man and horse were tired out by forced marches, and the night was impenetrably dark. At Etham, Jehovah had vouchsafed to guide His people by a cloud during the day, and fire by night, as Eastern armies still follow, in many cases, signals of fire and smoke at the front of the march. This light, which Pharaoh may have taken as a signal common to advancing armies at night, had moved from before, to the rear of the Hebrews, quickening and guiding laggards and stragglers, while misleading the Egyptians as to the progress of the host, as a body. Thinking that the storm would keep the waters back, and seeing the prey so near, the passion of the pursuers overcame their prudence. Their squadrons therefore rushed to the ford, rank pressing on rank, after those who claimed to know the way, towards the light which they might well fancy marked the leader's place in front. Meanwhile, according to Josephus, a terrible storm of rain, with dreadful thunder and lightning, broke out, and helped, with the loud and fierce wind, to bewilder the charioteers. Advance was henceforth hopeless, but so also was retreat; for the wheels sank in the water-covered sand, and bent or snapped the axles, hurling the charioteers headlong from their places, "like stones from a sling." Ere long, the chariots and the heavily mailed soldiers of Pharaoh, held in the remorseless grip of the yielding sands, were overwhelmed, and miserably perished.

Next morning all was over, and the triumphant Hebrews "saw the Egyptian dead lying in heaps upon the shore."

CUNNINGHAM GEIKIE.

4. THE FIRST CONSTITUTION.

(B. C. 1491.)

The promulgation of "The Law of Moses," introduced the Hebrew people to the obligations of responsible citizenship, and established the test by which they were to be proven worthy of a permanent government. From that day until the present, the principles of that organic law have been the basis of all well-balanced society. Its introduction in a volume designed to lead youth to aspire after good citizenship is suggestive of the highest possible attainment within their reach.

THE TEN COMMANDMENTS.

I am the Lord thy God who brought thee out of the land of Egypt, out of the house of bondage.

I. Thou shalt have no other gods before me.

II. Thou shalt not make unto thee any graven image, or any likeness of anything that is in heaven above, or that is in the earth beneath, or that is in the waters under the earth; thou shalt not bow down thyself unto them, nor serve them: for I the Lord thy God am a jealous God, visiting the iniquity of the fathers upon the children, upon the third and upon the fourth generation of them that hate me: and showing mercy unto thousands of them that love me and keep my commandments.

III. Thou shalt not take the name of the Lord thy God in vain: for the Lord wilt not hold him guiltless that taketh his name in vain.

IV. Remember the sabbath day, to keep it holy. Six days shalt thou labor and do all thy work; but the seventh day is the sabbath of the Lord thy God. In it thou shalt not do any work, thou, nor thy son, nor thy daughter, thy man-servant, nor thy maid-servant, nor thy cattle, nor thy stranger that is within thy gates; for in six days the Lord made heaven and earth, the sea, and all that in them is, and rested the seventh day: wherefore the Lord blessed the seventh day and hallowed it.

V. Honor thy father and thy mother; that thy days may be long upon the land which the Lord thy God giveth thee.

VI. Thou shalt not kill.

VII. Thou shalt not commit adultery.

VIII. Thou shalt not steal.

IX. Thou shalt not bear false witness against thy neighbor.

X. Thou shalt not covet thy neighbor's house: thou shalt not covet thy neighbor's wife, nor his man-servant nor his maid-servant, nor anything that is thy neighbor's.

5. THE FIRST CIVIL CODE.

The police and social regulations of the Hebrew Commonwealth exalted the dignity of the State, honored the rights of the stranger as well as those of the humblest native citizen, and still survive, by enactment in the codes of all highly civilized States. They were especially associated with a formal repetition of the original "Ten Commandments," and announced the true standard by which to estimate the greatness, wisdom, and justice of organized society. The following are selections which retain their essential features in the statutes of most American States. The Preamble, or Introduction, gives the general reputation which a nation acquires among the nations of the world when its people observe the principles of these divinely accredited statutes, and stands as addressed to all mankind, in all ages.

PREAMBLE.

"Hearken unto the statutes and the judgments which I shall give you! Keep them and do them; for this is your wisdom and your understanding in the sight of all nations. They shall hear all these statutes, and say, Surely this great nation is a wise and understanding people. And what nation is so great that it hath statutes and judgments so righteous as all this law which I set before you this day?"

"Keep thy soul diligently, lest thou forget the things which thou hast seen; but teach them to thy sons and thy son's sons. These words which I command thee this day shall be in thy heart. Thou shalt teach them diligently to thy children and shalt talk of them when thou sittest in thy house, and when thou walkest by the way; when thou liest down, and when thou risest up. Thou shalt write them upon the posts of thine house and on the gates."[1]

STATUTES.

"Judges and officers shalt thou make throughout all thy tribes, and they shall judge the people with just judgment. They shall not wrest judgment, neither take a gift; for a gift doth blind the eyes of the wise and pervert the words of the righteous. That which is altogether just, that shalt thou follow."

"One witness shall not rise up against a man for any iniquity; but at the mouth of two witnesses, or three witnesses, shall a matter be established. If a false witness rise up [testify] against a man, the judge shall make diligent inquiry; and if the witness be found to be a false witness, then shall be done to him, as he had thought to have done to his brother. Then they which remain [citizen spectators] shall hear, and fear, and shall thenceforth commit no such evil among you."

"Ye shall do no unrighteousness in judgment [cases before a magistrate] in mete-yard [length and surface measure] nor in weight, nor in measure. Thou shalt not have in thy bag divers weights, a great and a small one, nor in thy house different measures, a great and a small; but thou shalt have a just and perfect weight, a perfect and just measure shalt thou have."

[1] Courts were held at the gates of the cities; and there bargains were made; and there also proclamations were made, or posted, for the information of the people. — ED.

"Thou shalt not lend upon usury [excessive interest] to thy brother [thy fellow-citizen] either usury of money, usury of victuals, or usury of anything that is lent upon interest."

"Thou shalt not remove thy neighbor's landmarks, which they of old have set up in thine inheritance."

"The poor shall never cease out of thy land; therefore, I command thee, saying, Thou shalt open thine hand wide unto thy brother, to thy poor, and to thy needy in thy land."

"No man shall take the mill-stone, the lower, or the upper, to pledge [as security] for he then taketh a man's life [his means of making his daily bread] in pledge."

"When thou buildest a new house, thou shalt make a battlement for thy roof, that thou shalt not bring blood [responsibility for accident] upon thy house, if any man fall from thence."

"Thou shalt not see thy brother's ox or sheep go astray and hide thyself from them. Thou shalt in every case bring them to thy brother." (This is the basis of the modern "Pound Law" for stray stock.)

"Thou shalt not oppress a hired servant that is poor and needy, whether he be of thy brethren, or of the stranger that is in thy land, and therefore I command thee to open thy hand wide [be generous] to thy brother, to the poor and needy in thy land."

NOTE. — A sound Bankrupt Law; a Statute of Limitations; a careful distinction between murder and manslaughter, as when the head of an axe slip off the helve and kill a man; a coroner's inquest over a person found dead; arbitration, in closely balanced cases; enrolment and classification of the militia; special drafts of men and money in emergencies; regimental organizations of a thousand men, with ten companies and each of two platoons of fifty each, — were among the features of the ancient Hebrew Code. When, about the year 30 A. D., the Saviour, in order to feed a vast multitude, ordered them to be seated upon the grass, they, involuntarily, "seated themselves by hundreds and by fifties."

6. THE HEBREW CODES DEVELOPED.

The marvellous devotion of the Hebrew people to their new country was never effaced by their contact with other nations, even when the vices and idol-worship of those nations corrupted their lives and disgraced their history. The national sentiment was intensely patriotic; and they hopefully looked for some divinely commissioned leader of their own blood and faith, who should be to them both deliverer and king. Their sacred books were full of delineations of the character of the expected Messiah; but there was nothing in their stately temple-worship, or in the gorgeous Roman ceremonials, to inspire that purity of personal life which their own history had proven to be the sole condition of the best national life. The early democracy of equal rights had passed away, and the exactions of their own officials were hardly less severe than those of Rome.

The Christ, from whose birth all history is now reckoned, appeared at the "due time," and all the conditions of blood, nativity, family, and physical surroundings, harmonized with their prophetic books; but their thirst for political restoration had closed their eyes to the moral blessings of verified promise. His utterances recognized their whole history, but adapted its scope to its fullest meaning, that "all the nations of the earth should partake of its realized glories." Those utterances voice human hope and human destiny, just as the "Beatitudes," given in the Book of Matthew, are followed by His development of the earlier Hebrew Codes.

THE GOSPEL CODE ANNOUNCED.

"Think not that I am come to destroy the law and the prophets. I am not come to destroy, but to fulfil."

"Till heaven and earth shall pass away, one jot or one tittle shall in no wise pass from the law, till all be fulfilled."

"Ye have heard that it hath been said [Leviticus xix. 18], Thou shalt love thy neighbor as thyself, and hate thine enemy; but I say unto you, Love your enemies; bless them that curse you; do good to them that hate you; and pray for them which despitefully use you and persecute you." "Therefore, all things whatsoever ye would that men should do to you, do ye also unto them: for this is the law and the prophets."

"And whosoever shall give to drink unto one of these little ones a cup of water, only in the name of a disciple, he shall in no wise lose his reward."

"The first of all the commandments is, Hear, O Israel. The Lord our God is one Lord: and thou shalt love the Lord thy God with all thy heart, and with all thy soul, and with all thy strength." "This is the first and great commandment.

"The second is like; namely, Thou shalt love thy neighbor as thyself. There is none other commandment, greater than these."

---

7. A SKETCH OF MOSES.

Moses led the world's first emancipation movement, liberating three million slaves.

Moses organized this horde of bondmen into the world's first republic, the United States of Israel, with local self-government, citizen soldiery, popular and compulsory education, elective judiciary, primary, and appellate courts, courts of the last resort, and most of the various advantages of which modern republics boast.

Moses legislated for the first constitutional monarchy, a government of laws and not of men, where rulers as well as the people were alike amenable to law.

Moses made every citizen a land-holder, with inalienable rights; introduced Homestead Exemption; cancelled debts after six years; gave every weary toiler a weekly rest; legislated for the protection of the poor and infirm; made the person of every citizen sacred; guarded captives from outrage and abuse; protected bondmen from bodily abuse; prohibited usury; forbade cruelty to animals; and ordained a system of legislation more humane than any the world has ever known.

Moses organized the world's first Total Abstinence Society, with stringent rules and "iron-clad" pledges.

Moses introduced a sanitary system so wise and salutary that the science of the present day has only begun to appreciate its advantages.

HORACE LORENZO HASTINGS.

8. THE BURIAL OF THE DELIVERER.

(B. C. 1350.)

The story of the death of Moses alone, by himself, on Mount Nebo, has no more tender notice than the lines of Mrs. Alexander.

By Nebo's lonely mountain, on this side Jordan's wave,
In a vale in the land of Moab, there lies a lonely grave;
And no man knows that sepulchre, and no man saw it e'er,
For the Angels of God turned up the sod, and laid the dead
    man there.

That was the grandest funeral that ever passed on earth;
But no man heard the trampling, or saw the train go forth:
So, without sound of music, or voice of them that wept,
Silently down from the mountain crown the great procession
    swept.

. . . .

This was the truest warrior that ever buckled sword, —
This the most gifted poet that ever breathed a word:
And never earth's philosopher traced from his gilden pen,
On the deathless page, truths half so sage, as he wrote down for men.

And had he not high honor, — the hillside for a pall, —
To lie in state while angels wait, — with stars for tapers tall, —
In that strange grave without a name, whence his uncoffined clay
Shall break again, O wondrous thought, before the Judgment Day?

O lonely grave in Moab's land! O dark Beth-Peor's hill!
Speak to these curious hearts of ours, and teach them to be still:
God hath His mysteries of grace, His ways that we can never tell;
He hides them deep, like the hidden sleep of him He loved so well.

CECIL FRANCES (HUMPHREY) ALEXANDER.

9. NO MAN KNOWETH HIS SEPULCHRE.

Thus, still, whene'er the good and just
　Close the dim eye on life and pain,
Heaven watches o'er their sleeping dust
　Till the pure spirit comes again.

Though nameless, trampled, and forgot,
　His servant's humble ashes lie,
Yet God hath marked and sealed the spot,
　To call its inmate to the sky.

WILLIAM CULLEN BRYANT.

10. THE NEW COUNTRY OCCUPIED.

JOSHUA, THE PATRIOT GENERAL.

(B. C. 1451-1443.)

The discipline of the wilderness had done its work. For a generation, Israel had led a nomadic life, passing from place to place, as pasturage invited, though Kadesh had been its centre. The men who had come down from Egypt gradually died out; and their sons, under the inspiration of Moses and those associated with him, had grown into a strong and vigorous nation. He had given them a constitution which was democratic in its noblest sense. Every Israelite, whether rich or poor, was equal before the law and a free man. They had been taught to believe themselves the people of God, and that to treat them as slaves, as the Pharaohs treated the Egyptians, was a crime against Jehovah.

Moses, though their leader and dictator, bore himself as only the instrument and voice of God, from whom their laws came, and to whom, supremely, they owed both temporal and spiritual obedience. All the legislation given them had been based on the recognition of the highest moral law, and embodied the purest and loftiest conceptions of duty to God and man. Love of their neighbor, brotherly fellowship, equality as Israelites, gentleness and absolute uprightness, were the ideal he had set before them. Such maxims and laws were impressed on them until they became almost instinctively recognized, although sometimes violated or forgotten. In the words of the prophet, "These years saw the kindness of their youth, and the love of their espousal to Jehovah, when, as His betrothed bride, they followed the pillar of His Presence through the wilderness, in a land that was not sown."

Nor were their manly virtues less strengthened and developed than their religious ideas. The energies called forth by the necessities and perils of a desert life, the quickening breath of the pure air of the wilderness, a love of freedom quickened into a passion by its enjoyment for a generation, the interdependence fostered by common action as a people, the free constitution they enjoyed, and, above all, the grand religious conceptions which aroused all that was noble in the soul, had effaced the servile taunts of Egypt, called out the slumbering qualities of the race, and restored to them the vigorous tone of their shepherd ancestors.

But it was necessary that this wandering life should end, now that it had served its purpose; and the command was given to prepare to take possession of the long-promised land of Canaan.

The supreme authority over the nation and the army had been intrusted by Moses, before his death, to Joshua. This wise, patriotic, and accomplished leader, born about the time when his great master fled to Midian, was in the prime of life, had been intrusted with repelling the attack of Amalek, at Rephidim, and realized the most brilliant success. With no claim to be a prophet, he bore himself as a skilful soldier, with a difficult task to accomplish, and resolute to carry it out. He fulfilled his task, and the great war of the conquest of Canaan was over, and the occupation was complete.

The early Hebrew aversion to the authority of any individual was universal and profound. Patriotism, in a large sense, could hardly exist when each village was practically self-governing. In only two cases — namely, in difficult legal questions, and in the event of a general war — was any higher immediate authority than the heads of families, or clans, felt to be needed. For the first, Moses had provided; but nothing had been determined as to the latter. But Joshua, impressed by the magnitude of the country occupied, its infinite capacities and the necessity for the cohesive force of a truly national spirit, gathered the people in two large masses on the opposite, confronting mountains of Ebal and Gerizim, where he commanded them to recite aloud, responsively, the true conditions of permanent national independence.

Such a scene, transacted about twelve hundred years before the First Punic War, and a thousand years before the birth of Socrates, is unique in the world's history. When did any other nation thus pledge itself to a high religious life as the recognized conditions of prosperity, wherein disobedience to parents, inhumanity to the blind, to strangers, widows, and orphans, and even removal of the landmarks of neighbors, were made crimes as well as murder? Even modern legislation is slowly striving toward a standard as generous, exalted, and pure.

It was then — his work accomplished, his duty done — that Joshua, appointing no successor to his dignities and claiming no rank for his family or heirs, calmly retired to his inheritance, to spend the closing days of his life in modest privacy, satisfied to remain a contented citizen of the mighty Hebrew Commonwealth.

CUNNINGHAM GEIKIE.

NOTE. — The late J. Dorman Steele, in his "Ancient and Mediæval Peoples," justly states the strategical movements of Joshua, as follows: "Joshua's plan of crossing the Jordan, capturing Jericho, taking the heights beyond, by a night-march, and delivering the crushing blow at Bethoron (Joshua, x. 9), was a masterpiece of strategy, and ranks him among the greatest generals of the world. His first movement placed him in the centre of the country, where he could prevent his enemies from massing against him, and, turning in any direction, cut them up in detail."

The principle is the same which illustrates the military character of Washington, as defined in Part v., No. 6, of this volume. — ED.

11. RUTH AND NAOMI.

No story in the progress of the Hebrew nation is more pathetic in its sentiment and incidents than that of the great-grandmother of King David, — Ruth, the daughter-in-law of Naomi, a Hebrew widow. Thirty generations later, the recognized family line closed with the birth of Jesus.

FAREWELL? Oh, no! It may not be;
   My firm resolve is heard on high!
I will not breathe farewell to thee,
   Save only in my dying sigh.
I know not that I now could bear
   Forever from thy side to part,
And live without a friend to share
   The treasured sadness of my heart.

I will not boast a martyr's might
   To leave my home without a sigh, —
The dwelling of my past delight,
   The shelter where I hoped to die.
In such a duty, such an hour,
   The weak are strong, the timid brave;
For love puts on an angel's power,
   And faith grows mightier than the grave.

For rays of heaven serenely bright
   Have gilt the caverns of the tomb;
And I can ponder with delight
   On all its gathering thoughts of gloom.
Then, mother, let us haste away
   To that blest land to Israel given,
Where faith, unsaddened by decay,
   Dwells nearest to its native heaven.

For where thou goest, I will go;
   With thine my earthly lot is cast;

> In pain and pleasure, joy and woe,
>   Will I attend thee to the last.
> That hour shall find me by thy side,
>   And where thy grave is, mine shall be:
> Death can but for a time divide
>   My firm and faithful heart from thee.
>
> W. B. O. PEABODY.

12. DAVID, THE PATRIOTIC KING.

(B. C. 1056-1014.)

The conquest of the "Promised Land" did not prevent long and painful contests with adjoining nations, hostile to the Hebrew sway and impatient of a moral influence so repugnant to their licentious and cruel habits, their idolatry, and their thirst for power. But at last peace prevailed throughout their borders. The limits of the Hebrew kingdom, after it succeeded the original commonwealth in form of government, had been Dan and Beersheba, on the north and south. But David reigned from the river of Egypt to the Euphrates, from Gaza on the west to Thapsacus on the east. The whole region between the Mediterranean and the Euphrates had been ablaze with war at the same moment. The address of Joab before the first battle of Medeba, gave the key to the feeling which animated the people, — "Be of good courage, and let us play the man, for our people and the cities of our God!"

Zeal for Jehovah as their God, and for their country and brethren as His land and His people, had become a deep-rooted passion in every heart. It was, in fact, a revival of the ancient fervor of the days of Joshua, such as had burst forth in the darkest days of the past. This enthusiasm might have been chilled and well-nigh lost when the nation was in close contact with heathenism; but in the lonely mountain valley of central Palestine, and in the secluded pastures of Judah and the South, the heart of the people still beat sound.

The great deeds of Deborah, Gideon, and Jephthah, would have been impossible but for the slumbering religious life which they knew how to arouse to a vigorous enthusiasm. This latent fervor and hereditary loyalty to Jehovah had been at last rekindled in such power that it henceforth became the passionate, almost the fanatical glory of the nation.

Of this restoration of the spiritual glory of Israel, David, the anointed of Samuel, was a supreme illustration. In an age especially Puritan, says Geikie, he was the prominent representative of its spirit. With him, as with it, religion was the first thought in all relations in life, public or private. The whole community — citizen, soldier, magistrate, and king — alike moved in an atmosphere of the supernatural. All that was most heroic in David's age arose from this trust in God, and it fired the souls of the Maccabees, centuries later, for man never rises to his grandest or noblest in war, except when he believes in the sacredness of the cause for which he contends.

David was never more at the height of his glory. His enemies had been subdued. He had now a vast empire. Alliances were sought by neighboring powers; but with every temptation to play the part of the Eastern tyrant-despot, he bore himself, on the whole, with a tender moderation which never invaded the ancient liberties of the nation, endeared him in life, and made his memory sacred among his people forever.

His errors and faults never weakened his devotion to country; and his loftiest songs, of sweetest measure, were of Zion's heights and the deeds of the fathers.

SELECTIONS FROM GEIKIE.

13. THE PATRIOT KING IN MOURNING.

(B C. 1023.)

King David's limbs were weary. He had fled
From far Jerusalem; and now he stood,
With his faint people, for a little rest
Upon the shore of Jordan.

Oh, when the heart is full, — when bitter thoughts
Come crowding thickly up for utterance,
And the poor, common words of courtesy
Are such a very mockery, — how much
The bursting heart may pour itself in prayer!

He prayed for Israel; and his voice went up
Strongly and fervently. He prayed for those
Whose love had been his shield; and his deep tones
Grew tremulous. But oh, for Absalom! —
For his estranged, misguided Absalom,
The proud, bright being, who had burst away
In all his princely beauty, to defy
The heart that cherished him! — for him he poured
In agony that would not be controlled,
Strong supplication; and forgave him there,
Before his God, for his deep sinfulness.

. . . .

The pall was settled! He who slept beneath
Was straightened for the grave; and as the folds
Sank to the still proportions, they betrayed
The matchless symmetry of Absalom.
The king stood still; then throwing off
The sackcloth from his brow, and laying back
The pall from the still features of his child,
He bowed his head upon him, and broke forth
In the resistless eloquence of woe.

"Alas, my noble boy! that thou shouldst die, —
Thou, who wert made so beautifully fair;
That death should settle in thy glorious eye,
And leave his stillness in this clustering hair;
How could he mark thee for the silent tomb,
My proud boy, Absalom!
Cold is thy brow, my son, and I am chill,
As to my bosom I have tried to press thee.
How was I wont to feel my pulses thrill
Like a rich harp-string, yearning to caress thee,
And hear thy sweet 'My father!' from these dumb lips
And cold, Absalom!
The grave hath won thee! I shall hear the gush
Of music and the voices of the young;
And life will pass me in the mantling blush
And the dark tresses to the soft winds flung;
But thou no more with thy sweet voice shalt come
To meet me, Absalom!

And oh, when I am stricken, and my heart
Like a bruised reed is waiting to be broken,
How will its love for thee, as I depart,
Yearn for thine ear to drink its last deep token;
It were so sweet amid death's gathering gloom
To see thee, Absalom!
And now, farewell! 'T is hard to give thee up,
With death so like a gentle slumber on thee;
And thy dark sin — oh, I could drink the cup,
If from this woe its bitterness had won thee!
May God have called thee, like a wanderer, home,
My erring Absalom!"

. . . .

He covered up his face, and bowed himself
A moment on his child; then, giving him
A look of melting tenderness, he clasped
His hands convulsively, as if in prayer;

And, as a strength were given him by God,
He rose up calmly, and composed the pall
Firmly and decently, and left him there,
As if his rest had been a breathing sleep.

NATHANIEL PARKER WILLIS.

---

14. SAUL AND JONATHAN.

SAUL, king of the great Hebrew nation, and Prince Jonathan, his son, brother-in-law and the most intimate friend of David, fell in battle with the Philistines, about the year 1056 B.C. The lament of David is unrivalled in its appreciative regard and tenderness for the fallen heroes, and anxiety lest the honor of the nation should suffer.

Thy glory, O Israel, is slain upon thy high places!
How are the mighty fallen!
Tell it not in Gath,
Publish it not in the streets of Askelon,
Lest the daughters of the Philistines rejoice,
Lest the daughters of the uncircumcised triumph!
Ye mountains of Gilboa,
Let there be no dew nor rain upon you,
Neither fields of offerings;
For there the shield of the mighty was vilely cast away,
The shield of Saul, as of one not anointed with oil.

From the blood of the slain, from the fat of the mighty,
The bow of Jonathan turned not back,
And the sword of Saul returned not empty.

Saul and Jonathan were lovely and pleasant in their lives,
And in their death they were not divided;
They were swifter than eagles,
They were stronger than lions;
Ye daughters of Israel, weep over Saul,
Who clothed you in scarlet, delicately,
Who put ornaments of gold upon your apparel.

How are the mighty fallen in the midst of the battle!
Jonathan is slain upon thy high places!
I am distressed for thee, my brother Jonathan;
Very pleasant hast thou been unto me:
Thy love to me was wonderful,
Passing the love of women;
How are the mighty fallen,
And the weapons of war perished!

REVISED VERSION.

15. SOLOMON, THE WISE KING.
(B. C. 1033-975.)

SOLOMON, "the wise man," the son and successor of King David, surpassed all contemporary monarchs in wisdom, wealth, and glory. He married a daughter of Pharaoh, King of Egypt; and a cordial alliance with Hiram, King of Tyre, enabled him to enlist the interest of that prince in beautifying his capital, Jerusalem, and its magnificent Temple for the worship of Jehovah. Even the present rulers of Abyssinia proudly count as their ancestor the famous Queen of Sheba, who so freely acknowledged the wisdom and glory of Solomon, and scholars of all ages, including those of Arabia, India, and the farthest East, have made use of his concise maxims for the regulation of national and personal life.

SELECTIONS FROM SOLOMON'S PROVERBS.

WISDOM is the principal thing; therefore get wisdom, and with all thy getting, get understanding. Exalt her and she shall promote thee; she shall bring thee to honor, when thou dost embrace her. She shall give to thine head an ornament of grace; a crown of glory shall she deliver to thee.

KEEP thy heart with all diligence, for out of it are the issues of life.

LET thine eyes look right on, and let thine eyelids look straight before thee.

PONDER the path of thy feet, and let all thy ways be established.

Turn not to the right hand or to the left; remove thy feet from evil. The way of the wicked is as darkness; they know not at what they stumble: but the path of the just is as the shining light, that shineth more and more, unto the perfect day.

Train up a child in the way he should go, and when he is old he will not depart from it.

16. THE HEBREW CAPITAL DESPOILED.

Jerusalem was captured and the temple destroyed by Nebuchadnezzar, King of Chaldea, about 588 b. c.

Is this thy place and city, this thy throne,
Where the wild desert rears its craggy stones,
While suns, unblessed, their angry lustre fling,
And way-worn pilgrims seek the scanty spring?
Where now thy pomp, which kings with envy viewed?
Where now thy might, which all those kings subdued?
No suppliant nations in thy temple wait!
No prophet bards, thy glittering courts among,
Wake the full lyre and swell the tide of song;
But lawless Force and meagre Want is there,
And the quick-darting eye of restless Fear,
Where cold Oblivion, 'mid thy ruin laid,
Folds his dark wing beneath the ivy shade.
. . . .
Yet shall she rise; but not by war restored,
Nor built in murder, planted by the sword.
Yes, Salem, thou shalt rise; thy Father's aid
Shall heal the wound His chastening hand has made,
Shall judge the proud oppressor's ruthless sway;
Then on your tops shall deathless verdure spring.
Break forth, ye mountains! and ye valleys, sing!

No more your thirsty rocks shall frown forlorn,
The unbeliever's jest, the heathen's scorn;
The sultry sands shall tenfold harvests yield,
And a new Eden deck the thorny field.

Bishop Reginald Heber.

---

17. THE DESPOILER DOOMED.

The prediction of the prophet Isaiah, 712 B. C., was subsequently verified with most minute exactness.

On the lofty mountain, elevate the banner,
Lift up the voice to them, wave the hand,
That they may enter into the gates of the tyrants.
I have given my orders to my consecrated ones [warriors],
I have ordered my heroes to execute my indignation,
My proud exulters [deliverers]!
Hark!
      The noise of a multitude upon the mountain,
Like that of a great nation!
The tumult of kingdoms, of trembling nations!
Jehovah, God of hosts, mustereth his army for battle.
They come from a distant land, from the end of the heaven,
Jehovah and the instruments of his indignation,
To lay waste the whole country.

Behold, I will raise against them the Medes,
Who make no account of silver,
And as to gold, they regard it not.
Their bows shall strike down the youth,
Their eye shall not pity the children.
So shall Babylon, the pride of kingdoms,
The boast and glory of the Chaldeans,
Be like Sodom and Gomorrah, which God destroyed;
It shall never more be inhabited nor dwelt in,
From generation to generation.

There the Arab shall not pitch his tent,
Nor the shepherds make their flocks to lie down there.
But there the wild beasts of the desert shall lie down,
And howling monsters shall fill their houses;
There the ostriches shall dwell,
And the satyrs shall revel there.
The jackals shall howl in their palaces,
And the dragons in their magnificent pleasure-houses;
For her time is near,
And her days shall not be prolonged.
. . . .

Then it shall come to pass, that thou shalt
Utter this song over the king of Babylon, and say,
How hath the oppressor, the exactor of golden tribute ceased!
Jehovah hath broken the staff of the wicked,
The rod of the tyrants.
The whole earth is at rest, they break forth into song.
The fir-trees also exult over thee, Babylon,
And the cedars of Lebanon say,
Since thou art cast down, no axe-man has come up against us.
All the kings of the nations will accost thee, and say,
Art thou also become feeble, as we are,
And become like unto us?
Those that gaze upon thee shall say,
Is this the man who made the earth to quake,
And legions to tremble?
Who made the earth a desert,
And laid waste the cities thereof?
Who dismissed not his prisoners to their homes?

All the kings of the nations, yea, all, repose in glory,
Every one in his own place;
But thou art cast out from thy sepulchre
As a loathsome branch; as the raiment of those
That are slain, thrust through with the sword,
That go down to the stones of the pit;
As a carcass trodden under foot!

I will make it, Babylon, a possession for the porcupine
And for pools of water, and will sweep it with the
Besom of destruction, saith Jehovah, Lord of hosts!
Moses Stuart's Translation.

---

18. THE HEBREW MINSTREL'S LAMENT.

From the hills of the West, as the sun's setting beam
Cast his last ray of glory o'er Jordan's lone stream,
While his fast-falling tears with its waters were blent,
Thus poured a poor minstrel his saddened lament : —

"Awake, harp of Judah, that slumbering hast hung
On the willows that weep where thy prophets have sung ;
Once more wake for Judah thy wild notes of woe,
Ere the hand that now strikes thee lies mouldering and low.

"Ah, where are the choirs of the glad and the free
That woke the loud anthem responsive to thee,
When the daughters of Salem broke forth in the song,
While Tabor and Hermon its echoes prolong ?

"And where are the mighty, who went forth in pride
To the slaughter of kings, with their ark at their side ?
They sleep, lonely stream, with the sands of thy shore,
And the war-trumpet's blast shall awake them no more.

"O Judah, a lone, scattered remnant remain,
To sigh for the graves of their fathers in vain,
And to turn toward thy land with a tear-brimming eye,
And a prayer that the advent of Shiloh be nigh.

"No beauty in Sharon, on Carmel no shade ;
Our vineyards are wasted, our altars decayed ;
And the heel of the heathen, insulting, has trod
On the bosoms that bled for their country and God."
New England Magazine, 1832, page 60. "Z."

19. JERUSALEM AVENGED.

 Babylon was captured by the Persians about the year 538 b. c., during a night of royal debauchery, when the king, Belshazzar, made conspicuous use of the golden vessels of the Jewish Temple, which Nebuchadnezzar had stolen. King Cyrus, the Persian, diverted the Euphrates River from its bed, and entered the city by the empty channel. The prediction of Isaiah, uttered about the year 712 b. c., was fulfilled as to Babylon, and every new discovery adds confirmation to its accuracy.

The king was on his throne ; the satraps thronged the hall ;
A thousand bright lights shone o'er that high festival.
A thousand cups of gold, in Judah deemed divine, —
Jehovah's vessels, — held the godless heathen's wine.

In that same hour and hall, the fingers of a hand
Came forth against the wall, and wrote as if in sand ;
The fingers of a man, a solitary hand,
Along the letters ran, and traced them like a wand.

The monarch saw and shook, and bade no more rejoice ;
All bloodless waxed his look, and tremulous his voice :
"Let the men of lore appear, the wisest of the earth,
And expound the words of fear which mar our royal mirth."

Chaldea's seers are good, but here they have no skill,
And the unknown letters stood untold and awful still.
And Babel's men of age are wise and deep in lore,
But now they were not sage ; they saw, but knew no more.

A captive in the land, a stranger and a youth,
He heard the king's command, he saw that writing's truth.
The lamps around were bright, the prophecy in view ;
He read it on that night ; the morning proved it true :

"Belshazzar's grave is made, his kingdom passed away ;
He, in the balance weighed, is light and worthless clay ;
The shroud his robe of state, his canopy in stone ;
The Mede is at his gate, the Persian on his throne."

             Byron.

20. A NATION'S STRENGTH.

Psalm xxxiii.

Let all the earth fear the Lord :
Let all the inhabitants of the earth stand in awe of him :
For He spake and it was done. He commanded and it stood
 fast.
The Lord bringeth the counsels of nations to naught,
He maketh the thoughts of the people to be of no effect.

The counsel of the Lord standeth forever,
The thoughts of his heart to all generations.

Blessed is that nation whose God is the Lord,
The people whom he hath chosen as his inheritance.

The Lord looketh down from heaven,
He beholdeth all the sons of men ;
From the place of his habitation he looketh forth
Upon all the inhabitants of the earth, —
He that fashioneth the hearts of them all,
That considereth all their works.

There is no king that is saved by the multitude of an host,
A mighty man is not delivered by great strength ;
An horse is a vain thing for safety,
Neither shall he deliver any by his great power.

Behold, the eye of the Lord is upon them that fear him,
Upon them that hope in his mercy.
                                    Revised Version.

21. THE PATRIOT'S CRY.

PARAPHRASE OF PSALM CXXXVII.

Verses 1, 2, and 3.

By Babylon's still waters we sat down and wept;
   Yea, we wept as we thought of Zion, our pride;
And we hung our mute harps, once in harmony swept,
   On the willows that mournfully bent o'er the tide:
For they who had carried us captives away
   Would awaken our bosoms to gladness once more,—
Our spoilers commanded that Salem's sweet lay
   Should be breathed from our lips on Assyria's shore.

Verses 4, 5, and 6.

But how could we sing the high song of the Lord
   In the land of the stranger, or yield us to mirth,
When back to our bosoms, on every loved word,
   Would cluster regrets for the land of our birth?
O Jerusalem dear, when no remembrance shall come
   Of thy splendors and glories to darken my heart,
Let my tongue be in silence perpetual dumb,
   Let my hand be forgetful of cunning or art.

Verses 7, 8, and 9.

Remember the children of Edom, O God,
   When the day of Jerusalem's vengeance is found.
Oh, blast with thy lightning, and smite with thy sword,
   All who shouted, "Raze, raze her proud walls to the ground!"
And thou, O daughter of Babylon, doomed to the dust,
   Blest ever be he that rewardeth thy crime,
Who meteth thee measure thou gavest to us,
   And leaveth thee, shattered, to ruin and time!

HENRY B. CARRINGTON.

PART II.

OLD ROME AND HER RIVALS.

1. HORATIUS AT THE BRIDGE.

(About B. C. 500.)

According to a Roman legend which Macaulay has fully unfolded in the "Lays of Ancient Rome," Horatius Cocles, with two comrades, defended the Sublician bridge across the Tiber, before that city, until the bridge itself could be destroyed, and then saved his own life by swimming, although heavily armed. The same writer, with equal vividness, describes the monument which honors the noted exploit.

> It stands in the Comitium,
>   Plain for all folks to see :
> Horatio in his harness,
>   Halting upon one knee ;
> And underneath is written
>   In letters all of gold,
> How valiantly he kept the bridge
>   In the brave days of old.
> And still his name sounds stirring
>   Unto the men of Rome,
> As the trumpet-blast that cries to them
>   To "charge the Volscians home ;"
> And wives still pray to Juno
>   For boys with hearts as bold
> As his who kept the bridge so well
>   In the brave days of old.
> And in the nights of winter,
>   When the cold winds blow,

And the long howling of the wolves
    Is heard amidst the snow ;
When round the lonely cottage
    Roars loud the tempest's din,
And the good logs of Algidus
    Roar louder yet within ;
When the oldest cask is opened,
    And the largest lamp is lit ;
When the chestnuts glow in the embers,
    And the kid turns on the spit ;
When young and old in circle
    Around the firebrands close ;
When the girls are weaving baskets,
    And the lads are shaping bows ;
When the good man mends his armor,
    And trims his helmet's plume ;
When the goodwife's shuttle merrily
    Goes flashing through the loom, —
With weeping and with laughter
    Still is the story told,
How well Horatius kept the bridge
    In the brave days of old.

                          Thomas Babington Macaulay.

Note. — The Sublician bridge was the most ancient bridge of Rome, and the last in order, in following the course of the river. As its name implies, it was built of wood. It was raised by Ancus Martius, and dedicated with great pomp and ceremony by the Roman priests. It was afterwards rebuilt by Æmilius Lepidus, whose name it assumed. It was afterwards injured by an overflow of the river; and the Emperor Antonius, who repaired it, made it all with white marble. Some vestiges of this bridge still remain. — Ed.

2. REPRESENTATIVE GOVERNMENT TRUSTWORTHY.

This memorable appeal finds special application in the history of the American Republic. Paulus Æmilius had been called to the command of the Roman army, B.C. 168, under peculiar circumstances of responsibility. He had also been assigned to the territory, or department, which demanded the greatest wisdom, and involved the greatest risk. His address to the people at large, before taking the field, might well have been that of General Grant when he assumed command, and the criticisms of "stay-at-home critics" are almost precisely those of General Sherman, who offered free transportation to all scolding advisers who would not fight where fighting brought danger.

You seem to me, Romans, to have expressed more joy when Macedonia fell to my lot than when I was elected and entered upon office. And to me, your joy seemed to be occasioned by the hopes you conceived that I should put an end, worthy of the grandeur and reputation of the Roman people, to a war which in your opinion had already been of too long continuance. I shall do my utmost not to fall short of your anticipations.

The Senate has wisely regulated everything necessary to the expedition I am charged with; and, as I am ordered to set out immediately, I shall make no delay. I know that my colleague, Caius Lentulus, out of his great zeal for the public service, will raise and march off the troops appointed for me, with as much ardor and expedition as if they were for himself. I shall take care to transmit to you as well as to the Senate, an exact account of all that passes; and you may rely upon the certainty and truth of my letters. But, I beg you, as a great favor, that you will not give credit to, or lay any weight, out of credulity, upon the light reports which are frequently spread abroad without any author.

There are those who, in company and even at table, command armies, make dispositions, and provide all the operations of the campaign. They know, better than we, where we should camp and what posts it is necessary for us to seize; at what time and by what defile we should enter Macedonia; whether it be proper that we have magazines; from whence, either by sea or land, we are to bring provisions; when we are to fight the enemy, or lie still. They not only prescribe what is best to do; but, deviating ever so little from their plans, they make it a crime in their Consul General, and cite him before their tribunal. But know, Romans, that this is of very bad effect with your generals. All have not the resolution and constancy of Fabius, to despise impertinent reports.

I am far from believing that generals stand in no need of advice, and think, on the contrary, that whoever would conduct everything alone, upon his own opinion, and without counsel, shows more presumption than prudence. But some may ask, "How, then, shall we act reasonably?" I answer, "By not suffering anybody to obtrude their advice upon your generals but such as are, in the first place, versed in the art of war, and have learned from experience what it is to command; and in the second place, who are upon the spot, who know the enemy, are witnesses in person to all that passes, and are sharers with us in all the dangers.

If there be any one who conceives himself capable of assisting me with his counsels in the war you have charged me with, let him not refuse to do the Republic that service; but let him go with me into Macedonia. Ships, horses, tents, provisions, shall be provided for him at my charge. But if he will not take so much trouble, and prefer the tranquillity of the city to the dangers and fatigue of the field, let him not take upon him to hold the helm, and continue in the port. The city of itself supplies sufficient matter of discourse on other subjects; but as for these, let it be silent upon them, and know that we pay no regard to any counsels but such as shall be given us in the camp itself.

PLUTARCH.

---

3. FABRICIUS REFUSES BRIBES.

Pyrrhus, King of Epirus, in Northwestern Greece, a formidable enemy of Rome, attempted in vain to bribe Caius Luscinus, a Roman ambassador, who visited his court to negotiate conditions of peace. When, afterwards, about 280 B. C., Fabricius was approached by the physician of Pyrrhus, with offers of money, to poison his master, the high-minded Roman exposed the plot to the king. Afterwards he became Consul and Censor; and for fear that money would tempt officials to wrong-doing, he actually banished Cornelius Rufinus, a senator, because he kept a large service of silver plate. At his death, the Roman people gave dowry to his two daughters when they became of age.

With regard to my poverty, the king has been justly informed. My whole estate consists in a house of but mean appearance, and a little spot of ground, from which, by my labor, I draw my support. But if by any means thou hast been persuaded to think that this poverty renders me of less consequence in my own country, or in any degree unhappy, thou art greatly deceived.

I have no reason to complain of fortune. She supplies me with all that my nature requires, and if I am without superfluities, I am also free from the desire of them. With these, I confess I should be more able to succor the necessitous,—the only advantage for which the wealthy are to be envied; but small as my possessions are, I can still contribute something to the support of the State and the assistance of my friends. With respect to honors, my country places me, poor as I am, upon a level with the richest; for Rome knows no qualifications for great employments but virtue and ability. She appoints me to officiate in the most august ceremonies of religion; she confides to my care the most important negotiations.

My poverty does not lessen the weight and influence of my counsels in the Senate. The Roman people honor me for that very poverty which King Pyrrhus considers a disgrace. They know the many opportunities I have had to enrich myself without censure; they are convinced of my disinterested zeal for their prosperity; and if I have anything to complain of, it is only in the excess of their applause.

What value, then, can I put upon thy gold and thy silver? What king can add anything to my fortune? Always attentive to discharge the duties incumbent upon me, I have a mind free from self-reproach, and I have an honest fame.

PLINY.

4. VINDICATION OF VIRGINIUS.

VIRGINIA, the beautiful daughter of Lucius Virginius, a brave Roman general, and betrothed to Lucius Icilius, a Roman tribune, was claimed by Marcus Claudius as a slave; and he submitted the question of title to the decemvir, Appius Claudius, on whose behalf he had seized the maiden. Virginius reached the tribunal only in time to find that she had been declared a slave. To save her from dishonor, he thrust his dagger through her breast. The people dragged Claudius to prison, where he killed himself. Virginius joined his command in the field, where he fully vindicated his action, about the year 449 B. C.

HOLDING aloft the bloody knife, he exclaimed, "With this dagger I have slain my child, my only child, to preserve her from dishonor!"

(Yells of horror and bitter execration rose from the whole army; and a thousand swords flashed in the sun's bright beams).

"Soldiers," he cried, "I am like this blasted tree! Two years ago, the Ides of May (May 15th), three lusty sons went with me to the field. In one illustrious fight they perished. A daughter, beautiful as the day, yet remained. 'T is but a week ago you saw her here, bearing to her aged sire home-comforts, prepared by her own hands, and sharing with him the evening meal; and you blessed her as she passed. You'll never more see her that weekly came, with the soft music of her voice and spells of home, to cheer our hearts.

"As on the way to school she crossed the forum, Appius Claudius, through his minion, Marcus, claimed her as his slave. With desperate haste I rode to Rome. Holding my daughter by my hand, and by my side her uncle, her aged grand-sire, and Icilius, her betrothed, I claimed my child. The judge, that he might gain his end, decides that in his house and custody she must remain till I, by legal process, prove my right! The guards approach. Trembling, she clings about my neck, her hot tears upon my cheeks. Snatching this knife from a butcher's stall, I plunged it in her breast, that her pure virgin soul might go free and unstained to her mother and her ancestors.

"And this is the reward a grateful country gives her soldiers! Soldiers, the deadliest foes of our liberties are behind, not before us. They are not the Equi, the Volschi, and the Sabines, who meet us in fair fight; but that pampered aristocracy who chain you by the death-penalty to the camp, that in your absence they may work their will among those whom you have left behind.

"But why do I seek to kindle a fire in ice? Why seek to arouse the vengeance of those who care for no miseries but their own, and are enamoured of their fetters? I, indeed, can lose no more. Misfortune hath emptied her quiver. She hath no other shaft for this bleeding breast. But flatter not yourselves that the lust of Appius Claudius has expired with the defeat of his purpose. Your homes also invite the destroyer. Into your folds the grim wolf will leap. Among the lambs of your flock will he revel, his jaws dripping with blood. For you, also, the bow is bent, the arrow drawn to its head, and the string impatient of its discharge.

"By all that I have lost, and that you imperil by delay, avenge this accursed wrong! If you have arms, use them; liberties, vindicate them; patriotism, save the tottering State; natural affection, protect the domestic hearth; piety, appease the wrath of the gods by avenging the blood that cries to Heaven!

"To arms! to arms! or your swords will leap from their scabbards, the trumpets sound the onset; and the standards, of themselves, advance to rebuke your delay!"

ELIJAH KELLOGG.

5. REGULUS BEFORE THE ROMAN SENATE.

REGULUS, a Roman consul during the First Punic War against Carthage, begun about the year 264 B. C., after several victories in Africa, was captured, but was sent back to Rome to negotiate terms of peace, on the condition that in case of failure to secure satisfactory terms, he should return to captivity. He denounced the proposed treaty, returned to Carthage, and there suffered a cruel death. His address to the Roman Senate is memorable as one of the most exalted illustrations of self-immolation for the sake of country.

It ill becomes me, Senators of Rome, me, Regulus, after having so often stood in this venerable Assembly, clothed with the supreme dignity of the republic, to stand before you to-day, a captive, — the captive of Carthage. Though outwardly free, though no fetters encumber the limbs or gall the flesh, yet the heaviest of chains, the pledge of a Roman Consul, makes me the bondsman of the Carthaginians. They have my promise to return to them in the event of the failure of this their embassy.

But, Conscript Fathers, Senators, there is but one course to be pursued. Abandon all thought of peace! Reject the overtures of Carthage! Reject them wholly and unconditionally! What? What? Give back to her a thousand able-bodied men, and receive in return this one, attenuated, war-worn, fever-wasted frame, — this weed, whitened in a dungeon's darkness, pale and sapless, which no kindness of the sun, no softness of the summer breeze, can ever restore to life and vigor? It must not, shall not be! Oh, were Regulus what he was once, before captivity had unstrung his sinews and enervated his limbs, he might pause; he might think he were worth a thousand of the foe; he might say, "Make the exchange, Rome shall not lose by it!" But now, alas, 't is gone, — that impetuosity of strength which could once make him a leader indeed, to penetrate a phalanx, or guide a pursuit. His very armor would be a burden now! His battle-cry would be drowned in the din of onset! His sword would fall harmless upon his opponent's shield!

But if he cannot live, he can at least die, for his country. Do not deny him this supreme consolation. Consider! Every indignity, every torture which Carthage shall heap on his dying hours, will be better than a trumpet's call to your armies. They will remember only Regulus, that fellow-soldier and their leader. They will forget his defeats. They will regard only his services to the Republic. Tunis, Sicily, Sardinia, every well-fought field, won by his blood and theirs, will flash on their remembrance and kindle their avenging wrath!

And so shall Regulus, though dead, fight as he never fought before against the foe.

Conscript Fathers, there is another theme, — my family. Forgive the thought. To you and to Rome, I commit them. I leave them no legacy but my name, no testament but my example.

And you, ambassadors of Carthage, now in this august presence, I have spoken, not as you expected. I am your captive. Lead me back to whatever fate may await me. Doubt not that you shall find that to Roman hearts country is dearer than life, and integrity more precious than freedom.

Epes Sargent.

6. SEPARATION FROM TRAITORS.

Extract from the address of Marcus Tullius Cicero, before the Roman Senate, b. c. 62, upon the exposure of the conspiracy of Catiline.

It is now a long time, Conscript Fathers, that we have trod amidst the perils and plots of this conspiracy. I do not know how it comes to pass; but the full maturity of all these crimes and of this long-ripening rage and insolence has broken forth now, in the period of my consulship. If Catiline alone shall be removed from this powerful band of traitors, it may abate, perhaps, for a while, our fears and our anxieties; but the danger will still remain and continue to lurk in the veins and vitals of the Republic.

For, as men, oppressed with a severe fit of sickness and laboring under the raging heat of fever, are, at first, seemingly relieved by a draught of cold water, but afterwards find the disease return upon them with redoubled fury, so this distemper which has seized the Commonwealth, eased a little by the punishment of this traitor, Catiline, will, from his surviving associates, soon assume new force. Wherefore, let the wicked retire. Let them separate themselves from the honest. Let them rendezvous in one place. In fine, as I have often said, let a wall be between them and us. Let them cease to lay snares for the Consul in his own house; to beset the tribunal of the city Prætor; to invest the Senate with armed ruffians, and prepare fire-balls and torches for burning the city. In short, let every man's sentiments with regard to the public be inscribed on his forehead.

This I engage for and promise, Conscript Fathers, that by the diligence of the Consuls, the weight of your authority, the courage and firmness of the Roman people, and the unanimity of all honest men, Catiline being driven from the city, you shall behold all his treason detected, exposed, crushed, and punished.

With these omens, Catiline, of prosperity to the Republic, but of destruction to thyself and of all those who have joined themselves with thee in all kinds of parricide, go thy way to this impious and abominable war.

Meanwhile, thou, Jupiter, whose religion was established with the foundations of this city, whom we truly call Stator, the stay and the prop of this empire, wilt drive this man and his accomplices from thy altars and thy temples, from the houses and walls of the city, and from the lives and fortunes of us all. Thou wilt destroy with eternal punishments, both living and dead, all the haters of good men, the enemies of their country, the plunderers of Italy, now confederated in this detestable league and partnership of villany.

Harper's Trans.

THE LAW OF VIRTUE.

THE law of virtue is the same in God and man, and in no other disposition. This virtue is nothing else than a nature perfect in itself, and wrought up to the most consummate excellence. Because of this similitude, what connection can there be which concerns us more nearly, and is more certain?

CICERO.

7. ROMAN LIBERTY IN PERIL.

THE warfare between Rome and Carthage, her chief rival for supremacy along the shores of the Mediterranean Sea, was one of the most brilliant in history; and the careers of the rival generals are fully illustrated by selections from their appeals to their troops and their mutual correspondence. Hannibal crossed the Alps and threatened Rome.

PUBLIUS SCIPIO TO THE ROMAN ARMY.

(B. C. 216.)

NOT because of their courage, O soldiers, but because an engagement is now inevitable, do the enemy prepare for battle. Two thirds of their infantry and cavalry have been lost in the passage of the Alps. Those who survive hardly equal in numbers those who have perished. Should any one say, "Though few, they are stout and irresistible," I reply, Not so! They are the veriest shadows of men; wretches, emaciated by hunger and benumbed with cold; bruised and enfeebled among the rocks and crags; their joints frost-bitten, their sinews stiffened by the snow, their armor battered and shattered, their horses lame and powerless. Such is the cavalry, such the infantry, against which you have to contend; not enemies, but remnants and shreds of enemies. And I fear nothing more than that when you have fought Hannibal, the Alps may seem to have been beforehand, and to have robbed you of the renown of a victory. But perhaps it was fitting that the gods themselves, irrespective of human aid, should commence and carry forward a war against a leader and a people who violate the faith of treaties; and that we, who, next to the gods, have been most injured, should complete the contest thus commenced and nearly finished.

I would, therefore, have you fight, O soldiers, not only with that spirit with which you are wont to encounter other enemies, but with a certain indignation and resentment, such as you might experience if you should see your slaves suddenly taking up arms against you. We might have slain these Carthaginians when they were shut up in Eryx by hunger, the most dreadful of human tortures. We might have carried our victorious fleet to Africa, and in a few days destroyed Carthage without opposition. We yielded to their prayer for pardon; we released them from the blockade; we made peace with those whom we had conquered; and we afterwards held them under our protection when they were borne down by the African war. In return for these benefits they come, under the lead of hot-brained youth, to lay waste our country. Ah, would that the contest on your side were now for glory, and not for safety! It is not for the possession of Sicily and Sardinia, but for Italy, that you must fight, nor is there another army behind, which, should we fail to conquer, can resist the enemy; nor are there other Alps, during the passage of which, fresh forces may be procured. Here, soldiers, here we must make our stand! Here we must fight, as if we fought before the walls of Rome!

Let every man bear in mind that it is not only his own person, but his wife and children he must now defend. Now let the thought of them alone possess his mind! Let him remember that the Roman Senate, the Roman people, are looking with anxious eyes to our exertions; and that, as our valor and our strength shall be this day, such will be the fortune of Rome, such the welfare, nay, the very existence of our country!

Trans. from Livy.

SELF-RESPECT.

I CAN afford to despise critics so long as I am conscious that I exercise supreme unselfishness in all my dealings with God and man. CATO

8. CARTHAGE IN PERIL.

The adventures of Hannibal, extending through the islands of the Mediterranean Sea as well as through Spain, are full of thrilling interest. Although he was not sufficiently supported by the authorities of Carthage to perfect his triumphs, his genius and courage have made him one of the most conspicuous and successful military leaders of human history.

HANNIBAL'S ADDRESS TO HIS ARMY.

(B. C. 216.)

Here, soldiers, you must either conquer or die. On the right and on the left, two seas enclose you; and you have no ships to flee to for escape. The river Po around you, larger and more imperious than the Rhone; the Alps behind, scarcely passed by you when fresh and vigorous, hem you in. Fortune has granted you the termination of your labors. Here she will bestow a reward worthy of the service you have undergone. All the spoil that Rome has amassed by so many triumphs will be yours. Think not that in proportion as this war is great in name, the victory will be difficult.

From the Pillars of Hercules, from the ocean, from the remotest limits of the world, over mountains and rivers, you have advanced victorious, and through the fiercest nations of Spain and Gaul. And with whom are you now to fight? With a raw army, which this very summer was beaten, conquered, and surrounded,—an army unknown to their leader, and he to them. Shall I compare myself, almost born and certainly bred in the tent of my father, that illustrious commander,—myself, who was the pupil of you all, before I became your commander,—to this six months general? Or shall I compare his army with mine?

On whatsoever side I turn my eyes, I behold all full of confidence, courage, and strength,—a veteran infantry; a most gallant cavalry; you, our allies, most faithful and valiant; you, Carthaginians, whom not only your country's cause, but the justest anger, impel to battle. The valor, the confidence of invaders, are ever greater than those of the defensive party. As the assailants in this war, we pour down with hostile standards upon Italy. We bring the war. Suffering, indignity, and injury fire our minds. First, they demanded me, your leader, for punishment; and then all of you who had laid siege to Saguntum. And had we been given up, they would have visited us with the severest tortures. Cruel and haughty nation; Everything must be yours, and at your disposal. You are to prescribe to us with whom we shall make war! with whom, peace. You are to shut us up by boundaries of mountains and rivers which we must not pass. But you,—you are not to observe the limits you yourselves have appointed. "Pass not the Iberus!" What next? Saguntum is on the Iberus. You must not move a step in that direction.

Is it a small thing that you have deprived us of our most ancient provinces, Sicily and Sardinia? Will you take Spain also? Should we yield Spain, you will cross over into Africa. "Will cross," did I say? They have sent the two Consuls of this year, one to Africa, and the other to Spain.

Soldiers there is nothing left us in any quarter but what we can vindicate with our swords! Let those be cowards who have something to look back upon; whom, flying through safe and unmolested roads, their own country will receive. There is a necessity for us to be brave. There is no alternative but victory or death; and if it must be death, who would not rather encounter it in battle than in flight? The immortal gods could give no stronger incentive to victory! Let but these truths be fixed in your minds; and once I again proclaim, you are conquerors.

Trans. from Livy

9. HANNIBAL PLEADS FOR PEACE.

BEFORE THE BATTLE OF ZAMA.

(B. C. 202.)

Since fate has so ordained it that I, who began the war, and have so often been on the point of ending it by a complete conquest, should now come, of my own motion, to ask a peace, I am glad that it is of you, Scipio, I have the fortune to ask it. Nor will this be among the least of your glories, that Hannibal, victorious over so many Roman generals, submitted at last to you.

I could wish that our fathers, and we, had confined our ambition within the limits which Nature seems to have prescribed to it, — the shores of Africa and the shores of Italy. The gods did not give us that mind. On both sides, we have been so eager after foreign possessions as to put our own to the hazard of war. Rome and Carthage have had, each in turn, to turn the enemy at her gates.

But, since errors past may be more easily blamed than corrected, let it now be the work of you and me to put an end, if possible, to the contention. For my own part, my years, and the experience I have had of the instability of Fortune incline me to leave nothing to her determination which reason can decide. But much I fear, Scipio, that your youth, your want of like experience, and your uninterrupted success, may render you averse to thoughts of peace.

He whom Fortune has never failed, rarely reflects upon her inconstancy. Yet without referring to former examples, my own perhaps may suffice to teach you moderation. I am the same Hannibal who, after the victory at Cannae, became master of the great part of your country, and deliberated with myself what fate I should decree to Italy and Rome.

And now, see the change! Here in Africa, I am come to treat with a Roman for my own preservation and my country's. Such are the sports of Fortune. Is she then to be trusted because she smiles? An advantageous peace is preferable to the hope of victory. The one is in your power; the other at the pleasure of the gods. Should you prove victorious, it would add little to your glory, or the glory of your country; if vanquished, you lose in one hour all the honor and reputation you have been so many years in acquiring.

But what is my aim in all this? That you should content yourself with our cession of Spain, Sicily, Sardinia, and all islands between Italy and Africa. A peace on these conditions will, in my opinion, not only secure the tranquillity of Carthage, but be sufficiently glorious for you and for the Roman name. And do not tell me that some of our citizens dealt fraudulently with you in the late treaty. It is I, Hannibal, that now ask a peace. I ask it, because I think it expedient for my country; and thinking it expedient, I will inviolably maintain it.

Trans. from Livy.

---

10. SCIPIO DECLINES HANNIBAL'S OVERTURES FOR PEACE.

BEFORE THE BATTLE OF ZAMA.

(B. C. 202.)

I KNOW very well, Hannibal, that it was the hope of your return which emboldened the Carthaginians to break the truce with us and lay aside all thoughts of peace, when it was just upon the point of being concluded; and your present proposal is a proof of it. You retrench from their concessions everything but what we are and have been long in possession of.

But as it is your care that your fellow-citizens should feel under obligation to you of being eased of a great part of their burdens, so it devolves upon me that they draw no advantage from their perfidy. Nobody is more sensible than myself of the weakness of man and the power of Fortune, and that whatever we undertake is subject to a thousand chances.

If, before the Romans passed over into Africa, you had of your own accord made the offers you now make, I believe that they would not have been rejected. But as you have been forced out of Italy, and we are masters here of the open country, the situation of things is much altered. But this is chiefly to be considered, that the Carthaginians, by the late treaty which we made at their request, were, over and above what you offer, to have released to us prisoners, without ransom; to have delivered up their ships of war; to have paid us five thousand talents, and to have given us hostages for the performance of all. The Senate accepted these conditions, but Carthage failed on her part. Carthage deceived us. What is, then, to be done? Are the Carthaginians to be released from the most important articles of the treaty, as a reward for this breach of faith? No, certainly, no!

If, to the conditions before agreed upon, you had added some new articles to our advantage, there would have been matter of reference to the Roman people; but when, instead of adding, you retrench, there is no room for deliberation. The Carthaginians, therefore, must submit to us at discretion, or must vanquish us in battle.

SCIPIO AFRICANUS.

11. CÆSAR'S DEATH JUSTIFIED.

The assassination of Cæsar by Brutus occurred March 15, B. C. 44, and was publicly justified by Caius Cassius, as follows: —

Soldiers and Fellow-Citizens, — The unjust reproaches of our enemies we could easily disprove, if we were not, by our numbers and the swords which we hold in our hands, in condition to despise them. While Cæsar led the armies of the Republic against the enemies of Rome, we took part in the same service with him, we obeyed him, we were happy to serve under his command. But when he declared war against the Commonwealth, we became his enemies; and when he became an usurper and tyrant, we resented, as an injury, even the favors which he presumed to bestow upon ourselves.

Had he fallen as a sacrifice to private resentment, we should not have been the proper actors in the execution of the sentence against him. He was willing to have indulged us with preferments and honors; but we were not willing to accept as the gift of a master what we were entitled to claim as free citizens. We conceived that he, in presuming to confer the honors of the Roman Republic, encroached on the prerogatives of the Roman people and insulted the authority of the Roman Senate. Cæsar cancelled the laws and overturned the constitution of his countrymen; he usurped all the powers of the Commonwealth; he set up a monarchy and affected to be a king. This our ancestors, at the expulsion of Tarquin, bound themselves and their posterity, by the most solemn oaths and by the most direful imprecations, never to endure. The same obligation has been entailed upon us, as a debt, by our fathers; and we, having faithfully paid and discharged it, have performed the oath and averted the consequences of failure from ourselves and from our posterity.

In the station of soldiers, we might have committed ourselves, without reflection, to the command of an officer whose abilities and valor we admired; but in the character of Roman citizens, we have a far different part to sustain. I must suppose that I now speak to the Roman people and to the citizens of a free Republic; to men who have never learned to depend upon others for gratifications and favors; who are not accustomed to own a superior, but who are themselves the masters, the dispensers of fortune and of honor, and the givers of all those dignities and powers by which Cæsar himself was exalted, and of which he assumed the entire disposal.

Recollect from whom the Scipios, the Pompeys, and even Cæsar himself derived his honors: from your ancestors, whom you now represent, and from yourselves; to whom, according to the laws of the Republic, we who are now your laborers in the field address ourselves as your fellow-citizens in the Commonwealth, and as persons depending on your pleasure for the just reward of our services. We are happy in being able to restore to you what Cæsar had the presumption to appropriate to himself, the power and dignity of your fathers; and happy in being able to secure to every Roman citizen that justice which, under the late usurpation of Cæsar, was withheld even from the sacred person of the magistrates themselves.

An usurper is the common enemy of all good citizens, but the task of removing him could be the business of only a few. The Senate and the Roman people, as soon as it was proper for them to declare their judgment, pronounced their approbation of those who were concerned in the death of Cæsar, by the honors and rewards which they bestowed upon them. They are now become the prey to assassins and murderers. These respectable citizens, we trust, will soon, by your means, be restored to a condition in which they can enjoy, together with you, all the honors of a free people; concur with you in bestowing, and partake with you in receiving, the rewards which are due to such eminent services as you are now engaged to perform.

CAIUS CASSIUS.

---

12. THE DEGENERACY OF ATHENS.

(B. C. 322.)

DEMOSTHENES, the greatest of Grecian orators, and born about the year 380 B. C., commenced the study of oratory at the age of seventeen, although having weak lungs, imperfect articulation, and awkward gestures. He is reported to have trained his voice by declamation near the seashore, with pebbles in his mouth, so as to gain mastery of his voice, and increase its distinctness and compass. His patriotic appeals against the encroachments of King Philip are among the most memorable examples of patriotic eloquence; and the purity, welfare, and independence of his countrymen were the burden of his life. He died at the age of sixty years, B. C. 320.

CONTRAST, O men of Athens, your conduct with that of your ancestors. Loyal towards the people of Greece, religious towards the gods, faithful to the rule of civic equality, they mounted by a sure path to the summit of prosperity. What is your condition under your present complaisant rulers? Has it in any respect changed? In how many?

I confine myself to this simple statement: Sparta prostrate; Thebes occupied elsewhere; able, in fact, in the peaceable possession of our domain, to be the umpire of other nations, — what have we done? We have lost our own provinces, and dissipated with no good result more than fifteen hundred talents. The allies which we have gained by war, your counsellors have deprived us of by peace, and we have trained up to power our formidable foe. Whoever denies this, let him stand forth and tell me where has this Philip drawn his strength, if not from the very bosom of Athens?

Ah, but surely, if abroad we have been weakened, our interior administration is more flourishing. And what are the evidences of this? A few whitewashed ramparts, repaired roads, fountains, — mere trifles, bagatelles! Turn, turn your eyes upon the functionaries to whom we owe these vanities. One of them has passed from misery to opulence; one, from obscurity to splendor; and another has had built for him sumptuous palaces which look down upon the edifices of State. Indeed, the more our public fortunes have declined, the more have theirs ascended. Tell us the meaning of these contrasts! Why is it that formerly all prospered, while now all is in jeopardy! It is because formerly the people itself, daring to wage war, was master of its officials, the sovereign dispenser of all favors. It is because individual citizens were then glad to receive from the people honors, magistracies, benefits. How are times changed! All favors are in the gift of our officials; everything is under their control; while you, — you, the people! — enervated in your habits, mutilated in your means, and weakened in your allies, stand like so many supernumeraries and lackeys, too happy if your worthy chiefs distribute to you the fund for the theatre, — if they throw to you a meagre pittance!

And, last degree of baseness, you kiss the hand which thus makes largess to you of your own! Do they not imprison you within your own walls, beguile you to your own ruin, tame you and fashion you to their yoke? Never, oh, never, can a manly pride and noble courage impel men subjected to vile and unworthy actions! The life is necessarily the image of the heart. And your degeneracy — by Heaven, I should not be surprised, if I, in charging it home upon you, exposed myself, rather than those who brought you to it, to your resentment! To be candid, frankness of speech does not every day gain the entrance of your ears; and that you suffer it now, may well be matter of astonishment.

DEMOSTHENES.

13. VIRTUE UNCORRUPTED BY FORTUNE.

THE incident mentioned by the eminent historian Quintus Curtius is also described by both Justinian and Diodorus. A Macedonian by the name of Hephestion was so intimate with Alexander the Great that, when he died, special honors were paid to his memory, and the physician who attended him was put to death, upon the claim that he had been negligent in his medical attendance, about 325 B. C.

THE city of Sidon having surrendered to Alexander, he ordered Hephestion to bestow the crown on him whom the Sidonians should think most worthy of that honor. Hephestion, living at the time with two men of distinction, offered them the crown. They declined the honor, as contrary to the law of that country, which excluded all but such as were related to the royal family from accepting such an honor.

Admiring their disinterested spirit, he requested them to name some person of the royal blood who should receive the crown at their hands. Overlooking many who would have been ambitious of the honor, they selected Abdalonimus, who was remotely related to the royal family, but had been reduced by misfortunes to the humble work of cultivating a small garden in the suburbs of the city, for a mere pittance in money.

While Abdalonimus was busily weeding his garden, the two friends of Hephestion approached him, bearing the crown of royalty, and saluted him as king. Repeating Alexander's instructions, they required him immediately to exchange his rusty garb and utensils of industry for the regal robe and sceptre. All this only seemed to him like an illusion of the fancy, or a cruel, deliberate insult to his poverty. Persuaded of the sincerity of the proposition, he assumed office, being first enjoined not to forget the humble condition from which he had been raised, when he should occupy a throne with a nation in his power.

He had hardly taken possession of the government when the pride and envy of his enemies whispered murmurs of complaint in every sphere of society, until they reached the ears of Alexander himself. He at once commanded the newly-elected prince to be sent for, and abruptly inquired of him, not how he conducted his official duty, but with what temper of mind he had borne his previous life and its condition of poverty. "Would to Heaven," was the reply, "that I may be able to bear my crown with equal moderation! for when I possessed little, I wanted nothing. These hands supplied me with whatever I desired." From this answer, Alexander formed so high an opinion of his wisdom that he not only confirmed his title, but annexed a neighboring province to the government of Sidon.

QUINTUS CURTIUS.

14. MERIT BEFORE BIRTH.

THE promotion of Caius Marius to the command of the Roman army in the campaign against Jugurtha, the Numidian usurper, aroused desperate opposition on the part of the aristocracy, to which Marius replied in most emphatic terms.

You have committed to my conduct, O Romans, the war against Jugurtha. The Patricians take offence. They say, "Why, he has no family statues. He can point to no illustrious ancestors." What of that? Will dead ancestors or motionless statues fight battles? Can your general appeal to them in the hour of extremest danger? How wise it would be, surely, to intrust your army to some untried person without a single scar, but with any number of ancestral statues, — who knows not the simplest rudiments of military service, but is very perfect in pedigree! I have known such holiday heroes, raised, because of family, to positions for which they had no fitness. But, then, in the moment of action they were obliged, in their ignorance and trepidation, to intrust every movement, even the most simple, to some subaltern, some despised plebeian.

What they have seen in books, I have seen written on battle-fields, with steel and blood. They sneer at my mean origin. Where, — and may the gods bear witness, — where, but in the spirit of man, is nobility lodged? Tell these despicable railers that their haughty lineage cannot make them noble, nor will my humble birth make me base. I profess no indifference to noble descent; but when a descendant is dwarfed in the comparison, it should be a shame, and not a matter to boast of! I can show the standards, the armor, and the spoils which I have in person wrested from the vanquished. I can show the scars of many wounds received in combating the enemies of Rome. These are my statues! These are my honors, to boast of; not inherited by accident, but earned by toil, by abstinence, by valor, amid clouds of dust and seas of blood. Their very titles date from similar acts of their ancestors; but these detractors did not even dare to appear on the field as spectators. These are my credentials! These, O Romans, are my titles of nobility! Tell me, are they not as respectable, are they not as valid, are they not as deserving of your confidence and reward as those of which any patrician of them all can boast?

Trans. from Sallust.

15. PRINCE ADHERBAL BEFORE THE ROMAN SENATE.

A PLEA FOR OUTRAGED HOSPITALITY.

(B. C. 102.)

KING MICIPSA, of the African kingdom of Numidia, of which the present Algiers formed a part, was aided by Rome in a struggle with Carthage, Rome's chief rival, and before his death left his sons Adherbal and Hiempsal to the charge of his adopted son, Jugurtha, with instructions to be faithful to Rome, which in return would prove to be to them a complete defence against all enemies, "better than armies, fortifications, and treasure." Jugurtha murdered the younger brother; and the appeal of Adherbal to the Roman Senate for protection has few equals in pathos and dignity. The gold of Jugurtha was too powerful for Rome to withstand; but after the murder of Adherbal, the Commonwealth was driven to a disastrous war, until Jugurtha himself was subdued and dragged in chains through the streets of Rome after the chariot of Marius.

SENATORS OF ROME,—Whither, oh, whither shall I fly? I return to the royal palace of my ancestors; but my father's throne is seized by the murderer of my brother. What can I there expect but that Jugurtha should hasten to imbrue, in my blood, those hands which are now reeking with my brother's? If I were to fly for refuge or assistance to any other court, from what prince can I hope for protection if the Roman Commonwealth give me up? From my own family or friends I have no expectations! My royal father is no more! He is beyond the reach of violence, and out of hearing of the complaints of his unhappy son. Were my brother alive, our mutual sympathy would be some alleviation of my woe. But he is hurried out of life in his early youth, by the very hand which should have been the last to injure any of the royal family of Numidia.

The bloody hand of Jugurtha has butchered all whom he suspected to be in my interest. Some have been destroyed by the lingering torment of the cross; others have been given a prey to wild beasts, and their anguish made the mere sport of men more cruel than wild beasts. If there be any yet alive, they are shut up in dungeons, there to draw out a life more intolerable than death itself.

Look down, illustrious senators of Rome, from that height of power to which you are raised, on the unexampled distresses of a prince, who is, by the cruelty of a wicked intruder, become an outcast from all mankind. Let not the crafty insinuations of him who returns murder for adoption prejudice your judgment. Do not listen to the wretch who has butchered the son and relations of a king who gave him power to sit on the same throne with his sons. If ever the time comes when the vengeance due from above shall overtake him, then he who now, hardened in wickedness, triumphs over those whom his violence has laid low, will in his turn feel distress, and suffer for his impious ingratitude to my father and his blood-thirsty cruelty to my brother.

O murdered, butchered brother! O dearest to my heart, now gone forever from my sight! But why should I lament his death? He is, indeed, deprived of the blessed light of heaven, of life, of kingdom, by the very person who ought to have been the very first to hazard his own life in defence of any of Micipsa's family. But as things are, my brother is not so much deprived of these comforts as delivered from terrors, from flight, from exile, and the endless train of miseries which render life to me a burden. He lies full low, gored with wounds and festering in his own blood. But he lies in peace. He feels none of the miseries which rend my soul with agony and distraction: while I am set up as a spectacle to all mankind of the uncertainty of human affairs. So far from having it in my power to punish his murderer, I am not the master of means of securing my own life. So far from being in a condition to defend my kingdom from the violence of the usurper, I am obliged to apply for foreign protection, even for my own person.

Fathers, Senators of Rome, the arbiters of nations! To you I fly for refuge from the murderous fury of Jugurtha. By your affection for your children; by your love for your country; by your own virtues; by the majesty of the Roman Commonwealth; by all that is sacred, and all that is dear to you, — deliver a wretched prince from undeserved, unprovoked injury, and save the kingdom of Numidia, which is your own property, from being the prey of violence, usurpation, and cruelty.

Trans. from Caius Crispus Sallust.

16. THE WAIL OF JUGURTHA.

When the Roman Senate, upon the plea of Adherbal, insisted, through a heavy bribe, that his cousin Jugurtha should still hold half the kingdom of Numidia, that prince, determined to rule alone, besieged Adherbal in Cirta, its capital, — the modern Constantina, — and put him to death. War with Rome followed. Led to Rome, chained to the chariot of the victorious Marius, Jugurtha was sentenced by the Roman Senate to be starved in prison, and died B. C. 108. Sallust's record of Adherbal's lofty and pathetic appeal to Rome is hardly more thrilling than Wolfe's picture of Jugurtha in his cell. Both have historic lessons, and both burn with emotion.

Well, is the rack prepared, — the pincers heated?
Where is the scourge? How, — none employed in Rome?
We have them in Numidia. Not in Rome?
I 'm sorry for it; I could enjoy it now!
I might have felt them yesterday; but now —
Now I have seen my funeral procession!
The chariot-wheels of Marius have rolled over me;
His horses' hoofs have trampled me in their triumph;

I have attained that terrible consummation,
My soul could stand aloof, and from on high
Look down upon the ruins of my body,
Smiling in apathy ;
     I feel no longer ;
I challenge Rome to give another pang !

Oh, how he smiled when he beheld me pause
Before his car and scowl upon the mob !
The curse of Rome was burning on my lips,
And I had gnaw'd my chain and hurl'd it at them,
But that I knew he would have smiled again.
 . . . .

Look here, thou caitiff, if thou canst, and see
The fragments of Jugurtha ! View him wrapt
In the last shred he borrowed from Numidia ;
'T is covered with the dust of Rome ; behold
His rooted gaze upon the chains he wears,
And on the channels they have wrought upon him ;
Then look around upon his dungeon walls,
And view yon scanty mat on which his frame
He flings, and rushes from his thoughts to sleep !
            Sleep !
I 'll sleep no more until I sleep forever :
When I slept last, I heard Adherbal scream.
I 'll sleep no more ! I 'll think until I die :
My eyes shall pore upon my miseries,
Until my miseries shall be no more.
Yet wherefore did he scream ? Why, I have heard
His living scream, — it was not half so frightful !
Whence comes the difference ?
         When the man was living,
Why, I did gaze upon his couch of torments
With placid vengeance, and each anguished cry
Gave me stern satisfaction. Now he 's dead,
And his lips move not ; yet his voice's image
Flashed such a dreadful darkness o'er my soul,

I would not hear that fearful cry again
For the high glory of Numidia's throne.
But ah! 't was I that caused that living scream,
And therefore did its echo seem so frightful.
If 't were to do again, I would not kill thee;
Wilt thou not be contented? But thou say'st,
"My father was to thee a father also;
He watched thy infant years, and gave thee all
That youth could ask; and scarcely manhood came,
Than came a kingdom also; and yet thou didst —"

Oh, I am faint! They have not brought me food —
How did I not perceive it until now?
Hold! my Numidian cruse is still about me.
No drop within — O faithful friend, companion
Of many a weary march and thirsty day,
'T is the first time thou hast failed my lips.
Gods! I 'm in tears! I did not think of weeping.
Oh, Marius, wilt thou never feel like this?
Ha! I behold the ruin of a city;
And on a craggy fragment sits a form
That seems in ruin also. How unmoved,
How stern, he looks! Amazement! it is Marius.
Ha! Marius, thinkest thou now upon Jugurtha?
He turns! he 's caught my eye! I see no more.

CHARLES WOLFE.

PART III.

OUR FATHERS AND THEIR HOMES.

1. OLD ENGLAND.

Nurse of the Pilgrim sires who sought,
   Beyond th' Atlantic's foam,
For fearless truth and honest thought
   A refuge and a home,
Who would not be of them or thee
   A not unworthy son,
That hears amid the chained or free
   The name of Washington?

Cradle of Shakspeare, Milton, Knox,
   King-shaming Cromwell's throne,
Home of the Russells, Watts, and Lockes,[1]
   Earth's greatest are thine own;
And shall thy children forge base chains
   For men that would be free?
No! by the Eliots, Hampdens, Vanes,
   Pyms, Sydneys, yet to be.

No! for the blood which kings have gorged
   Hath made their victims wise;
While every lie that Fraud hath forged
   Veils wisdom from his eyes;
But time shall change the despot's mood;
   And mind is mightier now than then,
When turning evil into good,
   And monsters into men.

[1] Eminent friends of liberty. See Vocabulary.

If round the soul the chains are bound
    That hold the world in thrall ;
If tyrants laugh when men are found
    In brutal fray to fall ;
Lord, let not Britain arm her hands
    Her sister States to ban,
But bless through her all other States, —
    The family of man !

For freedom if thy Hampden fought ;
    For peace if Falkland fell ;
For peace and love if Bentham wrote,
    And Burns sang wildly well ;
Let Knowledge, strongest of the strong,
    Bid Hate and Discord cease ;
Be this the burden of my song, —
    Love, Liberty, and Peace.

EBENEZER ELIOT.

2. ERIN AND THE DAYS OF OLD.

MALACHI, monarch of Ireland in the tenth century, is reported to have taken a gold collar from the neck of a Danish champion of an invading army. At that time the Red Knights flourished, claiming to have occupied Ulster before the time of Christ. The round towers referred to by the poet still remain, scattered through Ireland; and according to ancient legends, the waters of Lough Neagh, once a fountain, revealed other towers when the waters were placid.

LET Erin remember the days of old,
    Ere her faithless sons betrayed her ;
When Malachi wore the collar of gold
    Which he won from her proud invader ;
When her kings, with standard of green unfurled,
    Led the Red Branch knights to danger ;
Ere the emerald gem of the western world
    Was set in the crown of the stranger.

> On Lough Neagh's banks, as the fisherman strays
>   When the clear cold eve 's declining,
> He sees the round towers of other days
>   In the waves beneath him shining;
> Thus shall memory often in dream sublime
>   Catch a glimpse of the days that are over;
> Thus, sighing, look through the waves of time,
>   For the long faded glories they cover.
>
> Thomas Moore.

3. OUR RELATIONS WITH ENGLAND.

What reflecting American does not acknowledge the incalculable advantages derived to this land out of the deep foundations of civil, moral, and intellectual truth from which we have drawn in England? What American does not feel proud that his fathers were the countrymen of Bacon, of Newton, and of Locke? Who does not know that every pulse of civil liberty in the heart of our ancestors, the sobriety, the firmness, and the dignity with which the cause of free principles came into existence here, constantly found encouragement from the friends of Liberty there? For myself, I can truly say that, after my native land, I feel a strong reverence for that of my fathers. The pride I take in my own country makes me respect that from which we sprang. The sound of my native language beyond the sea is a music to my ears beyond the richest strains of Tuscan softness or Castilian majesty. I tread with reverence the spots where I can retrace the footsteps of our suffering fathers. The pleasant land of their birth has a claim on my heart. It seems to me a classic, yea, a holy land; rich in the memory of the great and the good, the champions and the martyrs of Liberty, the exiled heralds of truth, and richer, as the parent of this land of promise in the west.

I am not the panegyrist of England. I am not dazed by her riches, nor awed by her power. Nor is my admiration awakened by her armies, mustered for the battles of Europe; her navies overshadowing the ocean; nor her empire grasping the farthest East. It is these, and the price of guilt and blood by which they are too often maintained, which are the causes why no friend of Liberty can salute her with undivided affections. But it is the cradle and the refuge of free principles, though often persecuted; the school of religious liberty, the more precious for the struggles through which it has passed; the tombs of those who have reflected honor upon all who speak the English language; the birthplace of our fathers; the home of the Pilgrims, — it is these which I love and venerate in England. I should feel ashamed of an enthusiasm for Italy and Greece, did I not also feel it for a land like this. In an American, it would seem to me degenerate and unthankful to hang with rapture and passion upon the traces of Homer and Virgil, and follow, without emotion, the nearer and plainer footsteps of Shakspeare and Milton. I should think him cold in his love for his native land, who felt no melting in his heart for that other native country which holds the ashes of his forefathers.

EDWARD EVERETT

4. NEW ENGLAND.

HAIL to the land whereon we tread,
   Our fondest boast;
The sepulchre of mighty dead,
The truest hearts that ever bled,

Who sleep on glory's brightest bed,
   A fearless host!
No slave is here, — our unchained feet
Walk freely as the waves that beat
   Our coast.

Our fathers crossed the ocean's wave
   To reach this shore,
They left behind the coward slave,
To welter in his living grave;
With hearts unbent and spirits brave,
   They sternly bore
Such toils as meaner souls had quelled;
But souls like these, such toils impelled
   To soar.

Hail to the morn when first they stood
   On Bunker's height,
And, fearless, stemmed the invading flood,
And wrote our dearest rights in blood,
And mowed in ranks the hireling brood,
   In desperate fight!
Oh, 't was a proud, exulting day,
For e'en our fallen fortunes lay
   In light.

There is no other land like thee,
   Nor dearer shore;
Thou art the shelter of the free;
The home, the port of Liberty
Thou hast been, and shalt ever be,
   Till Time is o'er.
Ere I forget to think upon
Thy land, shall mother curse the son
   She bore.

>   Thou art the firm, unshaken rock
>   On which we rest;
>   And rising from thy hardy stock,
>   Thy sons the tyrant's frowns shall mock,
>   And slavery's galling chains unlock,
>   And free the oppressed:
>   All, who the wreath of Freedom twine
>   Beneath the shadow of their vine,
>   Are blest.
>
>   We love thy rude and rocky shore,
>   And here we stand.
>   Let foreign navies hasten o'er,
>   And on our heads their fury pour,
>   And peal their cannon's loudest roar,
>   And storm our land;
>   They still shall find, our lives are given
>   To die for home; and leant on heaven
>   Our hand.
>
>   JAMES GATES PERCIVAL.

5. ENGLAND'S RELATIONS TO AMERICA.

THE laws of England, founded on principles of liberty, are still in substance the code of America. Our writers, our statutes, the most modern decisions of our judges, are quoted in every court of justice from the St. Lawrence to the Mississippi. English law, as well as English liberty, is the foundation on which the legislation of America is founded. The authority of our jurisprudence may survive the power of our government for as many ages as the laws of Rome commanded respect and the reverence of Europe after the subversion of her empire.

Our language is as much that of America as it is that of England. As America increases, the glory of the great writers of England increases with it; the admirers of

Shakspeare and Milton are multiplied; and the fame of every future Englishman is widely spread. Is it unreasonable, then, to hope that these ties of birth, of liberty, of laws, of language, and of literature, may in time prevail over vulgar, ignoble, and ruinous prejudice? Their ancestors were as much the countrymen of Bacon and Newton, of Hampden and Sydney, as ours. They are entitled to their full share of that inheritance of glory which has descended from our common ancestors.

Neither the liberty of England, nor her genius, nor the noble language which that genius has consecrated, is worthy of their disregard. All these honors are theirs if they choose to preserve them. The history of England, till the adoption of counsels adverse to liberty, is their history. We may still preserve or revive kindred feelings. They may claim noble ancestors, and we may look forward to noble descendants.

JAMES MACINTOSH.

6. NEW ENGLAND AND VIRGINIA.

THERE are circumstances of peculiar and beautiful correspondence in the careers of Virginia and New England, which must ever constitute a bond of sympathy, affection, and pride between their children. Not only did they form respectively the great northern and southern rallying points of civilization on this continent; not only was the most friendly competition or the most cordial co-operation, as circumstances allowed, kept up between them during their early colonial existence, — but who forgets the generous emulation, the noble rivalry, with which they continually challenged and seconded each other in resisting the first beginnings of British aggression, in the persons of their James Otises and Patrick Henrys?

Who forgets that while that resistance was first brought to a practical test in New England, at Lexington and Concord and Bunker Hill, Fortune reserved for Yorktown of Virginia the last crowning battle of Independence? Who forgets that while the hand by which the original Declaration of Independence was drafted, was furnished by Virginia, the tongue by which the adoption of that instrument was defended and secured, was furnished by New England, — a bond of common glory, upon which not Death alone seemed to set his seal, but Deity, I had almost said, to affix an immortal sanction, when the spirits by which that hand and voice were moved, were caught up together to the clouds on the same great Day of the Nation's Jubilee.

ROBERT CHARLES WINTHROP.

7. THE PILGRIMS OF NEW ENGLAND.

WE meet again, the children of the Pilgrims, to remember our fathers. The two centuries and more which interpose to hide them from our eye — centuries so brilliant with progress, so crowded with incidents, so fertile in accumulations — dissolve for the moment as a curtain of cloud, and we are once more at their side. The grand and pathetic series of their story unrolls itself about us, vivid as if with the life of yesterday. All the stages by which they were slowly formed from the general mind and character of England, the tenderness of conscience, the sense of duty, force of will, trust in God, the love of truth, and the spirit of liberty by which they were advanced from Englishmen to Pilgrims, from Pilgrims to the founders of a free church, and the fathers of a free people, in a new world, come before us.

The voyage of the "Mayflower;" the landing; the slow

winter's night of disease and famine in which so many, the good, the beautiful, the brave, sank down and died, giving place at last to the spring-dawn of health and plenty, — come before us. The meeting with the old red race on the hill beyond the brook; the treaty of peace unbroken for half a century; the organization of a Republican form of government in the "Mayflower's" cabin; the planting of these kindred, coeval, and auxiliary institutions, without which such a government could no more live than the uprooted tree can put forth leaf and flower, — come before us. And with these come institutions to diffuse pure religion, good learning, austere morality, plain living, and high thinking; the laying deep and sure, far down on the Rock of Ages, the foundation-stone of that imperial structure whose dome now swells towards Heaven.

All these things, high, holy, and beautiful, come thronging fresh on our memories, such as we have heard them from our mother's lips; such as we have heard them in the history of kings, of religion, and of liberty. They gather themselves about us, familiar, certainly, but of an interest that can never die, — an interest heightened by their relations to that eventful future into which they have expanded, and through whose light they shine.

It is their festival we have come to keep to-day. It is their tabernacle we have come to build. It is not ourselves, our present, or our future; it is not political economy, or political philosophy, of which you would have me to-day say a word. We would speak of certain valiant, good peculiar men, our fathers. We would wipe the dust from a few old, noble urns. We would recall the forms and the lineaments of the honored dead, — forms and features which the grave has not changed; over which the grave has no power; robed in the vestments and all radiant with the hues of an assured immortality.

RUFUS CHOATE.

8. THE PURITAN.

The Puritans were men who derived a peculiar character from the daily contemplation of superior beings and eternal interests. Not content with acknowledging in general terms an overruling Providence, they habitually ascribed every event to the will of the Great Being, for whose power nothing was too vast, for whose inspection nothing was too minute. To know Him, to serve Him, to enjoy Him, was with them the great end of existence. They rejected with contempt the ceremonious homage which other sects substituted for the pure worship of the soul. They aspired to gaze upon the intolerable brightness of the Deity, and to commune with Him, face to face. Hence their contempt for worldly distinctions. The difference between the greatest and the meanest seemed to vanish, when compared with the boundless interval which separated the whole race from Him on whom their eyes were constantly fixed. If they were unacquainted with the works of philosophers and poets, they were deeply read in the oracles of God.

Thus the Puritan was made up of two different men: one, all self-abasement, penitence, gratitude, passion; the other, proud, calm, inflexible, sagacious. People who saw nothing of the godly but their uncouth visages, and heard nothing from them but their groans and their hymns, might laugh at them. But those had little reason to laugh who encountered them in the hall of debate, or on the field of battle. They brought to civil and military affairs a coolness of judgment and an immutability of purpose which some writers have thought inconsistent with their religious zeal, but which were, in fact, the effects of it. The intensity of their feelings on one subject made them tranquil on every other. Death had lost its terrors, and pleasure its charms. They had their smiles and their tears, their raptures and their sorrows; but not for the things of the world. Enthusiasm had made them stoics, had cleared their minds from vulgar passion and prejudice, and raised them above the influence of danger and corruption. It sometimes might lead them to pursue unwise ends, but never to choose unwise means. We acknowledge that the tone of their minds was often injured by straining after things too high for mortal reach, and they too often fell into the vices of intolerance and extreme austerity. Yet, when all circumstances are taken into consideration, we do not hesitate to pronounce them a brave, a wise, an honest and useful people.

MACAULAY.

9. FATHERLAND.

God, who gave iron, purposed ne'er,
    That man should be a slave;
Therefore the sabre, sword, and spear
    In his right hand he gave;
Therefore he gave his fiery mood,
    Fierce speech, and free-born breath
That he might fearlessly the feud
    Maintain through blood and death.

Therefore will we, what God did say,
    With honest truth maintain,
And ne'er a fellow-creature slay,
    A tyrant's pay to gain.
But he shall perish by stroke of brand
    Who fighteth but for sin and shame,
And not inherit the German land,
    With men of the German name.

O Germany, bright Fatherland,
  O German love so true,
Thou sacred land, thou beauteous land,
  We swear to thee anew!
Outlawed, each knave and coward shall
  The crow and raven feed;
But we will to the battle all,
  Revenge shall be our meed.

Flash forth! flash forth! whatever can,
  To bright and flaming life:
Now all ye Germans, man for man,
  Forth in the holy strife!
Your hands lift upward to the sky,
  Your hearts shall upward soar;
And, "man for man," let each one cry,
  Our slavery is o'er!

Let sound, let sound, whatever can,
  Trumpet and fife and drum;
This day our sabres, "man for man,"
  To stain with blood we come, —
With hangman's and with coward's blood.
  O glorious day of ire,
That to all Germans seemeth good,
  Day of our great desire.

Let wave! let wave! whatever can,
  Standard and banner wave!
Here will we purpose, "man for man "
  To grace a hero's grave.
Advance, ye brave ranks, hardily,
  Your banners wave on high,
We'll gain us freedom's victory,
  Or freedom's death we'll die.

ERNST MORITZ ARNDT.

10. THE FATHERLAND.

Where is the true man's fatherland?
Is it where he, by chance, was born?
Doth not the yearning spirit scorn
In such scant borders to be spanned?
Oh, yes, his fatherland must be
As the blue heaven, wide and free!

Is it alone where freedom is,
Where God is God, and man is man?
Doth he not claim a broader span
For the soul's love of home than this?
Oh, yes, his fatherland must be,
As the broad heaven, broad and free!

Where'er a human heart doth wear
Joy's myrtle wreath, or sorrow's gyves;
Where'er a human spirit strives
After a life more true and fair, —
There is the true man's birthplace grand:
His is a world-wide fatherland!

Where'er a single slave doth pine,
Where'er one man may hold another —
Thank God for such a birthplace, brother, —
That spot of earth is thine and mine;
There is the true man's birthright grand:
His is a world-wide fatherland!

James Russell Lowell.

11. WE WERE BOYS TOGETHER.

We were boys together,
   And never can forget
The school-house on the heather,
   In childhood where we met;
The humble home to memory dear,
   Its sorrows and its joys,
Where woke the transient smile or tear,
   When you and I were boys.

We were youths together,
   And castles built in air;
Your heart was like a feather,
   And mine weighed down with care;
To you came wealth with manhood's prime,
   To me it brought alloys
Foreshadowed in the primrose time,
   When you and I were boys.

We're old men together;
   The friends we loved of yore,
With leaves of autumn weather,
   Are gone for evermore.
How blest to age the impulse given, —
   The hope Time ne'er destroys, —
Which led our thoughts from earth to heaven,
   When you and I were boys.

GEORGE P. MORRIS.

The soul of Jonathan was knit with the soul of David, and Jonathan loved him as his own soul.

I. Samuel, xviii. 1.

12. FATHER-LAND AND MOTHER-TONGUE.

Our Father-land! And wouldst thou know
   Why we should call it Father-land?
It is, that Adam here below
   Was made of earth by Nature's hand;
And he, our father, made of earth,
   Hath peopled earth on every hand;
And we, in memory of his birth,
   Do call our country "Father-land."

At first, in Eden's bowers, they say,
   No sound of speech had Adam caught,
But whistled like a bird all day,
   And maybe 't was for want of thought;
But Nature, with resistless laws,
   Made Adam soon surpass the birds:
She gave him lovely Eve, because,
   If he'd a wife, they must have words.

And so, the native land, I hold
   By male descent, is proudly mine;
The language, as the tale was told,
   Was given in the female line.
And thus, we see, on either hand
   We name our blessings whence they're sprung:
We call our country "Father-land,"
   We call our language "Mother-tongue."

Samuel Lover.

13. THE LAND OF MY BIRTH.

There 's a magical tie to the land of our home,
Which the heart cannot break, though the footsteps may roam ;
Be that land where it may, at the Line or the Pole,
It still holds the magnet that draws back the soul.
'T is loved by the freeman, 't is loved by the slave ;
'T is dear to the coward, more dear to the brave !
Ask of any the spot they like best on earth,
And they 'll answer with pride, "The land of my birth."

O England, thy white cliffs are dearer to me
Than all the famed coasts of a far, foreign sea !
What emerald can peer or what sapphire can vie
With the grass of thy fields or thy summer-day sky ?
They tell me of regions where flowers are found,
Whose perfume and tints spread a paradise round ;
But brighter to me cannot garland the earth
Than those that spring forth in the land of my birth.

Did I breath in a clime where the bulbul is heard,
Where the citron-tree nestles the soft humming-bird,
Oh, I 'd covet the notes of my nightingale still,
And remember the robin that feeds at my sill.
Did my soul find a feast in the gay "land of song,"
In the gondolier's chant, or the carnival's throng,
Could I ever forget, 'mid their music and mirth,
The national strain of the land of my birth ?

Eliza Cook.

OUR OWN THE BEST

'T is with our judgment, as our watches ; none go just alike, yet each believes his own.

14. ROCKS OF MY COUNTRY.

Rocks of my country, let the cloud
    Your created heights array,
And rise ye, like a fortress proud,
    Above the surge and spray;
My spirit greets you as ye stand,
    Breasting the billow's foam;
Oh, thus forever guard the land,
    The severed land of home!

I have left rich blue skies behind,
    Lighting up classic shrines,
And music in the southern wind,
    And sunshine on the vines.
The breathings of the myrtle-flowers
    Have floated o'er my way,
The pilgrim's voice at vesper hours
    Hath soothed me with its lay.

The isles of Greece, the hills of Spain,
    The purple heavens of Rome, —
Yes, all are glorious; yet again
    I bless thee, land of home!
For thine the Sabbath peace, my land,
    And thine the guarded hearth;
And thine the dead, the noble band,
    That makes thee holy earth.

Their voices meet me in thy breeze,
    Their steps are on thy plains;
Their names by old, majestic trees
    Are whispered round thy fanes.
Their blood hath mingled with the tide
    Of thine exulting sea;
Oh, be it still a joy, a pride,
    To live and die for thee!

                  FELICIA DOROTHEA HEMANS

15. THE HOUSE WHERE I WAS BORN.

I remember, I remember,
  The house where I was born;
The little window where the sun
  Came peeping in at morn.
He never came a wink too soon,
  Nor brought too long a day;
But now I often wish the night
  Had borne my breath away.

I remember, I remember,
  The roses red and white,
The violets and the lily-cups, —
  Those flowers made of light, —
The lilacs where the robin built,
  And where my brother set
The laburnums on his birthday:
  The tree is living yet.

I remember, I remember,
  Where I was used to swing,
And thought the air must rush as fresh
  To swallows on the wing;
My spirit flew in feathers then,
  That is so heavy now,
And summer pools could hardly cool
  The fever on my brow.

I remember, I remember,
  The fir-trees dark and high;
I used to think their slender tops
  Were close against the sky.
It was a childish ignorance;
  But now 't is little joy
To know I 'm farther off from heaven
  Than when I was a boy.

THOMAS HOOD.

16. AT THE OLD HOME AGAIN.

Lines written on re-visiting the Country.

I stand upon my native hills again,
  Broad, round, and green, that in the summer sky
With garniture of waving grass and grain,
  Orchards, and beechen forests, basking lie,
While deep the sunless glens are scooped between,
Where brawl o'er shallow beds the streams unseen.
  . . . .

Here, I have 'scaped the city's stifling heat,
  Its horrid sounds, and its polluted air;
And, where the season's milder fervors beat,
  And gales, that sweep the forest border, bear
The song of bird, and sound of running stream,
Am come awhile to wander and to dream.

Ay, flame thy fiercest, Sun! thou canst not wake,
  In this pure air, the plague that walks unseen.
The maize leaf and the maple bough but take,
  From thy fierce heats, a deeper, glossier green;
The mountain wind, that faints not in thy ray,
Sweeps the blue streams of pestilence away.

The mountain wind! most spiritual of all
  The wide earth knows; when in the sultry time
He stoops him from his vast cerulean hall,
  He seems the breath of a celestial clime;
As if from heaven's wide-open gates did flow
Health and refreshment on the world below.

William Cullen Bryant.

Remove not the ancient landmarks which thy fathers have set up.

Proverbs, xxii. 28.

17. THE NORWEGIAN WEDDING-MARCH, OF GRIEG, IN VERSE.

The rapidly increasing emigration to America of the honest, hardy, and industrious people of Norway and Sweden, gives special interest to their home customs, and none is more impressive than the country wedding which is portrayed in Grieg's famous Wedding-March. The early stir in the village, the chimes, the incidents of the march, until the chapel closes upon the procession, vividly reproduce the scene.

Afar off, confusèd sounds salute the quiet air,
Commingling with noisy clanging of a chime:
Starting on the outskirts of a mountain village, where
A Norway peasant crowd assembles at sweet eventime.

My house half way up the winding village road
Is situate; the village church a full mile further on,
Where priest and people at an altar meet to worship God,
And solemn rites of life and death are spoken for the town.

To-day, bells chime for nuptial vows of groom and bride:
The happy groom, the happy woman at his side,
Clasp hands, and lead the way to chapel door:
Behind them join a glad procession of dear friends,
With rustic band, chanting in unison, o'er and o'er,
A sweet, sad bride-song, oft heard in Norway fiords and glens.

I hear the voices rising, falling, then the drums;
And shouts of laughter, and the tramp of lightsome feet;
The piercing clarionet, the brasses: onward comes the
Merry crowd. My windows, opening on the street,
Let in the noises and the music, which impel my soul
To cheerful contemplation of life's start and goal.

Just now they've passed behind a heavy clump of wood;
The noise is almost hushed; I only feel the tread
Of feet; the bride-song's lost. Oh, is it surely dead?

And have dark clouds of strife shut out the rainbow-hued?
Ah, no; the mellow sunshine and the music again illume the
    road!

The bride, in meditation sweet, with rapture scarcely under-
    stood,
Glances backward 'cross her years of fresh young life,
Through childhood, girlhood, up to budded womanhood.
Memory weaves again the fairy tales with folk-lore rife,
Of Scandia's loving muses, songs of the sea, and vikings gone,
Fills her blue eyes with tears. Her way unknown, an instant
    seemeth long;

But that strong man, whom she hath chosen for her lord,
Has pressed her trembling hand against his rugged breast
And calmed her fears: now 'mong the company her voice is
    heard, —
Her sweet voice, higher and more gladsome than the rest.

Again, emerging 'gainst the lurid sunset sky,
The happy crowd comes on! Out blares the band!
The song swells forth! and now they pass my windows by,
Swinging hats in air, and dancing hand in hand.
The little church appears in view, and every happy voice
And every happy instrument joins the merry din.
Passing from me up the road, a thousand joys
I wish them, as their boisterous songs to die away begin.

Fainter and fainter grows the bride-song evermore,
Louder and louder throb the heart-beats of that groom and
    bride.
With bowed heads they reach the threshold of the sacred
    door
And enter, and the bride-song's hushed anon — inside.

                                        CHARLES W. JOHNSON.

18. THE OLD OAKEN BUCKET.

How dear to this heart are the scenes of my childhood
    When fond recollection presents them to view!
The orchard, the meadow, the deep-tangled wildwood,
    And every loved spot which my infancy knew;
The wide-spreading pond, and the mill which stood by it,
    The bridge, and the rock where the cataract fell;
The cot of my father, the dairy-house by it,
    And e'en the rude bucket which hung in the well:
The old oaken bucket, the iron-bound bucket,
    The moss-covered bucket which hung in the well.

That moss-covered bucket I hail as a treasure;
    For often, at noon, when returned from the field,
I found it the source of an exquisite pleasure,
    The mutest and sweetest that nature can yield.
How ardent I seized it, with hands that were glowing,
    And quick to the white pebbled bottom it fell;
Then soon, with the emblem of truth overflowing,
    And dripping with coolness, it rose from the well:
The old oaken bucket, the iron-bound bucket,
    The moss-covered bucket, arose from the well.

How sweet from the green mossy rim to receive it,
    As, poised on the curb, it inclined to my lips!
Not a full blushing goblet could tempt me to leave it,
    Though filled with the nectar that Jupiter sips.
And now, far removed from the loved situation,
    The tear of regret will intrusively swell,
As fancy reverts to my father's plantation,
    And sighs for the bucket that hangs in the well:
The old oaken bucket, the iron-bound bucket,
    The moss-covered bucket, that hangs in the well.

. . SAMUEL WOODWORTH.

19. WOODMAN SPARE THAT TREE.

Woodman spare that tree!
 Touch not a single bough!
In youth it sheltered me,
 And I'll protect it now.
'T was my forefather's hand
 That placed it near the cot;
Then, woodman, let it stand,
 Thy axe shall harm it not.

That old familiar tree,
 Whose glory and renown
Are spread o'er land and sea,
 And wouldst thou hew it down?
Woodman, forbear thy stroke;
 Cut not its earth-bound ties:
Oh, spare that aged oak,
 Now towering to the skies!

When but an idle boy,
 I sought its grateful shade;
In all their gushing joy
 Here, too, my sisters played.
My mother kissed me here,
 My father pressed my hand;
Forgive this foolish tear,
 But let that old oak stand.

My heart-strings round thee cling,
 Close as thy bark, old friend!
Here shall the wild bird sing,
 And still thy branches bend.
Old tree, the storm still brave!
 And, woodman, leave the spot:
While I've a hand to save,
 Thy axe shall harm it not.
GEORGE P. MORRIS

20. THE OLD HOME AND THE NEW.

Impromtu lines, written after fifty years' residence in America, upon the arrival of the Scotch cutter "Thistle" in the harbor of New York.

"The Thistle," the thistle, the bonnie brown thistle,
    Has come to our shores from the "Land of the cake,"[1]
With a trim little hull and the wings of a gull,
    For a race o'er the bay, to fraternally make.

From the home of my childhood "The Thistle" has come,
    Her name bearing emblem, to Scot ever dear,
And memories tender of the years that have gone
    Since I wended my journey to home over here.

Thus the land of my birth with fresh zeal I recall,
    And the mother who taught that land to adore,
Who bade me to honor, whate'er might befall,
    The home I adopted on Columbia's shore.

So the "Thistle" that bristles with challenge so bold,
    And reminds me of heather and bonnie blue bell,
Of Scotland's great names, and her glories of old,
    Only strengthens new ties I'm loving so well.

For the crags of old Scotland, endeared in the past,
    Are shorn of the glories the minstrel once sung;
But their echoes shall linger, forever to last,
    In words bold and sweet, of the same mother tongue.

Robert Bleakie.

21. OUR GARDENER'S BURIAL.

This is the grave prepared: set down the bier.
Mother, a faithful son we bring thee here,
In loving ease to lie beneath thy breast,
Which many a year with loving toil he drest;

---

[1] The Oat meal, loaf or cake, in common use.

His was the eldest craft, the simple skill
That Adam plied, ere good was known by ill.
The throstle's song at dawn his spirit tuned;
He set his seeds in hope, he grafted, pruned,
Weeded, and mowed, and, with a true son's care,
Wrought thee a mantle of embroidery rare.
The snowdrop and the winter aconite
Came to his call ere frosts had ceased to bite.
He bade the crocus flame as with a charm;
The nestling violets bloomed, and feared no harm,
Knowing that for their sakes a champion meek
Did bloodless battle with the winter bleak;
But when the wealthier months with largess came,
His blazoned beds put heraldry to shame,
And on the summer air such perfume cast
As Saba or the Spice Isles ne'er surpassed.
The birds all loved him, for he would not shoot
Even the wingèd thieves that stole his fruit:
And he loved them, the little fearless wren,
The red-breasts, curious in the ways of men,
The pilgrim swallow, and the dearer guest
That sets beneath our eaves her plastered nest;
The merry white-throat, bursting with his song,
Fluttered within his reach, and feared no wrong;
And the mute fly-catcher forgot her dread,
And took her prey beside his stooping head.
Receive him, Mother Earth: his work is done.
Blameless he lived, and did offence to none;
Blameless he died, forbidding us to throw
Flowers in his grave, because he loved them so:
But bloom among the grasses on his mound, —
He would not have them stifle underground.
We that have loved must leave him: Mother, keep
A faithful watch about him in his sleep.

London Spectator.

22. MY FATHERLAND.

FAITHFUL love till death enduring,
    Pledge I thee with heart and hand;
All my being, all my having,
    Owe I thee, my fatherland.

Not in words and ditties only,
    Would my heart my thanks outpour,
For with deeds I fain would prove it,
    In the dark, fierce strife of war.

So in joy and so in sorrow,
    Friend and foe, I'll tell it now,
We for aye are bound together,
    And my pride and joy art thou.

Faithful love till death enduring,
    Pledge I thee with heart and hand,
All my being, all my having,
    Owe I thee, my fatherland.

HOFFMANN VON FALLERSLEBEN

23. HOME.

WHERE burns the loved hearth brightest,
    Cheering the social breast?
Where beats the fond heart lightest,
    Its humblest hopes possessed?
Where is the smile of sadness,
    Of meek-eyed patience born,
Worth more than those of gladness,
    Which mirth's bright cheeks adorn?
Pleasure is marked by fleetness
    To those who ever roam;
While grief itself has sweetness
    At Home, dear Home!

There blend the ties that strengthen
  Our hearts in hours of grief,
The silver links that lengthen
  Joy's visits when most brief.
There eyes in all their splendor
  Are vocal to the heart,
And gladness, gay or tender,
  Fresh eloquence impart.
Then dost thou sigh for pleasure;
  Oh, do not widely roam,
But seek that hidden treasure
  At Home, dear Home!

Does pure religion charm thee
  Far more than aught below?
Wouldst thou that she should arm thee
  Against the hour of woe?
Think not that she dwelleth only
  In temples built for prayer;
For home itself is lonely
  Unless her smiles be there.
The devotee may falter,
  The bigot blindly roam,
If worshipless her altar
  At Home, dear Home!

Love over it presideth
  With meek and watchful awe;
Its daily service guideth,
  And shows its perfect law.
If there thy faith shall fail thee,
  If there no shrine be found,
What can thy prayers avail thee,
  With kneeling crowds around?
Go, — leave thy gift unoffered
  Beneath Religion's dome,
And be her first-fruits offered
  At Home, dear Home!

                      BERNARD BARTON.

24. HOME! HOME! SWEET HOME!

'Mid pleasures and palaces though we may roam,
Be it ever so humble, there's no place like home.
A charm from the skies seems to hallow us there,
Which, seek through the world, is ne'er met with elsewhere.
    Home! home! sweet home!
    There's no place like home!

An exile from home, splendor dazzles in vain.
Oh, give me my lowly thatched cottage again!
The birds singing gayly, that came to my call!
Oh, give me sweet peace of mind, dearer than all!
    Home! home! sweet home!
    There's no place like home!

JOHN HOWARD PAYNE.

25. LOVE OF COUNTRY.

Breathes there the man, with soul so dead,
Who never to himself hath said,
  "This is my own, my native land!"
Whose heart hath ne'er within him burned,
As home his footsteps he hath turned
  From wandering on a foreign strand?
If such there breathe, go, mark him well;
For him no minstrel raptures swell;
High though his titles, proud his name,
Boundless his wealth as wish could claim,—
Despite those titles, power, and pelf,
The wretch, concentred all in self,
Living, shall forfeit fair renown,
And, doubly dying, shall go down
To the vile dust, from whence he sprung,
Unwept, unhonored, and unsung.

SIR WALTER SCOTT

PART IV.

AMERICAN INDEPENDENCE.

───•───

1. SEVENTY-SIX.

WHAT heroes from the woodland sprung,
   When, from the fresh-awakened land,
The thrilling cry of Freedom rung,
And to the work of warfare strung
   The yeoman's iron hand!

Hills flung the cry to hills around,
   And ocean-mart replied to mart;
And streams, whose springs were yet unfound,
Pealed far away the startling sound
   Into the forest's heart.

Then marched the brave from rocky steep,
   From mountain river swift and cold :
The borders of the stormy deep,
The vales where gathered waters sleep,
   Sent up the strong and bold,

As if the very earth again
   Grew quick with God's creating breath,
And from the sods of grove and glen
Rose ranks of lion-hearted men,
   To battle to the death.

Already had the strife begun:
  Already blood on Concord's plain
Along the springing grass had run,
And blood had flowed at Lexington,
  Like brooks of April rain.

That death-stain on the vernal sward
  Hallowed to Freedom all the shore:
In fragments fell the yoke abhorred;
The footsteps of a foreign lord
  Profaned the soil no more.

WILLIAM CULLEN BRYANT.

2. INDEPENDENCE DAY.

THE United States is the only country with a known birthday. All the rest begun, they know not when, and grew into power, they know not how. If there had been no Independence Day, England and America combined would not be so great as each actually is. There is no "Republican," no "Democrat," on the Fourth of July, — all are Americans. All feel that their country is greater than party.

JAMES GILLESPIE BLAINE.

AMERICA AN AGGREGATE OF NATIONS.

GIANT aggregate of nations, glorious whole, of glorious parts,
Unto endless generations live united, hands and hearts.
Be it storm or summer weather, peaceful calm or battle-jar,
Stand in beauteous strength together, sister States, as now
  ye are.

MARTIN FARQUHAR TUPPER.

3. CAROLINA AND MECKLENBURG.

It is believed that the first Englishman ever landed upon our shores was sent by Sir Walter Raleigh to Roanoke Island, on the 4th day of July ("prophetic coincidence"), 1584, before the Pilgrims landed at Plymouth or Jamestown was settled. The first blood shed in resistance to British oppression was at Alamance, May 7, 1771; and the first Proclamation looking to Independence was made at Charlotte, Mecklenburg County, North Carolina, May 20, 1775. The following tribute to this beautiful and patriotic State is in harmony with the facts.

  Tell me, ye winds, if e'er ye rest
   Your wings on fairer land,
  Save when, near Araby the blest,
   Ye scent its fragrant strand?
  Tell me, ye spirits of the air:
   Know ye a region anywhere,
  By night or day that can compare
   With Carolina, bright and fair?

  Her feet she plants on Ocean's plane;
   Her arms the hills embrace;
  In mountain's snow, or mist, or rain,
   She laves her smiling face;
  Turns then to greet Aurora's dawn,
   Ere yet on sea the day is born;
  And stars that die at birth of morn
   Kiss her "good-by," and then are gone!

  Fair Ceres smiles o'er waving fields,
   On hillside and on plain;
  The generous soil abundance yields,
   With sunshine and with rain.
  Tell me, ye rivers, creeks, and rills:
   Know ye a land the farmer tills,
  That larger barns and granaries fills
   Than Carolina's vales and hills?

Beneath her soil, just hidden, lie
　Treasures of priceless worth,
Which in their value well may vie
　With richest mines of earth.
Then list, as blithe Hygeia sings:
　"Long life and health are in our springs!
Drink deep; each draught new vigor brings,
　Backward old Time shall turn his wings,
　　Death lose his stings!"

On Mecklenburg's historic ground,
　All hail! our Charter Tree;
Where Freedom's voice was first to sound
　The watchword, "Man is free!"
That clarion note the nation caught;
　Our sires, emboldened by the thought,
All that they had and were they brought,
　For altars, homes, and honor fought,
　　And freedom bought!

JAMES A. DELKE.

4. THE FOURTH OF JULY.

Extract from Address delivered by DANIEL WEBSTER, July 4th, 1851, at laying the corner-stone of the new wing of the Capitol.

THIS is that day of the year which announced to mankind the great fact of American Independence! This fresh and brilliant morning blesses our vision with another beholding of the birthday of our Nation; and we see that Nation, of recent origin, now among the most considerable and powerful, and spreading from sea to sea over the continent.

On the Day of the Declaration of Independence, our illustrious Fathers performed the first scene in the last Act of this drama, — one, in real importance, infinitely exceeding that for which the great English poet invoked, —

> "A muse of fire, a kingdom for a stage,
> Princes to act,
> And monarchs to behold the swelling scene."

The Muse inspiring our Fathers was the Genius of Liberty, all on fire with a sense of oppression, and a resolution to throw it off. The whole world was the stage, and higher characters than princes trod it. Instead of monarchs, countries and nations and the age beheld the swelling scene. How well the characters were cast, and how well each acted his part, and what emotions the whole performance excited, let history now and hereafter tell.

On the Fourth Day of July, 1776, the representatives of the United States of America, in Congress assembled, declared that these Colonies are, and ought to be, free and independent States. This declaration, made by most patriotic and resolute men, trusting in the justice of their cause and the protection of Heaven, — and yet not without deep solicitude and anxiety, — has now stood for seventy-five years. It was sealed in blood. It has met dangers and overcome them. It has had detractors, and abashed them all. It has had enemies, and conquered them. It has had doubting friends, but it has cleared all doubts away; and now, to-day, raising its august form higher than the clouds, twenty millions of people contemplate it with hallowed love, and the world beholds it, and the consequences that have followed from it, with profound admiration.

This anniversary animates and gladdens all American hearts. On other days of the year we may be party men, indulging in controversies more or less important to the public good. We may have likes and dislikes, and we may maintain our political differences, often with warm, and sometimes with angry, feelings. But to-day we are Americans all; and all, nothing but Americans.

As the great luminary over our heads, dissipating fogs and mist, now cheers the whole atmosphere, so do the associations connected with this day disperse all sullen and cloudy weather in the minds and feelings of true Americans. Every man's heart swells within him. Every man's port and bearing becomes somewhat more proud and lofty as he remembers that seventy-five years have rolled away, and that the great inheritance of Liberty is still his, — his, undiminished and unimpaired; his, in all its original glory; his to enjoy, his to protect, his to transmit to future generations.

5. THE FIRST AMERICAN CONGRESS.

THERE never was, in any age or nation, a body of men who, for general information, for the judicious use of civil and religious liberty, for true dignity, elevation, and grandeur of zeal, could stand comparison with the First American Congress.

Whom do I behold? A Hancock, a Jefferson, a Henry, a Lee, a Rutledge! Glory to their immortal spirits! On you depend the destinies of your country; the fate of three millions of men, and of the countless millions of their posterity. Shall these be slaves? Or will you make a noble stand for liberty against a power whose triumphs are already co-extensive with the earth; whose legions trample on thrones and sceptres; whose thunders bellow on every ocean? How tremendous the occasion! How vast the responsibilities!

The President and all the members of this august assembly take their seats. Every countenance tells the mighty struggle within. Every tongue is silent. It is a pause in nature, — that solemn, awful stillness which precedes the earthquake or tornado. At length one arises, and one equal to the occasion, — Patrick Henry, the Virginia Demosthenes. What dignity! What majesty! Every eye fastens on him. Firm, erect, undaunted, he rolls on the torrent of his mighty eloquence. What a picture does he draw of the horrors of servitude and the charms of freedom!

At once, he gives full rein to all his gigantic powers, and pours his own heroic spirit into the minds of his auditors. They become as one man, actuated by one soul; and the universal shout is, "Liberty or Death!"

This single speech of this illustrious man gave an impulse which probably decided the fate of America. His eloquence seized and moved the assembled sages, as the descending hail-storm, bursting in thunder, rending the forests, and shaking the mountains!

God bestows on nations no greater gift than great and good men, endowed with the high and commanding powers of eloquence. Such a man as Patrick Henry, may, on some great occasion, when the happiness or misery of millions depend on a single decision, render more important service to a nation than all the generations of a century.

JONATHAN MAXCY.

If we are not this day wanting in our duty to our country, the names of these American legislators will be placed by posterity at the side of all those whose memory has been and will be forever dear to virtuous men and good citizens.

RICHARD HENRY LEE.

6. THE PRINCIPLES OF THE REVOLUTION.

When we speak of the glory of our fathers, we mean not that vulgar renown to be attained by physical strength; nor yet that higher fame, to be acquired by intellectual power. Both often exist without lofty thought, pure intent, or generous purpose. The glory which we celebrate was strictly of a moral and religious character: righteous as to its ends; just as to its means.

The American Revolution had its origin neither in ambition, nor avarice, nor envy, nor in any gross passion; but in the nature and relation of things, and in the thence-resulting necessity of separation from the parent State. Its progress was limited by that necessity. Our fathers displayed great strength and great moderation of purpose. In difficult times they conducted with wisdom; in doubtful times, with firmness; in perilous times, with courage; under oppressive trials, erect; amidst temptations, unseduced; in the dark hour of danger, fearless; in the bright hour of prosperity, faithful.

It was not the instant feeling and pressure of despotism that roused them to resist, but the principle on which that arm was extended. They could have paid the impositions of the British government, had they been increased a thousand-fold; but payment acknowledged right, and they spurned the consequences of that acknowledgment. But, above all, they realized that those burdens, though light in themselves, would, to coming ages, — to us, their posterity, — be heavy, and probably insupportable. They preferred to meet the trial in their own times, and to make the sacrifices in their own persons, that we and our descendants, their posterity, might reap the harvest and enjoy the increase.

Generous men, exalted patriots, immortal statesmen! For this deep moral and social affection, for this elevated self-devotion, this bold daring, the multiplying millions of your posterity, as they spread backward to the lakes, and from the lakes to the mountains, and from the mountains to the western waters, shall annually, in all future time, come up to the temple of the Most High, with song and anthem, and thanksgiving, with cheerful symphonies and hallelujahs, to repeat your names; to look steadfastly on the brightness of your glory; to trace its spreading rays to the points from which they emanate; and to seek in your character and conduct a practical illustration of public duty in every occurring social exigency.

Josiah Quincy.

7. THE LESSON OF THE REVOLUTION.

Happy was it for America, happy for the world, that a great name, a guardian genius, presided over her destinies in war, combining more than the virtues of the Roman Fabius and the Theban Epaminondas, and compared with whom the conquerors of the world, the Alexanders and the Cæsars, are but pageants, crimsoned with blood and decked with the trophies of slaughter, objects equally of the wonder and the execration of mankind. The hero of America was the conqueror only of his country's foes and the hearts of his countrymen. To the one he was a terror; and in the other he gained an ascendancy, supreme, unrivalled, the tribute of admiring gratitude, the reward of a nation's love.

The American armies, compared with the embattled legions of the old world, were small in numbers; but the soul of a whole people centred in the bosom of those more than Spartan bands, and vibrated quickly and keenly with every incident that befell them, whether in their feats of valor, or the acuteness of their sufferings. The country itself was one wide battle-field, in which not merely the life-blood, but the dearest interests, the sustaining hopes of every individual, were at stake. It was not a war of pride and ambition between monarchs, in which an island or a province might be the reward of success. It was a contest for personal liberty and civil rights, coming down, in its principles, to the very sanctuary of home and the fireside, and determining for every man the measure of responsibility he should hold over his own condition, possessions, and happiness. The spectacle was grand and new, and may well be cited as the most glowing page in the annals of progressive man.

JARED SPARKS.

8. THE AMERICAN CONSTITUTION.

AFTER all our doubts, our suspicions and speculations on the subject of government, we must at last return to this important truth, — that when we have formed a constitution on free principles, we may, with safety, furnish it with all the powers necessary to answer, in the most ample manner, the purposes of government.

The great objects desired are a free representation and mutual checks. When these can be obtained, all the apprehensions as to the extent of powers are unjust and imaginary. What, then, is the structure of this American Constitution? One branch of the Legislature is to be elected by the people, — by the same people who choose your State Representatives. Its members are to hold office for two years, and then return to their constituents. Here the people govern. Here they act by their immediate representatives. You also have a Senate, constituted by your State Legislatures, by men in whom you place the highest confidence, and forming another representative branch. Then, again, you have an Executive Magistrate, created by a form of election which merits universal admiration. You find all the checks which the greatest politicians and the best writers have ever conceived. What more can reasonable man desire? The Legislative authority is lodged in three distinct branches, and the Judicial is still reserved as an independent body who hold their offices during good behavior. This organization is all so skilfully contrived that it is next to impossible that an impolitic or wicked measure should pass its scrutiny with success.

What do gentlemen mean by coming forward and declaiming against this government? Why do they say that we ought to limit its powers and destroy its capacity for blessing the people? Has philosophy suggested, has experience taught, that such a government ought not to be intrusted with everything necessary for the good of society? When you have divided and balanced the departments of government; when you have strongly connected the virtue of your rulers with their interests; when, in short, you have rendered your system as perfect as human forms can be, — you must place confidence; and you must give power.

ALEXANDER HAMILTON.

If I have a wish dearer to my soul than that my ashes may be mingled with those of a Warren and a Montgomery, it is, that these American States will never cease to be free and independent.

SAMUEL ADAMS.

9. THE AMERICAN CONSTITUTION TESTED.

(From Inaugural Address of President John Adams, 1797.)

EMPLOYED in the service of my country abroad, I first saw the Constitution of the United States in a foreign country. Irritated by no literary altercation, animated by no public debate, heated by no party animosity, I read it with great satisfaction, as the result of good heads, prompted by good hearts. I saw in it an experiment better adapted to the genius, character, situation, and relations of this nation and country than any other that had been suggested. In its general principles and outline it was conformable to such a system of government as I had ever most esteemed, and my own State in particular had contributed to establish.

Returning to the bosom of my country after a painful separation from it for ten years, I had the honor to be elected to a station under the new order of things, and I have repeatedly laid myself under the most serious obligations to support the Constitution.

The operation of it has equalled the most sanguine expectations of its friends; and from a habitual attention to it, satisfaction in its administration, and delight in its effects upon the peace, order, prosperity, and happiness of the nation, I have acquired an habitual attachment to it, and veneration for it. What other form of government, indeed, can so well deserve our esteem and love?

To a benevolent mind, there can be no spectacle more pleasing, more noble, majestic, and august, than an Assembly like that which has so often been seen in this and the other Chamber in Congress,—of a government in which the Executive authority, as well as that of all branches of the Legislature, are exercised by citizens selected at regular periods by their neighbors, to make and execute laws for the general good. Can anything essential, anything more than mere ornament and decoration, be added to this by robes or diamonds? Can authority be more amiable or respectable when it descends from accidents or remote antiquity, than when it springs fresh from the hearts and judgments of an honest and enlightened people? It is the people that are represented. It is their power and majesty that is reflected, and only for their good, in every legitimate government, under whatever form it may appear.

The existence of such a government as ours, for any length of time, is a full proof of the general dissemination of knowledge and virtue throughout the whole body of the people. What object more pleasing than this can be presented to the human mind? If national pride is ever justifiable or excusable, it is when it springs, not from power or riches, grandeur or glory, but from a conviction of national innocence, information, and benevolence.

10. THE AMERICAN CONSTITUTION NO EXPERIMENT.

We are told that our constitution is a mere experiment. I deny it, utterly. He that says so, shows that he has not studied it at all, or has studied to little purpose the history and genius of our institutions. The great cause of their prosperous results is precisely to the contrary. It is because our fathers made no experiments, and had no experiment to make, that their work has stood. They were forced, by a violation of their historical, hereditary rights under the old Common Law of their race, to dissolve their connection with the mother country; but the whole constitution of society in the States, the great body and bulk of their public law with all its maxims and principles, — in short, all that is Republican in our institutions, — remained after the Revolution, and remains now, with some very subordinate modifications, what it was from the beginning.

Our written constitutions do nothing but consecrate and fortify "the plain rules of ancient liberty," handed down with Magna Charta, from the earliest history of our race. It is not a piece of paper, it is not a few abstractions engrossed on parchment, that makes free governments. No! The law of Liberty must be inscribed on the heart of the citizen. "The Word," if I may use the expression, without irreverence, "must become flesh." You must have a whole people trained, disciplined, bred, yea, born as our fathers were, to institutions like ours.

Before the Colonies existed, the Petition of Rights, that Magna Charta of a more enlightened age, had been presented by Lord Coke and his immortal compeers, in 1628. Our founders brought it with them, and we have not gone a step beyond them. They brought these maxims of civil liberty in their souls, not in their libraries, as rules of conduct, as a symbol of public duty and private right, to be adhered to with religious fidelity. The very first pilgrim that set his foot upon the rock of Plymouth, stepped forth a living constitution, armed at all points to defend and to perpetuate the liberty to which he had devoted his whole being.

HUGH SWINTON LEGARE.

POPULATION OF THE UNITED STATES AT DIFFERENT PERIODS.

First	Census	(1790),	3,929,214	Seventh	Census	(1850),	23,191,876
Second	"	(1800),	5,308,483	Eighth	"	(1860),	31,443,321
Third	"	(1810),	7,239,881	Ninth	"	(1870),	38,558,371
Fourth	"	(1820),	9,633,822	Tenth	"	(1880),	50,155,783
Fifth	"	(1830),	12,866,020	Eleventh	"	(1890),	62,622,250
Sixth	"	(1840),	17,069,453				

PART V.

WASHINGTON.

―――◆―――

1. WASHINGTON'S TRAINING.

Among the mountain passes of the Blue Ridge and the Alleghanies, a youth is seen employed in the manly and invigorating occupation of a surveyor, and awakening the admiration of the backwoodsmen and savage chieftains by the strength and endurance of his frame and the resolution and energy of his character. In his stature and conformation he is a noble specimen of a man. In the various exercises of muscular power, on foot or in the saddle, he excels all competitors. His admirable physical traits are in perfect accordance with the properties of his mind and heart; and over all, crowning all, is a beautiful and, in one so young, a strange dignity of manners, and of mien, — a calm seriousness, a sublime self-control, which at once compels the veneration, attracts the confidence, and secures the favor of all who behold him. That youth is the Leader whom Heaven is preparing to conduct America through her approaching trial.

As we see him voluntarily relinquishing the enjoyments, luxuries, and ease of the opulent refinement in which he was born and bred, and choosing the perils and hardships of the wilderness; as we follow him fording swollen streams, climbing rugged mountains, breasting the forest storms, wading through snow-drifts, sleeping in the open air, living upon the coarse food of hunters and of Indians, we trace with devout admiration the divinely appointed education he was receiving to enable him to meet and endure the fatigues, exposures, and privations, of the War of Independence.

Soon he was called to a more public sphere of action; and we again follow him in his romantic adventures as he travels the far-off wilderness, a special messenger to the French commander on the Ohio, and afterwards, when he led forth the troops of Virginia in the same direction, or accompanied the ill-starred Braddock to the blood-stained banks of the Monongahela. Everywhere we see the hand of God conducting him into danger, that he might extract from it the wisdom of an experience not otherwise to be attained, and develop those heroic qualities by which alone danger and difficulty can be surmounted; but all the while covering him with a shield.

When we think of him, at midnight and in mid-winter, thrown from a frail raft into the deep and angry waters of a wide and rushing western river, thus separated from his only companion through the wilderness, with no aid for miles and leagues about him, buffeting the rapid current and struggling through driving cakes of ice; when we behold the stealthy savage, whose aim against all other marks is unerring, pointing his rifle deliberately at him, and firing, over and over again; when we see him riding through showers of bullets on Braddock's fatal field, and reflect that never, during his whole life, was he ever wounded, or even touched by a hostile force, — do we not feel that he was guarded by an unseen hand, warding off every danger? No peril by flood or field was permitted to extinguish a life consecrated to the hopes of humanity, and to the purposes of Heaven.

For more than sixteen years he rested from his warfare, amid the shades of Mount Vernon, ripening his mind by reading and reflection, increasing his knowledge of practical affairs, entering into the whole experience of a citizen, at home, and on his farm, and as a delegate to the Colonial Assembly. When, at last, the war broke out and the unanimous voice of the Continental Congress invested him, as the exigency required, with almost unbounded authority, as their Commander-in-chief, he blended, although still in the prime of his life, in the mature bloom of his manhood, the attributes of a sage with those of a hero. A more perfectly fitted and furnished character has never appeared on the theatre of human action, than when, reigning up his war-horse beneath the majestic and venerable elm, still standing at the entrance of the Watertown road to Cambridge, George Washington unsheathed his sword, and assumed the command of the gathered armies of American Liberty.

Charles Wentworth Upham.

2. THE UNSELFISHNESS OF WASHINGTON.

To the pen of the historian must be resigned the more arduous and elaborate tribute of justice to those efforts of heroic and political virtue which conducted the American people to peace and liberty. The vanquished foe retired from our shores, and left to the controlling genius who repelled them the gratitude of his own country, and the admiration of the world. The time had now arrived which was to apply the touchstone to his integrity, which was to assay the affinity of his principles to the standard of immutable right.

On the one hand, a realm to which he was endeared by his services almost invited him to empire; on the other, the liberty to whose protection his life had been devoted, was the ornament and boon of human nature.

Washington could not depart from his own great self. His country was free. He was no longer a general. Sublime spectacle! more elevating to the pride of virtue than the sovereignty of the globe united to the sceptre of the ages! Enthroned in the hearts of his countrymen, the gorgeous pageantry of prerogative was unworthy the majesty of his dominion. That effulgence of military character which in ancient states has blasted the rights of the people whose renown it had brightened, was not here permitted, by the hero from whom it emanated, to shine with so destructive a lustre. Its beams, though intensely resplendent, did not wither the young blossoms of our Independence; and Liberty, like the burning bush, flourished, unconsumed by the glory which surrounded it.

To the illustrious founder of our Republic it was reserved to exhibit the example of a magnanimity that commanded victory, of a moderation that retired from triumph. Unlike the erratic meteors of ambition, whose flaming path sheds a disastrous light on the pages of history, his bright orb, eclipsing the luminaries among which it rolled, never portended "fearful change" to religion, nor from its "golded tresses" shook pestilence on empire.

What to other heroes has been glory, would to Washington have been disgrace. To his intrepidity, it would have added no honorary trophy, to have waded, like the conqueror of Peru, through the blood of credulous millions, to plant the standard of triumph at the burning mouth of a volcano. To his fame, it would have erected no auxiliary monument to have invaded, like the ravager of Egypt, an innocent though barbarous nation, to inscribe his name on the pillar of Pompey.

ROBERT TREAT PAINE.

3. A STAR IN THE WEST.

There 's a star in the West that shall never go down
    Till the record of valor decay;
We must worship its light, though it is not our own,
    For liberty burst in its ray.
Shall the name of a Washington ever be heard
    By a freeman, and thrill not his breast?
Is there one out of bondage that hails not the word
    As the Bethlehem Star of the West?

"War! war to the knife! Be enthralled, or ye die!"
    Was the echo that woke in his land;
But it was not his voice that prompted the cry,
    Nor his madness that kindled the brand.
He raised not his arm, he defied not his foes,
    While a leaf of the olive remained;
Till, goaded with insult, his spirit arose,
    Like a long-baited lion unchained.

He struck with firm courage the blow of the brave,
    But sighed o'er the carnage that spread;
He indignantly trampled the yoke of the slave,
    But wept for the thousands that bled.
Though he threw back the fetters and headed the strife,
    Till man's charter was fairly restored,
Yet he prayed for the moment when Freedom and Life
    Would no longer be pressed by the sword.

Oh, his laurels were pure! and his patriot name
    In the page of the future shall dwell,
And be seen in all annals, the foremost in fame,
    By the side of a Hofer and Tell.
The truthful and honest, the wise and the good,
    Among Britons, have nobly confessed
That his was the glory, and ours was the blood,
    Of the deeply stained field of the West.

                        Eliza Cook.

4. WASHINGTON A MODEL FOR YOUTH.

To Americans the name of Washington will be forever dear, — a savor of sweet incense, descending to every succeeding generation. The things which he has done are too great, too interesting, ever to be forgotten. Every object which we see, every employment in which we are engaged, every comfort which we enjoy, reminds us daily of his character.

Every ship bears the fruit of his labors on its wings and exultingly spreads its streamers to his honor. The student meets him in the still and peaceful walk; the traveller sees him in all the smiling and prosperous scenes of his journey; and our whole country, in her thrift, order, safety, and morals, bears inscribed in sunbeams, on all her hills and plains, the name and glory of Washington.

By him are our rulers at the present time, and at every future period, taught how to rule. The same conduct will ever produce substantially the same effects, the same public well-being, the same glory, the same veneration. To be wise and good; to forget or restrain the dictates of passion and obey those of duty; to seek singly the public welfare, and lose in it personal gratification; to resist calmly and firmly the passions, and only pursue the interests of a nation, is the greatest secret of ruling well.

The youth of our country who wish to become great, useful, and honorable will here find the best directions and the most powerful incitements. To be great, useful, and honorable they must resemble him. Let them remember that greatness is not the result of mere chance or genius; that it is not the flash of brilliancy, nor the desperate sally of ambition; that it is, on the contrary, the combined results of strong mental endowments, vigorous cultivation, honorable design, and wise discretion. It is not the glare of a meteor, glittering, dazzling, consuming, and vanishing, but the steady and exalted splendor of the sun, — a splendor, which, while it shines with pre-eminent brightness, warms, also, enlivens, adorns, improves, and perfects the objects on which it shines; glorious indeed by its lustre, but still more glorious in the useful effects produced by its power. Of this great truth the transcendent example before us is a most dignified exhibition.

Let our youth imitate, therefore, the incessant attention, the exact observation, the unwearied industry, the scrupulous regard to advice, the slowness of decision, the cautious prudence, the nice punctuality, the strict propriety, the independence of thought and feeling, the unwavering firmness, the unbiassed impartiality, the steady moderation, the exact justice, the unveering truth, the universal humanity, and the high veneration for religion and for God always manifested by this great man.

Then will future Washingtons arise to bless our country.

Timothy Dwight.

---

5. WASHINGTON AS A LEADER.

> To thee, beneath whose eye
> Each circling century
>   Obedient rolls,
> Our nation, in its prime,
> Looked with a faith sublime,
> And trusted in "the time
>   That tried men's souls,"

When from this gate of heaven
People and priests were driven,
  By fire and sword;
And where thy saints had prayed,
The harnessed war-horse neighed
And horseman's trumpet brayed
  In harsh accord.

Nor was our fathers' trust,
Thou Mighty One and Just,
  Then put to shame;
"Up to the hills" for light
Looked they in peril's night,
And from yon guarded height
  Deliverance came.

There, like an angel form
Sent down to still the storm,
  Stood Washington!
Clouds broke and rolled away;
Foes fled in wild dismay;
Wreathed were his brows with bay,
  When war was done.

God of our sires and sons,
Let other Washingtons
  Our country bless,
And, like the brave and wise
Of by-gone centuries,
Show that true greatness lies
  In righteousness.

                JOHN PIERPONT.

6. WASHINGTON AS A SOLDIER.

From the "North American Review" of October, 1882.

The conflict which tried Washington and gave birth to the Republic was not to develop new principles of war, but to illustrate those which do not change with the physical appliances of force. It began without formal declaration on either side. Great Britain struck her first blows at local rebels, and did not see that revolt was universal. The people everywhere struck back, as if they were rightfully free. The policy which, through secret orders to the Colonial governors, had sought first to disarm, and then subdue, only intensified the popular longing to be free. Each colony committed overt, disloyal acts, before the clash at Lexington was known at the South. However tardily the world realized the fact, the war, from the first, was that of Great Britain against three millions of strong people, already practically a nation. Her right policy was that which would have directed her arms in a war against any independent State. To seize all commercial and social centres at once, so that combined resistance could not be successfully organized, was as important as for the Colonies to demonstrate the universal unity and activity of their assertion of independence.

It was as well settled then, as since, that geographical elements shape strategical and tactical movements; and that, as armies have their right, centre, and left divisions, so in countries of large extent there are right, centre, and left zones, or belts of operation, geographically taken, which strategy must respect. The right zone embraced New England, sharply severed from the centre by the Hudson River, as the left zone was defined by the waters of the Delaware and Chesapeake. From New York as a base, there was quick access by water to Newport, within striking distance of Boston; and the control of tide-waters, well supported, left New England powerless to aid the centre. As early as 1775, Lord Dartmouth advised the evacuation of Boston, the occupation of New York and Newport, and "the seizure of some respectable port to the southward, from which to attack sea-coast towns in the winter. The struggle for New York was the practical beginning of the war upon a scientific basis. To isolate the American forces in the three zones, was true British policy. It was the policy of Washington to hold his forces in each zone to the closest possible co-operation, and thus prevent a conflict in three zones at the same time, or beyond his effective reach and control. It is by holding these propositions in view that we apprehend the full significance of operations in New Jersey, which practically linked the three zones, and became the strategic battle-field of the war.

The British army left Boston, March 17, 1775, for Halifax, to refit. On the 18th, Washington despatched General Heath's division to New York, and on the 23d, when the British army actually put to sea, the entire army, except a police garrison, followed. The movements which resulted in the Battle of Long Island, the retreat to White Plains, and the opening of the first New Jersey campaign are familiar. "Retreat" is a misnomer for that march: it was generalship. At every stage of the advance, the troops were so disposed that only a wilful detention by General Lee, of his large division, prevented a direct engagement with Howe. Instead of a purpose to reach Philadelphia, Washington, as early as December 12, determined to take the offensive. The Battle of Trenton was the blow he struck. Howe wrote to England for reinforcements, and New Jersey was delivered. Contemporaries honored the exploit. The "Fabian Policy," so called, had been enlivened by sudden brilliant acts, each of which was like an inspiration in its fitness, and a lightning stroke in its execution. Brooklyn and the retreat, Harlem and the withdrawal, Chatterton Hill and White Plains, the march itself, Trenton and Princeton, suggest all; and these were crowned by such art in choice of a mountain camp, that, as at the hub of a wheel, he alike threatened the Hudson, communicated with New England, kept New York and Staten Island under alarm, and covered the capital. These were so clasped within easy reach that Howe could attack neither without risk to his base.

The campaign of 1777 was equally disastrous to General Howe, and on the 3d of July he again took refuge in New York. The transfer of operations to the middle zone, in August, evoked marvellous acts of consummate military skill. To face 18,000 British regulars with less than 12,000, and contest the field at the Brandywine; to cross the Schuylkill and threaten the rear of the successful foe; to take the offensive at Germantown, and again at Monmouth, until the entire British army was again at New York, but still threatened by that central post in New Jersey, harmonized with the true philosophy and the settled purpose of Washington to win final victory. The practical transfer of active operations to the southern zone, in 1779, did not divert the great leader from his theory of the proper conduct of the war. On the 18th of May, 1781, Lafayette took command in Virginia, but Washington with his French allies still threatened New York, and Clinton demanded immediate reinforcements from Cornwallis, being "threatened with siege." Meanwhile, brick ovens were erected opposite Staten Island, and Washington allowed the enemy to capture fictitious despatches, threatening the city. On the 21st, the American army, and, on the 25th, the French army crossed the Hudson. On August 30th, Washington was at Philadelphia, *not missed* by Clinton. He passed Philadelphia with his whole army, on the 2d of September, *not missed* by Clinton. On the 5th he reached Chester, and learned that the expected French fleet of De Grasse had entered the Chesapeake, and still he had *not* been *missed* by Clinton. On the 6th, but too late, Clinton understood it all.

That grasp of the New Jersey fastnesses, which held supreme direction of operations and defeated all British combinations during five years of war, was at last relaxed, only that it might assure that permanent triumph which its consummate strategy had made possible. On the 14th of September, Washington joined Lafayette; and on the 19th of October, Cornwallis surrendered. The war was at an end! Against every possible obstacle, in spite of small levies, scarce supplies, general corruption, universal bankruptcy, jealous subordinates, and factious politicians, there had been manifested, wherever Washington appeared, such strategical adjustments as assured the highest attainable advantages over the theatre of war, as a whole; such tactical action as made the most of the troops engaged, with no signal disaster in the extremest hour of peril; such prompt management of supplies as best to utilize the means furnished by Congress; such appliances in engineering as met emergencies; and such instruction in minor tactics that the Continental troops were rarely in fault. Add to these, that military policy, or statesmanship in war, which was so clear and penetrating that Congress and subordinates only advanced the war as its suggestions were accepted as influential and paramount, and the summary seems complete.

Upon such premises of fact, it is affirmed, that there was one mind, that of Washington, which absolutely penetrated all the signal issues of the war for American Independence by its magnetic force, and, from Boston to Yorktown, so controlled and developed those issues that victory became the logical necessity of its philosophy and action, and made him, indeed, " First in War."

Henry B. Carrington.

7. MOUNT VERNON, THE HOME OF WASHINGTON.

The following lines were written on the back of a picture at Mount Vernon, by Rev. William Day.

There dwelt the Man, the flower of human kind,
Whose visage mild bespoke his nobler mind.

There dwelt the Soldier, who his sword ne'er drew
But in a righteous cause, to Freedom true.

There dwelt the Hero, who ne'er killed for fame,
Yet gained more glory than a Cæsar's name.

There dwelt the Statesman, who, devoid of art,
Gave soundest counsels from an upright heart ;

And, O Columbia, by thy sons caressed,
There dwelt the Father of the realms he blessed ;
Who no wish felt to make his mighty praise,
Like other chiefs, the means himself to raise ;
But there retiring, breathed in pure renown,
And felt a grandeur that disdained a crown.

8. CROWN OUR WASHINGTON.

On the 22d day of February, 1894, was inaugurated the patriotic custom of placing the portrait of Washington in our public schools. An appropriate programme was prepared for the occasion by the "Youth's Companion," which was enthusiastically carried out in every State.

The following poem, taken, by permission, from that programme, was written for the ceremony attending the placing a crown of laurel or evergreen above the portrait of Washington. Captain J. G. B. Adams, Commander in Chief of the Grand Army of the Republic, initiated this beautiful ceremony. North, South, East, and West responded with equal zeal, and the custom may well become annual and universal throughout the land.

The "Companion," as early as 1888, organized the movement of placing the American flag in, or over, every school building in the land. It also organized the National Columbian Public School Celebration. On that day the United States flag was raised over school buildings, generally, and will pass into history as a day of wide patriotic observance. (See Index, Upham.)

Arise! 't is the day of our Washington's glory;
 The garlands uplift for our liberties won.
Oh, sing in your gladness his echoing story,
 Whose sword swept for freedom the fields of the sun!
   Not with gold, nor with gems,
   But with evergreens vernal,
And the banners of stars that the continent span,
Crown, crown we the chief of the heroes eternal,
Who lifted his sword for the birthright of man!

He gave us a nation to make it immortal;
 He laid down for Freedom the sword that he drew,
And his faith leads us on through the uplifting portal
 Of the glories of peace and our destinies new.
   Not with gold, nor with gems,
   But with evergreens vernal,
And the flags that the nations of liberty span,
Crown, crown him the chief of the heroes eternal,
Who laid down his sword for the birthright of man.

Lead, Face of the Future, serene in thy beauty,
  Till o'er the dead heroes the peace star shall gleam,
Till Right shall be Might in the counsels of duty,
  And the service of man be life's glory supreme.
      Not with gold, nor with gems,
      But with evergreens vernal,
And the flags that the nations in brotherhood span,
Crown, crown we the chief of the heroes eternal,
Whose honor was gained by his service to man !

O Spirit of Liberty, sweet are thy numbers !
  The winds to thy banners their tribute shall bring
While rolls the Potomac where Washington slumbers,
  And his natal day comes with the angels of spring.
      We follow thy counsels,
      O hero eternal !
To highest achievement the school leads the van,
And, crowning thy brow with the evergreen vernal,
We pledge thee our all to the service of man !

HEZEKIAH BUTTERWORTH.

9. GENERAL WASHINGTON'S RESIGNATION.

On the 23d day of December, 1783, General Washington surrendered to Congress his commission as Commander in Chief of the Army, in the following address: —

MR. PRESIDENT, — The great events on which my resignation depended having at length taken place, I have now the honor of offering my sincere congratulations to Congress, and of presenting myself before them to surrender into their hands the trust committed to me, and to claim the indulgence of retiring from the service of my country.

Happy in the confirmation of our independence and sovereignty, and pleased with the opportunity afforded the United States of becoming a respectable nation, I resign with satisfaction the appointment I accepted with diffidence, — a diffidence in my abilities to accomplish so arduous a task, which, however, was superseded by a confidence in the rectitude of our cause, the support of the supreme power of the Union, and the patronage of Heaven.

The successful termination of the war has verified the most sanguine expectations; and my gratitude for the interposition of Providence, and the assistance I have received from my countrymen, increases with every review of the momentous contest. While I repeat my obligations to the Army in general, I should do injustice to my own feelings not to acknowledge, in this place, the peculiar services and distinguished merits of the gentlemen who have been attached to my person during the war. It was impossible the choice of confidential officers to compose my family should have been more fortunate. Permit me, Sir, to recommend in particular those who have continued in the service to the present moment, as worthy of the favorable notice and patronage of Congress.

I consider it an indispensable duty to close this last solemn act of my official life by commending the interests of our beloved country to the protection of Almighty God; and those who have the superintendence of them, to His holy keeping.

Having now finished the work assigned me, I retire from the great theatre of action; and, bidding an affectionate farewell to this august body, under whose orders I have so long acted, I here offer my commission, and take my leave of all the employments of public life.

G. WASHINGTON.

PART VI.

INCENTIVES TO PATRIOTISM.

———•———

1. THE TRUE GRANDEUR OF NATIONS.

CASTING our eyes over the history of nations, we discern with horror the succession of numerous slaughters by which their progress has been marked. Even as the hunter traces the wild beast to his lair by the drops of blood upon the hearth, so do we follow man, weary and staggering with wounds, through the black path of the past which he has reddened with his gore.

Oh, let it not be in future ages as in the past! Let the grandeur of man be discerned, not in bloody victories or in ravenous conquests, but in the blessings which he has secured, in the good he has accomplished, in the triumphs of justice and benevolence, in the establishment of perpetual peace.

As the ocean washes every shore and with all-embracing arm clasps every land, while on its heaving bosom it bears the products of various climes, so peace surrounds, protects, and upholds all other blessings. Without it commerce is vain, the ardor of industry is restrained, happiness is blasted, virtue slackens and dies. Peace has its peculiar victories, in comparison with which, Marathon, Bannockburn, and Bunker Hill, fields sacred in the history of human freedom, shall lose their lustre. Our own Washington rises to a truly heavenly stature, not when we follow him over the ice in the Delaware to the capture of Trenton; not when we behold him victorious over Cornwallis at Yorktown; but when we regard him, in noble deference to justice, refusing the crown which a faithful soldiery proffered, and at a later day upholding the peaceful neutrality of the country, while he received, unmoved, the clamor of the people wickedly crying for war.

CHARLES SUMNER.

2. THE COST OF LIBERTY.

LIBERTY has been bought with a great price. Trace it along the centuries; mark the prisons where captives for it pined; mark the graves to which victims for it went down despairing; mark the fields whereon its heroes battled; mark the seas whereon they fought; mark the exile to which they fled; mark the burned spots where men gave up the ghost in torture, to vindicate the integrity of their souls; add sufferings which have found no record, and imagine, if you can, the whole. Liberty has cost more than all these!

Is there value for the cost? Consult the purchaser, if you are able to pay the cost. Awaken from the prisons those who have perished in them, and from the graves those broken-hearted by oppression. Call from the field of blood those who choose death rather than bonds. Invoke from the caverns of the deep those whom the ocean swallowed, in braving the invader. Summon back from exile those who sank unseen in savage wilds. Pray for those to come once more to earth, who bore testimony to the truth in agony.

Then you will marshal a host of witnesses which no man can number. All these, aforetime, through manifold afflictions, maintained even unto death the cause of Liberty. Inquire if they repent? Ask them if the boon which they have given us was worthy of the sufferings with which they bought it? Ask the speakers who proclaimed freedom, the thinkers who made law for it, the reformers who purified it, if that for which they toiled was worth the labor which they spent? "It was!" all will exclaim with triumphant note. "It was!" will come with glad consent, with one glad "Amen," from this glorious company of Apostles, this goodly fellowship of prophets, this noble band of martyrs.

HENRY GILES.

3. NO PEACE WITHOUT LIBERTY.

Is the present condition of Europe, peace? Or is the murmur of discontent from all the nations peace? I believe the Lord has not created the world to be in such a peaceful condition. No! The present condition of the world is not peace! It is a condition of oppression on the European continent. And because there is this condition of oppression, there cannot be peace; for, so long as men and nations are discontented, there cannot be peace; there cannot be tranquillity.

War, like a volcano, everlastingly boiling, will at the slightest opportunity break out again, and sweep away all the artificial props of peace, and of those interests on which peace depend. Europe is continually a great battle-field, a great barrack. Such is its condition; and, therefore, let not those who call themselves men of peace say they will not help Europe, because they love peace!

Let them confess truly, that they are not men of peace, but only the upholders of the oppression of nations. With me and my principles is peace, because I will always uphold the principles of liberty; and only on the principles of liberty can nations be contented; and only with the contentment of nations can there be peace on the earth. With me and with my principles there is peace, — lasting peace, consistent peace! With the tyrants of the world there is oppression, struggle, and war.

LOUIS KOSSUTH.[1]

[1] LOUIS KOSSUTH, the Hungarian patriot during the revolution of 1848-1849, visited the United States in 1851, and by eloquent appeals sought to arouse American interest in behalf of the oppressed peoples of Europe, claiming that the great standing armies were a perpetual foe to the peace of the world. During October, 1893, he reaffirmed his conviction that the most fearful war of human history was hanging over the suffering peoples of the Old World, in which all nations of the earth might be involved. His death in exile, near Turin, Italy, on the 25th of March, 1894, awakened a fresh appreciation of his sublime devotion to his native land. His remains were attended to their burial at Buda Pest, on the 1st day of April, by immense multitudes, and a wave of tender emotion seemed to sweep over the entire population of Hungary. The vision of Kossuth, elsewhere noticed, has been more than avenged, in the spontaneous, irresistible wail of sorrow over his departure.

4. THE PEOPLE TRIUMPHANT.

In the efforts of the people, of the people struggling for their rights, moving not in organized, disciplined masses, but in their spontaneous action, man for man, and heart for heart, there is something glorious. They can then move forward without orders, act together without combination, and brave the flaming lines of battle without intrenchments to cover, or walls to shield them. No dissolute camp has worn off from the feelings of the youthful soldier the freshness of that home, where his mother and sisters sit waiting, with tearful eyes and aching hearts, to hear good news from the wars. No long service in the ranks of the conqueror has turned the veteran's heart into marble. Their valor springs not from recklessness, from habit, from indifference to the preservation of a life knit by no pledges to the lives of others; but in the spirit and the strength of the cause alone, they act, contend, and bleed. In this, they conquer!

The people always conquer! They always must conquer! Armies may be defeated; kings may be overthrown; and new dynasties be imposed by foreign arms, on an ignorant and slavish race, that care not in what language the covenant of their subjugation runs, nor in whose name the deed of their barter and sale is made out. But the people never invade; and when they rise against the invader, are never subdued. If they are driven from the plains, they fly to the mountains. Steep rocks and everlasting hills are their castles; the tangled, pathless thicket their palisade; and nature, God, is their ally. Now He overwhelms the hosts of their enemies beneath His drifting mountains of sand; now He buries them under a falling atmosphere of polar snows. He lets loose His tempests on their fleets. He puts a folly into their counsels, a madness into the hearts of their leaders; and He never gave, and never will give, a final triumph over a virtuous and gallant people, resolved to be free.

EDWARD EVERETT

5. AMERICAN NATIONALITY.

By the side of all antagonisms, higher than they, stronger than they, there rises colossal the fine sweet spirit of nationality, — the nationality of America! See there the pillar of fire which God has kindled and lifted and moved for our hosts and our ages. Gaze on that, worship that, worship the highest in that.

Think of it as it fills your mind and quickens your heart, and as it fills the mind and quickens the hearts of millions around you. Instantly, under such an influence, you ascend above the smoke and stir of this small local strife; you tread upon the high places of the earth and of history; you think and feel as an American for America. Her power, her eminence, her consideration, her honor, are yours; your competitors, like hers, are kings; your home, like hers, is the world; your path, like hers, is on the highway of empires. Our charge, her charge, is of generations and ages; your record, her record, is of treaties, battles, voyages, beneath all the constellations. Her image, immortal, golden, rises on your eye, as our western star at evening rises on the traveller from his home. No lowering cloud, no angry river, no inundated city or plantation, no tracts of arid sand are on that surface, but all blended and softened into one beam of kindred rays, the image, harbinger, and promise of love, hope, and a brighter day!

But if you would contemplate nationality, not merely as a state of consciousness, but as an active virtue, look around you. Is not our history one witness and record of what it can do? The glory of the fields of that war, the eloquence of that revolution, this one wide sheet of flame which wrapt tyrant and tyranny, and swept all that escaped from it away forever; the courage to fight, to advance, to guard the young flag by the young arm and the young heart's blood, to hold up and to hold on till the magnificent consummation crowned the work, -- were not all these imparted or inspired by this imperial sentiment? Has it not here begun the master-work of man, the creation of a national life? Aye, did it not, indeed, call out that prodigious development of wisdom, -- the wisdom of constructiveness which illustrated the years after the war, and the framing and adoption of the American Constitution?   RUFUS CHOATE.

6. OUR NATIONALITY.

Our nationality has its charter and seal, not in a written constitution so much as in the trend of a coast, the trough of a glorious valley, grooved by the finger of Providence, the most princely domain of the globe, the course and sweep of a history more manifestly Providential than any since the deliverance from Egypt and the settlement of Palestine.

If we feel what traditions mean, if we are open to the inspiration of great characters, noble as any in the secular annals of our planet, if we are not dead to the call of a long-compacted and holy trust, we shall confess that we have one great duty, one supreme privilege, rather, to devote all that we have, and are, and hope to be, to the maintenance of the nation which God has delivered in its fresh magnificence to the keeping of our patriotism and valor. Make the preservation of nationality the goal of all action, the touchstone of all politics. Stand for everything that serves that. Resist everything, reject everything, pour impassioned scorn upon everything that opposes that. If a man talks State Sovereignty, say that the only real sovereignty a State can have is in consenting to fit, like a rib, into the national backbone. It loses its sovereignty when it sets up to be what God never made it to be,—a whole body. If a man talks of the Tennessee River, or the Cumberland, show him the Ohio into which they flow. If he talks of the Ohio, point him to Cairo, where it pours into a mightier tide. If he talks of the Yellowstone, or the Platte, or the Kansas, or the Arkansas, tell him that the nation holds, to-day, the springs of all these, and that they hurry, with their American contributions, to the stream over whose mouth the American banner floats secure. If he talks of the

Sacramento in the dialect of State Sovereignty, tell him that he had better smother his breath in the muddiest of its waters.

"Our Union is river, lake, ocean, and sky;
Man breaks not the medal when God cuts the die."

The Constitution of the United States is stereotyped in granite ranges and river grooves. God has cut into the die the branches of the Chesapeake, the windings of the Delaware, the Potomac, and the Shenandoah, the trendings of the Alleghanies, and the mighty armlets of the Mississippi, that State lines and customs of latitude shall be overruled. It is as if the one word "America," and the constructive motto, *E Pluribus Unum*, "from many, one," were stamped in letters for a telescope to discern at the distance of the moon, on the whole land, from the Rocky Mountains to the Hudson.

THOMAS STARR KING.

7. INDIVIDUAL PURITY THE HOPE OF THE STATE.

IF there be on earth one nation more than another whose institutions must draw their life-blood from the individual purity of its citizens, that nation is our own. In our country, where almost every man, however humble, bears to the omnipotent ballot-box his full portion of the sovereignty, where at regular periods the ministers of authority who went forth to rule, return, to be ruled, and lay down their dignities at the feet of the monarch-multitude, — where, in short, public sentiment is the absolute lever that moves the political world, the purity of the people is the rock of political safety.

We may boast, if we please, of our exalted privileges, and fondly imagine that they will be eternal; but whenever those vices shall abound which undeniably tend to debasement, steeping the poor and ignorant still lower in poverty and ignorance, and thereby destroying that wholesome mental equality which can alone sustain a self-ruling people, it will be found, by woful experience, that our happy system of government, the best ever designed for the intelligent and good, is the very worst to be intrusted to the degraded and the vicious. The great majority will then become, indeed, a many-headed monster, to be tamed and led at will. The tremendous power of suffrage, like the strength of the eyeless Nazarine, so far from being their protection, will but serve to pull down upon their heads the temple their ancestors reared for them.

Demagogues will find it an easy task to delude those who have deluded themselves; and the freedom of the people will finally be buried in the grave of their virtues. National greatness may survive. Splendid talents and brilliant victories may fling their delusive lustre abroad. These can illumine the darkness that hangs around the throne of the despot; but their light will be like the baleful flame that hovers over decaying humanity, and tells of the corruption that festers beneath. The immortal spirit will have gone; and along our shores, and among our hills, hallowed by the uncoffined bones of the patriot, — even there, in the ears of their degenerate descendants, shall ring the knell of departed Liberty.

CHARLES SPRAGUE.

SINCERITY AND TRUTH.

SINCERITY and pure truth in every age still pass current.

MONTAIGNE.

8. CHRISTIANITY AS A POLITICAL FORCE.

THE influence of Christianity upon the political condition of mankind, though silent and almost imperceptible, has been one of the most powerful instruments of its amelioration. The principles and rules of practical conduct which it prescribes; the doctrine of the natural equality of men, with a common origin, a common responsibility, and a common fate; the lessons of humility, gentleness, and forbearance which it teaches, — are as much at war with political as they are with all moral injustice, oppression, and wrong.

During century after century, excepting for brief intervals, the world too often saw the system marred by the fiercest intolerance and the grossest deprivation. It has been made the confederate of monarchs in carrying out schemes of oppression and fraud. Under its banner armed multitudes have been banded together, and led on by martial prelate to wars of desolation and revenge. Perpetrators of the blackest crimes have purchased immunity from punishment.

But nearly two thousand years have passed away, and no trace is left of the millions who, under the influence of bad passions, have dishonored its holy precepts, or of the far smaller number who, in seasons of general deprivation, have drunk its current of living water on the solitary mountain, or in the living rock. Its simple maxims, outliving them all, are silently working out a greater revolution than any which the world has yet seen; and long as the period may seem since its doctrines were first announced, it is almost imperceptible when regarded as one of the divisions of that time which is of endless duration.

To use the language of an eloquent and philosophical writer, "The movements of Providence are not restricted to narrow bounds. It is not anxious, to-day, to deduce the consequences of the premises it laid down yesterday. It may defer this for ages, till the fulness of time has come. Its logic will not be less conclusive for reasoning slowly. Providence moves through time, as the gods of Rome moved through space. It makes a step, and years have rolled away. How long a time, how many circumstances intervened before the regeneration of the moral powers of man by Christianity exercised its great, its legitimate function upon his social condition! Yet who can doubt or mistake its power?

John A. Dix.

9. REVERENCE FOR LAW.

By efforts of patriotism alone can this great and growing Republic be preserved. Happy is that country, and only that country, where the laws are not only just and equal, but supreme and irresistible; where selfish interests and disorderly passions are curbed by an arm to which they must submit.

We look back with horror and affright to the dark and troubled ages, when a gloomy and cruel superstition tyrannized over the peoples of Europe; dreaded alike by kings and people, by governments and individuals; before which the law had no force, justice no respect, and mercy no influence.

The sublime principles of morality, the kind and endearing charities, the true and rational reverence for a bountiful Creator, which are the elements and life of our religion, were trampled down, in the reckless career of ambition, pride, and lust of power. Nor was it much better when the arm of the warrior and the sharpness of his sword determined every question of right, and held the weak in bondage to the strong; when the revengeful feuds of the great involved in one common ruin themselves and their humblest vassals.

But those disastrous days are gone, never to return. There is no power but law, which is the power of all; and those who administer it are the masters, the ministers of all.

JOSEPH HOPKINSON (Author of "Hail Columbia").

---

10. THE IDEAL CITIZEN.

Extract from "Civics."

THE ideal citizen is the man who believes that all men are brothers, and the nation is merely an extension of his family, to be loved, respected, and cared for accordingly. Such a man attends personally to all civic duties with which he deems himself charged. Those which are within his own control he would no more trust to his inferiors than he would leave the education of his children to kitchen servants. The public demands upon his time, thought, and money, come upon him suddenly, and often they find him ill-prepared; but he nerves himself to the inevitable, knowing that in the village, State, and nation, any mistake or neglect upon his part must impose a penalty, sooner or later, upon those whom he loves.

The ideal citizen is "good for all demands" justly made upon him; never shirks work, or assumes that what he neglects to attend to will be made right by his fellow-citizens. He knows how, in civic affairs, to apply the point of the old saying that "a stitch in time saves nine," and, conversely, that if stitches are not taken in time, there may be rents and exposures which newly aroused industry cannot repair in time to prevent disgrace and loss.

The ideal citizen always "wants to know why." His conscience may be better than his education, but he loses no opportunity to discover what has been the stumbling-block of other communities and nations, and if he does not find this task easy, he perseveres, knowing that when one is in a fight, it is better to be beaten than to dodge responsibility by running away.

In politics the ideal citizen takes sides with a party, but makes his partisan affiliations through principle, instead of prejudice or the partiality that comes through personal acquaintance. He finds this hard work at times, but, somehow, everything worth doing or having, requires a great deal of personal effort, and not a little self-sacrifice; yet he realizes that to be led by the nose is unmanly, even if the leader be a wiser man, and a personal friend besides. He may respect men who differ in opinion, but it is not necessary on that account that he should respect their erroneous ideas. He is not to be held to account for others' opinions, but simply for his own.

Sometimes the ideal citizen finds himself obliged to vote with a party which he previously has opposed, and in which his associates are his old political enemies. In such cases his position is painful; for, as a rule, the more thoughtful and earnest the man, the dearer to him are the old ties of sympathy and association. It needs bravery to make an ideal citizen. He knows that local necessities have no possible connection with national issues, and acts accordingly. Like Washington, he votes for measures, not men. He has seen great abuses develop from small neglects; so, instead of concentrating his attention and spending his money, once in four years, to elect the Presidential candidate of his party, he attends all the primary meetings, and never fails to vote at an election simply because the offices seem of small importance.

The ideal citizen is always a disturbing factor in his own political field. He is in the position of the missionary to a congregation of Southern negroes, who persisted in preaching against theft and other violations of the ten commandments, while his hearers were longing only to hear of the wonders described in the Book of Revelation, and to exult in anticipation of rambling through the golden streets and stately mansions of the great hereafter. It is much the same way in politics. The man who in time of peace prepares for war, and tries to urge his party associates to forego selfish desires, and incite all to a more earnest effort for the public good, is always sure to be regarded as a nuisance. Consequently, the ideal citizen must be prepared to become a martyr.

The greatest men are seldom those who receive the greatest formal recognition. Neither Webster, Clay, nor Calhoun became President, and Moses was driven out of Egypt for avenging the wrongs of one of his race. The ancient Greeks banished all their wise men; and as for Jesus, He was crucified instead of crowned.

Finally, the ideal citizen looks out not for himself alone, but regards himself as but part of the community in which he lives. To make money out of politics seems as bad to him as living on the earnings of his parents and children; for he knows that the community or nation has no money of its own, but only what it extracts from the pockets of the people, the poorest as well as the richest. His compensation consists in the sense of duty well done; and the more he does, the less the reward he thinks himself entitled to.

JOHN HABBERTON.

11. LIBERTY OF THE PRESS.

The liberty of the press is the highest safeguard of all free government. Ours could not exist without it. It is like a great exulting and abounding river. It is fed by the dews of heaven, which distil their sweetest drops to form it. It gushes from the rill, as it breaks from the deep caverns of the earth. It is augmented by a thousand affluents, that dash from the mountain-top, to separate again into a thousand bounteous and irrigating streams around. On its broad bosom it bears a thousand barks. There genius spreads its purpling sail. There poetry dips its silver oar. There art, invention, discovery, science, morality, religion, may safely and securely float. It wanders through every land. It has a genial, cordial source of thought and inspiration, wherever it touches, whatever it surrounds. Upon its borders there grows every flower of grace and every fruit of truth. Sometimes that river oversteps its bounds. Sometimes that stream becomes a dangerous torrent, and destroys towns and cities upon its bank. But, without it, civilization, humanity, government, — all that makes society itself, — would disappear, and the world would return to its ancient barbarism.

Edward D. Baker.

12. IDLENESS A CRIME.

Extract from "Civics."

A fallacy lies at the root of the labor question; that is, the illogical admission that a man has a right to be idle, if he so prefer. The choice of employment and the right to demand a just wage for work done, does not rest upon a dogma so pernicious. The law of labor is an inherent obligation as well as a necessity. Personal self-support, to the extent of personal ability, is a duty. Individual support at the expense of others violates the principle that aggregated labor is essential to the public good. The aggregate of protection which society insures, is the measure of the obligation which exacts willing industry, and makes voluntary idleness a crime. This is not a question of morals or ethics, but every just code of laws demands that every man should share in the protection of all, and in the protection of the rights of all, as well as his own. No citizen is exempt from a summons to the national defence. He is equally required to contribute to the common good, through the equally important ordinary relations with which every-day labor is allied.

Obedience to law is a paramount obligation, or anarchy ensues; and anarchy is simple madness. Optional obedience to law is a senseless paradox. There is no right of choice here. At the instant a man says, "I will be idle, and take the consequences," he becomes dependent upon others, and forces them to do for him that which he is bound to do for himself. Even the readiness of the subject of law to bear the penalty of its infraction, does not convert the wrong to right.

This position must not be misunderstood. Delay to work, pending terms and conditions, is a matter of judgment or contract, incident to the changing relations of labor and product; but it may be protracted until it becomes suicidal and ruinous. A margin must be conceded to reasonable competition, and the desire of all men to get the best out of the same relative labor; but a failure to reach the full measure of satisfaction desired, must not efface the purpose to realize the best attainable results.

Innocent idleness is a practicable impossibility. To see a man drown, and decline to rescue, is, substantially, to drown him. Cessation of labor, for rest, or change of terms or conditions, is rational and honorable. In any other sense, idleness involves a condition of actual violence to all faithful workers. Mental faculties and physical forces will not lie dormant. Remove the incentives to labor for justly attainable ends, and at once all animal elements which have been softened and subjected through legitimate exercise will assert their presence, and their power to harm. The idle element will tear down, but never re-build! Even if the popular fallacy that a man may work or not, at his pleasure, had a technical basis of merit, it loses all proper recognition when it asserts a claim to suspend other labor than his own. No despotism on earth is so destructive as the sway of a multitude which asserts its voice, and demands recognition without the sanction of law. And this is equally true in *all* social grades. The idleness of those without means, is matched by the profligacy of such as have abundant means, but live only for self and passion. Neither can excuse the mischief done, and neither can impart substantial good to individual or society.

The spirit of sound law is equally repressive of violent invasion of the rights of honest acquisition. The industrious will always save! The improvident will always waste! The motive to industry must be acquisition, for future use, or human life would be more abject than that of animal instinct. Accumulated resources are only to be valued for their uses, and enforced inactivity of those resources cripples many who live upon their distributions to society. It is not to be unnoticed that hoarded acquisitions rapidly segregate themselves in this country, so that the names once associated with large acquisitions are soon found at the beginning-point again. This harmonizes with the theory of free, honest, and patient labor. The highest type of social and domestic happiness, in any Christian civilization, is found among the classes whose prosperity depends upon faithful industry. False gauges are those which declare acquisition, for its own sake, to be the true test, or measure of success. Uniformity of acquisition, or wage, is equally incompatible with the very type of mental and physical skill which energizes labor. No arbitrary wage relations can be made uniform, or independent of changing times and conditions. In no other country can national good and happiness be so directly secured to individual effort. Emigrants do not realize at once, that, as a rule, substantial independence is obtainable by honest industry, and that the acquisition is then safe. A changeable wage rate is unavoidable.

A wise adjustment will be proportionate to the harmony between *realized labor* and *expectant labor*. The former is simply capital. At sunset, the industrious man has *realized capital*, by the difference of the measure of profit over expense. The thriftless and idler are in arrears! The contrast will deepen daily; but the fact is only made more definite, that there will always be remunerative wage for all who work cheerfully and faithfully by and up to the measure of demand. Extraordinary conditions demand extraordinary and mutual fraternities, so that both capital and labor may adjust their relations to the highest security, order, peace, and happiness of all.

Henry B. Carrington.

POVERTY OF THE SOUL.

The want of goods is easily repaired; but the poverty of the soul is irreparable.

Montesquieu.

13. NATIONAL INJUSTICE.

Do you know how empires find their end? Yes. The great States eat up the little. As with fish, so with nations. Come with me! Let us bring up the awful shadows of empires buried long ago, and learn a lesson from the tomb!

Come, old Assyria, with the Ninevitish dove upon thy emerald crown! What laid thee low? "I fell by my own injustice! Thereby Nineveh and Babylon came with me to the ground!"

O queenly Persia, flame of the nations! Wherefore art thou so fallen! thou who troddest the people under thee, bridgest the Hellespont with ships, and pourest thy temple-wasting millions on the western world? "Because I trod the people under me; because I bridged the Hellespont with ships, and poured my temple-wasting millions on the western world. I fell by my own misdeeds!"

And thou, muse-like, Grecian queen, fairest of all thy classic sisterhood of States, enchanting yet the world with thy sweet witchery, speaking in art, and most seductive in song, why liest thou there with the beauteous yet dishonored brow reposing on thy broken harp? "I loved the loveliness of flesh, embalmed in Parian stone. I loved the loveliness of thought, and treasured that more than Parian speech. But the beauty of justice, the loveliness of love, I trod down to earth. Lo! therefore have I become as those barbarian states, and as one of them."

O manly, majestic Rome, with thy sevenfold mural crown all broken at thy feet, why art thou here? 'T was not injustice brought thee low, for thy great Book of Law is prefaced with these words, "Justice is the unchanging, everlasting will to give each man his right." It was not the saint's ideal. It was the hypocrite's pretence. "I made iniquity my law! I trod the nations under me! Their wealth gilded my palaces, where now thou may'st see the fox and hear the owl. It fed my courtiers and my courtesans. Wicked men were my cabinet counsellors. The flatterer breathed his poison in my ear. Millions of bondmen wet the soil with tears and blood! Do you not hear it crying yet to God? Lo! here have I my recompense, tormented with such downfalls as you see. Go back and tell the new-born child[1] who sitteth on the Alleghanies, laying his either hand upon a tributary sea, and a crown of stars upon his youthful brow, — tell him there are rights which States must keep, or they shall suffer wrongs. Tell him there is a God who keeps the black man and the white, and hurls to earth the loftiest realm that breaks His just, eternal law. Warn the young empire, that he come not down, dim and dishonored, to my shameful tomb. Tell him that Justice is the unchanging, everlasting will, to give each man his right. I know it. I broke it. Bid him keep it, and be forever safe."

THEODORE PARKER.

14. A REPUBLIC DEFINED.

WE establish the Republic. It is the government that most needs the continued inspiration and benediction of God; for if the reason of the people should be obscured or misled, there is no longer a sovereign. Then comes an inter-regnum, anarchy, death.

In order that a government may be durable, and worthy of the sanction of religion, it must contain a principle that is true, that is divine, that is best adapted to the welfare of the many. Without this, the Constitution is a dead

---

[1] America.

letter. It is nothing more than a collection of laws. It is without soul. It no longer lives. It no longer produces fruit.

The new principle of the Republic is political equality among all classes of citizens. This principle has for its exponent, universal suffrage; for its result, the sovereignty of all; for its moral consequence, fraternity among all. We reign according to the full measure of our reason, of our intelligence, of our virtue. We are all sovereigns over ourselves, and of the Republic. But to draft a Constitution, and to swear to it, is not all: a people is needed to execute it.

Citizens! All progress requires effort. Every effort is painful, and attended with painful embarrassments. Political transformations are laborious. The people are the artificers of their own future. Let them reflect upon that. The future awaits, and observes them. Shame upon the cowards who would draw back! Prudence belongs to the inconsiderate who would precipitate society into the unknown!

Glory be to the good, to the wise, to the persevering! May God be with them!

ALPHONSE DE LAMARTINE.

15. THE TORCH OF LIBERTY.

I saw it all in Fancy's glass, —
  Herself the fair, the wild magician,
Who bade this splendid day-dream pass,
  And named each gilded apparition.
'T was like a torch-race, such as they
  Of Greece performed in ages gone,
When the fleet youths, in long array,
  Passed the bright torch triumphant on.

I saw the expectant nations stand,
  To catch the coming flame, in turn;
I saw, from ready hand to hand,
  The clear, though struggling, glory burn.
And oh, their joy, as it came near,
  'T was, in itself, a joy to see;
While Fancy whispered in my ear,
  "That torch they pass is Liberty."

And each, as she received the flame,
  Lighted her altar with its ray;
Then, smiling, to the next who came,
  Speeding it on its sparkling way.
From Albion first, whose ancient shrine
  Was furnished with the fire already,
Columbia caught the boon divine,
  And lit a flame, like Albion's, steady.

   .   .   .   .   .   .

"Shine, shine forever, glorious flame,
  Divinest gift of gods to men!
From Greece thy earliest splendor came,
  To Greece thy ray returns again.
Take, Freedom, take thy radiant round;
  When dimmed, revive; when lost, return;
Till not a shrine through earth be found,
  On which thy glories shall not burn!"

THOMAS MOORE.

TRUE LIBERTY.

LIBERTY is not idleness, but an unconstrained use of time; the choice of work and of exercise. To be free, in a word, is not to be doing nothing; but to be one's own master as to what one ought or ought not to do.

BRUYERE.

16. AMERICA.

FAIREST OF FREEDOM'S DAUGHTERS.

Read at the dedication of the Bartholdi Statue, New York Harbor, October 28, 1888.

Night's diadem around the head,
   The world upon thee gazing,
Beneath the eye of heroes dead
   Thy queenly form up-raising,
Lift up, lift up thy torch on high,
   Fairest of Freedom's daughters!
Flash it against thine own blue sky,
   Flash it across the waters!

Stretch up to thine own woman's height,
   Thine eye lit with truth's lustre,
As though from God, Himself a-light,
   Earth's hopes around thee cluster.
The stars touch with thy forehead fair;
   At them thy torch was lighted.
They grope to find where truth's ways are,
   The nations long benighted.

Thou hast the van in earth's proud march,
   To thee all nations turning;
Thy torch against thine own blue arch,
   In answer to their yearning!
Show them the pathway thou hast trod,
   The chains which thou hast broken;
Teach them thy trust in man and God,
   The watchwords thou hast spoken.

Not here is heard the Alp-herd's horn,
   The mountain stillness breaking;
Nor do we catch the roseate morn,
   The Alpine summits waking.

Is Neckar's vale no longer fair,
  That German hearts are leaving?
Ah! German hearts from hearthstones tear,
  In thy proud star believing.

Has Rhineland lost her grape's perfume,
  Her waters green and golden?
And do her castles no more bloom
  With legends rare and olden?
Why leave, strong men, the Fatherland?
  Why cross the cold blue ocean?
Truth's torch in thine uplifted hand,
  Ha! kindles their devotion.

God, home, and country be thy care,
  Thou queen of all the ages!
Belting the earth is this one prayer:
  Unspotted be thy pages!
Lift up, lift up thy torch on high,
  Fairest of Freedom's daughters!
Flash it against thine own blue sky,
  Flash it across the waters!

JEREMIAH E. RANKIN.

17. THE GREAT AMERICAN REPUBLIC A CHRISTIAN STATE.

Contributed by CARDINAL GIBBONS, from Address, "The Religious Element in American Civilization."

At first sight it might seem that religious principles were entirely ignored by the fathers of the Republic in framing the Constitution, as it contains no reference to God, and makes no appeal to religion. And so strongly have certain religious sects been impressed with this fact that they have tried to get the name of God incorporated into that document. But the omission of God's holy name affords no just criterion of the religious character of the founders of the Republic, or of the Constitution which they framed. Nor should we have any concern to have the name of God imprinted in the Constitution, so long as the Instrument itself is interpreted by the light of Christian revelation. I would rather sail under the guidance of a living captain than of a figure-head at the prow of the ship. Far better for the nation that His Spirit should animate our laws, that He should be invoked in our Courts of Justice, that He should be worshipped in our Sabbaths and thanksgivings, and that His guidance should be implored in the opening of our Congressional proceedings.

But the Declaration of Independence is one of the most solemn and memorable professions of political faith that ever emanated from the leading minds of any country. It has exerted as much influence in foreshadowing the spirit and character of our Constitution and public policy as the Magna Charta exercised on the Constitution of Great Britain. A devout recognition of God and of His overruling Providence pervades that momentous document from beginning to end. God's holy name greets us in the opening paragraph, and is piously invoked in the last sentence of the Declaration; and thus it is, at the same time, the corner-stone and the keystone of this great monument to freedom. The illustrious signers declared that "when, in the course of human events, it becomes necessary for one people to dissolve the political bands that have connected them with another, and to assume among the powers of the earth the separate and equal station to which the laws of nature and of nature's God entitle them, a decent respect for the opinions of mankind requires that they should declare the causes that impel them to the separation." They acknowledge one

Creator, the source of "life, liberty, and of happiness." They "appeal to the Supreme judge of the world" for the rectitude of their intentions, and they conclude in this solemn language: "For the support of this declaration, with a firm reliance on the protection of Divine Providence, we mutually pledge to each other our lives, our fortunes, and our sacred honor."

The laws of the United States are so intimately interwoven with the Christian religion that they cannot be adequately expounded without the light of revelation. "The common law," says Kent, "is the common jurisprudence of the United States, and was brought from England and established here, so far as it was adapted to our institutions and circumstances. It is an incontrovertible fact that the common law of England is, to a great extent, founded on the principles of Christian ethics. The maxims of the Holy Scriptures form the great criterion of right and wrong in the civil courts.

The Puritans who founded New England, the Dutch who settled in New York, the Quakers and Irish who established themselves in Pennsylvania, the Swedes in Delaware, the English Catholics who colonized Maryland, the English Episcopalians who colonized Virginia, Georgia, and North Carolina, the Irish Presbyterians who also emigrated to the last-named State, the French Huguenots and the English colonists who planted themselves in South Carolina, the French and Spanish who took possession of Louisiana and Florida, — all these colonists made an open profession of Christianity in one form or other, and recognized religion as the basis of society. The same remark applies with equal truth to that stream of population which, from the beginning of the present century, has been constantly flowing into this country from Ireland and Germany, and extending itself over the entire land. We have grown up, not as distinct, independent, and conflicting communities, but as one corporate body, breathing the same atmosphere of freedom, governed by the same political rights.

I see in all this a wonderful manifestation of the humanizing and elevating influence of Christian civilization. What is the secret of our social stability and order? It results from wise laws, based on Christian principles, and which are the echo of God's eternal law. What is the cohesive power that makes us one body politic out of so many heterogeneous elements? It is the religion of Christ. We live as brothers, because we recognize the brotherhood of humanity, — one Father in heaven, one origin, one destiny.

Note. — The oath of the President of the United States before he assumes the duties of office; that administered in courts of justice, not only to witnesses, but also to the judge, jury, lawyers, and officers of the court, in accordance with the Constitution, — implies a belief in God and forms of acts of worship. It is a national tribute to the universal sovereignty of the Creator. By the act of taking an oath a man makes a profession of faith in God's unfailing truth, absolute knowledge, and infinite sanctity. The Christian Sabbath is revered, as a day of rest and public prayer, throughout the land. This is national homage to the Christian religion.

---

18. THE FLOWER OF LIBERTY.

WHAT flower is this that greets the morn,
Its hues from Heaven so freshly born?
With burning star and flaming brand
It kindles all the sunset land.
Oh, tell us what its name may be!
Is this the Flower of Liberty?
    It is the Banner of the Free,
    The starry flower of Liberty!

In savage Nature's fair abode,
Its tender seed our fathers sowed;
The storm-winds rocked its swelling bud,
Its opening leaves were streaked with blood;
Till lo! earth's tyrants shook to see
The full-blown Flower of Liberty!
    Then hail the Banner of the Free,
    The starry Flower of Liberty!

Behold its streaming rays unite,
One mingling flood of braided light:
The red that fires the Southern rose,
With spotless white from Northern snows,
And, spangled o'er its azure, see,
The sister stars of Liberty.
    Then hail the Banner of the Free,
    The starry Flower of Liberty!

The blades of heroes fence it round;
Where'er it springs is holy ground;
From tower and dome its glories spread;
It waves where lonely sentries tread;
It makes the land, as ocean, free;
And plants an empire on the sea!
    Then hail the Banner of the Free,
    The starry Flower of Liberty!

Thy sacred leaves, fair Freedom's flower,
Shall ever float on dome and tower,
To all their heavenly colors true,
In blackening frost, or crimson dew;
And God love us as we love thee,
Thrice holy Flower of Liberty!
    Then hail the Banner of the Free,
    The starry Flower of Liberty!

OLIVER WENDELL HOLMES.

19. OUR COUNTRY.

Our country, 't is a glorious land,
    With broad arms stretched from shore to shore :
The proud Pacific chafes her strand,
    She hears the dark Atlantic's roar ;
And, nurtured on her ample breast,
    How many a goodly prospect lies
In Nature's wildest grandeur drest,
    Enamelled with her loveliest dyes!

Rich prairies, decked with flowers of gold,
    Like sunlit oceans roll afar ;
Broad lakes her azure heavens behold,
    Reflecting clear each trembling star ;
And mighty rivers, mountain-born,
    Go sweeping onward, dark and deep,
Through forests where the bounding fawn
    Beneath their sheltered waters leap.

And, cradled 'mid her clustering hills,
    Sweet vales in dream-like beauty hide,
Where love the air with music fills,
    And calm content and peace abide ;
For Plenty here her fulness pours
    In rich profusion through the land,
And, sent to seize her generous stores,
    There prowls no tyrant's hireling band.

Great God, we thank thee for this home,
    This bounteous birthland of the free,
Where wanderers from afar may come
    And breathe the air of liberty.
Still may her flowers untrampled spring,
    Her harvests wave, her cities rise ;
And yet, till Time shall fold her wing,
    Remain Earth's loveliest Paradise.

William J. Peabody.

20. PATRIOTS AND MARTYRS.

Patriots have toiled, and in their country's cause
Bled nobly ; and their deeds, as they deserve,
Receive proud recompense. We give in charge
Their names to the sweet lyre. Th' historic muse,
Proud of the treasure, marches with it down
To latest times ; and Sculpture, in her turn,
Gives bond in stone and ever-during brass
To guard them, and t' immortalize her trust.

But fairer wreaths are due, though never paid,
To those who, posted at the shrine of truth,
Have fallen in her defence. A patriot's blood,
Well spent in such a strife, may earn, indeed,
And for a time insure to his loved land,
The sweets of liberty and equal laws ;
But martyrs struggle for a higher prize,
And win it with more pain.

Their blood is shed
In confirmation of the noblest claim, —
Our claim to feed upon immortal truth,
To walk with God, to be divinely free,
To soar, and to anticipate the skies !
Yet few remember them. They lived unknown,
Till persecution dragged them into fame
And chased them up to heaven.

Their ashes flow,
No marble tells us whither. With their names
No bard embalms and sanctifies his song.
And history, so warm on meaner themes,
Is cold on this. She execrates, indeed,
The tyranny that doomed them to the fire,
But gives the glorious sufferers little praise.

Nelson M. Holbrook

21. THE RICHEST PRINCE.

All their wealth and vast possessions
    Vaunting high in choicest terms,
Sat the German princes, feasting
    In the mighty hall at Worms.

"Mighty," cried the Saxon ruler,
    "Are the wealth and power I wield
In my country's mountain gorges,
    Sparkling silver lies concealed."

"See my land with plenty glowing,"
    Quoth the Palgrave of the Rhine:
"Bounteous harvests in the valleys;
    On the mountains, noble wine."

"Spacious towns and wealthy convents,"
    Louis spake, Bavaria's lord,
"Make my land to yield me treasures
    Great as those your fields afford."

Wurtemburgh's beloved monarch,
    Eberard the bearded, cried:
"See! my land hath little cities.
    'Mong my hills no metals hide;

Yet one treasure it hath borne me, —
    Sleeping in the woodland free,
I may lay my head in safety
    On my lowliest vassal's knee."

Then, as with a single utterance,
    Cried aloud these princes three:
"Bearded Count, thy land hath jewels
    Thou art wealthier far than we."

                  Andreas Justinus Korner

22. PATRIOTIC SONG.

Heart so light, eye so bright,
Arm so stalwart in the fight,
Seeking fame, all whose name
From great Herman came,
Singing, shouting, brothers, come!
   Let us gayly wander home.
      "Strong and free,
      True are we!"
   Shall our watchword be.

Hear it soar the wildwood o'er,
Through the oak-tree gray and hoar,
Loud and long swells the song,
From youthful throng.
Singing, shouting, brothers, come!
   Let us gayly wander home.
      "Strong and free,
      True are we!"
   Shall our watchword be.

Stars appear, shining clear;
Let us all be brothers here!
Fatherland, holy band,
Lead us hand in hand.
Singing, shouting, brothers, come!
   Let us gayly wander home.
      "Strong and free,
      True are we!"
   Shall our watchword be.

                                Kinkle.

23. NO SLAVE BENEATH THE FLAG.

No slave beneath that starry flag,
    The emblem of the free!
No fettered hand shall wield the brand
    That smites for liberty!
No tramp of servile armies
    Shall shame Columbia's shore,
For he who fights for freedom's rights
    Is free for evermore!

No slaves beneath these glorious folds
    That o'er our fathers flew,
When every breath was dark with death,
    But every heart was true!
No serfs of earth's old empires
    Knelt 'neath its shadow then;
And they who now beneath it bow,
    For evermore are men!

. . . .

Go tell the brave of every land,
    Where'er that flag has flown —
The tyrant's fear, the patriot's cheer,
    Through every clime and zone —
That now no more forever
    Its stripes are slavery scars;
No tear-drops stain its azure plain
    Nor dim its golden stars!

No slave beneath that grand old flag!
    Forever let it fly,
With lightning rolled in every fold,
    And flashing victory!
God's blessing breathe around it!
    And when all strife is done,
May freedom's light, that knows no night,
    Make every star a sun!

                  GEORGE LANSING TAYLOR

24. LAUS DEO.

It is done!
　Clang of bell and roar of gun
Send the tidings up and down.
　How the belfreys rock and reel,
　How the great guns, peal on peal,
Fling the joy from town to town!

　Ring, O bells!
　Every stroke exulting tells
Of the burial hour of crime.
　Loud and long, that all may hear,
　Ring for every listening ear
Of Eternity and Time!

　Let us kneel;
　God's own voice is in that peal,
And this spot is holy ground.
　Lord, forgive us! What are we,
　That our eyes this glory see,
That our ears have heard the sound?

　For the Lord
　On the whirlwind is abroad;
In the earthquake he hath spoken;
　He has smitten with his thunder
　The iron wall asunder,
And the gates of brass are broken!

　Did we dare,
　In our agony of prayer,
Ask for more than He has done?
　When was ever His right hand,
　Over any time or land,
Stretched as now, beneath the sun?
　.　　.　　.　　.　　.　　.　　.

It is done!
  In the circuit of the sun
Shall the sound thereof go forth;
  It shall bid the sad rejoice,
  It shall give the dumb a voice,
It shall belt with joy the earth!

  Ring and swing,
  Bells of joy! On morning's wing
Send the song of praise abroad;
  With a sound of broken chains,
  Tell the Nations that He reigns,
Who alone is Lord and God!

JOHN GREENLEAF WHITTIER.

---

25. OUR HERITAGE.

. . . .

WHAT doth the poor man's son inherit?
  Stout muscles and a sinewy heart,
A hardy frame, a hardier spirit;
  King of two hands, he does his part
  In every useful toil and art:
A heritage, it seems to me,
A king might wish to hold in fee.

What does the poor man's son inherit?
  Wishes o'erjoyed with humble things,
A rank adjudged to toil-worn merit,
  Content that from employment springs,
  A heart that in his labor sings:
A heritage, it seems to me,
A king might wish to hold in fee.

What doth the poor man's son inherit?
　　A patience learned by being poor;
Courage, if sorrow come, to bear it;
　　A fellow-feeling that is sure
　　To make the outcast bless his door:
A heritage, it seems to me,
A king might wish to hold in fee.

O rich man's son! there is a toil
　　That with all other level stands;
Large charity doth never soil,
　　But only whitens, soft white hands;
　　This is the best crop from thy lands:
A heritage, it seems to me,
A king might wish to hold in fee.

O poor man's son! scorn not thy state;
　　There is worse weariness than thine,
In being merely rich and great
　　Toil only gives the soul to shine,
　　And makes rest fragrant and benign:
A heritage, it seems to me,
Worth being poor to hold in fee.

Both, heirs to some six feet of sod,
　　Are equal in the earth at last;
Both, children of the same great God,
　　Prove title to your heirship vast
　　By record of a well-filled past:
A heritage, it seems to me,
Well worth a life, to hold in fee.
　　　　　　　　　　JAMES RUSSELL LOWELL.

26. THE ROMAN SENATE AND THE AMERICAN CONGRESS.

From Address of Louis Kossuth, Ex-Governor of Hungary, before the Congress of the United States, in 1851.

As once Cineas of Epirus stood among the senators of Rome, who, with a word of conscious authority and majesty, arrested kings in their ambitious march, thus full of admiration and of reverence, I stand before you, legislators of the new capitol, that glorious hall of your people's collected majesty. The capitol of old yet stands, but the spirit has departed from it and has come over to yours, purified by the air of liberty. The old stands, a mournful monument of the fragility of human things; yours, as a sanctuary of eternal rights.

The old beamed with the red lustre of conquest, darkened by the gloom of oppression; yours is bright with freedom. The old absorbed the world into its own centralized glory; yours protects your own nation from being absorbed even by itself. The old was awful with unrestricted power; yours is glorious by having restricted it. At the view of the old, nations trembled; at the view of yours, humanity hopes. To the old, misfortune was introduced with fettered hands, to kneel at triumphant conquerors' feet; to yours, the triumph of introduction is granted to the unfortunate exiles who are invited to the honor of a seat. And, where kings and Cæsars never will be hailed for their power and wealth, there the persecuted chief of a down-trodden people is welcomed as your great Republic's guest, precisely because he is persecuted, helpless, and poor. In the old, the terrible *væ victis*, " woe to the conquered."

27. THE PATRIOT PRESIDENT.

Extract from Mark Lemon's *Tribute to Abraham Lincoln, in the London "Punch."*

How humble, yet how hopeful he could be!
   How in good fortune and in ill the same!
Nor bitter in success nor boastful he,
   Thirsty for gold, nor feverish for fame.
He went about his work — such work as few
   Ever had laid on head and heart and hand —
As one who knows where there's a task to do,
   Man's honest will must Heaven's good grace command.

So went he forth to battle, on the side
   That he felt clear was Liberty's and Right's,
As in his peasant boyhood he had plied
   His warfare with rude Nature's warring mights.
The uncleared forest, the unbroken soil,
   The iron bark that turns the lumb'rer's axe,
The rapid that o'erbears the boatman's toil,
   The prairie hiding the mazed wanderer's tracks,
The ambushed Indian, and the prowling bear, —
   Such were the needs that helped his youthful train:
Rough culture, but such trees large fruit may bear,
   If but their stocks be of right girth and grain.

So he grew up, — a destined work to do,
   And lived to do it, four long-suffering years;
Ill fate, ill feeling, ill report lived through,
   And then he heard the hisses change to cheers,
The taunts to tributes, the abuse to praise,
   And took both with the same unwavering mood;
Till, as he came on light, from darkening days,
   And seemed to touch the goal from where he stood,

A felon had, between the goal and him,
  Reached from behind his back, a trigger pressed,
And those perplexed and patient eyes were dim ;
  Those gaunt, long-laboring limbs were laid to rest.

. . . .

The old world and the new, from sea to sea,
  Utter one voice of sympathy and shame.
Sore heart, so stopped when it at last beat high !
  Sad life, cut short just as its triumph came !
Yet with a martyr's crown is crowned a life
  With much to praise, little to be forgiven !

---

28. THE PATRIOTIC PRINCE.

Frederick Wilhelm Ludwig von Hohenzollern, late Emperor of Germany, was born March 22, 1797, and died March 9, 1888. Almost at his last moments, when advised to rest, he replied, "*I have no time for rest. What I have to say for my country, I must say now.*" These last words of a wise Christian ruler were the key to a marvellous patriotic life, the chief facts of which are embodied in the following tribute. In boyhood as well as in later life an exile from home, he was ever an impassioned lover and servant of his Fatherland. William was crowned Emperor, January 18, 1871, at the palace of Versailles, Paris, on the anniversary of the coronation of his ancestor Frederick I.

The Nation's sire, four-score of years had toiled
In service of the grand old Fatherland,
Since time when, exiled from ancestral halls,
His loving father bade him dress with care
In the Prussian garb of martial service.

"No time for rest," as forth he firmly strode, —
In years an untried youth, at heart a man ;
His spirit tempered by the solemn hour
Which witnessed vows " his country to redeem ; "
And, nerved by purpose never lost,
He moved serenely forward to the goal.

"No time for rest" when queenly mother, firm,
In earnest tones her son addressed,
And bade him, "through love for her, the honor of
The Prussian State, avenging justice stern,
And all his hopes for earth and heaven beyond,
To rise above the age degenerate,
And action take, — his utmost will exert,
Prussia to restore, reproach to cancel,
And raise again the prostrate Fatherland."

"No time for rest," as feeble limb and arm,
Nurtured and trained by well-timed exercise,
Put on the strength of ripened manhood,
And, beardless as a child, he faced the fires
Of hottest fight, an order to obey;
And "Bar-sur-Aube" its proudest honor sent
Unsought, but nobly earned, to youthful prince
Who knew no fear when country bade him do.

"No time for rest." when fatal Auerstadt,
Sad supplement to Jena's battle waste,
Enforced the stern demand that every nerve
And force of body, spirit, soul, and mind,
Must consecrated be anew, at once,
Or Prussia as a State be ever lost.

"No time for rest," when surging armies came
To rend his country, despoil her homes and halls,
And parcel out to cold usurping hosts
The heritage for which so long he fought, —
The heritage of an honored name and fame.

"No time for rest" when, wrongly judged by those
Who could not sound a mind so truly great,
Enforced to second exile from his home,
From Britain's genial, kind, and friendly care
He bent his homeward way, no more to roam.

"No time for rest" when, scarcely joined, as yet,
The whirlwind of a causeless war broke forth,
The grand old Fatherland to swiftly smite
Before its allied States could blend as one
Their treasures, their affections, and their prayers,
And, blending all, defy the ruthless storm.

"No time for rest" when, foremost at the front,
He stemmed the tide of battle's flow,
Reversed its course, and, mounting on the wave,
O'erflowed the invader's boasted seat of power,
And in the palace of his foe, dethroned,
Proclaimed to all the world, fruition full
Of years of restless toil, the work complete, —
United Germany.

"No time for rest. No time for rest."
The four-score years had filled their measure full,
When summons to a higher seat than throne
On earth, a broader realm than Fatherland,
Employs his earnest thought, as failing flesh
Withdraws its tenement from the lingering soul.

And yet, as breathed upon by breath divine,
The Christian monarch, hero, friend, and sire
Revives again, in wise and tender words
His country and his people there to bless,
Invoking "peace with all the world besides;"
"No more" himself "to toil with them on earth,"
But, parting, rise with white-winged messenger
Sent from the upper skies, from care set free,
To enter upon his rest at last, — Eternal Rest.

HENRY B. CARRINGTON.

29. TUBAL CAIN.

Old Tubal Cain was a man of might
  In the days when the earth was young ;
By the fierce red light of his furnace bright
  The strokes of his anvil rung ;

And he lifted high his brawny hand
  On the iron growing clear,
Till the sparks rushed out in scarlet showers,
  As he fashioned the sword and spear.

And he sang, "Hurrah for my handiwork !
  Hurrah for the spear and the sword !
Hurrah for the hand that shall wield them well,
  For he shall be king and lord ! "
   .   .   .   .

But a sudden change came o'er his heart
  Ere the setting of the sun ;
And Tubal Cain was filled with pain
  For the evil he had done.
He saw that men, with rage and hate,
  Made war upon their kind ;
That the land was red with the blood they shed
  In their lust for carnage blind.
And he said, "Alas ! that I ever made,
  Or that skill of mine should plan,
The spear and the sword for men whose joy
  Is to slay their fellow-man ! "
   .   .   .   .

And men, taught wisdom from the past,
  In friendship joined their hands,
Hung the sword in the hall, the spear on the wall,
  And ploughed the willing lands ;
And sang, "Hurrah for Tubal Cain !
  Our stanch good friend is he ;

And for the ploughshare and the plough,
  To him our praise shall be.
But while oppression lifts its head,
  Or a tyrant would be lord,
Though we may thank him for the plough,
  We'll not forget the sword."

CHARLES MACKAY.

30. SONG OF THE UNION.

ERE Peace and Freedom, hand in hand,
Went forth to bless this happy land
  And make it their abode,
It was the foot-stool of a throne;
But now no master here is known.
  No king is feared, but God.

Americans uprose in might,
And triumphed in the unequal fight,
  For Union made them strong;
Union, the magic battle-cry
That hurled the tyrant foeman high,
  And crushed his hireling throng.

That word since then has shone on high,
In starry letters on the sky, —
  It is our country's name.
What impious hands shall rashly dare
Down from its lofty peak to tear
  The banner of her fame?

The spirits of the heroic dead,
Who for Columbia fought and bled,
  Would curse the dastard son
Who should betray their noble trust,
And madly trample in the dust
  The charter which they won.

From vast Niagara's gurgling roar
To Sacramento's golden shore,
   From East to Western wave,
The blended vows of millions rise;
Their voice re-echoes to the skies:
   "The Union we must save!"

The God of Nations, in whose name
The sacred laws obedience claim,
   Will bless our fond endeavor
To dwell as brethren here below;
"The Union," then, "come weal, come woe,"
   We will preserve forever!

JEREMIAH W. CUMMINGS.

31. OUR FLAG IS THERE.

Written by an American naval officer, 1812.

OUR flag is there, our flag is there,
   We'll hail it with three loud huzzas.
Our flag is there, our flag is there,
   Behold the glorious Stripes and Stars.
Stout hearts have fought for that bright flag,
   Strong hands sustained it mast-head high,
And, oh, to see how proud it waves,
   Brings tears of joy in every eye.

That flag has stood the battle's roar,
   With foemen stout, with foemen brave;
Strong hands have sought that flag to lower,
   And found a speedy, watery grave.
That flag is known on every shore,
   The standard of a gallant band;
Alike unstained in peace or war,
   It floats o'er Freedom's happy land.

PART VII.

MEMORABLE BATTLE-FIELDS AND INCIDENTS.

1. THE BATTLE-FIELD.

ONCE this soft turf, this rivulet's sands,
   Were trampled by a hurrying crowd,
And fiery hearts and armed hands
   Encountered in the battle-cloud.

Ah, never shall the land forget
   How gushed the life-blood of her brave, —
Gushed, warm with hope and valor yet,
   Upon the soil they sought to save!
   . . . .

Soon rested those who fought; but thou,
   Who minglest in the harder strife
For truths which men receive not now,
   Thy warfare only ends with life.
   . . . .

Yet, nerve thy spirit to the proof,
   And blench not at thy chosen lot.
The timid good may stand aloof,
   The sage may frown, yet faint thou not!
   . . . .

Truth, crushed to earth, shall rise again:
   The eternal years of God are hers;
But Error, wounded, writhes with pain,
   And dies among his worshippers.

Yea, though thou die upon the dust,
   When those who helped thee flee in **fear**,
Die full of hope and manly trust,
   Like those who fell in battle here.

Another hand thy sword shall wield,
   Another hand the standard wave,
Till from the trumpet's mouth is pealed
   The blast of triumph o'er the grave!

WILLIAM CULLEN BRYANT.

2. THE HONORED DEAD.

THEY that die for a good cause are redeemed from death. Their names are gathered and garnered. Their memory is precious. Each place grows proud for them who were born there. Children shall grow up under more sacred inspirations whose elder brothers, dying nobly for country, left a name that honored and inspired all who bore it. Orphan children shall find thousands of fathers and mothers to love and help those whom dying heroes left as a legacy to the gratitude of the public.

Oh, tell me not that they are dead, that generous host, that airy army of invisible heroes! They hover as a cloud of witnesses above this nation. Are they dead who speak louder than we can speak, and a more universal language? Are they dead that yet move upon society, and inspire the people with nobler motives and more heroic patriotism?

Ye that mourn, let gladness mingle with your tears. He was your son; but now he is the nation's. He made your household bright; now his example inspires a thousand households. Dear to his brothers and sisters, he is now brother to every generous youth in the land. Before, he was narrowed, appropriated, shut up to you; now he is augmented, set free, and given to all. He has died from the family, that he might live to the nation!

Neither are they less honored who shall bear through life the marks of wounds and sufferings. So strange is the transforming power of patriotic ardor that men shall almost covet disfigurement; and buoyant children shall pause in their noisy games, and with loving reverence honor them whose hands can work no more, and whose feet are no longer able to march, except upon that journey which brings good men to honor and immortality.

Oh, mother of lost children! set not in darkness nor sorrow whom a nation honors! Oh, mourners of the early dead! they shall live again, and forever! The Nation lives, because you gave it men that loved it better than their own lives. And when a few more days shall have cleared the perils from around the Nation's brow, and she shall sit in unsullied garments of liberty, with justice upon her forehead, love in her eyes, and truth upon her lips, she shall not forget those whose blood gave vital currents to her heart, and whose life, given to her, shall live with her life, till time shall be no more.

Every mountain and hill shall have its treasured name, every river shall keep some solemn title, every valley and every lake shall cherish its honored register; and till the mountains are worn out, and the rivers forget to flow, till the clouds are weary of replenishing springs, and the springs forget to gush, and the rills to sing, shall their names be kept fresh with reverent honors, which are inscribed upon the book of National Remembrance!

HENRY WARD BEECHER.

3. THE BIVOUAC OF THE DEAD.

The muffled drum's sad roll has beat
    The soldier's last tattoo;
No more on life's parade shall meet
    That brave and fallen few.
On Fame's eternal camping-ground
    Their silent tents are spread,
And glory guards with solemn round
    The bivouac of the dead.

No rumor of the foe's advance
    Now swells upon the wind;
No troubled thought at midnight haunts
    Of loved ones left behind;
No vision of the morrow's strife
    The warrior's dream alarms;
No braying horn or screaming fife
    At dawn shall call to arms.

Their shivered swords are red with dust;
    Their plumed heads are bowed;
Their haughty banner, trailed in dust,
    Is now their martial shroud;
And plenteous funeral tears have washed
    The red stains from each brow;
And the proudest forms, by battle gashed,
    Are free from anguish now.

The neighing troop, the flashing blade,
    The bugle's stirring blast,
The charge, the dreadful cannonade,
    The din and shout, are passed.
Nor war's wild note, nor glory's peal,
    Shall thrill with fierce delight
Those breasts that nevermore may feel
    The rapture of the fight.

Like the fierce northern hurricane
  That sweeps his great plateau,
Flushed with the triumph yet to gain,
  Came down the serried foe.
Who heard the thunder of the fray
  Break o'er the field beneath,
Knew well the watchword of that day
  Was, "Victory or Death!"

Full many a mother's breath hath swept
  O'er Angostura's plain,
And long the pitying sky has wept
  Above its molder'd slain.
The raven's scream, or eagle's flight,
  Or shepherd's pensive lay,
Alone now wake each solemn height
  That frowned o'er that dread fray.

Sons of the "dark and bloody ground,"[1]
  Ye must not slumber there,
Where stranger steps and tongues resound
  Along the heedless air!
Your own proud land's heroic soil
  Shall be your fitter grave:
She claims from war its richest spoil, —
  The ashes of her brave.

Thus, 'neath their parent turf they rest,
  Far from the gory field,
Borne to a Spartan mother's breast
  On many a bloody shield.
The sunshine of their native sky
  Smiles sadly on them here,
And kindred eyes and hearts watch by
  The heroes' sepulchre.

[1] Kentucky, in the Indian wars.

Rest on, embalmed and sainted dead!
  Dear as the blood ye gave;
No impious footstep here shall tread
  The herbage of your grave;
Nor shall your glory be forgot
  While Fame her record keeps,
Or Honor points the hallowed spot
  Where Valor proudly sleeps.

Yon marble minstrel's voiceless stone
  In deathless song shall tell,
When many a vanished year hath flown,
  The story how ye fell.
Nor wreck, nor change, nor winter's blight,
  Nor Time's remorseless doom,
Can dim one ray of holy light
  That gilds your glorious tomb.
                    THEODORE O'HARA.

---

4. THE REVIEW OF THE DEAD.

As revised by author for "Beacon Lights of Patriotism."

'T was night. A lurid light
Made field and wood seem of some other world.
Before rising winds the vapors whirled,
Wild, spectre-like; and in deep gulfs afar,
  Star after star
Shone fugitive: — the white moon shuddered through
  The clouds that flew.

  Below, with dismal flow,
The Shenandoah swept the hills between;
The boding night-wind woke with wings unseen
The spirit-murmurs in the shadowy pines,
  And down their lines.
Far off, in softest cadences of sound,
  The whispers wound.

  A shade, in mist arrayed,
Came on the winds o'er moorland, tarn, and scaur, —
His mantle streaming in the night, his war
Steed shod with silence; in his dusky hand,
  A sabre; and,
As distant thunders on our slumbers fall,
  He made his call: —

  "Awake, lost legions! Shake
Oblivion's dreamless slumbers off! Their threnes
The pines sing o'er you now. The mock-bird preens
Where ye are laid, and round you, soft and clear,
  Year after year,
Murmur sweet streams, all lulled to rest — but come!
  I call you home!"

  A sound that shook the ground
Went forth through earth. 'T was like the hollow roar
Of cannon dying in the hills; and o'er
Night's broad expansions breathed the trumpet's tone,
  Blent with the moan
Of winds. Faint strains of martial music stole
  Into the soul.

  Along the vale they throng,
As clouds across the moon at midnight drift —
Dark, wavering volumes, fleecy scuds — with swift
Unechoing footfalls toward an awful hush.
  On, on they rush!
The vision raised his blade, and waved them on
  With, "Lo, the dawn!"

  And anxiously the ranks
Closed in dense columns down the misty vale;
Battalion on battalion, riders pale,
On dim, mysterious chargers, hurried past,
  And in that vast
Dumb pageant melted as the stars away
  Into the day.

                The form upon his arm
Bent low his head in grief.   The mystic band
Died in that river's roar, which through the land
Seems blent with children's crying, and the moan
        Of widows lone,
Lamenting for the ones that glad the door
        Of home no more.
                                HENRY JEROME STOCKARD.

5. OUR MARTYRED DEAD.

IN MEMORIAM.

Our martyred dead:
On each low bed,
Green be the chaplet,
Fresh the roses;
Oh, lightly rest,
On each calm breast,
The turf where each
In peace reposes.

Hail, hero shades!
Your battle blades
A wall of steel
Our homes surrounded;
Your deeds have won,
From sire to son,
Love, joy, and gratitude
Unbounded.

No marble cold
May guard your mould,
But living hearts
Around, are swelling;

> Each daring deed
> Shall gain the meed
> Of praise from all hearts
> Richly flowing.
>
> Your sacred dust
> Be the choice trust
> Of Freedom's grateful
> Sons and daughters;
> While future days
> Your fame shall raise,
> From Atlantic's
> To Pacific's waters.
>
> Rev. Mark Trafton.

6. THE MOURNING HERO'S VISION.

To-day is the fourth anniversary of the revolution in Hungary. Anniversaries of revolutions are almost always connected with the recollections of some patriots, death-fallen on that day, like the Spartans at Thermopylæ, martyrs of devotion to their fatherland. In almost every country there is some lofty monument, or some proud tombstone, adorned on such a day by a garland of evergreen, — the pious offering of patriotic tenderness.

I passed the night in a sleepless dream; and my mind wandered on the magnetic wings of the past, home to my beloved, bleeding land. I saw, in the dead of the night, dark veiled shades, with the paleness of eternal grief upon their sad brows. Yet they were terrible in the tearless silence of that great grief, gliding over the church-yards of Hungary, and kneeling down at the head of the graves and depositing the pious tributes of green cypress upon them. I beheld them, after a short prayer, rising with clinched fists and gnashing teeth, then stealing away, because the bloodhounds of my country's murderers lurked from every corner on that night, and on this day, to lead to prison those who dare to show a pious remembrance of the beloved dead.

To-day, a smile on the lips of a Magyr is taken for a crime of defiance to tyranny, and a tear in his eye is equivalent to a revolt; and yet I have seen, with my wandering soul, thousands performing the work of patriotic gratitude.

And I saw more. When the pious offerers had stolen away, I saw the honored dead, half risen from their tombs, looking to the offerings, and whispering gloomily, "Still a cypress, and still no flower of joy? Is there still the chill of winter and the gloom of night over thee, Fatherland? Are we not yet revenged?"

And the sky of the East reddened suddenly, and boiled with bloody flames; and from the far, far west, a lightning flashed like a star-spangled stripe, and within its light a young eagle mounted and soared toward the bloody flames of the East; and as he drew near, upon his approaching, the boiling flames changed into a radiant morning sun. Then a voice was heard from above, in answer to the question of the dead: "Sleep, sleep yet a little time. Mine is the revenge! I will make the stars of the West the sun of the East; and when ye next awake, ye will find the flower of joy upon your cold bed."

And the dead took the twig of cypress, the sign of resurrection, into their bony hands, and lay down.

Louis Kossuth.[1]

---

[1] The visit of Kossuth to the United States was so cordially responded to by the American people, that, in addition to popular ovations, the enthusiasm of Congress and many State Legislatures induced the patriot to expect material aid to Hungary in her struggle for independence. Bonds were issued, and many were sold, in aid of his plans.

7. THE SOLDIER'S WIDOW.

   Woe for my vine-clad home,
That it should ever be so dark to me,
With its bright threshold and its whispering tree; —
   That I should ever come,
Fearing the lonely echo of a tread,
Beneath the roof-tree of my glorious dead!

   Lead on, my orphan boy,
Thy home is not so desolate to thee,
And the low shiver in the linden-tree,
   May bring to thee a joy;
But, oh, how dark is the bright home before thee,
To her who with a joyous spirit bore thee!

   Lead on, for thou art now
My sole remaining helper. God hath spoken,
And the strong heart I leaned upon is broken;
   And I have seen his brow,
The forehead of my upright one and just,
Trod by the hoof of battle, to the dust.

   He will not meet thee there,
Who blessed thee at the even-tide, my son;
And when the shadows of the night steal on,
   He will not call to prayer:
The lips that melted, giving thee to God,
Are in the icy keeping of the sod.

   Ay, my own boy, thy sire
Is with the sleepers of the valley cast,
And the proud glory of my life hath past,
   With his high glance of fire.
Woe, that the linden and the vine should bloom,
And a just man be gathered to his tomb!

                    NATHANIEL PARKER WILLIS.

8. DIRGE FOR THE SOLDIER.

Close his eyes ; his work is done.
  What to him is friend or foeman,
Rise of moon, or set of sun,
  Hand of man, or kiss of woman ?
    Lay him low ; lay him low,
    In the clover or the snow !
What cares he ? He cannot know.
    Lay him low !

As man may, he fought his fight,
  Proved his truth by his endeavor ;
Let him sleep in solemn right, —
  Sleep forever and forever.
    Lay him low ; lay him low,
    In the clover or the snow !
What cares he ? He cannot know.
    Lay him low !

Fold him in his country's stars,
  Roll the drum, and fire the volley ;
What to him are all our wars, —
  What but death-bemocking folly ?
    Lay him low ; lay him low,
    In the clover or the snow !
What cares he ? He cannot know ;
    Lay him low !

Leave him to God's watching eye,
  Trust him to the hand that made him :
Mortal love sweeps idly by ;
  God alone has power to aid him.
    Lay him low ; lay him low,
    In the clover or the snow !
What cares he ? He cannot know.
    Lay him low !

George H. Boker.

9. THE BRAVE AT HOME.

The maid who binds her warrior's sash,
   With smile that well her pain dissembles,
The while beneath her drooping lash
   One starry tear-drop hangs and trembles, —
Though Heaven alone records the tear,
   And fame shall never know her story,
Her heart has shed a drop as dear
   As e'er bedewed the field of glory.

The wife who girds her husband's sword,
   'Mid little ones who weep or wonder,
And bravely speaks the cheering word, —
   What though her heart be rent asunder,
Doomed nightly, in her dreams, to hear
   The bolts of death around him rattle,
Hath shed as sacred blood as e'er
   Was poured upon the field of battle.

The mother who conceals her grief,
   While to her breast her son she presses,
Then breathes a few brave words and brief,
   Kissing the patriot brow she presses,
With no one but her secret God
   To know the pain that weighs upon her,
Sheds holy blood as e'er the sod
   Received on Freedom's field of honor.

Thomas Buchanan Read.

THE NOISE OF ARMS.

The noise of arms deafens the voice of the laws.

Montaigne.

10. THE SCOURGE OF WAR.

Hark! the cry of Death is ringing
   Wild from the reeking plain;
Guilty Glory, too, is flinging
   Proudly forth her vaunting strain;
Thousands on the field are lying,
   Slaughtered in the ruthless strife;
Wildly mingled, dead and dying
   Show the waste of human life.

Christian, can you idly slumber,
   While this work of death goes on?
Can you idly sit and number
   Fellow-beings, one by one,
On the field of battle falling,
   Sinking to a bloody grave?
Up! the God of Peace is calling, —
   Calling upon you to save!

Listen to the supplications
   Of the widowed ones of earth;
Listen to the cry of nations,
   Ringing loudly, wildly forth, —
Nations bruised and crushed forever
   By the iron heel of war.
God of Mercy, wilt thou never
   Send deliverance from afar?

Yes, a light is faintly gleaming
   Through the cloud that hovers o'er;
Soon the radiance of its beaming,
   Full upon our land will pour.
'T is the light that tells the dawning
   Of the bright Millennial Day,
Heralding its blessed morning
   With its peace-bestowing ray.

God shall spread abroad His banner, —
   Sign of universal peace;
And the earth shall shout Hosanna,
   And the reign of blood shall cease.
Man no more shall seek dominion
   Through a sea of human gore;
War shall spread its gloomy pinion
   O'er the peaceful earth no more.

WILLIAM HENRY BURLEIGH.

11. TRUE GLORY.

THEY err, who count it glorious to subdue
By conquest far and wide, to overrun
Large countries, and in field great battles win,
Great cities by assault. What do these worthies
But rob and spoil, burn, slaughter, and enslave
Peaceable nations, neighboring or remote?
Made captive, yet deserving freedom more
Than those, their conquerors, who leave behind
Nothing but ruin, wheresoe'er they rove,
And all the flourishing works of peace destroy:
Then swell with pride, and must be titled gods,
Great benefactors of mankind, deliverers,
Worshipped with temple, priest, and sacrifice.
But if there be in glory aught of good,
It may by means far different be attained,
Without ambition, war, or violence:
By deeds of peace, by wisdom eminent,
By patience, temperance.
Who names not now with honor, patient Job?
Poor Socrates (who next, more honorable?)
By what he taught, and suffered for so doing,
For truth's sake suffering death unjust, lives now
Equal in fame to proudest conquerors.

JOHN MILTON (In "Paradise Regained").

12. THE WARRIOR'S WREATH.

Behold the wreath which decks the warrior's brow:
Breathes it a balmy fragrance sweet? Ah, no!
    It rankly savors of the grave!
  'T is red, but not with roseate hues;
    'T is crimsoned o'er
    With human gore!
  'T is wet, but not with heavenly dews.

'T is drenched in tears, by widows, orphans, shed:
Methinks in sable weeds I see them clad,
    And mourn in vain for husbands slain,
  Children beloved, or brothers dear;
    The fatherless
    In deep distress,
  Despairing, shed the scalding tear.

I hear, 'mid dying groans, the cannon's crash;
I see, 'mid smoke, the musket's horrid flash;
    Here famine walks, there carnage stalks,
  Hell in her fiery eye; she stains
    With purple blood
    The crystal flood,
  Heaven's altars, and the verdant plains.

Scenes of domestic peace and social bliss
Are changed to scenes of woe and wretchedness;
    The votaries of vice increase, —
  Towns sacked, whole cities wrapt in flame!
    Just Heaven, say,
    Is this the "bay"
  Which warriors gain? Is this called Fame?

From "National Preceptor." *Anon.* 1835.

13. MIGHT MAKES RIGHT.

A sparrow, perched upon a bough,
Spied a poor beetle creep below,
And picked it up. "Ah, spare me, spare!"
The insect prayed: but vain its prayer.
"Wretch!" cries the murderer, "hold thy tongue,
For thou art weak, and I am strong."

A hawk beheld him, and in haste
Sharpens his beak for a repast,
And pounces plump upon him. "Oh,"
Exclaims the sparrow, "let me go!"
"Wretch!" cries the murderer, "hold thy tongue,
For thou art weak, and I am strong."

The hawk was munching up his prey,
When a stout eagle steered that way,
And seized upon him. "Sure, comrade,
You'll spare my life, — we're both a trade!"
"Wretch!" cries the murderer, "hold thy tongue,
For thou art weak, and I am strong."

A sportsman saw the eagle fly:
He shot, and brought him from the sky.
The dying bird could only groan,
"Tyrant, what evil have I done?"
"Wretch!" cries the murderer, "hold thy tongue,
For thou art weak, and I am strong."

'T is thus that man to man behaves:
Witness the planter and his slaves.
'T is thus that State oppresses State,
And infant freedom meets its fate.
"Wretch!" cries the stronger, "hold thy tongue,
For thou art weak, and I am strong."

From "National Preceptor." Anon. 1835.

14. THE REIGN OF PEACE.

BEAUTIFUL vision ! how bright it rose, —
Vision of peaceful and calm repose !
Well might it brighten the rapt seer's eye,
And waken his heart to an ecstasy !
'T was earth, glad earth, when her strife was o'er,
Her conflict ended, and war no more.

Households are grouped in the fig-tree's shade,
None to molest them or make afraid ;
Securely rest 'neath the house-side vine,
Parent and child from the noon sunshine ;
Nations rejoice in the blest release,
And the voice of Earth is a voice of peace.

Beautiful vision ! and shall it be
Surely accomplished, O Earth, in thee ?
The sword of war, shall it scathe no more
The peaceful scenes of the softest shore ?
And light stream down from the radiant skies
On scenes of the war-god's sacrifice ?

Ay ! for the word of the prophet is true.
Fair was the vision ; but full in view,
The Moslem's sabre, all keen and bright,
Burnished and bare for the ready fight ;
Sheathe it he will, and in spirit be
Like the turtle-dove in his cypress-tree.

The vines of Judah shall then be pruned,
Her broken harp be again attuned ;
And listening Earth, from her farthest shore,
Startled not now by the cannon's roar,
Songs of the angels shall hear again :
" Peace on earth, and good will to men! "

ELIZA THORNTON.

15. BANNOCKBURN.

The defeat of Edward II., King of England, at Bannockburn, A. D. 1314, will ever be memorial of the intense patriotism of the Scotch people, and their loyalty to the traditions of their fathers.

At Bannockburn the English lay;
The Scots, they were na far away,
But waited for the break of day
   That glinted in the east.

But soon the sun broke through the heath,
And lighted up that field of death;
When Bruce, wi' soul-inspiring breath,
   His heralds thus addressed:

"Scots wha hae wi' Wallace bled,
Scots wham Bruce has aften led,
Welcome to your gory bed,
   Or to glorious victory!

"Now 's the day, and now 's the hour;
See the front of battle low'r;
See approach proud Edward's power, —
   Edward, chains, and slavery!

"Wha will be a traitor knave?
Wha can fill a coward's grave?
Wha sae base as be a slave?
   Traitor! coward! turn and flee!

"Wha for Scotland's king and law
Freedom's sword will strongly draw,
Freeman stand, or freeman fa'?
   Caledonian, on wi' me!

"By oppression's woes and pains,
By your sons in servile chains,
We will drain our dearest veins,
   But they shall be, shall be, free!

"Lay the proud usurpers low!
Tyrants fall in every foe;
Liberty's in every blow!
   Forward! Let us do or die!"

ROBERT BURNS.

16. MARATHON BY STARLIGHT.

THE victory of Miltiades over the Persians, B. C. 490, delivered the Grecian States from great danger, and united them in a common defence.

No vesper-breeze is floating now,
   No murmurs shake the air;
A gloom hath veiled the mountain's brow,
   And quietude is there;
The night-beads on the dew-white grass
   Drop brilliant as my footsteps pass.

No hum of life disturbs the scene,
   The clouds are rolled to rest;
'T is like a calm where grief hath been,
   So welcome to the breast.
The warring tones of day have gone,
   And starlight glows on Marathon.
   . . . .

'T was here they fought; and martial peals
   Once thundered o'er the ground,
And gash and wound from plunging steels
   Endewed the battle-mound;
Here Grecians trod the Persian dead,
   And Freedom shouted while she bled.

But gone the day of Freedom's sword,
    And cold the patriot brave
Who mowed the dastard-minded horde
    Into a gory grave,
While Greece arose sublimely free,
    And dauntless as her own dark sea.

Still starlight sheds the same pale beam
    For aye upon the plain,
And musing breasts might fondly dream
    The Grecian free again;
For empires fall, and Freedom dies,
    But dimless beauty robes the skies.

May He whose glory gems the sky,
    God of the slave and free,
Hear every patriot's burning sigh
    That's offered here for thee!
For thee, sad Greece, and every son
    That braves a Turk on Marathon.

RICHARD MONTGOMERY.

17. JOAN OF ARC'S FAREWELL TO HOME.

This patriotic girl, at the age of eighteen, rescued her country, in the year 1429.

FAREWELL, ye mountains, ye beloved glades,
Ye lone and peaceful valleys, fare ye well!
Through you Joanna never more may stray!
For aye, Joanna bids you now farewell.
Ye meads which I have watered, and ye trees
Which I have planted, still in beauty bloom!
Farewell, ye grottos, and ye crystal springs!
Sweet echo, vocal spirit of the vale,
Who sang'st responsive to my simple strain,
Joanna goes, and ne'er returns again.

He who in glory did on Horeb's height
Descend to Moses in the bush of flame,
And bade him stand in Royal Pharaoh's sight;
Who once to Israel's pious shepherd came,
And sent him forth, his champion in the fight;
Who aye hath loved the lowly shepherd train, —
He, from these leafy boughs, thus spake to me:
"Go forth! Thou shalt on earth my witness be.

"Thou in rude armor must thy limbs invest,
A plate of steel upon thy bosom bear.
Vain earthly love may never stir thy breast,
Nor passion's sinful glow be kindled there,
But war's triumphant glory shall be thine.
Thy martial fame all women shall outshine!

" For when in fight the stoutest hearts despair,
When direful ruin threatens France, forlorn,
Then thou aloft my oriflamme shalt bear,
And swiftly as the reaper mows the corn,
Thou shalt lay low the haughty conqueror;
His fortune's wheel thou rapidly shalt turn,
To Gaul's heroic sons deliv'rance bring,
Relieve beleaguered Rheims, and crown thy king!"

The Heavenly Spirit promised me a sign:
He sends the helmet. — it hath come from Him.
Its iron filleth me with strength divine;
I feel the courage of the cherubim.
As with the rushing of a mighty wind
It drives me forth to join the battle's din;
The clanging trumpets sound, the chargers rear,
And the loud war-cry thunders in mine ear.

SCHILLER.

18. LEONIDAS.

The heroism of the Spartan patriot Leonidas, and the willing self-sacrifice of his little band of three hundred veterans at the Pass of Thermopylæ, along the northern shore of the Mediterranean Sea, B. C. 480, are among the most emphatic expressions of true patriotism to be found in human history. All the later struggles of Greece against Turkish oppression have equally aroused the sympathy of England and America.

Shout for the mighty dead
   Who died along this shore,
Who died within this mountain glen!
For never nobler chieftain's head
Was laid on valor's crimson bed,
   Nor ever prouder gore
Sprang forth, than theirs who won the day
Upon thy strand, Thermopylæ!

Shout for the mighty men
   Who on the Persian tents,
Like lions from their midnight den,
Bounded on the slumbering deer;
Rush'd, a storm of sword and spear,
   Like the roused elements
Let loose from an immortal hand,
To chasten or to crush a land!

But there are none to hear:
   Greece is a hopeless slave.
Leonidas! no hand is near
To lift thy fiery falchion now;
No warrior makes the warrior's vow
   Upon thy sea-washed grave.
The voice that should be raised by men
Must now be given by wave and glen.

                                   GEORGE CROLY.

19. FALL OF THE INDIAN HEROES.

"They come! they come! the paleface come!"
The chieftain shouted, where he stood
Sharp-watching at the margin wood,
And gave the war-whoop's treble yell,
That like a knell on fair hearts fell,
Far watching from their rocky home.

No nodding plumes and banners fair
Unfurled or fretted in the air;
No screaming fife or rolling drum
Did challenge brave of soul to come:
But, silent, sinew-bows were strung,
And, sudden, heavy quivers hung,
And swiftly to the battle sprung
Tall, painted braves, with tufted hair,
Like death-like banners in the air.

And long they fought, and firm and well,
And silent fought, and silent fell,
Save when they gave the fearful yell
Of death, defiance, or of hate.
But what were feathered flints to fate?
And what were yells to seething lead?
And what the few and feeble feet
To troops that came with martial tread,
And stood by wood and hill and stream
As thick as people in a street,
As strong as spirits in a dream?

From pine and poplar, here and there,
A cloud, a crash, a flash, a thud,
A warrior's garments rolled in blood,
A yell, that rent the mountain air,
Of fierce defiance and despair
Did tell who fell, and when, and where:

Then tighter drew the coils around,
And closer grew the battle-ground,
And fewer feathered arrows fell,
And fainter grew the battle-yell,
Until upon the hill was heard
The short, sharp whistle of the bird.

The calm that cometh after all,
Looked sweetly down at shut of day,
Where friend and foe commingling lay
Like leaves of forest as they fall.
. . . .
The mighty chief at last was down,
The broken breast of brass and pride:
The hair all dust, the brow a-frown,
And proud mute lips compressed with hate
To foes, — yet all content with fate;
While circled round him thick the foe,
Had folded hands in dust, and died.
His tomahawk lay at his side,
All blood, beside his broken bow;
One arm stretched out as over-bold,
One hand, half-doubled, hid in dust,
And clutched the earth, as if to hold
His hunting-grounds still in his trust.

Here tall grass bowed its tasselled head,
In dewy tears above the dead;
And there they lay in crooked fern,
That waved and wept above by turn;
And further on, by sombre trees,
They lay, wild heroes of wildest deeds,
In shrouds alone of weeping weeds,
Bound in a never-to-be-broken peace.

JOAQUIN MILLER.

20. THE DYING TRUMPETER.[1]

Upon the field of battle the dying trumpeter lay,
And from his side the life-blood was streaming fast away.
His deadly wound is burning, and yet he cannot die
Till his company, returning, brings news of victory.

Hark! as he rises, reeling upon the bloody ground,
Hark! o'er the field is pealing a well-known trumpet sound.
It gives him life and vigor; he grasps his horse's mane;
He mounts, and lifts his trumpet to his dying lips again.
And all his strength he gathers, to hold it in his hand,
Then pours, in notes of thunder, "Victoria!" o'er the land.

"Victoria!" sounds the trumpet: "Victoria!" all around;
"Victoria!" like the thunder, it rolls along the ground.
And in that blast so thrilling the trumpeter's spirit fled;
He breathed his last breath in it, and from his steed fell dead.

> The company, returning,
> Stood silent round their friend;
> "That," said the old field-marshal,
> "That was a happy end!"

JULIUS MOSEN.

---

21. ALAMANCE.

The bloody skirmish with the British at Alamance, North Carolina, was prior to that at Lexington, Mass., — viz., May 7, 1771; and John Ashe, Speaker of the Assembly, headed the people in armed resistance to the issuing of government stamps, six years earlier than the encounter still honored by the people of the "Old North State" as the Battle of Alamance.

No stately column marks the hallowed place
   Where silent sleeps, un-urned, their sacred dust:
The first free martyrs of a glorious race,
   Their fame a people's wealth, a nation's trust.

[1] Translated by Epes Sargent.

The rustic ploughman at the early morn
  The yielding furrow turns with heedless tread,
Or tends with frugal care the springing corn,
  Where tyrants conquered and where heroes bled.

Above their rest the golden harvest waves,
  The glorious stars stand sentinels on high,
While in sad requiem, near their turfless graves,
  The winding river murmurs, mourning, by.

No stern ambition waved them to the deed:
  In Freedom's cause they nobly dared to die.
The first to conquer, or the first to bleed,
  "God and their country's right" their battle-cry.

But holier watchers here their vigils keep
  Than storied urn or monumental stone;
For Law and Justice guard their dreamless sleep,
  And Plenty smiles above their bloody home.

Immortal youth shall crown their deathless fame;
  And as their country's glories shall advance,
Shall brighter blaze, o'er all the earth, thy name,
  Thou first-fought field of Freedom, — Alamance.

Seymour W. Whiting.

---

22. THE DEATH OF OSCEOLA.

Osceola, a principal chief of the Seminole Indians of Florida, was captured while bearing a flag of truce, and died in prison, after seven years of war with the whites in defence of his home and people.

In a dark and dungeon room
  Is stretched a tawny form,
And it shakes in its dread agony
  Like a leaf in the autumn storm.

No pillared palmetto hangs
  Its tufts in the clear, bright air,
But a sorrowing group, and the narrow wall,
  And a smouldering fire is there.

For his own green forest home
  He had struggled long and well;
But the soul that breasted a nation's arms,
  At the touch of a fetter fell.
He had worn wild Freedom's crown
  On his bright unconquered brow,
Since he first saw the light of his beautiful skies:
  It was gone forever, now.

But in his last dread hour,
  Did not bright visions come, —
Bright visions that shed a golden gleam
  On the darkness of his doom?
They calmed his throbbing pulse,
  And they hung on his muttering breath:
The spray thrown up from life's frenzied flood,
  Plunging on to the gulf of death.

The close walls shrunk away:
  Above was the stainless sky,
And the lakes with their fluttering isles of flowers,
  Spread glittering to his eye.
O'er his hut the live oak spread
  Its branching, gigantic shade,
With its dots of leaves, and its robes of moss,
  Broad blackening on the glade.

But a sterner sight is found:
  Battle's wild torrent is there;
The tomahawk gleams, and the red blood streams,
  And the war-whoops rend the air.

At the head of his faithful band,
    He peals forth his terrible cry,
And he fiercely leaps 'mid the slaughtered heaps
    Of the foe that but fought to die.

One gasp, and the eye is glazed,
    And still is the stiffening clay:
The eagle soul of the chief had passed
    On the battle's flood away.
                    ALFRED BILLINGS STREET.

23. THE BOY OF RATISBON.

You know we French stormed Ratisbon;
    A mile or so away,
On a little mound, Napoleon
    Stood, on our storming day;
With neck out-thrust, — you fancy how, —
    Legs wide, arms locked behind,
As if to balance the prone brow
    Oppressive with its mind.

Just as perhaps he mused, "My plans
    That soar, to earth may fall,
Let once my army leader, Lannes,
    Waver at yonder wall," —
Out 'twixt the battery-smokes there flew
    A rider, bound on bound,
Full galloping; nor bridle drew
    Until he reached the mound.

Then off there flung, in smiling joy,
    And held himself erect,
Just by his horse's mane, a boy;
    You hardly could suspect —

(So tight he kept his lips compressed,
   Scarce any blood came through)
You looked twice, ere you saw his breast
   Was almost shot in two.

"Well," cried he, "Emperor, by God's grace
   We've got you Ratisbon!
The Marshal's in the market-place,
   And you'll be there anon,
To see your flag-bird flap his vans
   Where I, to heart's desire,
Perched him." The chief's eyes flashed; his plans
   Soared up again like fire.

The chief's eyes flashed; but presently
   Softened itself, as sheathes
A film the mother eagle's eye
   When her bruised eaglet breathes.
"You're wounded!" "Nay," his soldier's pride
   Touched to the quick, he said;
"I'm killed, sire!" and, his chief beside,
   Smiling, the boy fell dead.

ROBERT BROWNING.

24. THE BURIAL OF SIR JOHN MOORE.

At the close of a battle between the French and English at Corunna, Spain, January 16, 1809, Sir John Moore was buried in a hastily made grave upon the English ramparts, late at night, and wrapped in his military clothing. He had repeatedly said that, if killed in battle, he wished to be buried where he fell.

Not a drum was heard, not a funeral note,
   As his corse to the rampart we hurried;
Not a soldier discharged his farewell shot
   O'er the grave where our hero we buried.

We buried him darkly at dead of night,
    The sods with our bayonets turning;
By the struggling moonbeam's misty light
    And the lantern dimly burning.

No useless coffin enclosed his breast,
    Nor in sheet nor in shroud we wound him;
But he lay like a warrior taking his rest
    With his martial cloak around him.

Few and short were the prayers we said,
    And we spoke not a word of sorrow,
But we steadfastly gazed on the face that was dead,
    And we bitterly thought of the morrow.

We thought as we hollowed his narrow bed,
    And smoothed down his lonely pillow,
That the foe and the stranger would tread o'er his head,
    And we far away on the billow.

Lightly they'll talk of the spirit that's gone
    And o'er his cold ashes upbraid him;
But little he'll reck, if they let him sleep on
    In the grave where a Briton has laid him.

But half of our heavy task was done
    When the clock struck the hour for retiring;
And we heard the distant and random gun
    That the foe was suddenly firing.

Slowly and sadly we laid him down,
    From the field of his fame fresh and gory;
We carved not a line, and we raised not a stone —
    But we left him alone with his glory.

                              CHARLES WOLFE.

25. THE BATTLE OF LINDEN.

HOHENLINDEN, Bavaria, near which the Austrians, under Archduke John, were defeated by the French and Bavarians under General Moreau, December 3, 1800, at the close of a raging snow-storm.

On Linden, when the sun was low,
All bloodless lay the untrodden snow;
And dark as winter was the flow
   Of Iser rolling rapidly.

But Linden saw another sight,
When the drum beat at dead of night
Commanding fires of death to light
   The darkness of her scenery.

By torch and trumpet fast arrayed,
Each horseman drew his battle-blade,
And furious every charger neighed,
   To join the dreadful revelry.

Then shook the hills with thunder riven;
Then rushed the steed, to battle driven;
And louder than the bolts of Heaven
   Far flash'd the red artillery.

But redder yet that light shall glow
On Linden's hills of blood-stained snow;
And bloodier yet the torrent flow
   Of Iser, rolling rapidly.

'T is morn; but scarce yon level sun
Can pierce the war-clouds, rolling dun,
While furious Frank and fiery Hun
   Shout in their sulphurous canopy.

The combat deepens. On, ye Brave
Who rush to glory, or the grave.
Wave, Munich, all thy banners wave,
   And charge with all thy chivalry!

> Few, few shall part where many meet!
> The snow shall be their winding-sheet,
> And every turf beneath their feet
>   Shall be a soldier's sepulchre.
>
> Thomas Campbell.

---

26. THE BATTLE OF WATERLOO.

There was a sound of revelry by night,
And Belgium's capital had gathered then
Her beauty and her chivalry, and bright
The lamps shone o'er fair women and brave men;
A thousand hearts beat happily; and when
Music arose with its voluptuous swell,
Soft eyes looked love to eyes which spake again,
And all went merry as a marriage bell.
But hush! hark! a deep sound strikes like a rising knell!

Did ye not hear it? — No! 'T was but the wind,
Or the car rattling o'er the stony street;
On with the dance! Let joy be unconfined;
No sleep till morn, when Youth and Pleasure meet
To chase the glowing hours with flying feet —
But hark! — that heavy sound breaks in once more,
As if the clouds its echo would repeat;
And nearer, clearer, deadlier than before!
Arm! Arm! it is — it is — the cannon's opening roar!

. . . .

Ah! then and there was hurrying to and fro,
And gathering tears, and tremblings of distress,
And cheeks all pale, which but an hour ago
Blushed at the praise of their own loveliness;
And there were sudden partings, such as press
The life from out young hearts, and choking sighs
Which ne'er might be repeated; who could guess
If ever more should meet those mutual eyes,
Since upon night so sweet such awful morn should rise!

And there was mounting in hot haste: the steed,
The mustering squadron, and the clattering car,
Went pouring forward with impetuous speed,
And swiftly forming in the ranks of war;
And the deep thunder peal on peal afar;
And near, the beat of the alarming drum
Roused up the soldier ere the morning star;
While thronged the citizens with terror dumb,
Or whispering with white lips,—
"The foe! They come! They come!"

. . . .

Last noon beheld them full of lusty life,
Last eve, in beauty's circle proudly gay;
The midnight brought the signal-sound of strife,
The morn, the marshalling in arms; the day
Battle's magnificently stern array!
The thunder-clouds close o'er it, which when rent
The earth is covered thick with other clay,
Which her own clay shall cover, heaped and pent,
Rider and horse,—friend, foe,—in one red burial blent.

BYRON.

27. THE BATTLE OF LEXINGTON.

The skirmish at Alamance, N. C., is elsewhere noticed. The subsequent resistance by the militia of Massachusetts to the aggressive action of the British troops at Boston, precipitated the War for Independence. The glowing description of this first resistance, with the purpose to dare open war, is given in the language of the historian Weems, who, if not always accurate in detail, never failed to honor the zeal of the revolutionary veterans.

APRIL the 19th, 1775, was the fatal day marked out by mysterious Heaven for tearing away the stout infant colonies from the old mother country. Early that morning, General Gage sent a detachment of about 1,000 men from

Boston to destroy some military stores which the Americans had accumulated in the town of Concord, near Lexington.

On coming to the place they found the town militia assembled on the green, near the road. "*Throw down your arms and disperse, you rebels!*" was the cry of the British officer [Pitcairn], which was immediately followed by a general discharge from the soldiers, whereby eight of the Americans were killed, and several wounded. The provincials retired; but, finding that the British still continued their fire, they returned it with good interest, and soon strewed the green with the dead and wounded. Such fierce discharges of musketry produced the effect that might have been expected in a land of freemen, who saw their gallant brothers suddenly engaged in the strife of death. Never before had the bosoms of the swains experienced such a tumult of heroic passions. Then, throwing aside the implements of husbandry, and leaving their teams in the half-finished furrows, they flew to their houses, snatched up their arms, and bursting forth from their wild, shrieking wives and children, hastened to the glorious field where Liberty, heaven-born goddess, was to be bought with blood. Pouring in now from every quarter, were seen crowds of sturdy peasants, with flushed cheeks and flaming eyes, eager for battle. Even age forgot its wonted infirmities, and hands long palsied with years threw aside the cushioned crutch and grasped the deadly firelock. Fast as they came up, their ready muskets began to pour forth the long red streams of fiery vengeance.

The enemy fell back appalled. The shouting farmers, swift-closing on their rear, followed their steps with death, while the British, as fast as they could load, wheeling on their pursuers, returned the deadly fire. But their flight was not in safety! Every step of their retreat was stained with blood: every hedge or fence by which they passed, concealed a deadly foe.

They would, in all probability, have been cut off to a man, had not General Gage *luckily recollected* that, born of Britons, these Yankees might possess some of the family valor, and therefore sent one thousand men to support the detachment. This re-inforcement met the poor fellows, faint with fear and fatigue, and brought them safely into Boston.

Mason L. Weems.

28. BUNKER HILL.

Oh, is not this a holy spot!
   'T is the high place of Freedom's birth!
God of our fathers, is it not
   The holiest spot of all the earth?

Quenched is thy flame on Horeb's side;
   The robber roams o'er Sinai now;
And those old men, thy seers, abide
   No more on Zion's mournful brow.

But on this hill thou, Lord, hast dwelt,
   Since round its head the war-cloud curled,
And wrapt our fathers, where they knelt
   In prayer and battle for the world.

Here sleeps their dust: 't is holy ground;
   And we, the children of the brave,
From the four winds are gathered round,
   To lay our offerings on their grave.

Free as the winds around us blow,
   Free as the waves below us spread,
We rear a pile that long shall throw
   Its shadow on their sacred bed.

But on their deeds no shade shall fall,
   While o'er their couch thy sun shall flame;
Thine ear was bowed to hear their call,
   And Thy right hand shall guard their fame.

JOHN PIERPONT.

29. VALLEY FORGE.

From Centennial Address of Henry Armitt Brown, delivered at Valley Forge, June 19, 1878.

THE century that has gone by has changed the face of Nature, and wrought a revolution in the habits of mankind. We to-day behold the dawn of an extraordinary age. Man has advanced with such astounding speed, that, breathless, we have reached a moment when it seems as if distance had been annihilated, time made as nought, the invisible seen, the intangible felt, and the impossible accomplished. Already we knock at the door of a new century, which promises to be infinitely brighter and more enlightened and happier than this.

We know that we are more fortunate than our fathers. We believe that our children shall be happier than we. We know that this century is more enlightened than the past. We believe that the time to come will be better and more glorious than this. We think, we believe, we hope, but we do not know. Across that threshold we may not pass; behind that veil we may not penetrate. It may be vouchsafed us to behold it, wonderingly, from afar, but never to enter in. It matters not. The age in which we live is but a link in the endless and eternal chain. Our lives are like sands upon the shore; our voices, like the breath of this summer breeze that stirs the leaf for a moment, and is forgotten. The last survivor of this mighty multitude shall stay but a little while. The endless generations are advancing to take our places as we fall. For them, as for us, shall the years march by in the sublime procession of the ages.

And here, in this place of sacrifice, in this vale of humiliation, in this valley of the shadow of death, out of which the life of America rose regenerate and free, let us believe, with an abiding faith, that to them union will seem as dear, and liberty as sweet, and progress as glorious, as they were to our fathers, and are to you and me, and that the institutions which have made us happy, preserved by the virtue of our children, shall bless the remotest generation of the time to come. And unto Him who holds in the hollow of His hand the fate of nations, and yet marks the sparrow's fall, let us lift up our hearts this day, and unto His eternal care commend ourselves, our children, and our country.

---

30. THE STORMING OF MONTEREY.

We were not many, we who stood
    Before the iron sheet that day;
Yet many a gallant spirit would
Give half his years, if he but could
    Have been with us at Monterey.

Now here, now there, the shot is hailed
    In deadly drifts of fiery spray;
Yet not a single soldier quailed,
When wounded comrades round them wailed
    Their dying shout at Monterey.

And on, still on our column swept,
   Through walls of flame, its withering way;
Where fell the dead the living stepped,
Still charging on the guns that swept
   The slippery streets of Monterey.

The foe himself recoiled aghast,
   When, striking where the strongest lay,
We swooped his flanking batteries past,
And, braving full their murderous blast,
   Stormed home the towers of Monterey.

Our banners on those towers wave
   And there our evening bugles play,
Where orange boughs above their grave
Keep green the memory of the brave
   Who fought and bled at Monterey.

We were not many, we who pressed
   Beside the brave who fell that day;
But who of us had not confessed
He'd rather share their warrior rest
   Than not have been at Monterey?

CHARLES FENNO HOFFMAN.

31. HIGHTIDE AT GETTYSBURG.

A CLOUD possessed the hollow field:
The gathering battle's smoky shield.
   Athwart the gloom the lightning flashed,
   And through the cloud some horsemen dashed,
And from the heights the thunder pealed.

Then, at the brief command of Lee,
Moved out that matchless infantry,
   With Pickett leading grandly down,
   To rush against the roaring crown
Of those dread heights of destiny.

Far heard above the angry guns,
A cry across the tumult runs, —
   The voice that rang through Shiloh's woods
   And Chickamauga's solitudes:
The fierce South, cheering on her sons.

Ah, how the withering tempest blew
Against the front of Pettigrew!
   A Khamsin wind that scorched and singed,
   Like that infernal flame that fringed
The British squares at Waterloo!

"Once more in Glory's van with me!"
Virginia cries to Tennessee,
   "We two together, come what may,
   Shall stand upon those works to-day!"
(The reddest day in history.)

But who shall break the guards that wait
Before the awful face of Fate?
   The tattered standards of the South
   Were shrivelled at the cannon's mouth,
And all her hopes were desolate.

In vain the Tennesseean set
His breast against the bayonet.
   In vain Virginia charged and raged,
   A tigress in her path uncaged.
Till all the hill was red and wet!

Above the bayonets, mixed and crossed,
Men saw a gray, gigantic ghost
   Receding through the battle-cloud,
   And heard across the tempest loud
The death-cry of a nation lost!

The brave went down! Without disgrace
They leaped to Ruin's red embrace;
   They only heard Fame's thunders wake,
   And saw the dazzling sun-burst break
In smiles on Glory's bloody face.

They fell, who lifted up a hand
And bade the sun in heaven to stand!
   They smote and fell, who set the bars
   Against the progress of the stars,
And stayed the march of Motherland.

They stood, who saw the future come
On through the fight's delirium!
   They smote and stood, who held the hope
   Of nations on that slippery slope,
Amid the cheers of Christendom!

God lives! He forged the iron will
That clutched and held that trembling hill.
   God lives and reigns! He built and lent
   The heights for Freedom's battlement,
Where floats her flag in triumph still!

Fold up the banners! Smelt the guns!
Love rules. Her gentler purpose runs.
   A mighty mother turns in tears
   The pages of her battle years,
Lamenting all her fallen sons!
WILL H. THOMPSON.

32. ONCE AT BATTLE EVE.

THE poetess describes an incident which occurred on the banks of the Tennessee River, during the year 1863.

AFTER the hard and hurried march,
   The army lay encamped at night
Among the hills, upon whose crest
   Still burned the sunset's fading light;
And through the soft unclouded blue
   The stars came slowly, one by one,
Deepening as all the bright clouds changed
   To ashes o'er the buried sun.

The air was fragrant with the scents
   That fill the waking woods in spring, —
Of dewy grass, of spicy buds,
   Of flowers that May and sunshine bring;
Upon a trembling spray a thrush
   Piped softly, ere it sought its nest,
A tender strain of brooding love,
   A tuneful prophecy of rest.

Over the long pontoon that bound
   The lapsing river, shore to shore,
The horses' tread with rumbling wheels
   Blent in a deep, continuous roar;
The soldiers gathered round their fires:
   Tall and grotesque their shadows danced
Against the tents, while sudden gleams
   On bayonet and sabre glanced.

Each face was grave, each voice was hushed:
   Dear thoughts of home filled every breast,
And only faint, reluctant smiles
   Came at some grim, foreboding jest.

Each knew, ere night should fall again,
    They, or a stubborn foe, would yield
Life, honor, all that men hold dear,
    Upon a blood-drenched battle-field.

The drums were beating the "tattoo,"
    When through it, suddenly, there rang
A pealing Psalm in unison.
    A thousand swelling voices sang,
Like those who wait in fearless faith,
    "Eternal are thy mercies, Lord;"
The echoing valleys answered back,
    "Eternal truth attends Thy Word."

"Thy praise shall sound from shore to shore,"
    Their comrades heard with bated breath, —
"Till suns shall rise and set no more:"
    'T was victory assured o'er death.
They met the shock of fierce attack,
    Of frenzied charge, we know how well,
For graves and scars and empty homes,
    Of that day's fierce encounter tell.

Long years have come and gone since then:
    Peace followed peril and distress,
And still the words they sang come back,
    Like some dead voice that speaks to bless.
What they achieved, in purer laws
    And freer power, is ours, to-day;
And Truth and Mercy still doth God
    Affirm, in His appointed way.

MARY HANNAH KROUT.

33. TO THEE, O COUNTRY!

Written by the author, now Mrs. J. B. King, in her 15th year, and set to music by Julius Eichberg, and used by permission of Messrs. O. Ditson & Co.

>To thee, O country, great and free,
>   With trembling hearts we cling;
>Our voices tuned by joyous love,
>   Thy power and praises sing.
>
>Upon thy mighty, faithful heart
>   We lay our burdens down.
>Thou art the only friend who feels
>   Their weight without a frown.
>
>For thee we daily work and strive,
>   To thee we give our love,
>For thee with fervor deep we pray
>   To Him who dwells above.
>
>O God preserve our Fatherland!
>   Let peace its ruler be,
>And let her happy kingdom stretch
>   From north to southmost sea.

ANNA PHILIPINE EICHBERG.

PART VIII.

EMPHATIC APPEALS TO DUTY.

1. THE NATIONAL ENSIGN.

Behold it! Listen to it! Every star has a tongue; every stripe is articulate. "There is no language or speech where their voices are not heard." There is magic in the web of it. It has an answer for every question of duty. It has a solution for every doubt and perplexity. It has a word of good cheer for every hour of gloom or of despondency.

Behold it! Listen to it! It speaks of earlier and of later struggles. It speaks of victories, and sometimes of reverses, on the sea and on the land. It speaks of patriots and heroes among the living and the dead. But before all and above all other associations and memories, whether of glorious men, or glorious deeds, or glorious places, its voice is ever of Union and Liberty, of the Constitution and the Laws.

Behold it! Listen to it! Let it tell the story of its birth to these gallant volunteers, as they march beneath its folds by day, or repose beneath its sentinel stars by night! Let it recall to them the strange, eventful history of its rise and progress; let it rehearse to them the wonderful tale of its trials and its triumphs, in peace as well as in war; and never let it be prostituted to any unworthy or unchristian purpose of revenge, depredation, or rapine!

And may a merciful God cover the head of each one of its brave defenders in the hour of battle!

Robert Charles Winthrop.

2. THE BENDED BOW.

In early British times, emblems were used as messengers to the people when sudden danger demanded their aid in national defence, as the mountain fires of Switzerland were signals for rallying in behalf of liberty, and as the watchmen of the ancient Hebrews communicated similar alarms, from mountain peak to mountain peak, as invaders threatened the passes and valleys. The inspiring words of Mrs. Hemans illustrate the enthusiasm with which the ancient Briton rallied to the call of the "bended bow," the call "To Arms."

There was heard the sound of a coming foe,
There was sent through Britain a bended bow,
And a voice was poured on the free winds far,
As the land rose up at the sound of war!

Heard ye not the battle-horn?
Reaper, leave thy golden corn!
Leave it for the birds of heaven!
Swords must flash, and spears be riven:
Leave it for the winds to shed, —
Arm! ere Britain's turf grows red!
  And the reaper armed, like a freeman's son;
  And the bended bow and the voice passed on.

Hunter, leave the mountain chase!
Take the falchion from its place!
Let the wolf go free to-day;
Leave him for a nobler prey!
Let the deer ungalled sweep by, —
Arm thee! Britain's foes are nigh!
  And the hunter armed, ere the chase was done;
  And the bended bow and the voice passed on.

Chieftain, quit the joyous feast!
Stay not until the song hath ceased:
Though the mead be foaming bright,
Though the fire gives ruddy light,

Leave the hearth and leave the hall, —
Arm thee! Britain's foes must fall!
   And the chieftain armed, and the horn was blown;
   And the bended bow and the voice passed on.

Prince, thy father's deeds are told
In the bower and in the hold, —
Where the goatherd's lay is sung,
Where the minstrel's harp is strung.
Foes are on thy native sea, —
Give our bards a tale of thee!
   And the prince came armed, like a leader's son;
   And the bended bow and the voice passed on.

Mother, stay not thou thy boy!
He must learn the battle's joy.
Sister, bring the sword and spear;
Give thy brother words of cheer!
Maiden, bid thy lover part, —
Britain calls the strong in heart!
   And the bended bow and the voice passed on;
   And the bards made song of a battle won.

FELICIA DOROTHEA HEMANS.

---

3. THE BOSTON MASSACRE.

(March 5th, 1770.)

BRITISH taxation of the American Colonists, without representation on their part in the British Parliament, resulted in a collision between the soldiers and citizens, ever memorable as one of the exciting causes of the Revolutionary War. John Hancock, one of the most vigorous denunciators of the tragedy, afterwards presided over the Continental Congress, and signed the Declaration of American Independence. — ED.

TELL me, ye bloody butchers! ye villains, high and low! ye wretches who contrived, as well as you who executed, the inhuman deed! do you not feel the goads and stings of conscious guilt pierce through your savage bosoms? Though some of you may think yourselves exalted to a height that bids defiance to the arms of human justice, and others shroud yourselves beneath the mask of hypocrisy, and build your hopes of safety on the low arts of cunning, chicanery and falsehood; yet do you not sometimes feel the gnawings of that worm which never dies? Do not the injured shades of Maverick, Gray, Caldwell, Attucks, and Carr, attend you in your solitary walks, arrest you even in the midst of your debaucheries, and fill even your dreams with terror?

Ye dark, designing knaves, ye murderers, parricides! how dare you tread upon the earth which has drunk in the blood of slaughtered innocents, shed by your wicked hands? How dare you breathe that air which wafted to the ear of Heaven the groans of those who fell a sacrifice to your accursed ambition? But, if the laboring earth does not extend her jaws; if the air you breathe is not commissioned to be the minister of Death, yet, hear it and tremble! The eye of Heaven penetrates the darkest chambers of the soul, traces the leading clew through all the labyrinths which your industrious folly has devised; and you, however you may have screened yourselves from mortal eyes, must be arraigned, must lift your hands, red with the blood of those whose death you have procured, at the tremendous bar of God.

JOHN HANCOCK.

NOTE. — At the trial of ten British soldiers, at the November term of the Suffolk County Court of Assizes, Boston, Mass., 1770, for the murder, by shooting, of Maverick, Gray, Caldwell, Attucks, and Cary, Robert Treat Paine, Esq., and Samuel Quincy, Esq., appeared as counsel for the Crown. John Adams, Esq., Mr. Josiah Quincy, and Mr. Sampson Salter Blowers appeared as counsel for the prisoners. A verdict of "not guilty" was rendered against eight, but the remaining two were found guilty of "manslaughter."

4. SCORN TO BE SLAVES.

GENERAL JOSEPH WARREN, physician, soldier, statesman, and patriot, fell in the Battle of Bunker Hill, June 17th, 1775.

His appeal to the people after the "Boston Massacre" deserves perpetual remembrance. After the excitement of the tragedy abated, resentment against the soldiers gave place to a more decided arraignment of the British government for that arbitrary policy which precipitated the collision.

THE voice of your father's blood calls from the ground: "My sons, cease to be slaves! In vain we met the frowns of tyrants; in vain we crossed the boisterous ocean, found a new world, and prepared it for the happy residence of Liberty; in vain we fought; in vain we toiled; we bled in vain, if you, our offspring, want valor to repel the assaults of her invaders."

Stain not the glory of your worthy ancestors; but, like them, resolve never to part with your birthright! Be wise in your deliberations, and determined in your exertions for the preservation of your liberty! Follow not the dictates of passion, but enlist yourselves under the sacred banner of reason. Use every method in your power to secure your rights! At least, prevent the curses of posterity from being heaped upon your memories.

If you, with united fortitude and zeal, oppose the torrent of oppression; if you feel the true fire of patriotism burning in your breasts; if you, from your souls, despise the most gaudy dress that slavery can wear; if you really prefer the lonely cottage, while blessed with liberty, to gilded palaces surrounded with the ensigns of slavery, you may have the full assurance that tyranny, with her accursed train, will hide her accursed head in confusion, shame, and despair!

JOSEPH WARREN.

5. WARREN'S SUPPOSED ADDRESS AT BUNKER HILL.

Stand! the ground's your own, my braves!
Will ye give it up to slaves?
Will ye look for greener graves?
Hope ye mercy still?
What's the mercy despots feel?
Hear it in that battle peal!
See it in yon bristling steel!
Ask it, ye who will!

Fear ye foes who kill for hire?
Will ye to your homes retire?
Look behind you! they're afire!
And, before you, — see
Who have done it! From the vale
On they come! and will ye quail?
Leaden rain and iron hail
Let their welcome be!

In the God of battles trust!
Die we may, and die we must;
But, oh! where can dust to dust
Be consigned so well
As where heaven its dew shall shed
On the martyred patriot's bed,
And the rocks shall raise their head,
Of his deeds to tell?

John Pierpont.

6. PATRIOTISM.

Bereft of patriotism, the heart of a nation will be cold, and cramped, and sordid; the arts will have no enduring impulse, and commerce no invigorating soul; society will degenerate, and the mean and vicious will triumph. Patriotism is not a wild and glittering passion, but a glorious reality. The virtue that gave to Paganism its dazzling lustre, to Barbarism its redeeming trait, to Christianity its heroic form, is not dead. It still lives to console, to sanctify humanity. It has its altar in every clime, its worship and its festivities.

On the heathered hills of Scotland the sword of Wallace is yet a bright tradition. The genius of France in the brilliant literature of the day pays its high homage to the piety and heroism of the young Maid of Orleans. In her new Senate-Hall, England bids her sculptor place among the effigies of her greatest sons, the images of Hampden and of Russell. In the gay and graceful capital of Belgium, the daring hand of Geefs has reared a monument full of glorious meaning to the three hundred martyrs of the Revolution.

By the soft blue waters of Lake Lucerne stands the chapel of William Tell. On the anniversary of his revolt and victory, across those waters, as they glitter in the July sun, skim the light boats of the allied Cantons. From the prows hang the banners of the Republic, and as they near the sacred spot, the daughters of Lucerne chant the hymns of their old poetic land. Then ·bursts forth the glad Te Deum, and Heaven again hears the voice of that wild chivalry of the mountains which, five centuries ago, pierced the white eagle of Vienna, and flung it bleeding on the rocks of Uri.

At Innspruck, in the black aisle of the old cathedral,

the peasant of the Tyrol kneels before the statue of Andreas Hofer. In the defiles and valleys of the Tyrol, who forgets the day on which he fell within the walls of Mantua? It is a festive day throughout his quiet, noble land. In that old cathedral his inspiring memory is recalled amid the pageantries of the altar; his image appears in every house; his victories and virtues are proclaimed in the songs of the people; and when the sun goes down, a chain of fires, in the deep red light of which the eagle spreads his wings and holds his giddy revelry, proclaims the glory of the chief whose blood has made his native land a sainted spot in Europe.

Shall not all join in this glorious worship?

Shall not all have the faith, the duties, the festivities of patriotism?

THOMAS FRANCIS MEAGHER.

7. THE MARCH OF FREEDOM.

It is not for men long to hinder the march of human freedom. I believe in the Infinite God. You may make your statutes. An appeal always lies to a Higher Law, and decisions averse to that get set aside in the flight of the ages. Your statutes cannot hold Him. You may gather all the dried grass and all the straw in both continents; you may bind it into ropes to bind down the sea: while it is calm, you may laugh, and say, "Lo! I have chained the ocean, and hold down the law of Him who holds the universe as a rosebud in His hand, its very ocean as but a drop of dew."

"How the waters suppress their agitation," you may say. But when the winds blow their trumpets, the sea rises in His strength, snaps asunder the bands that have confined its mighty limbs, and the world is littered with the idle hay.

Stop the human race in its development and march to freedom? As well might the boys of Boston, some lustrous night, mounting to the steeples of the town, call on the stars to stop their course. Gently but irresistibly the Greater and the Lesser Bear move around the Pole; Orion in his mighty mail comes up the sky; the Bull, the heavenly Twins, the Crab, the Maid, the Scales, and all that shining company pursue their march all night; and the new day discovers the idle urchins in their lofty places, all tired, sleepy, and ashamed.

THEODORE PARKER.

8. ADDRESS OF GENERAL WOLFE BEFORE QUEBEC.

(A. D. 1759.)

I CONGRATULATE you, my countrymen and fellow-soldiers, on the spirit and success with which you have executed this important part of our enterprise. The formidable Heights of Abraham are now surmounted; and the city of Quebec, the object of all our toils, now stands in full view before us. A perfidious enemy, who dared to exasperate you by their cruelties, but not to oppose you on equal ground, are now constrained to face you on the open plain, without ramparts or intrenchments to shelter them.

You know too well the forces which compose their army to dread their superior numbers. A few regular troops from old France, weakened by hunger and sickness, who, when fresh, were unable to withstand the British soldiers, are their general's chief dependence. Those numerous companies of Canadians, insolent, mutinous, unsteady, and undisciplined, have exercised his utmost skill to keep them together to this time; and as soon as their irregular ardor is dampened by one firm fire, they will instantly turn their backs, and give you no further trouble but in the pursuit. As for those savage tribes of Indians, whose horrid yells in the forest have struck many a bold heart with affright, terrible as they are with a tomahawk and a scalping-knife to a flying and prostrate foe, you have experienced how little their ferocity is to be dreaded by resolute men upon fair and open ground. You can now only consider them as the just objects of a severe revenge for the unhappy fate of many slaughtered countrymen.

This day puts it in your power to terminate the fatigue of a siege which has so long employed your courage and patience. Possessed with a full confidence of the certain success which British valor must gain over such enemies, I have led you up these steep and dangerous rocks, only solicitous to show you the foe within your reach. The impossibility of a retreat makes no difference in the situation of men resolved to conquer or die; and believe me, my friends, if your conquest could be bought with the blood of your general, he would most cheerfully resign a life which he has so long devoted to his country.

---

9. ADDRESS OF CARADOC THE BARD.

Nothing in history can surpass the bravery of the ancient Briton, or the devotion of their professional singers, who introduced battles and followed up victories by songs of appeal or triumph.

Hark to the measured march! The Saxons come!
  The sound earth quails beneath the hollow tread;
Your fathers rushed upon the swords of Rome
  And climbed her warships, when the Caesars fled.
The Saxons come! Why wait within the wall?
They scale the mountain. Let the torrent fall.

Hark! Ye have swords and shields, and armor, Ye!
　No mail defends the Cymrian Child of Song;
But, where the warrior, there the bard should be!
　All fields of glory to the bard belong.
His realm extends wherever godless strife
Spurns the base death, and wins immortal life.

Unarmed, he goes, — his guard, the shield of all:
　Where he bounds, foremost, on the Saxon spear.
Unarmed, he goes, that falling, e'en his fall
　Shall bring no shame, and shall bequeath no fear!
Does the song cease? Avenge it by the deed.
And make the sepulchre, a Nation freed.
　　　　　　　　　EDWARD GEORGE LYTTON BULWER.

---

10. BOADICEA.

PRASUTAGUS, king of the Icenians, who occupied what now constitutes the counties of Norfolk, Suffolk, Cambridgeshire, and Huntingdonshire, England, having faith in Roman honor, made the emperor of Rome joint heir with Boadicea, his wife. The queen's heroism after being scourged, and the violation of her daughters by Roman officials, is vividly depicted by Tacitus, as, "seated in her chariot, with her daughters, she traverses the battle-field, not to recover her throne and treasures, but for vengeance." After a terrible defeat, near London, A. D. 61, she put an end to her life. "*Annals.*" *Book XIV.*

WHEN the British warrior queen,
　Bleeding from the Roman rods.
Sought, with an indignant mien,
　Counsel of her country's gods,
Sage, beneath a spreading oak,
　Sat the Druid, hoary chief;
Every burning word he spoke
　Full of rage, and full of grief.

" Princess, if our aged eyes
　Weep upon thy matchless wrongs,
'T is, because resentment ties
　All the terror of our tongues.

Rome shall perish! Write that word
　　In the blood that she has spilt;
Perish, hopeless and abhorred,
　　Deep in ruin as in guilt.
Rome, for empire far renowned,
　　Tramples on a thousand States;
Soon her pride shall kiss the ground —
　　Hark! the Gaul is at her gates!
Other Romans shall arise,
　　Heedless of a soldier's name;
Sounds, not arms, shall win the prize,
　　Harmony the path to fame.
Then the progeny that springs
　　From the forests of our land,
Armed with thunder, clad with wings,
　　Shall a wider world command.
Regions Cæsar never knew
　　Thy posterity shall sway;
Where his eagles never flew,
　　None invincible as they."

Such the bard's prophetic words,
　　Pregnant with celestial fire,
Bending, as he swept the chords
　　Of his sweet but awful lyre.

She, with all a monarch's pride,
　　Felt them in her bosom glow;
Rushed to battle, fought and died;
　　Dying, hurled them on the foe.

"Ruffians, pitiless as proud,
　　Heav'n awards the vengeance due;
Empire is on us bestowed,
　　Shame and ruin wait for you."

　　　　　　　　　　　　COWPER.

11. LET THERE BE LIGHT.

The Greek rhetorician Longinus quotes from the Mosaic account of the Creation what he calls the sublimest passage ever uttered: "God said, 'Let there be light;' and there was light."

From the centre of black immensity, effulgence shone forth. Above, beneath, on every side, its radiance streamed out, silent, yet making each spot in the vast concave brighter than the line which the lightning pencils upon the midnight cloud. Darkness fled as the swift beams spread onward and outward, in unending circumfusion of splendor. Onward and outward still they move to this day, glorifying, through wider and wider regions of space, the Infinite Author from whose power and beneficence they sprang.

But not only in the beginning, when God created the heavens and the earth, did He say, "Let there be light:" whenever a soul is born into the world, its Creator stands over it, and again pronounces the same sublime words, "Let there be light."

Magnificent, indeed, was the material creation, when, suddenly blazing forth in mid-space, the new-born sun dispelled the darkness of the ancient night. But infinitely more magnificent is it when the human soul rays forth its subtler and swifter beams; when the light of the senses irradiates all outward things, revealing the beauty of their colors, and the exquisite symmetry of their proportions and forms; when the light of reason penetrates to their invisible properties and laws, and displays all those hidden relations that make up the sciences; when the light of conscience illuminates the moral world, separating truth from error, and virtue from vice.

The light of the newly-kindled sun was glorious. It struck upon all the planets and wakened into existence their myriad capacities of life and joy. That light sped on beyond Sirius, beyond the pole-star, beyond Orion and the Pleiades, and is still spreading onward into the abysses of space. But the light of the human soul flies faster than the light of the sun, and outshines its meridian blaze. It can embrace not only the sun of our system, but all suns, and galaxies of suns; ay, the soul is capable of knowing and enjoying Him who created the suns themselves; and when these starry lustres that now glorify the firmament shall wax dim, and fade away like a wasted taper, the light of the soul shall still remain. Nor time, nor cloud, nor any power but its own perversity, shall ever quench its brightness.

Again I would say that whenever a human soul is born into the world, God stands over it and pronounces the sublime fiat, "Let there be light!"

May the time soon come when all human governments shall co-operate with the divine government in carrying this benediction and baptism into fulfilment!

HORACE MANN.

12. GUSTAVUS, KING OF SWEDEN, TO HIS SOLDIERS.

From an epic poem illustrating the ability, patriotism, and military prowess of Gustavus Vasa, grandfather of Gustavus Adolphus.

SWEDES! countrymen! behold at last,
After a thousand dangers past,
  Your chief, Gustavus, here!
Long have I sighed 'mid foreign bands;
Long have I roamed in foreign lands;
At length, 'mid Swedish hearts and hands,
  I grasp a Swedish spear!

Yet, looking forth, although I see
None but the fearless and the free,
   Sad thoughts the sight inspires;
For where, I think, on Swedish ground,
Save where these mountains frown around,
Can that best heritage be found, —
   The freedom of your sires?

Ay, Sweden pines beneath the yoke;
The galling chain our fathers broke
   Is round our country now.
On perjured craft and ruthless guilt
His power a tyrant Dane hath built;
And Sweden's crown, all blood-bespilt,
   Rests on a foreign brow.

On you your country turns her eyes, —
On you, on you, for aid relies,
   Scions of noblest stem!
The foremost place in rolls of fame
By right your fearless fathers claim;
Yours is the glory of their name, —
   'T is yours to equal them.

As rushing down, when winter reigns,
Resistless, to the shaking plains,
   The torrent tears its way,
And all that bars its onward course
Sweeps to the sea with headlong force,
So swept your sires the Dane and Norse:
   Can ye do less than they?

But no! your kindling hearts gainsay
The thought! Hark! I hear the bloodhounds bay!
   Yon blazing village see!
Rise, countrymen! awake! defy
The haughty Dane! your battle-cry
Be "Freedom!" We will do or die!
   On! Death or victory!

PIERRE FRANÇOIS LEFEVRE.

13. THE DEFIANT SEMINOLE CHIEF.

BLAZE, with your serried columns
    I will not bend the knee!
The shackles ne'er again shall bind
    The arm which now is free.
I've mailed it with the thunder,
    When the tempest muttered low;
And where it falls, ye well may dread
    The lightning of its blow!

I've scared ye in the city,
    I've scalped ye on the plain;
Go, count your chosen where they fell
    Beneath my leaden rain!
I scorn your proffered treaty!
    The pale face I defy!
Revenge is stamped upon my spear,
    And blood my battle-cry!

Ye've trailed me through the forest,
    Ye've tracked me o'er the stream;
And struggling through the everglade,
    Your bristling bayonets gleam;
But I stand as should the warrior,
    With his rifle and his spear,—
The scalp of vengeance still is red,
    And warns ye, "Come not here!"

I loathe ye with my bosom,
    I scorn ye with mine eye;
And I'll taunt ye with my latest breath,
    And fight ye till I die!
I ne'er will ask ye quarter;
    I ne'er will be your slave;
But I'll swim the sea of slaughter,
    Till I sink beneath the wave!

G. WILLIAM PATTEN.

14. PLEA OF THE POCOMTUC CHIEF.

WHITE man, there is eternal enmity between me and thee! I quit not the land of my fathers but with my life. In these woods where I bent my youthful bow, I will still hunt the deer. Over yonder waters I will still glide, unrestrained, in my bark canoe. By those dashing water-falls I will still lay up my winter's supply of food. On these fertile meadows I will still plant my corn.

Stranger, the land is mine! I understand not these paper rights. I gave not my consent when, as thou sayest, these broad regions were purchased, for a few bawbles, of my fathers. They could sell what was theirs; but they could sell no more. How could my fathers sell that which the Great Spirit sent me into the world to live upon? They knew not what they did.

The stranger came, a timid suppliant, few and feeble, and asked to lie down on the redman's bear-skin, and to warm himself at the redman's fire; to have a little piece of land to raise corn for his women and children; and now he is become strong and mighty and bold: he spreads out his parchment over the whole, and says, "It is mine!"

Stranger, there is not room for us both! The Great Spirit has not made us to live together. There is poison in the white man's cup. The white man's dog bites at the redman's heels. If I should leave the land of my fathers, whither should I fly? Shall I go to the South, and dwell among the graves of the Pequots? Shall I wander to the West? the fierce Mohawk, the man-eater, is my foe. Shall I fly to the East? the Great Water is before me. No, stranger; here I have lived, and here I will die; and if here thou abidest, there is eternal war between me and thee.

Thou hast taught me thy arts of destruction. For that alone I thank thee. And now take heed to thy steps: the redman is thy foe. When thou goest forth by day, my bullet shall whistle by thee; when thou liest down at night, my knife shall be at thy throat. The noonday sun shall not discover thy enemy, and the darkness of night shall not protect thy rest. Thou shalt plant in terror, and I will reap in blood; thou shalt sow the earth with corn, and I will strew it with ashes; thou shalt go forth with the sickle, and I will follow after with my scalping-knife; thou shalt build, and I will burn, till the white man, or the Indian, shall cease from the land. Go thy way, for this time, in safety, but remember, stranger, there is eternal war between me and thee.

EDWARD EVERETT.

15. BONAPARTE TO HIS ARMY IN ITALY.

The first Italian campaign in 1796 has few parallels in history for brilliant victories rapidly gained; and the address of Napoleon in no degree exaggerates the successes realized.

SOLDIERS: You have in a fortnight gained six victories, taken twenty-one stands of colors, seventy-one pieces of cannon, several strong places, and made fifteen thousand prisoners. You have fought battles without cannon, made forced marches without shoes, and, deprived of everything, have supplied everything. The republican phalanxes, the soldiers of Liberty, were alone capable of suffering what you have suffered. At the commencement of the campaign you were destitute of everything. Now you are amply provided. The magazines taken from your enemies are many. The artillery for the field and the siege are already here.

Soldiers, the country has a right to expect great things of you. Justify her expectations! The greatest obstacles are undoubtedly overcome; but you have battles still to fight, cities to take, rivers to pass. Is there one among you whose courage is diminished? Is there one among you who would prefer returning to the summits of the Alps and the Apennines? No! all burn with the desire of extending the glory of the French, to humble the proud kings who dare to meditate putting us again in chains, to dictate a peace that shall be glorious, and that shall indemnify the country for the immense sacrifice which she has made. All of you burn with a desire to say, on your return to your home, "I belong to the Army of Italy."

Friends, I promise this conquest to you; but there is one condition which you must swear to fulfil: that is, to respect the people whom you deliver, — to repress the horrible pillage which some wretches, instigated by our enemies, have practised. Unless you do this, you will no longer be the friends, but the scourge, of the human race. You will no longer form the honor of the French people! They will disavow you! Your victories, your successes, the blood of your countrymen who died in battle, — all, even honor and glory, will be lost. With respect to myself and the generals who possess your confidence, we shall blush to command an army without discipline, and who shall admit no other law than that of force.

People of Italy, the French Army comes to break your chains! The French people are the friends of all people. Come with confidence to them. Your property, religion, and customs shall be respected. We make war as generous enemies, and wish only to make war against the tyrants who oppress you.

Trans. from the French.

16. GRATTAN'S APPEAL FOR IRELAND.

I APPEAL to your sober senses; I appeal also to your love of freedom, to your pride as a nation, and to the feelings which belong to man. I give my opinion and advice.

I am attached, and ever will be attached, to England, so long as she upholds the liberties of Ireland; but I am, and ever will be, and ever ought to be, the enemy of England, if she attempts to keep Ireland in slavery. Therefore it is that I advise you to meet. Assemble in your parishes, villages, and hamlets! Resolve — petition — address! Petition against the demolition of your constitution! Your lives, your properties, those of your wives and children, — all may be at stake! Recollect that liberty consists not only in its actual enjoyment, but in the impossibility of another depriving you of it without your consent.

Habitual departures from freedom familiarize men with arbitrary power. What others permit to be inflicted upon us, they may at no distant day tolerate themselves. All is doubt, distrust, disgrace. Rely on it that the certain and fatal result in this instance will be to make Ireland hate the connection, contemn the council of England, and despise her power.

Call for an inquiry into the real or supposed crimes of Ireland, for which she is to be visited with this calamity. Challenge proof, and put yourselves on God and your country. If guilty, let us calmly abide the results, and peaceably submit to our sentence. But if we are traduced, and really be innocent, tell Ministers the truth, and strain every effort to avert their oppression. Do not descend to your graves with the damaging censure that you suffered the liberties of your country to be taken away, and that you were mutes as well as cowards.

Come forward like men, not alone in Heath, but in Ireland everywhere! Protest against this atrocious attempt! Look in the face the enemies of your country; and if our liberties are to be cloven down, if Ireland is again enthralled, let us at least stand firm and erect, while the assassins strike the blow; and if we fall, let it be like men who deserve to be free!

HENRY GRATTAN.

17. FREEDOM.

Men whose boast it is that we
Come of fathers brave and free,
If there breathe on earth a slave,
Are ye truly free and brave?
If ye do not feel the chain
When it works a brother's pain,
Are ye not base slaves indeed,—
Slaves unworthy to be freed?

If ye hear without a blush
Deeds to make the roused blood rush
Like red lava through your veins
For your sisters now in chains,
Answer,—are ye fit to be
Mothers of the brave and free?

Is true freedom but to break
Fetters for our own dear sake,
And with leathern heart forget
That we owe mankind a debt?
No! true freedom is to share
All the chains our brothers wear,
And with heart and hand to be
Earnest to make others free.

> They are slaves who fear to speak
> For the fallen and the weak?
> They are slaves who will not choose
> Hatred, scorning, and abuse,
> Rather than in silence shrink
> From the truth they needs must think;
> They are slaves who dare not be
> In the right with two or three.
>
> JAMES RUSSELL LOWELL.

---

18. "DEAD ON THE FIELD OF HONOR."

Extract from address delivered by Ex-Governor J. L. CHAMBERLAIN, at dedication of a soldiers' monument, August 8th, 1869, at Plymouth, Massachusetts.

You all know the story of La Tour d'Auvergne, "The First Grenadier of France," for whose inspiring heroism the Emperor Napoleon ordered that his name be called at every daily parade of his corps. At the call, the sergeant of his original company stepped to the front, and with his salute replied, "Dead on the field of honor." These were indeed, and ever will be, thrilling words. It is an instinct of the human heart to honor those who have overcome the fear of death, and especially those who have given their lives for a belief, a sentiment, an idea, a principle. All nations have their treasured rolls of martyrs and heroes; and it has been held worthy of the highest ambition to write one's name upon the scroll. It has been deemed a high necessity by the State to cherish the memory of those who have died in its behalf. Art, eloquence, and song, philosophy and religion, have conspired to perpetuate the fame and embalm the characters, if not the names, of those who died for the weal of others. Even those who profess to believe that passing pleasure is the end of life are constrained to yield to the force of heroic example; and the responsive heart of man responds that "it is sweet to die for country."

To be superior to cold, fatigue, and hunger, to rise above the care of self and the fear of death, to subdue the sense, — is a kind of regeneration, the very transfiguration of human nature. Whatever the final cause or object may be, the over-mastering of self is great; for such manliness is noble, and such devotion is sublime. But if we yield our admiration to the mere spectacle of such heroism, what honor shall we pay to those who were heroes for the sake of right, — the men who bear witness to their faith by dying for it; who go forth, in the full comprehension and communion of the truth, to stake their lives on its vindication! To die in a just cause, in attestation of faith in it, because of love for it, is indeed to die gloriously, — to die on the "field of honor."

And yet, this is not to die: it is rather to live with martyrs and heroes of the past, and in the memory, the gratitude, the benediction of the future. To be enrolled "dead in a just cause," — is not this to be triumphant over death, and after death? For human history is not a dead sea; it is a flowing river. There is a course and progress of human affairs, a development of society, — rational, spiritual, moral, and material; a slow but sure unfolding of the latent genius of the race; a destiny of man, a God of history.

So, standing here on Plymouth Rock, and looking out upon that sea which once bore hither a few brave spirits driven in scorn from the Old World's embrace, to unfold the New World's brighter destiny, — that same sea which to-day covers the delicate nerves that thrill the heart-beats between world and world, — I read the mighty lesson of the times. And what is whispered by the past, and what is thundered by the present, what I see in your countenances and read on those sealed lips, I proclaim to the expectant future, for Truth shall conquer, and those that fell for her defence she will lift to her triumph.

Stand, then, O monument! Resist the shock of the elements and the touch of time, eloquent with these deathless names. And ye, O martyrs, tell to after ages what virtue was in this! Tell to a delivered country how precious are her foundations! Tell to enfranchised humanity, Liberty can never die!

---

19. BE JUST, AND FEAR NOT.

CARDINAL WOLSEY, after losing the royal favor, A. D. 1529.
(KING HENRY VIII: Act III., Scene II.)

WOLSEY, *by himself.*

I have touch'd the highest point of all my greatness;
And from that full meridian of my glory,
I haste now to my setting: I shall fall
Like a bright exhalation in the evening,
And no man see me more.

. . . .

WOLSEY, *to Cromwell, who has entered.*

. . . .

Cromwell, I did not think to shed a tear
In all my miseries; but thou hast forc'd me,
Out of thy honest truth, to play the woman.
Let's dry our eyes: and thus far hear me, Cromwell;
And, — when I am forgotten, as I shall be,
And sleep in dull, cold marble, where no mention
Of me more must be heard of, — say, I taught thee;
Say, Wolsey, that once trod the ways of glory,
And sounded all the depths and shoals of honour —

Found thee a way, out of his wreck, to rise in;
A sure and safe one, though thy master miss'd it.
Mark but my fall, and that that ruin'd me.
Cromwell, I charge thee, fling away ambition:
By that sin fell the angels; how can man, then,
The image of his Maker, hope to win by 't?
Love thyself last: cherish those hearts that hate thee;
Corruption wins not more than honesty.
Still in thy right hand carry gentle peace,
To silence envious tongues: Be just, and fear not.
Let all the ends thou aim'st at be thy country's,
Thy God's, and Truth's: then if thou fallest, O Cromwell!
Thou fall'st a blessed martyr. Serve the King;
And — Pr'ythee, lead me in:
There take an inventory of all I have,
To the last penny; 't is the King's: my robe,
And my integrity to Heaven, is all
I dare now call mine own. O Cromwell, Cromwell!
Had I but served my God with half the zeal
I served my King, he would not in mine age
Have left me naked to mine enemies.

SHAKESPEARE.

---

20. A BURLESQUE CHALLENGE TO AMERICA.

This article, from the " London Punch," fitly suggests the absurdity of war between England and America.

LET us quarrel, American kinsmen. Let us plunge into war. We have been friends too long. We have too highly promoted each other's wealth and prosperity. We are too plethoric; we want depletion. To which end, let us cut each other's throats. Let us sink, burn, kill, and destroy, with mutual energy; sink each other's shipping, burn each other's arsenals, destroy each other's property at large. We will bombard your towns, and you shall bombard ours, if you can. Let us ruin each other's commerce as much as possible, — and that will be a considerable sum. Let our banks break, while we smite and slay one another; let our commercial houses smash right and left in the United States and the United Kingdom. Let us maim and mutilate one another; let us make of each other miserable objects, — cripples, halt, and blind, adapted for the town's end, to beg for life.

Come, let us render the wives of each other widows, and the mothers childless, and cause them to weep rivers of tears, amounting to an important quantity of "water-privilege." The bowl of wrath, the devil's punch-bowl, filled high as possible, share we with one another. This, with shot and bayonets, will be good in your insides and in my inside, in the insides of all us brethren.

Oh, how good it is! oh, how pleasant it is, for brethren to engage in internecine strife! What a glorious spectacle we Christian Anglo-Saxons, engaged in the work of mutual destruction, in the reciprocation of savage outrages, shall present to the despots and the fiends!

How many dollars will you spend? How many pounds sterling shall we? How much capital shall we sink on either side, on land as well as in the sea? How much we shall have to show for it in corpses and wooden legs! Never ask what other return we may expect for the investment. So, then, American kinsmen, let us fight; let us murder and ruin each other. Let demagogues come hot from their conclave of evil spirits, "cry havoc, and let slip the dogs of war," and do you be mad enough to be those mad dogs, and permit yourselves to be hounded upon us by them.

MARK LEMON.

21. DEATH OR LIBERTY.

Ex-President JOSEPH F. TUTTLE, of Wabash College, Indiana, contributes for this volume these notes of the thrilling address delivered at Cincinnati, in 1834, by Theodore D. Weld, when Mr. Weld was a student at Lane Seminary. President Tuttle, then a mere boy, was attracted to the meeting where Mr. Weld was mobbed for his views upon African slavery. Mr. Weld is the only survivor, since the death of Whittier, of a famous companionship of the early anti-slavery struggle.

ONE day, in one of the West India Islands, the sons and daughters of the planters went upon a sailing excursion. The day was glorious, and the sea scarcely rippled into waves under the gentle wind that bore the vessel along like some white-winged bird. It was a day of festivity and mirth, of wine and the dance; and all went merry as a marriage bell. The gay youth, taken up with pleasure, took no note of signs of approaching storm. Suddenly they were awakened from their dreams by a peal of thunder, like a signal gun for battle. The sky grew dark; the wind moaned and sobbed as if in agony; the lightnings flashed, and the thunder crashed through the sky. All was consternation; and yet, just in sight, were their homes. Oh, if they were there!

The calm is suddenly broken by the breath of the whirlwind which came swooping down like a bird of prey. And now the waves roll, and the vessel plunges wildly toward the reef of rocks, heedless of all efforts of the struggling helmsman. See it! How it flies toward the place of death! Every cheek is blanched in the presence of the King of Terrors! Look! it is almost there! See the waves yonder, breaking into foam, and flinging their waters to the heavens. See the vessel as the mad waves drive it furiously along! Hearken! do you not hear the roar of the breakers mingled with the shrieks of the poor creatures on the vessel's deck? One moment more, and she is dashed upon the rocks. And now the waves, as if inspired with madness, rush upon it to tear it in pieces, and swallow up those young lives. See those sons and daughters clinging to the wreck, and shrieking for help! It is a scene of unspeakable terror.

Meanwhile, on the shore yonder are gathered the parents whose children are thus stretching out their hands in supplication for help. Here are boats, but can they live in such a sea? And here are slaves, looking upon the terrible scene while their masters bid them man the boats and go to the rescue. And shall they go? And why shall they go? They look at their masters on the shore, and their young masters on the wreck. They look at the sea lashing and breaking on the shore in fury. Wherefore shall they go, as into the very jaws of death? They refuse. The masters entreat, and then command them to go. Nay, they use the dreadful whip to scourge them into obedience to that dreadful peril, but in vain! Not a slave will enter a boat. And must these children perish, without one single effort to save them?

One motive remained untried. These slaves belonged to the class supposed to have no longing for freedom, and now it shall be known whether that be so or not. In this extremity the planters held a hurried consultation; and then one of their number, leaping upon a rock, waved his hat and shouted, "Liberty! Liberty! Liberty! to every slave that shall man the boats and go to the rescue." Those men, those slaves, started as we may suppose the dead will start at the sound of God's last trumpet.

"Liberty! Liberty! Liberty!"

Those black faces were suffused with a new joy. Those poor dumb hearts beat with the pulsations of a new hope. A moment's hesitation, as if to see whether that were a real sound, — whether their own ears did indeed hear that wondrous word "Liberty," — and they started for the boats.

One was manned and pushed out into the waves that broke upon the shore; but it was swamped, — every man perishing in the attempt. Another was manned, but quickly shared the same fate; and yet this double catastrophe did not terrify men who had heard the word "Liberty," and who might win it by this perilous venture. And thus they ventured their lives in the tremendous contest; and though many of them died in the attempt, they rescued the imperilled youth, less noble than themselves. And yet there are those who say that the slave does not love Liberty.

THEODORE DWIGHT WELD.

22. PRESS ON!

Press on! there's no such word as fail!
  Press nobly on! the goal is near, —
Ascend the mountain! breast the gale!
  Look onward, upward, — never fear!
Why shouldst thou faint? Heaven smiles above,
  Though storm and vapor intervene;
That sun shines on, whose name is Love,
  Serenely o'er Life's shadowed scene.

Press on! Surmount the rocky steeps,
  Climb boldly o'er the torrent's arch;
He fails alone who feebly creeps, —
  He wins who dares the hero's march.
Be thou a hero! let thy might
  Tramp on eternal snows its way,
And through the ebon walls of night
  Hew down a passage unto day.

Press on ! If once or twice thy feet
    Slip back and stumble, harder try ;
From him who never dreads to meet
    Danger and Death, they 're sure to fly.
In coward ranks the bullet speeds;
    While on their breasts who never quail,
Gleams, guardian of chivalric deeds,
    Bright courage, like a coat-of-mail.

Press on ! If Fortune play thee false
    To-day, to-morrow she 'll be true;
Whom now she sinks, she now exalts,
    Taking old gifts, and granting new.
The wisdom of the present hour
    Makes up for follies past and gone ;
To weakness strength succeeds, and power
    From frailty springs. Press on ! press on !

Press bravely on, and reach the goal,
    And gain the prize, and wear the crown ;
Faint not ! for to the steadfast soul
    Come wealth and honor and renown.
To thine own self be true, and keep
    Thy mind from sloth, thy heart from soil ;
Press on ! and thou shalt surely reap
    A heavenly harvest for thy toil.

                        PARK BENJAMIN.

PART IX.

HINTS TO YOUNG AMERICA.

1. OUR COUNTRY.

When we speak of our country we mean the United States of America. The State in which we reside is a small part of that country, and the town in which we live is but a small part of the State. Our government is the offspring of the popular will. The people brought it into existence to impose salutary restraints upon the States, and to insure to the people in every State the benefits of a republican freedom. We are a nation, not by the sufferance of Delaware or Ohio, but by virtue of our historical and constitutional antecedents. Each State has its rights, but among them is not the right to break up this Union by secession. A four years' war, the fiercest in the world's history, has settled that question.

The most precious of our rights is that by which we claim the protection of the American flag, whether we stand on the Atlantic border of our beloved country, on the mountains of Colorado, or on the plains of Texas.

Why ought we to cherish this Union? Simply because it is the guarantee of our liberties. It is not true that a diminutive nationality is favorable to human freedom. Ancient Greece, broken up into independent States, perished because of the absence of a National Union like ours. No argument against our system can be drawn from the vast extent of our country. The steam-engine, the railroad, and the magnetic telegraph have annihilated space and time. Our grand republican experiment, already confirmed by the supreme test of civil war, and purged of one fatal inconsistency, is based on the Christian principle of justice, — the equality of all men before the law. Let us rise to the full benefit of this sacred teaching. Let us realize that it is our duty to do what we can constantly to raise up those beneath us to our own level of virtue and intelligence, and to welcome all men to the political benefits which we inherit.

That we live in the enjoyment of the fruits of our labors, that we live at all, perhaps, or live girt about by the blessings of civilization, we owe, under Providence, to our country. Let us prove ourselves true sons and daughters of such a mother! Let us lovingly uphold the symbol of her just authority, the glorious Flag of the United States! Let us labor to make her, by her noble example, the peaceful propagandist of justice and freedom throughout the world! Let us serve her with all our might, and defend her, should occasion summon, with our mortal lives!

Epes Sargent.

2. THE YOUNG AMERICAN.

Scion of a mighty stock, hands of iron, hearts of oak,
Follow with unflinching tread where the noble fathers led!
Craft and subtle treachery, gallant youth, are not for thee;
Follow thou, in word and deed, whither Truth and Conscience
    lead.

Honesty with steady eye, duty and simplicity,
Love that gently winneth hearts, — these shall be thy only
    arts;
Prudent in the council train, dauntless on the battle-plain,
Ready, at thy Country's need, for her glorious cause to bleed.

Where the dews of night distil upon Vernon's holy hill,
Where above it, gleaming far, Freedom lights her guiding
 star,
Thither turn the watchful eye, flashing with a purpose high;
Thither, with devotion meet, often turn the pilgrim feet.

Let thy noble motto be, Thy Country! Liberty!
Planted on Religion's rock, thou shalt stand through every
 shock;
Laugh at danger far or near, spurn at baseness, spurn at
 fear,
And, with persevering might, speak the truth and do the
 right.

So shall Peace, a charming guest, dove-like in thy bosom
 rest;
So shall Honor's steady blaze beam upon thy closing days:
Happy if celestial favor smile upon thy high endeavor,
Happy if it be thy call in the holy cause to fall.

ALEXANDER HILL EVERETT.

3. GETTING THE RIGHT START.

THE first great lesson a young man should learn is that he knows nothing and is nothing. Bred at home, he cannot readily understand that every one else can be his equal in talent and acquisition. This is a critical period of his history. If he bow to the conviction that his mind and person are but ciphers, and that whatever he is to be and is to win, must be achieved by hard work, there is abundant hope for him. If a huge self-conceit hold possession of him, or he sink discouraged upon the threshold of fierce competition and more manly emulations, he might as well be a dead man. The world has no use for such a man, and he has only to retire or be trodden upon.

The next thing for him to learn is that the world cares nothing for him, and that he must take care for himself. He will not be noticed till he does something to prove that he has an absolute value in society. No letter of recommendation will give him this, or ought to give him this. Society demands that a young man shall be somebody, and prove his right to the title, but will not take this upon trust, at least for a long time: it has been cheated too frequently. There is no surer sign of an unmanly spirit than a wish to lean upon somebody and enjoy the fruits of the industry of others. When a young man becomes aware that only by his own exertions can he rise into companionship and competition with the sharp, strong, and well-drilled minds around him, he is ready for work, and not before.

The next lesson is patience, thorough preparation, and contentment with the regular channels of business-effort and enterprise. This is one of the most difficult to learn, of all the lessons of life. It is natural for the mind to reach out eagerly for immediate results. Beginning at the very foot of the hill, and working slowly to the top, seems a very discouraging process; and precisely at this point have thousands of young men made shipwreck of their lives. Let this be understood, then, at starting, that the patient conquest of difficulties is not only essential to the successes which you seek, but to that preparation of mind which is requisite for the enjoyment of your successes, and for retaining them when gained. It is the general rule of Providence, the world over, and in all time, that unearned success is a curse. It is the process of earning success that shall be the preparation for its conservation and enjoyment.

So, day by day, and week by week, month after month,

and year after year, work on, and in that process gain strength and symmetry, and nerve and knowledge, that when success patiently and bravely worked for shall come, it may find you prepared to receive and keep it. The development which you will get in this brave and patient labor will prove itself in the end the most valuable of your successes. It will help to make a man of you. It will give you power and self-reliance. It will give you not only self-respect, but the respect of your fellows and the public.

Joseph Gilbert Holland.

4. THE SUPREMACY OF CONSCIENCE.

The arrangement of God which makes man's conscience his guide to action, is beneficent every way. It is beneficent for the individual. The results will be seen in the end, — as with the Puritan in this country, as with the Huguenots of France, as with the band of the persecuted in the Waldensian valleys, — in a purer piety; in a nobler self-devotion; in a grander and more powerful grasp of the principles of duty; in a more exalted communion with God in His holiness; in a higher disregard of the blandishments of time; in a mightier unfolding of all spiritual force; in a deeper impression on the history of the world.

It is beneficent for the State, as for the persons who compose it, that conscience thus decide. "The State." What is it? It is not lands, or ports, or capitals. It is the men who form and guide it! Where these are elevated, the State is flourishing. In Italy, in Russia, under the iron system of the old despots of France, has liberty advanced? Has intelligence been diffused?

Has morality grown purer? Has religion gained power? Has right been done? Has the State been ennobled? Has even a just stability of government been secured and established? Nay, verily! but in all these the reverse.

On the other hand, take any man, take any people, in the development of the system that nurtures and educates conscience, as the guide to man's duty, as the interpreter of God's law to him and for him, as the authority he must bow to, whatever man decrees, and Liberty there advances. The State grows in power as its citizens are enlightened. It becomes settled and established, on the basis of equity. Follow it in its career, and its progress shall be traced in beneficence and peace. From first to last its orbit shall be an orbit that brightens with the glow of knowledge and of heroism; and that closes in the splendor of a still culminating glory.

RICHARD SALTER STORRS.

5. THE TRUE ASPIRATION OF YOUTH.

HIGHER, higher, will we climb,
  Up the mount of glory,
That our names may live through time
  In our country's story;
Happy, when her welfare calls,
He who conquers, he who falls.

Deeper, deeper, let us toil
  In the mines of knowledge,—
Nature's wealth and Learning's spoil
  Win from school and college;
Delve we there for richer gems
Than the stars of diadems.

Onward, onward, will we press
   In the path of duty;
Virtue is true happiness,
   Excellence true beauty.
Minds are of celestial birth;
Let us make a heaven of earth.

Closer, closer, let us knit
   Hearts and hands together,
Where our fireside comforts sit
   In the wildest weather.
Oh, they wander wide who roam
For the joys of life from home!

Nearer, dearer, bands of love
   Draw our souls in union
To our Father's house above,
   To the saint's communion.
Thither every hope ascend;
There may all our labor end.
                     JAMES MONTGOMERY.

---

6. TO WHOM HONOR BE DUE.

LONG live who knows humanity,
   Its duties and its worth;
Who loves his brother-man as much
An' if he walk with beggar's crutch
   Or clad in purple forth.

Long live who ne'er hath bowed the knee
   To golden idol's pride;
Who owns for sordid self no care,
And not before a monarch's chair
   Hath ever fawned or lied.

But he whom inward voices ne'er
  To manly deeds did call,
Who leisure for dull sloth hath found,
While innocence stood waiting round,
  Full deeply he may fall.

Long live who hears the sick man's cry,
  The poor man's woes can feel;
Who, by no thought of money led,
Nightly repairs to sickness' bed,
  To comfort and to heal.

. . . .

Long live who waves for Fatherland
  The blood-stained banner high,
Who'll charge for freedom and the laws
(His shield the goodness of his cause)
  Upon the enemy!

Long live who'll wage the sterner war
  With error's direful night;
Who, though they "Crucify him!" cry,
Though king and priest stand threatening by,
  Will battle for the right!

And long live every honest man,
  Each man of dauntless mood,
Each monarch, and each serving-man,
Each citizen, each countryman,—
  Each man that doeth good!

From the German.

HASTE NOT, REST NOT.

Haste not! rest not! calmly wait,
  Meekly bear the storms of fate.
Duty be thy polar guide;
  Do the right, whate'er betide.
Haste not! rest not! conflicts past,
  God shall crown thy work at last.

GOETHE.

7. TRUE LIBERTY.

People talk of Liberty as if it meant the liberty to do just what a man likes. I call that man free who is able to rule himself. I call him free who fears doing wrong, but fears nothing else. I call that man free who has learned the most blessed of all truths, — that liberty consists in obedience to the power, and to the will, and to the law that his higher soul reverences and approves. He is not free because he does what he likes; but he is free because he does what he ought, and there is no protest in his soul against that doing.

Some people think there is no liberty in obedience. I tell you that there is no liberty except in loyal obedience, — the obedience of the unconstrained affections. Did you ever see a mother kept at home, a kind of prisoner, by her sick child, obeying its every wish and caprice? Will you call that mother a slave? Or is this the obedience of slavery? I call it the obedience of the highest liberty, — that of love.

We hear a great deal in these days respecting the right of private judgment, the rights of labor, the rights of property, and the rights of man. Rights are grand things, divine things, in this world of God's; but the way in which we expound those rights, alas! seems to be the very incarnation of selfishness. I can see nothing very noble in a man who is forever going about calling for his rights. I cannot see anything manly in the ferocious struggle between rich and poor, — the one to take as much, and the other to keep as much, as he can. The cry of "my rights and your duties," we should change to something nobler. If we can say, "my duties and your rights," we shall learn what real liberty is.

FREDERICK WILLIAM ROBERTSON.

8. THE AGE OF WORK.

This address, delivered in 1851, at the time of the first London Exposition, is especially appropriate since the Columbian Exposition, celebrating the completion of the first four centuries of American civilization.

WHAT mechanical inventions already crowd upon us! Look abroad, and contemplate the infinite achievements of steam-power. Reflect on all that has been done by the railroad. Pause to estimate, if you can, with all the help of the imagination, what is to be the result from the agency now manifested in operations of the telegraph. Cast a thought over the whole field of scientific, mechanical improvement and its application to human wants. How many comforts, how many facilities, it has given to man! What has it done for his food and his raiment! What for his communication with his fellow-man in every clime, for his instruction in books, for his amusement, his safety! What new lands has it opened, and what old ones are made accessible! How has it enlarged his sphere of knowledge and converse with his own species!

It is all a great, an astounding marvel, which oppresses the mind to think of. In all the desirable facilities of life, in the comfort that depends upon mechanism, in all that is calculated to delight the sense or instruct the mind, the man of moderate means of this day is placed far in advance of the most wealthy, powerful, and princely of ancient times, — yes, of the times less than a century ago.

We have only begun! We are but on the threshold of this, the mechanical epoch, the new era. A vast multitude of all peoples, nations, and tongues gathered but yesterday, under a magnificent crystal palace, in the greatest city of the world, to illustrate and distinguish the achievements of art, to dignify and exalt the great mechanical fraternity who filled that palace with wonders.

What is this but setting the great distinctive seal upon the nineteenth century? What is this but an advertisement of the fact that society has risen to a higher platform than ever before? What is this but a proclamation, announcing honor, honor immortal, to the workmen who fill the world with beauty, comfort, and power; honor to be forever embalmed in history, to be perpetuated in monuments, to be written in the hearts of this and succeeding generations?

JOHN PENDLETON KENNEDY.

9. SUCCESS IN LIFE.

I HAVE been requested to say something which may be of benefit to young men; and if anything I can say will help the young to lead good and useful lives, I am willing to say it. There is nothing miraculous in the success I have met with. If a man has good principles, and does his best to act up to them, he should not fail of success, though it may not be success of precisely the same kind or degree as mine. Good principles are just as good for the artist as for the mechanic, for the poet as for the farmer, for the man of business as for the clergyman. Would you learn the lesson of success? Here it is in three words. Would you climb the ladder? Here it is, just three rounds: Industry, Temperance, Frugality. Write these words upon your hearts, and practise them in your lives. It is a good thing to have a good motto, but it is better to live up to one. Five other mottoes have been helpful and encouraging to me throughout my busy life: " Be true," " Be kind," " Keep out of debt," " Do the best, and leave the rest," "What can't be cured must be endured."

I began to support myself when I was twelve years old, and I have never been dependent on others since. I had had some schooling, but not much. I came to Philadelphia with three dollars in my pocket. I found board and lodgings for two dollars and a half, and then I got a place in a bookstore for three dollars. That gave me a surplus of fifty cents a week. I did not merely do the work that I was required to do; but did all I could, and put my whole heart into it. I wanted my employer to feel that I was more useful to him than he expected me to be. I was not afraid to make fires, clean and sweep, and perform what some young gentlemen, nowadays, consider as menial work, and therefore beneath them. The Bible says that it is what cometh out of the mouth that defileth a man. It is not work, but character, that can be discreditable.

But a man can be industrious, and yet his industry may not achieve much valuable result. You must not only work, but you must select your work with intelligence. You must be preparing the way for what you intend to become, as well as do well what lies in your hand. While I was working as an errand-boy, I improved such opportunity as I had to read books, and attend book sales at night, so as to learn the market value of books, and anything else that might be useful hereafter in my business. I fixed my ambition high, so that I might at least be always tending upward. I lived near a theatre, and many of the actors knew me, so that I might have gone and witnessed the performances. Other boys did it, and I would have liked to do it. But I thought it over, and concluded I would not, and I never did. This self-denial, if it may be called that, did not make me morose or unhappy. You must not yield to the temptation to relax your efforts, and turn off and amuse yourself. I was always cheerful, took an interest in my work, and took pleasure in doing it well, and in the feeling that I was getting on in a way to become something. When, at last, I had an office in the Public Ledger Building, I believe I said to myself, "Some time I will own that paper." At any rate, I directed my work in such a way that, when the time came that I was able to buy it, I was also able to manage it properly.

I have always believed that it is possible to unite success in business with strict moral integrity. If the record of my life has any value, it is in showing that it is not necessary to success in business that a man should indulge in "sharp" practices. Riches cannot compensate a man for the consciousness of having lived a dishonorable and selfish life.

I cannot lay too strong a stress on the matter of strict temperance. You should have courage enough to say, "No," if you are asked to drink. There is no safety in moderate drinking; every one who touches it at all, is in danger. It does no good, and if the habit is continued, it is almost sure to lead to destruction and death.

Perhaps I ought to say a word about the companions a young man should choose for himself in life. You should try to make companions of the best people you can become acquainted with. It is not necessary for this purpose to be a genius, or to have remarkable talent or extraordinary erudition. But be yourself, and be a man, and learn to think of others before yourself, and you will have friends enough, and of the best. A man is known by the company he keeps, and those who know what friends you have will be able to form a very correct idea of what you yourself are. You should see to it that this estimate be as high as your opportunities may secure.

Perhaps I cannot better sum up my advice to young

people than to say that I have derived, and still find, the greatest pleasure in my life from doing good to others. Do good constantly, patiently, and wisely, and you will never have cause to say that your life was not worth living.

GEORGE W. CHILDS.

---

10. THE CRITICAL CONDITIONS OF LABOR.

EXTRACTS from Address of Ex-President BENJAMIN HARRISON, before the 28th graduating class of the Peirce School of Business and Shorthand, Philadelphia, December 20th, 1893.

THE demand for cheapness has compacted capital and consolidated small enterprises. In the old time, when shops were small, the owner knew every man in his employ, his name, his skill, his disposition, and, not unlikely, something of his home and family. He exchanged friendly greetings with him, and commended his work. And, on his part, the workman took a pride in the shop, and confidently went to his employer for advice as to the investment of his savings. The relation was of man with man, and often seasoned with friendly confidence. But when the fifty becomes five thousand, much of this becomes impossible, and the rest of it is rare. How shall the owner have personal touch with the multitude? How can the workmen be made to know if the truth be so; and if not, how can it be made true that the owner of the mill "thinketh upon them;" that their contentment, happiness, and prosperity are his concern; that he esteems them men, not implements, — not lesser cogs that can only feel the grinding contact of the master-wheels, but men who are moved by touch of brother's palm and heart.

And how shall the workman's heart be cleansed of envy and misjudgment, and to reciprocate every manifestation of interest on the part of the employer? Like the armed peace maintained in Europe, this situation is costly and dangerous. Every benevolent and thoughtful man is anxious and distressed. I suppose a just and perfect peace will not be established until the kingdom of the Elder Brother is set up throughout the world, and the Golden Rule becomes the law of life. But this war can be restricted, and its evils ameliorated. We ought to be able to settle upon one principle, if we cannot in every case agree as to the application.

We have our Gradgrinds, our snobs, our purse-proud sons of artisan fathers, our dudes and butterflies, our English counterfeiters; but the mass of our people, of the rich as well as the men of moderate means, have a generous, hearty human sympathy and fellowship with the honest sons of toil. The chief trouble is not want of heart or of right judgment, but to hold busy men long enough to hear the tale of wrong, and to discriminate between it and the false appeal that lies in wait for every man of wealth or influence. And, on the other hand, the American workmen — and by that I mean all, whether native or foreign born, who are in spirit and purpose American — are, as a body, intelligent, spirited, and patriotic. They will not bear patronizing, but they are hungry for fraternity.

The working-men, if you give these terms their proper shape, are the civil bulk of the nation. Everything is borne up and borne along by them. They are the musket bearers. The great Union Army was like the kingdom of Heaven in one respect, "not many mighty were enrolled." These sturdy sons will come again, should war's dread alarms again wake our streets and valleys. But why should not we call these "comrades" now? It was not the muster that created the companionship; that only revealed it. In the company we got the touch of the elbow and the cadenced step. Why cannot we have them in civil life, with all those who love our civil institutions? They are needed. They give strength and security as well as fellowship.

But with all this good disposition, in spite of the common interests that bind us together, the observant philanthropist and patriot is forced to admit that the seams which have marred the face of the social landscape seem to be widening into chasms. If these gulfs are to be filled, we must establish dumps on both sides of them. It will aid the work, if those on either side use the bridges to get a view of it from the other side.

What are the natural rights of man? The old declaration says that among them are life, liberty, and the pursuit of happiness. It is a fine summary. It sets the feet of a man in a larger place. They are said to be God's endowment, and it follows that they are inalienable. He gave me life, and I have no more right to sell it or throw it away than you have to take it; no more right to alienate my liberty than you have to rob me of it. It is quite as contrary to natural right to prevent me from working as to force me to work when I don't choose. If a greater success has been attained, envy is ignoble, and malice a crime. The indiscriminate denunciation of the rich is mischievous. It perverts the mind, poisons the heart, and furnishes excuse for crime. It is a most wholesome and saving fact in the United States, that the people so generally reject the teachings of anarchy. The workman is a producer; the anarchist is a destroyer, and fellowship is impossible. I would that there were fewer very rich men and fewer very poor men; but it would not help but greatly hurt, to take by force from the one what he has honestly acquired and bestow upon the other what he has not earned. We should destroy thrift, enterprise, industry; for men will not labor unless they can enjoy the fruit of their labors. We should destroy self-respect, manliness, personal pride; for he only feels himself a man, who eats his bread in the sweat of his brow, and not in another man's favor.

We see each other so seldom, our touch is so casual, that we do not understand each other's ways. It takes an earthquake, a famine, or a flood to get our attention. But there is no work that requires more thought or is more worthy of doing, than the work of burning the barriers of misconception and prejudice which now separate men. Benefactions are good for those who are past helping themselves. If the seamstress, when she leaves a good woman's house, takes with her the feeling that she may come back, if in perplexity or trouble, it is worth more to her than her wages. We need to get rid of the idea that the payment of stipulated wages entitles us to a receipt in full. In full of wages? Yes, but not in full of obligation! You are bound to make the employment as safe and healthful as its nature will permit. Society has awakened to interest in this matter, and laws have mitigated some of the needless perils of labor. These reforms should be made of good will and not of law.

We owe it to our employees that they shall not be abused in their person or in their self-respect. Foremen, not "bosses," should be set over them. Discipline? Yes, but no nagging! Reproof? Yes, but no damning! No employee should ever be compelled to choose between pocketing an insult and pocketing his wages. He should be required to act like a man, and be treated as one. If it is honorable to employ a man to do a particular thing, it must be honorable to do it. The late Senator Stanford would not have a swearing man about his stables at Palo Alto. He required that even his horses should be treated with respect. We should be under special restraints not to speak harshly or to act with injustice toward one who cannot retort or resent. No blood follows the blow: the hemorrhages are internal; but a spring of hatred has been opened. If we would have work well done, we must let the man see that he is not degraded in our opinion by doing it; that, indeed, commendation as well as wages are due the faithful worker. God does not esteem the gold and the glory of heaven enough for His servants. He crowns them with the benediction, "Well done, good and faithful servant!" And here, a man whose work praises him, should not miss a man to praise his work. The only way in this free land to be assured of one's rights is freely and generously to acknowledge other people's rights.

11. NO EXCELLENCE WITHOUT LABOR.

The moral and intellectual education of every individual must be chiefly his own work. Rely upon it that the ancients were right, that in morals and in intellect we give the final shape to our own fortunes. How else could it happen that young men who have had precisely the same opportunities, should be continually presenting us with such different results, and rushing to such opposite destinies?

Differences of talent will not solve it, because that very difference is often in favor of the disappointed candidate. You shall see issuing from the halls of the same college, — nay, sometimes from the bosom of the same family, — two young men, of whom the one shall be admitted to be a genius of high order, the other scarcely above the point of mediocrity; and yet you shall see the former sinking and perishing in poverty, obscurity, and wretchedness, while, on the other hand, you shall observe the latter plodding his slow but sure way up the hill of life, gaining steadfast footing at every step, and mounting at length to eminence and distinction, an ornament to his family, a blessing to his country.

Now, whose work is this? Manifestly their own. They are the architects of their respective fortunes. The best seminary that can open its portals to you, can do no more than afford you the opportunity of instruction. It must depend, at last, upon yourselves, whether you will be instructed or not, or to what point you will push your education. It may be declared as the result of observation that it is a settled truth that there is no real excellence without great labor. This is a fiat from which no power of genius can absolve you. Genius, unexerted, is like the poor moth that flutters around the candle, till it scorches itself to death. If genius be desirable at all, it is only of that great and magnanimous kind, which, like the condor of South America, pitches from the mountains of Chimborazo above the clouds, and sustains itself at pleasure in that empyreal region, with an energy rather invigorated than weakened by the effort. It is this capacity for high and continued exertion, this vigorous power of profound and searching investigation, this wide-spreading comprehension of mind, and these long reaches of thought that —

> "Pluck bright honor from the pale-faced moon,
> Or dive into the bottom of the deep,
> Where fathom-line could never touch the ground,
> And drag up honor by the locks."

This is the prowess, and these the hardy achievements, which are to enroll your names among the great men of earth.

WILLIAM WIRT.

12. LABOR HOURS HAVE LIMITS.[1]

If we consider man, in a commercial point of view, as a machine for productive labor, let us not forget what a piece of mechanism he is, — how "fearfully and wonderfully made." If we have a fine horse, we do not use him exactly as a steam-engine, and still less should we use a man so, especially in his younger years. The depressing labor that begins early in life and is continued too long, every day, enfeebles his body, enervates his mind, weakens his spirit, overpowers his understanding, and is incompatible with any good or useful degree of education.

A state of society in which such a system prevails, will inevitably, and in no short space, feel its baleful effects. What is it which makes one community more prosperous and flourishing than another? Not the soil; not its climate; not its mineral wealth, its natural advantages, its ports, or its great rivers. Is it anything in the earth, or in the air, that makes Scotland a richer country than Egypt; or Batavia, with its marshes, more prosperous than Sicily? No! but the Scotchman made Scotland what she is; and Dutchmen raised their marshes to such eminence. Look to America! Two centuries ago it was a wilderness of buffaloes and wolves. What has caused the change? Is it her rich mould? Is it her mighty rivers? Is it her broad waters? No! Her plains were then as fertile as now; her rivers were as numerous! Nor was it any great amount of capital that the emigrants carried with them. They took a mere pittance. What is it then that has effected the change? It is simply this. You have placed the Englishman instead of the red man upon the soil; and the Englishman, intelligent and energetic, cut

---

[1] Written in 1846, but never more timely than now.

down the forests, turned them into cities and fleets, and covered the land with harvests and orchards in their place.

But the question of limiting the hours of labor,— a question for the most part connected with persons of tender years, and a question in which public health is concerned as well as public morals, — is one which the State may properly interfere with, as of vast importance. As law-givers, we have errors of two kinds to repair. We have done that which we ought not to have done, and have left undone that which we ought to have done. We have regulated that which we ought to have left to regulate itself, and we have not regulated that which it was our business to have regulated. We have given to certain branches of industry a protection which was their bane. We have withheld from public health and from public morality a protection which it was our duty to have given. We have prevented the laborer from getting his loaf where he could get it cheapest; but we have not prevented him from prematurely destroying the health of his body and mind by inordinate toil. I hope that we are approaching the end of a vicious system of interference and of a vicious system of non-interference.

Thomas Babington Macaulay.

THE LAW OF LABOR.

Life, as a rule, is all work. The drone of a hive must die. A symmetrical life is one that has realized success through struggle and victory. Pleasure is but a style of rest to body or brain, and is the balm which soothes the strain of labor, and not only refreshes the worker, but gives new zest to work itself.

From " Crisis Thoughts."

13. TRUE NOBILITY.

What is noble? To inherit
   Wealth, estate, and proud degree?
There must be some other merit,
   Higher yet than these, for me ;
Something greater far must enter
   Into life's majestic span,
Fitted to create and centre
   True nobility in man !

What is noble? 'T is the finer
   Portion of our mind and heart,
Linked to something still diviner
   Than mere language can impart;
Ever prompting, ever seeing
   Some improvement yet to plan
To uplift our fellow-being,
   And like man to feel for Man !

What is noble? Is the sabre
   Nobler than the humble spade ?
There 's a dignity in labor,
   Truer than ever pomp arrayed !
He who seeks the mind's improvement
   Aids the world in aiding mind;
Every great commanding movement
   Serves not one, but all mankind.

O'er the forge's heat and ashes,
   O'er the engine's iron head,
Where the rapid shuttle flashes,
   And the spindle whirls its thread,
There is Labor, lowly tending
   Each requirement of the hour;
There is Genius, still extending
   Science and the world of power.

'Mid the dust and speed and clamor
   Of the loom-shed and the mill,
'Mid the click of wheel and hammer,
   Great results are growing still!
Though too oft by Fashion's creatures
   Work and workers may be blamed,
Commerce need not hide its features,—
   Industry is not ashamed!

What is noble! That which places
   Truth in its enfranchised will,
Leaving steps, like angel traces,
   That mankind may follow still!
E'en though Scorn's malignant glances
   Prove him poorest of his clan,
He's the noble who advances
   Freedom and the cause of man!

CHARLES SWAIN.

14. DON'T GIVE TOO MUCH FOR THE WHISTLE.

WHEN I was a child, says Dr. Franklin, my friends, on a holiday filled my little pockets with coppers. I went directly to a shop where they sold toys for children; and being charmed with the sound of a whistle in the hands of another boy whom I met by the way, I voluntarily offered and gave all my money for one. I then came home, and went whistling all over the house, much pleased with my whistle, but disturbing all the family. My brothers and sisters and cousins understanding the bargain I had made, told me I had given four times as much for it as it was worth. This, however, was afterwards of use to me, the impressions continuing on my mind; so that often when I was tempted to buy some unnecessary thing, I said to myself, "Don't give too much for the whistle!" As I grew up, came into the world and observed the actions of men, I thought I met with very many who gave too much for the whistle.

When I saw one too ambitious to court favors, wasting his time in attendance at levees, sacrificing his repose, his liberty, his virtue, and perhaps his friends, I said to myself, "This man gives too much for his whistle." When I saw another, fond of popularity, constantly employing himself in political bustles, neglecting his own affairs, and ruining them by that neglect, I said, "He pays, indeed, too much for his whistle."

If I knew a miser who gave up every kind of comfortable living, all the pleasure of doing good to others, all the esteem of his fellow-citizens, and the joys of benevolent friendship for the sake of accumulating wealth, "Poor man," said I, "you do indeed pay too much for the whistle."

When I met a man of pleasure, sacrificing every laudable improvement of his mind, or of his fortune, to mere corporal sensations, and ruining his health in the pursuit, "Mistaken man," said I, "you are providing pain instead of pleasure for yourself: you give too much for the whistle."

If I saw one fond of fine clothes, fine furniture, fine horses, fine equipage, all above his fortune, for which he contracted debts, and ended his career in prison, "Alas!" said I, "he has paid dear, very dear, for his whistle."

In short, I conceived that the greater part of the miseries of mankind were brought upon them by the false estimates they had made of the value of things, and by "giving too much for their whistles."

BENJAMIN FRANKLIN.

15. WHITTLING TYPICAL OF YOUNG AMERICA.

The Yankee boy, before he's sent to school,
Well knows the virtue of that magic tool,
The pocket-knife.
                To that his wistful eye
Turns, while he hears his mother's lullaby.
His hoarded cents he gladly gives to get it,
Then leaves no stone unturned till he can whet it;
And in the education of the lad
No little part that implement hath had.

His pocket-knife to the young whittler brings
A growing knowledge of material things.
Projectiles, music, and the sculptor's art,
His chestnut whistle, and his shingle dart,
His elder pop-gun, with its hickory rod,
Its sharp explosion, and rebounding wad,
His corn-stalk fiddle, and the deeper tone
That murmurs from his pumpkin-stalk trombone,
Conspire to teach the boy.
                  To these succeed
His bow, his arrow of a feathered reed;
His wind-mill, raised the passing breeze to win;
His water-wheel, that turns upon a pin;
Or, if his father lives upon the shore,
You'll see his ship, "beam ends upon the floor,"
Full rigged, with raking mast, and timbers staunch,
And waiting, near the wash-tub, for a launch.

Thus, by his genius and his jack-knife driven,
Ere long he'll solve you any problem given;
Make any gimcrack, musical or mute,
A plough, a couch, an organ, or a flute;

Make you a locomotive or a clock,
Cut a canal, or build a floating dock,
Or lead forth beauty from a marble block, —
Make anything, in short, for sea or shore,
From a child's rattle to a "Seventy-Four."[1]

Make it; said I? Ay! when he undertakes it,
He'll make the thing and the machine that makes it;
And when the thing is made, whether it be
To move on earth, in air, on land, or on the sea;
Whether on water, o'er the waves to glide,
Or upon land to roll, revolve, or slide;
Whether to whirl or jar, to strike or ring,
Whether it be a piston or a spring,
Wheel, pulley, tube sonorous, wood or brass,
The thing designed shall surely come to pass;
For, when his hand's upon it, you may know
That there's "go" in it, and he'll make it go.

JOHN PIERPONT.

16. THE ROAD TO HAPPINESS OPEN.

O HAPPINESS, our being's end and aim!
Good, Pleasure, Ease, Content! whate'er thy name;
That something still which prompts th' eternal sigh,
For which we bear to live, or dare to die;
Which still so near us, yet beyond us lies,
O'erlooked, seen double, by the fool and wise;
Plant of Celestial seed, if dropped below,
Say, in what mortal soil thou deign'st to grow?
Fair opening to some court's propitious shrine,
Or deep with diamonds in the flaming mine?
Twined with the wreaths Parnassian laurels yield,
Or reaped in iron harvests of the field?

---

[1] A "Line of Battle" ship, carrying seventy-four guns.

Where grows? Where grows it not? If vain our toil,
We ought to blame the culture, not the soil.
Fixed to no spot is Happiness sincere;
'T is nowhere to be found, or everywhere;
'T is never to be bought, but always free;
And, fled from monarchs, St. John, dwells with thee.

Ask of the learn'd the way? The learn'd are blind;
This bids to serve, and that to shun mankind;
Some place the bliss in action, some in ease;
Those call it Pleasure, and Contentment these;
Some, sunk to beasts, find pleasure end in pain;
Or, indolent, to each extreme they fall,
To trust in everything, or doubt of all.

Who thus define it, say they more or less
Than this, — that Happiness is Happiness?
Take Nature's path, and mad opinions leave;
All states can reach it, and all hands conceive.
Obvious her goods, in no extreme they dwell;
There needs but thinking right and meaning well;
And mourn our various portions as we please,
Equal is common sense and common ease.
Remember, man, "The universal cause
Acts not by partial, but by general laws;"
And makes what "Happiness" we justly call,
Subsist not in the good of one, but all.
Order is Heaven's first law; and this confest,
Some are, and must be greater than the rest,
More rich, more wise; but who infers from hence
That such are happier, shocks all common sense.
Heaven to mankind impartial we confess,
If all are equal in their happiness:
But mutual wants this happiness increase;
All Nature's difference keeps all Nature's peace.

ALEXANDER POPE.

17. NOT TO MYSELF ALONE.

"Not to myself alone,"
The little opening flower, transported, cries,—
"Not to myself alone I bud and bloom.
With fragrant breath the breezes I perfume,
And gladden all things with my rainbow dyes.
The bee comes sipping every eventide,
His dainty fill;
The butterfly within my cup doth hide
From threatening ill."

"Not to myself alone,"
The circling star with honest pride doth boast,—
"Not to myself alone I rise and set.
I write upon Night's coronal of jet
His power and skill who formed our myriad host;
A friendly beacon at heaven's open gate,
I gem the sky,
That man might ne'er forget, in every fate,
His home on high."

"Not to myself alone,"
The heavy-laden bee doth murmuring hum,—
"Not to myself alone, from flower to flower,
I roam the wood, the garden, and the bower,
And to the hive at evening weary come:
For man, for man, the luscious food I pile
With busy care,
Content if he repay my ceaseless toil
With scanty share."

"Not to myself alone,"
The soaring bird with lusty pinion sings,—
"Not to myself alone I raise my song.
I cheer the drooping with my warbling tongue,
And bear the mourner on my viewless wings;

I bid the hymnless churl my anthem learn,
    And God adore;
I call the worldling from his dross to turn,
    And sing and soar."

"Not to myself alone,"
The streamlet whispers on its pebbly way, —
"Not to myself alone I sparkling glide.
I scatter health and life on every side,
And strew the fields with herb and flow'ret gay.
    I sing unto the common, bleak and bare,
        My gladsome tune;
    I sweeten and refresh the languid air
        In droughty June."

"Not to myself alone:"
O man, forget not — thou, earth's honored priest.
Its tongue, its soul, its life, its pulse, its heart —
In earth's great chorus to sustain thy part!
Chiefest of guests at love's ungrudging feast,
    Play not the niggard; spurn thy native clod,
        And self disown.
    Live to thy neighbor; live unto thy God;
        Not to thyself alone!

                              J. RUSSELL WEBB.

18. THE MIGHTY WORD "NO."

THE most tremendous word in the English language is the short yet mighty word, "No." It has been the pivot on which innumerable destinies have turned for this world and the next. Spoken at the right moment, it has saved multitudes from disgrace, from ruin. The splendid career of Joseph turned on the prompt NO spoken at the very nick of time.

Nehemiah's simple, manly statement is, "So do not I, because of the fear of God." Nobly said. We wish some young man would write those sharp ringing words in his note-book, and determine to make the same answer whenever he is tempted to do a selfish or wicked act. Daniel might easily have said to himself, Oh, everybody about the Court here drinks wine and lives high on the king's meat. I do not want to be thought queer or puritanical." He dared to be singular. "So did not I," was the motto of this sturdy young teetotaler. If he had yielded to the current of temptation, and drifted with it, we never should have heard of such a man as Daniel.

All the people who make a marked success in life, and who achieve any good work for God, are the people who are not ashamed to be thought singular. The man who runs with the crowd counts for nothing. It is when he turns about and faces the multitude who are rushing on to do evil that he commands every eye. Then, by a bold protest, he may put a thousand to flight. Every young man must come out and be separate from sinners, if they wish to save their characters and their souls. The downward pull of sin is tremendous. To be able firmly to say, "Yet will not I," requires the grace from above in the heart. There is a subtle pull also in the drift of fashion and usage which carries away every one who is not established on a Bible conscience. Three fourths of all the persons who are drowned on the seashore are swept out by the undertow. This is the secret influence which takes hold of so many church-members and carries them off into extravagant living, into sinful amusements, and all manner of worldly conformities. The bottom of the great deep is strewed with backsliders. Every true Christian is bound to be a "non-conformist."

I would press the truth home upon every young man. Your salvation depends upon your ability to say NO.

The messmates of Captain Hedley Vicars sneered at him as a Methodist and a fanatic. A British soldier once told me that Vicars was a spiritual power in his regiment. We had just such Christian soldiers in our army during the war. In every school the difference is clearly marked between the boy who has moral pluck and the boy who is mere pulp. The one knows how to say, NO! The other is so afraid of being thought " verdant " that he soon kills everything pure and fresh and manly in his character, and dries up into a premature hardness of heart. I well remember the pressure brought to bear in college upon every young man to join in a wine dinner or to take a hand in some contraband amusement. Some timber got well seasoned. Some of the other got well-rotted, through sensuality and vice. The Nehemiahs at college have been Nehemiahs ever since. The boy was father of the man.

The only motive that could hold back the brave " nonconformist " at Jerusalem was a godly conscience. " So did not I, because of the fear of God." This ever fresh principle held him firm when temptation struck him as the undercurrents strike against the keel. Christ must be to you a pattern, and He must be to you a power. It is not enough to believe in Jesus. You must add to your faith "courage." Then, with Christ as your model, and Christ as your Inward Might, you will always be able to face down temptation with the iron answer, " So will not I."

THEODORE D. CUYLER, *Feb.* 17, 1894.

A PREVENTIVE "NO."

ENTER not into the path of the wicked, and go not in the way of evil men.

Avoid it, pass not by it, turn from it, and pass away.

Proverbs of Solomon.

19. BETTER THAN GOLD.

Better than grandeur, better than gold,
Than rank or titles a hundredfold,
Is a healthful body, a mind at ease,
And simple pleasures that always please;
A heart that can feel for a neighbor's woe,
And share in his joy with a friendly glow,
With sympathies large enough to infold
All men as brothers, is better than gold.

Better than gold is the sweet repose
Of the sons of toil when their labors close;
Better than gold is the poor man's sleep,
And the balm that drops on his slumbers deep;
Better than gold is a thinking mind,
That in realms of thought and books can find
A treasure surpassing Australian ore,
And live with the great and good of yore.

Better than gold is a peaceful home,
Where all the fireside charities come, —
The shrine of love, the haven of life,
Hallowed by mother or sister or wife;
However humble that home may be,
Or tried with sorrows by Heaven's decree,
The blessings that never were bought or sold,
And centre there, are better than gold.

Better than gold in affliction's hour
Is the balm of love with its soothing power;
Better than gold on a dying bed
Is the hand that pillows the sinking head.
When the pride and glory of life decay,
And earth and its vanities fade away,
The prostrate sufferer needs not to be told
That trust in Heaven is better than gold.

Alexander Smart.

20. WISDOM AND WEALTH.

I ONCE saw a poor fellow, keen and clever,
  Witty and wise: he paid a man a visit,
And no one noticed him, and no one ever
    Gave him a welcome. "Strange!" cried I. "Whence
      is it?"
      He walked on this side, then on that,
      He tried to introduce a social chat.
      Now here, now there, in vain he tried;
      Some formally and freezingly replied,
And some by their silence said, "Better stay at home!"

  A rich man burst the door, —
  As Crœsus rich, I'm sure.
He could not pride himself upon his wit;
And, as for wisdom, he had none of it.
  He had what some think better, — he had wealth.
What a confusion! All stand up erect;
  These crowd around to ask him of his health;
These bow in eager duty and respect;
    And these arrange a sofa or a chair,
    And these conduct him there.
    "Allow me, Sir, the honor!" then a bow
    Down to the earth. Is't possible to show
Meet gratitude for such kind condescension?

  The poor man hung his head,
  And to himself he said,
"This is indeed beyond my comprehension!"
  Then looking round,
  One friendly face he found,
And said, "Pray tell me, why is wealth preferred
  To wisdom?" "That's a silly question, friend,"
Replied the other. "Have you never heard
    A man may lend his store
    Of gold or silver ore,
  But wisdom none can borrow, none can lend?"

                      KHNEMNITZER (Ivan Ivanovich).

21. THE WORLD WOULD BE BETTER FOR IT.

If men cared less for wealth and fame,
    And less for battle-fields and glory;
If writ in human hearts a name
    Seemed better than in song or story;
If men, instead of nursing pride,
    Would learn to hate it and abhor it;
If more relied on love to guide,
    The world would be the better for it.

If men dealt less in stocks and lands,
    And more in bonds and deeds fraternal;
If Love's work had more willing hands,
    To link the world to the supernal;
If men stored up Love's oil and wine,
    And on bruised human hearts would pour it;
If "yours" and "mine" would once combine,
    The world would be the better for it.

If more would act the play of life,
    And fewer spoil it in rehearsal;
If Bigotry would sheathe its knife
    Till Good became more universal;
If Custom, gray with ages grown,
    Had fewer blind men to adore it;
If talent shone for truth alone,
    The world would be the better for it.

If men were wise in little things,
    Affecting less in all their dealings;
If hearts had fewer rusted strings
    To isolate their kindly feelings;

If men, when Wrong beats down the Right,
  Would strike together and restore it;
If Right made Might in every fight,
  The world would be the better for it.

H. M. COBB.

---

22. THE WORTH OF FAME.

Oh, who shall lightly say that Fame
Is nothing but an empty name,
While in that sound there is a charm
The nerves to brace, the heart to warm,
  As, thinking of the mighty dead,
The young from slothful couch shall start,
  And vow, with lifted hands outspread,
Like them to act a noble part?

Oh, who shall lightly say that Fame
Is nothing but an empty name,
  When but for those, our mighty dead,
All ages past a blank would be,
  Sunk in oblivion's murky bed,
A desert bare, a shipless sea?
  They are the distant objects seen,
  The lofty marks of what has been.

Oh, who shall lightly say that Fame
Is nothing but an empty name,
  When memory of the mighty dead,
To earth-worn pilgrim's wistful eye,
  The brightest rays of cheering shed
That point to immortality?

JOANNA BAILLIE.

23. THE THREE W'S,—WORK, WATCH, WAIT.

On a stormy night in New York, when the rivers were filled with floating ice, and a heavy sea-fog settled over the city, the steam-whistles, fog-horns, and bells resounded from all directions. The news-boys assembled in their hall, it being Sunday, for singing, and to listen to words of cheer and counsel. Three W's on their blackboard were thus explained.

Watch! boys, watch! The signal-lights are flashing,
To guide your boat through life to harbor sure;
Fear not the storms you meet, nor waves high dashing,
Nor rocks you press so near, while you endure;
But gird your belt, and steer your craft along,
By beacon light and faithful compass led;
The voyage o'er, you'll rest in peace at last,
On waters calm, with stormless skies o'erhead.
Watch! boys, watch!

Work! boys, work! The idler's task is never done:
The faithful rest when he has just begun.
Your hearts will bound with honest pride
As o'er the sea of life you safely glide,
If duty be your law, and work be fitly done,
Your God your guide, your hope, His spotless Son.
Work! boys, work!

Wait! boys, wait! Be sure you're right, then sail ahead;
Impatient zeal to victory never led.
With courage firm, and temper ever sweet,
With cheerful zest your every task to meet;
With kindness pure, for all who toil with you,
As good as brave, and only brave as true,—
Then shall you bless the world, and, by it blessed,
Depart from earth, and with the ransomed rest.
Wait! boys, wait!

Watch, work, and wait, boys! but waiting, watch and work!
There's lots of fun ahead, for all you boys,
Who, gathered in this cheerful hall, to-night,
Resolve to face the storms and ills of life,
With faith in God; and fearing ill to do, —
But that alone, — the right to still pursue.
Yes! watch, work, and wait, boys! beginning now;
And waiting, watch and work!

HENRY B. CARRINGTON.

24. HOW TO HAVE JUST WHAT WE LIKE.

Hard by a poet's attic lived a chemist,
  Or alchemist, who had a mighty
    Faith in the "Elixir Vitæ;"
And though unflattered by the dimmest
Glimpses of success, kept credulously groping
  And grubbing in his dark vocation;
    Stupidly hoping
To find the art of changing metals,
And so coin guineas from his pots and kettles,
  By mystery of "transmutation."

Our starving poet took occasion
  To seek this conjurer's abode;
    Not with encomiastic ode
Or laudatory dedication;
  But with an offer to impart;
    For twenty pounds, the secret art
Which should procure without the pain
  Of metals, chemistry, and fire,
What he so long had sought in vain,
  And gratify his heart's desire.

The money paid, poor bard was hurried
  To the philosopher's sanctorum,
Who, as it were, sublimed and flurried
  Out of his chemical decorum,
Crowed, capered, giggled, seemed to spurn his
Crucibles, retort, and furnace,
  And cried, as he secured the door,
And carefully put to the shutter,
  "Now, now, the secret, I implore!
For Heaven's sake, speak, discover, utter!"

With grave and solemn air the poet
Cried, "List, oh, list! for thus I show it;
  Let this plain truth those ingrates strike,
Who still, though blessed, new blessings crave:
  That we may all have what we like,
Simply by liking what we have!"

HORACE SMITH.

---

25. WHAT MIGHT BE DONE.

From Swett's "Common School Readings."

WHAT might be done if men were wise, —
What glorious deeds, my erring brother,
  Would they unite
  In love and right,
And cease the scorn of one another!

Oppression's heart might be imbued
With purest drops of loving kindness,
  And knowledge pour,
  From shore to shore,
Light on the eyes of mental blindness.

All slavery, warfare, lies, and wrongs,
All vice and crime might die together;
  All wine and corn,
  To each man born,
Be free as warmth in summer weather.

The meanest wretch that ever trod,
The deepest sunk in guilt and sorrow,
  Might stand erect
  In self-respect,
And share the teeming world to-morrow.

What might be done? This might be done,
And more than this, my suffering brother, —
  More than the tongue
  E'er said or sung,
If men were wise, and loved each other.

Anon.

---

26. HOW WE TAKE IT.

The world is quite as good a world
  As mortal man could make it;
If bad is tinctured with the good,
  Like honest men we take it.
To pine o'er evil here, and die,
  Is not a wise endeavor;
But we should seek a cure for wrong,
  And stand by right forever.

This world is not a place for man
  To triumph o'er the lowly,
Nor is it quite the wisest plan
  To count all things as holy;

For though we act a manly part
    And do good deeds sincerely,
How prone to err we mortals are, —
    E'en when life's sun shines clearly.

This world is fair to those who seek
    To dwell in peace and gladness,
Though oft the eyes are dim with tears,
    The heart bowed down with sadness.
Grief hath a brief abiding place,
    Where charms of earth are given,
And those who dwell in virtue's ways,
    Will find it next to heaven.

The world is what we make it, friends,
    A home of joy and gladness;
Or, if we turn from sunshine bright,
    A place of gloom and sadness.
No matter what our aim may be,
    True worth will bring us pleasure;
And if we live and act like men,
    Our bliss no words can measure.

The world is quite as good a world
    As man in sin can make it.
To help each other is our creed,
    Whate'er betides, we take it;
For when the night has passed away,
    The sun of morn is given,
To show us that each cross will bring
    Us one day nearer heaven.
THEODORE D. C. MILLER, M. D.

HOW TO TAKE IT.

PATIENCE and time do more than strength and passion.
RACINE.

27. AS THY DAY THY STRENGTH SHALL BE.

There are stepping-stones in the deepest waters
   That firmly meet the tides of human life;
And havens safe from every storm that gathers;
   And issues out of every human strife.

There is no cloud that sunshine does not follow,
   Nor pain without its solace in the end;
There is no day but that the coming morrow
   Will bring some balm, the passing ills to mend.

There are no ties so precious in the binding
   That threatened parting does not endear them,
Nor offerings of good that in the giving
   Return no mercies which they fitly emblem.

Ah, there are no hopes with full fruition here,
   Nor fears that compass half their fancied ills;
And there is no mortal scheme from doubting clear,
   Nor earthly joy that e'er the spirit fills.

But onward, upward, to cheer the tiresome way,
   There beams perennial Light above the grave;
And solace promised, a joy without alloy,
   To prove that trials here but bless and save.

From the "New York Churchman." (H. B. C.)

ALL-SUFFICIENT STRENGTH.

He who bridles the fury of the billows, knows how to put a stop to all the secret plans of the wicked.

Racine.

28. IF I WERE A VOICE.

If I were a voice, a persuasive voice,
   That could travel the wide world through,
I would fly on the beams of the morning light,
And speak to men with a gentle might,
   And tell them to be true.
I'd fly, I'd fly o'er land and sea,
Wherever a human heart might be,
Telling a tale, or singing a song,
In praise of the right, in blame of the wrong.

If I were a voice, a consoling voice,
   I'd fly on the wings of air;
The homes of sorrow and guilt I'd seek,
And calm and truthful words I'd speak,
   To save them from despair.
I'd fly, I'd fly o'er the crowded town,
And drop like the happy sunlight down
Into the hearts of suffering men,
And teach them to rejoice again.

If I were a voice, a pervading voice,
   I'd seek the kings of earth;
I'd find them alone on their beds at night,
And whisper words that should guide them right, —
   Lessons of priceless worth.
I'd fly more swift than the swiftest bird,
And tell them things they never heard, —
Truths which the ages for aye, repeat,
Unknown to the statesmen at their feet.

If I were a voice, an immortal voice,
   I'd speak in the people's ear;
And whenever they shouted "Liberty!"
Without deserving to be free,
   I'd make their error clear.

I'd fly, I'd fly on the wings of day,
Rebuking wrong on my world-wide way,
And making all the earth rejoice, —
If I were a voice, an immortal voice.

CHARLES MACKAY.

---

29. LOOK NOT UPON THE WINE.

Look not upon the wine when it is red within the cup!
Stay not for pleasure when she fills her tempting beaker up!
    Though clear its depths, and rich its glow,
    A spell of madness lurks below.

They say 't is pleasant on the lip, and merry on the brain;
They say it stirs the sluggish blood, and dulls the tooth of pain;
    Ay! but within its glowing deeps
    A stinging serpent, unseen, sleeps.

Its rosy lights will turn to fire, its coolness change to thirst;
And, by its mirth, within the brain a sleepless worm is nursed;
    There's not a bubble at the brim
    That does not carry food to him.

Then dash the brimming cup aside, and spill its purple wine;
Take not its madness to thy lip; let not its curse be thine.
    'T is red and rich, — but grief and woe
    Are in those rosy depths below.

NATHANIEL PARKER WILLIS.

30. THE ALCOHOLIC AND THE TOBACCO HABIT.

Written at Portland Maine, April 8, 1894, for "Beacon Lights of Patriotism," — "hoping these few lines may be useful to young people," — by General Neal Dow, immediately after his ninetieth birthday anniversary.

For many years it has been a matter of wonder to me that so little care is taken by parents and teachers to inform children and young people, and that, thoroughly, of the danger which invariably threatens all persons who contract the alcoholic and tobacco habits.

But very little, if anything was said about this when I was a boy, but, somehow, I escaped that great danger, while many, if not most of my playfellows and schoolmates, fell victims to those habits, and died from the effects, many years ago. My parents, and all my ancestors, both maternal and paternal, were Friends; and it is an important part of the discipline of those excellent people, so to live that their personal influence shall always be for the right, and never for the wrong. It is in that way, perhaps, that I imbibed the conviction, very early in life, that the use of intoxicating drinks of any kind, and of tobacco, as well, was always dangerous, and safe — never.

Young people cannot know much about the world, nor about men; and thus they are led to accept habits, manners, and customs as right and proper, because supported by the example and practice of very respectable people. That, surely, is a very dangerous rule to follow, because there are always a great many people who are called respectable, and yet it would be very perilous for young persons to follow their example and habits. No one was ever injured in health or morals by abstinence from tobacco and strong drink, while millions have been ruined by indulgence in both, or either of them.

Neal Dow.

PART X.

AMERICAN INDEPENDENCE CONSUMMATED.

---

1. PRESIDENT LINCOLN'S ADDRESS AT GETTYSBURG, November 19, 1864.

Fourscore and seven years ago, our Fathers brought forth upon this continent a new Nation, conceived in Liberty and dedicated to the proposition that all men were created equal. Now we are engaged in a great Civil War, testing whether that Nation, or any nation so conceived and so dedicated, can long endure. We are met on a great battle-field of the war. We are met to dedicate a portion of it as the final resting-place of those who have given their lives that that Nation might live.

It is altogether fitting and proper that we should do this; but, in a larger sense, we cannot dedicate, we cannot consecrate, we cannot hallow this ground. The brave men, living and dead, who struggled here have consecrated it far above our power to add or detract. The world will very little note, nor long remember, what we say here; but it can never forget what they did here.

It is for us, the living, rather, to be dedicated here to the unfinished work that they have thus far so nobly carried on. It is rather for us to be here dedicated to the great task remaining before us; that from these honored dead we take increased devotion to that cause for which they here gave the last full measure of devotion; that we here highly resolve that these dead shall not have died in vain, — that the Nation shall, under God, have a new birth of Freedom, and that government of the people, by the people, for the people, shall not perish from the earth.

---

2. THE PATRIOT DEAD.

Breathe balmy airs, ye fragrant flowers,
    O'er every silent sleeper's head;
Ye crystal dews and summer showers,
    Dress in fresh green each lowly bed.

Strew loving offerings o'er the brave,
    Their country's joy, their country's pride;
For us their precious lives they gave,
    For freedom's sacred cause they bled.

Each cherished name its place shall hold,
    Like stars that gem the azure sky;
Their deeds, on history's page enrolled,
    Are sealed for immortality.

Long, where on glory's fields they fell,
    May Freedom's spotless banner wave,
And fragrant tributes grateful tell
    Where live the free, where sleep the brave.

Samuel Francis Smith.

3. THE GREAT QUESTION SETTLED.

From Address of Hon. George W. Curtis, at Gettysburg, July 3, 1888.

The great question is settled. Upon this field, consecrated by American valor, we meet to consecrate ourselves to American Union. In this hallowed ground lie buried not only brave soldiers of the blue and the gray, but the passions of war, the jealousies of sections, and the bitter root of all our national differences,—human slavery. Other questions, indeed, remain which will sternly try our patriotism and our wisdom; but they will be appealed to the ordeal of battle no longer. They will be settled in those peaceful, popular, and parliamentary contentions which befit a patriotic and intelligent Republican people. Even the Civil War has but quickened and deepened our prosperous activities. Those mighty armies of the blue and the gray, marshalled for the warfare of a generation, if such had been decreed, swiftly and noiselessly disappeared; and all that military energy and discipline and skill, streaming into a thousand industries, are as beneficent in peace as they were terrible in war.

Can we wrest from the angel of this hour any blessing so priceless as the common resolution that we shall not have come to this consecrated spot only to declare our joy and gratitude, nor only to cherish proud and tender memories, but also to pledge ourselves to Union, in its sublimest significance? Then, indeed, in the field of Gettysburg as we now behold it, the blue and the gray blending in happy harmony, like the mingling hues of the summer landscape, we may see the radiant symbol of the triumphant America of our pride, our hope, and our joy!

4. GETTYSBURG.

A MECCA FOR THE BLUE AND GRAY.

From Address of General John B. Gordon, Governor of Georgia, July 3, 1888.

Of all the martial virtues, the one which is perhaps most characteristic of the truly brave is the virtue of magnanimity. That sentiment, immortalized by Scott in his musical and martial verse, will associate for all time the name of Scotland's king with those of the great spirits of the past. How grand the exhibitions of the same generous impulses that characterize this memorable battle-field! My fellow-countrymen of the North, if I may be permitted to speak for those whom I represent, let me assure you that in the profoundest depths of their nature, they reciprocate that generosity with all the manliness and sincerity of which they are capable. In token of that sincerity they join in consecrating, for annual patriotic pilgrimage, these historic heights, which drank such copious draughts of American blood, poured so freely in discharge of duty, as each conceived it, — a Mecca for the North, which so grandly defended, a Mecca for the South, which so bravely and persistently stormed it. We join you in setting apart this land as an enduring monument of peace, brotherhood, and perpetual union. I repeat the thought with emphasis, with singleness of heart and of purpose, in the name of a common country, and of universal liberty; and by the blood of our fallen brothers, we unite in the solemn consecration of these hallowed hills, as a holy, eternal pledge of fidelity to the life, freedom, and unity of this cherished Republic.

5. NO CONFLICT NOW.

From Address of General CHARLES DEVENS, at the Bunker Hill celebration, June 17, 1875, Charlestown, Mass.

THE conflict is over! Day by day the material evidences of war fade from sight; the bastions sink to the level of the ground which surrounded them; scarp and counterscarp meet in the ditch which divided them. So let them pass away, forever!

To-day it is the highest duty of all, no matter on what side they were, but, above all, of those who have struggled for the preservation of the Union, to strive that it become one of generous confidence, in which all the States shall, as of old, stand shoulder to shoulder, if need be, against the world in arms. Towards those with whom we were lately in conflict, and who recognize that the results are to be kept inviolate, there should be no feeling of resentment or bitterness. They join with us in the wish to make of this regenerated Union a power grander and more august than the founders ever dared to hope. All true men are with the South in demanding for her, peace, order, good and honest government, and encouraging her in the work of rebuilding all that has been made desolate. We need not doubt the issue. With the fire of her ancient courage, she will gird herself up to the emergencies of her new situation. Standing always in generous remembrance of every section of the Union, neither now nor hereafter will we distinguish between States or sections, in our anxiety for the glory and happiness of all. Together will we utter our solemn aspiration, in the spirit of the motto of the city which now encloses within its limits the battle-field, and town for which the battle was fought: "As God was to our fathers, so may He be to us."

6. SEPARATE AS BILLOWS, BUT ONE AS THE SEA.

From Address by Senator ALEXANDER STEPHENS, at Washington, upon the unveiling of Carpenter's picture representing President Lincoln signing the Emancipation Proclamation.

BEFORE the upturning of Southern society by the Reconstruction Acts, the white people there came to the conclusion that their domestic institution known as slavery had better be abolished. During the conflict of arms, I frequently almost despaired of the liberties of our country, both North and South. When secession was resorted to as a remedy, I went with my State, holding it my duty to do so, but believing all the time, that, if successful, when the passions of the hour and of the day were over, the great law which produced the Union at first, "mutual interest and reciprocal advantage," would reassert itself, and that at no distant day a new Union of some sort would again be formed.

And now, after the severe chastisement of war, if the general sense of the whole country shall come back to the acknowledgment of the original assumption that it is for the best interests of all the States to be so united, as I trust it will, the States being "separate as billows, but one as the sea," this thorn in the body politic being now removed, I can perceive no reason why, under such a restoration, we, as a whole, may not enter upon a new career, exciting increased wonder in the Old World by the peaceful and harmonious workings of our matchless system of American federal institutions of self-government.

All this is possible, if the hearts of the people be right. It is my earnest wish to see it. Fondly would I gaze upon such a picture of the future. With what rapture may we not suppose the spirits of our fathers would hail its opening scenes, from their mansions above! But if instead of this, sectional passions shall continue to bear sway, if prejudice shall rule the hour, if a conflict of classes, of capital and labor, or of the races, shall arise, or the embers of the late war be kept glowing until with new fuel they shall flame up again, then, hereafter, by some bard it may be sung, —

> 'The star of Hope shone brightest in the West,
> The hope of Liberty, the last, the best;
> It, too, has set upon her darkened shore,
> And Hope and Freedom light up Earth no more."

7. THE NINETEENTH CENTURY ENDS SLAVERY.

From Address of Justice Lamar, at dedication of monument to John C. Calhoun, Charleston, S. C., April 26, 1888.

SLAVERY is dead, — buried in a grave that never gives up its dead! Let it rest! Every benefit which slavery conferred upon those subject to it, all the ameliorating and humanizing tendencies it introduced into the life of the African, all the elevating agencies which lifted him higher in the scale of rational moral being, were the elements of the future and inevitable destruction of the system. The mistake that was made by the Southern defenders of slavery, was in regarding it as a permanent form of society, instead of a process of emergence and transition from barbarism to freedom. If at this day, the North or the American Union were to propose to re-establish the institution, it would be impracticable. The South could not, and would not, accept it as a boon. The existing industrial relations of capital and labor, had there been no secession, no war, would of themselves have brought about the death of slavery.

8. AGAIN BRETHREN AND EQUALS.

From Address at dedication of Soldiers' Monument at Manchester, N. H., by General James W. Patterson.

The true grandeur of passing historic events is not seen till the noise and obstruction of the fictitious and perishable are forgotten. So the relative importance of our late war is not realized.

The day is not far distant when the South, equally with the North, will perceive that they builded better than they knew. The sons of the South are of noble stock. We respect the honesty of their convictions, and the virility with which they defended them. We would seek the cordial and conciliatory course of kindred, and would let the "dead past bury its dead." As an exhibition of physical prowess, the contention was magnificent! Both armies fought for their convictions with a relentlessness of valor unsurpassed. The campaigns of the war and the subsequent financial achievements, have revealed to the world a strength and integrity worthy of the ancient mould of men. The blood of the North and the South has mingled in a conflict of political principles. May it nourish no root of bitterness; but may there henceforth be a union of affection and labors to advance and perpetuate the dignity and grandeur of a common country! I protest, in the name of the dead and the peace of posterity, that the issues adjudicated in honorable warfare shall not be raised again, like unquiet ghosts, into the arena of politics, to disturb the peace and prosperity of the nation.

We honor the valor and manliness of the South, and will respect her rights. We demand the same, and no more. On that platform we can stand together, and against the world.

9. OUR BANNER UNRENT: ITS STARS UNOBSCURED.

From Address of General LAWRENCE S. ROSS, Governor of Texas, July 4, 1887, at reunion of Hood's veterans.

WE see here to-day a free and independent mingling of men of every section of our broad domain, all prejudices of the past forgotten; and while our State has been fortunate in acquiring thousands of those who fought against us, and who are an honor both to the States which gave them birth, and ours which they have made their home, — it matters not whence they come, they can exult in the reflection that our country is the same, and they find floating here the same banner that waved above them there, with its "folds unrent" and its bright stars unobscured; and in its defence, if need be, the swords of these old Confederates, so recently sheathed, would leap forth with equal alacrity with those of the North. The fame of such men as Farragut, Stanley, Hood, and Lee, and the hundreds of private soldiers who were the true heroes of the war, belongs to no time or section, but is the common property of mankind. They were all cast in the same grand mould of self-sacrificing patriotism, and I intend to teach my children to revere their names as long as the love of country is respected as a noble sentiment in the human breast.

It is a remarkable fact that those who bore the brunt of the battle were the first to forget old animosities and consign to oblivion obsolete issues. And I emphasize the declaration that, in most instances, those whose hatred has remained implacable through all these years of peace, are men who held high carnival in the rear, and, after all danger had passed, emerged from their hiding-places, filled with ferocious zeal and courage, blind to every principle of wise statesmanship, to make amends for lack of deeds of valor by pressing to their lips the sweet cup of revenge, for whose intoxicating contents our country has already paid a price that would have purchased the goblet of the Egyptian queen.

---

10. BELLIGERENT NON-COMBATANTS.

From Decoration Day Address of General W. T. Sherman, at New York, May 30, 1878.

It is related of General Scott that when asked, in 1861, the probable length of the then Civil War, he answered, "The conflict of arms will last five years; but will be followed by twenty years of angry strife, by the "belligerent non-combatants."

Wars are usually made by civilians, bold and defiant in the forum; but when the storm comes, they go below, and leave their innocent comrades to catch the "peltings of the pitiless storm." Of the half-million of brave fellows whose graves have this day been strewn with flowers, not one in a thousand had the remotest connection with the causes of the war which led to their untimely death. I now hope and beg that all good men, North and South, will unite in real earnest to repair the mistakes and wrongs of the past; will persevere in the common effort to make this great land of ours to blossom as the garden of Eden!

I invoke all to heed well the lessons of this "Decoration Day," to weave each year a fresh garland for the grave of some beloved comrade or hero, and to rebuke any and all who talk of civil war, save as the "last dread tribunal of kings and peoples."

11. IMMORTAL MEMORIES.

From Address, and contributed by General GEORGE A. SHERIDAN.

WAR came! It was not the result of men's ambition, North or South. It was the clash of two civilizations, so antagonistic as to make impossible harmony of action or peaceful growth, side by side. One or the other must yield.

The land that had known but peace echoed to the tread of armed men. Up from the land of the orange and the myrtle came mighty hosts, harnessed for conflict, chanting songs of battle, eager for the fight, sweeping with as fiery courage and as dauntless bearing to the onset as of old the men out of whose loins they sprung charged Saracenic hosts or closed in deadly grapple with the knightly sons of France. From the land of the fir and the pine, down from its mountains and out from its valleys, glittering with steel and bright with countless banners, steady and strong, the men of the North marched to the conflict.

A hush as of death filled the land as the mighty hosts confronted each other. An instant,—and the heavens seemed rent asunder, and the solid globe to reel. North and South had met in shock of war! Blood deluged the land; the ear of pity deaf; the springs of love dried up; the throb of mighty guns; the gleam of myriad blades; the savage shouts of men grappling each other in relentness clutch; Death, pale, pitiless, tireless thrusting his awful sickle into harvest fields where the grain was human life; bells from every steeple in the land tolling out their solemn notes of sorrow for the slain; fathers, mothers, wives, and little ones smiting their palms together in agony, as they looked upon the features of their loved ones marbled in eternal sleep.

At last, the bells of liberty throughout the land rang out a joyous peal of welcome, and guns from fortress, field, and citadel proclaimed that America remained one and indivisible. Over all the land a single flag threw out its folds, index of a re-united people. Those who fought against us are now of us, and with us reverently acknowledge that above all the desires of men move the majestic laws of God, evolving alike from victory or defeat of nations, substantial good for all his children.

12. BENEFITS OF THE CIVIL WAR.

From Address of Hon. CHARLES M. BUSBEE, at Raleigh, N. C., Memorial Day, 1883.

THE war was not without its benefits to us, and even now we can discern them. It was inevitable! Sooner or later it had to come! It could no more have been avoided than you could have stayed the movements of the tides. It ought not to have been unavoidable, to be sure, just as man ought not to become diseased, but it was. So long as society remains irrational, so long as human governments are imperfect, will the sword be the final arbiter. It is a survival of the savage nature that the refining hand of time has never obliterated, a remnant of the ages long ago.

But the war, with all its dark catalogue of horrors, brought in its train many compensatory blessings. It developed the manly virtues of our people, their inherent fortitude and self-sacrifice. It is something to have illustrated the valor of a people, to have carried a nation's flag without dishonor through a hundred battles, to have set an example to coming ages of what unselfish heroism can accomplish, to have immortalized a State, to have accepted defeat with fortitude; and this we did.

Again, the war built upon more certain and enduring foundations the government of the United States, and it stands upon a broader and stronger basis than before. Were we honest in our convictions? Yes. Were we sincere in our allegiance to the Confederate States? Yes. Does this affect our loyalty to the government of the United States? Not at all. Loyalty, free and honest loyalty to the government as it is, is not repugnant to a past loyalty to that adolescent nation whose star shone with abnormal brilliancy for a few short years, and then vanished into the blackness of eternal night. The men who followed the "Stars and Bars" from Bethel to Appomattox with ceaseless devotion; defended them amid the whirlpool of blood that surged and eddied around Malvern Hill; carried them up the crimson slopes of Gettysburg; followed them into the jaws of death at Spottsylvania; shielded them like a tiger at bay over its young behind the earthworks of Petersburg, furled them at Appomattox forever and forever. The duties, the obligations, the allegiance of a citizen are not inconsistent with the sympathies and memories of a soldier; and if those dead heroes whose virtues and valor we to-day commemorate, could defile before us, in the glory of yon setting sun, in serried ghostly phalanx, they would declare the gospel of loyalty and peace and reconciliation.

And the day is not far distant, if it be not already come, when the courage and heroic deeds of both sides will be recognized as the common property of us all, the common heritage and common glory of a prosperous and patriotic people.

13. OUR HEROES.

The heart swells with unwonted emotion when we remember our sons and brothers, whose constant valor has sustained on the field the cause of our country, of civilization, and liberty. On the ocean, on the rivers, on the land, on the heights where they thundered down from the clouds of Lookout Mountain the defiance of the skies, they have graven with their swords a record imperishable.

The Muse herself demands the lapse of silent years to soften, by the influence of time, her too keen and poignant realization of the scenes of War, — the pathos, the heroism, the fierce joy, the grief of battle. But during the ages to come she will brood over their memory. Into the hearts of her consecrated priests she will breathe the inspirations of lofty and undying beauty, sublimity, and truth, in all the glowing forms of speech, of literature, and plastic art. By the homely traditions of the fireside, by the headstones in the church-yard consecrated to those whose forms repose far off in rude graves, or sleep beneath the sea, embalmed in the memories of succeeding generations of parents and children, the heroic dead will live on in immortal youth.

By their names, their character, their service, their fate, their glory, they cannot fail: —

"They never fail who die
  In a great cause; the block may soak their gore;
  Their heads may sodden in the sun, their limbs
  Be strung to city gates and castle wall;
  But still their spirit walks abroad.
                        "Though years
  Elapse, and others share as dark a doom,
  They but augment the deep and sweeping thoughts
  Which overpower all others, and conduct
  The world at last to Freedom."

The bell which rang out the Declaration of Independence has found at last a voice articulate, to "proclaim liberty throughout all the land unto all the inhabitants thereof." It has been heard across oceans, and has modified the sentiments of cabinets and kings. The people of the Old World have heard it, and their hearts stop to catch the last whisper of its echoes. The poor slave has heard it; and with bounding joy, tempered by the mystery of religion, he worships and adores. The waiting continent has heard it, and already foresees the fulfilled prophecy, when she will sit "redeemed, regenerated, and disenthralled by the irresistible Genius of Universal Emancipation."

JOHN ALBION ANDREW.

14. THE EVE OF DECORATION DAY.

On the afternoon before Decoration Day, about thirty young girls were seated on the carpet of the parlor of one of the patriotic daughters of the Revolution, working flowers into bouquets, and spontaneously singing snatches of the National Hymn, "My Country, 't is of Thee;" and this is the recognition of the spirit of their work. — S. F. SMITH.

SWEET in the innocence of youth,
  Born of the brave and free,
They wove fair garlands, while they sang,
  "My Country, 't is of thee."
How every bosom swelled with joy,
  And thrilled with grateful pride,
As fond the whispering cadence breathed,
  "Land where my fathers died!"

Fair flowers in sweet bouquets they tied, —
  Breaths from the vales and hills;
While childish voices poured the strain,
  "I love thy rocks and rills."

Each face grew radiant with the thought,
  "Land of the noble free;"
Each voice seemed reverent as it trilled,
  "Sweet land of Liberty."

And bud and bloom and leaf they bound,
  And bade the living keep
Unharmed and pure the cherished graves
  Where brave men calmly sleep;
And thus, while infant lips begin
  To lisp "sweet freedom's song,"
Manhood's deep tones, from age to age,
  Shall still "the sound prolong."

I hailed the promise of the scene;
  Gladness was in the strain;
The glorious land is safe while love
  Still swells the fond refrain;
And what shall be our sure defence?
  Who guards our liberty?
Not man, not arms alone; we look,
  "Our fathers' God, to Thee."

---

15. ODE FOR DECORATION DAY.

Flowers for the mourned ones, fresh in their bloom,
Gifts of the grateful, brighten their tomb.
Sing the glad anthems, loved they so well;
Speak of their loyalty, deeds of theirs tell;
Visit each grave with a floral oblation;
Leave, where they slumber, love's sweet decoration!

Tears for the brave ones, fallen in strife,
Liberty's martyrs, giving their life!

Patriot soldiers, loving their land,
Hasting to battle, — heroes so grand!
Honor their memories on History's pages;
Build for them monuments lasting thro' ages!

Dirges for brothers sleeping in death!
Faced they the cannon's sulphurous breath;
Feared not the foemen, never would yield;
Bled for their country, died on the field!
Precious their offering, — let it be cherished;
Gratitude give them, for nobly they perished!

Fame for the true hearts, true to the flag,
Strong for the Union, firm as a crag!
Fireblasts of battle, missiles of lead,
Turned them not backward, laying them dead!
Deeds of such daring with earth's choicest are blended,
Long as the flag waves, so bravely defended!

Garlands unfading give to our braves;
Flowers immortal bloom on their graves!
Veteran warriors, young hearts and bold,
Foremost in conflict, — silent and cold!
Memory keeps and rehearses their story;
Die not their names, star-lighted with glory!

Rest for the martyred, — rest in the grave;
Thunders of battle wake not the brave;
War-drum and shouting, musketry's roar,
Rolling loud o'er them, heeded no more!
Peace that they fought for came to us timely;
Freedom they died for triumphed sublimely.

S. DRYDEN PHELPS.

16. DECORATION DAY.

Sleep, comrades! sleep and rest
   On this field of grounded arms,
Where foes no more molest,
   Nor sentry's shot alarms.

Ye have slept on the ground before,
   And started to your feet
At the cannon's sudden roar,
   Or the drum's redoubling beat.

But in this camp of death
   No sound your slumber breaks;
Here is no fevered breath,
   No wound that bleeds and aches.

All is repose and peace;
   Untrampled lies the sod;
The shouts of battle cease,—
   It is the truce of God.

Rest, comrades! rest and sleep!
   The thoughts of men should be
As sentinels, to keep
   Your rest from dangers free.

Your silent tents of green
   We deck with fragrant flowers;
Yours has the suffering been,
   The memory shall be ours.

                                        Longfellow.

17. ABRAHAM LINCOLN.

Extract from address of Bishop John P. Newman, delivered February 12, 1894.

Human glory is often fickle as the winds, and transient as a summer day; but Abraham Lincoln's place in history is assured. All the symbols of this world's admiration are his. He is embalmed in song; recorded in history; eulogized in panegyric; cast in bronze; sculptured in marble; painted on canvas; enshrined in the hearts of his countrymen; and lives in the memories of mankind. Some men are brilliant in their times, but their words and deeds are of little worth to history; but his mission was as large as his country, vast as humanity, enduring as time. No greater thought can ever enter the human mind than obedience to law and freedom for all. Some men are not honored by their contemporaries, and die neglected. Here is one more honored than any other man while living, more revered when dying, and destined to be loved to the last syllable of recorded time. He has this threefold greatness,—great in life, great in death, great in the history of the world. Lincoln will grow upon the attention and affections of posterity, because he saved the life of the greatest nation, whose ever widening influence is to bless humanity. Measured by this standard, Lincoln shall live in history from age to age.

Great men appear in groups, and in groups they disappear from the vision of the world; but we do not love or hate men in groups. We speak of Gutenberg and his coadjutors, of Washington and his generals, of Lincoln and his cabinet: but when the day of judgment comes, we crown the inventor of printing; we place the laurel on the brow of the father of his country, and the chaplet of renown upon the head of the saviour of the Republic.

Some men are great from the littleness of their surroundings; but he only is great who is great amid greatness. Lincoln had great associates, — Seward, the sagacious diplomatist; Chase, the eminent financier; Stanton, the incomparable Secretary of War; with illustrious senators and soldiers. Neither could take his part nor fill his position. And the same law of the coming and going of great men is true of our own day. In piping times of peace, genius is not aflame, and true greatness is not apparent; but when the crisis comes, then God lifts the curtain from obscurity, and reveals the man for the hour.

Lincoln stands forth on the page of history, unique in his character, and majestic in his individuality. Like Milton's angel, he was an original conception. He was raised up for his times. He was a leader of leaders. By instinct the common heart trusted in him. He was of the people and for the people. He had been poor and laborious; but greatness did not change the tone of his spirit, or lessen the sympathies of his nature. His character was strangely symmetrical. He was temperate, without austerity; brave, without rashness; constant, without obstinacy. He put caution against hope, that it might not be premature; and hope against caution, that it might not yield to dread or danger. His marvellous hopefulness never betrayed him into impracticable measures. His love of justice was only equalled by his delight in compassion. His regard for personal honor was only excelled by love of country. His self-abnegation found its highest expression in the public good. His integrity was never questioned. His honesty was above suspicion. He was more solid than brilliant; his judgment dominated his imagination; his ambition was subject to his modesty; and his love of justice held the mastery over all personal considerations. Not excepting Washington, who inherited wealth and high social position, Lincoln is the fullest representative American in our national annals. He had touched every round in the human ladder. He illustrated the possibilities of our citizenship. We are not ashamed of his humble origin. We are proud of his greatness.

We are to judge men by their surroundings, and measure their greatness by the difficulties which they surmounted. Every age has its heroes, every crisis its master. Lincoln came into power in the largest and most violent political convulsion known to history. In nothing is the sagacity and might of Lincoln's statesmanship more apparent than in his determination to save the Union of these States. This was the objective point of his administration. He denied State Sovereignty as paramount to National Sovereignty. States have their rights and their obligations; and their chief obligation is to remain in the Union. Some political philanthropists clamored for the overthrow of slavery, and advocated the dissolution of the Union rather than live in a country under whose government slavery was tolerated. But Lincoln was a wiser and a better philanthropist than they. He would have the Union, with or without slavery. He preferred it without, and his preference prevailed. How incomparably worse would have been the condition of the slave in a Confederacy with a living slave for its corner stone, than in the Union of the States! Time has vindicated the character of his statesmanship, that to preserve the Union was to save this great nation for human liberty, and thereby advance the emancipated slave to education, thrift, and political equality.

18. DEATH THE PEACEMAKER.

THE BLUE AND THE GRAY.

A WASTE of land, a sodden plain,
    A lurid sunset sky,
With clouds that fled and faded fast
    In ghastly phantasy;
A field upturned by trampling feet,
    A field up-piled with slain,
With horse and rider blent in death
    Upon the battle-plain.

Two soldiers, lying as they fell
    Upon the reddened clay,—
In daytime, foes; at night, in peace,
    Breathing their lives away.
Brave hearts had stirred each manly breast;
    Fate only made them foes;
And lying, dying, side by side,
    A softened feeling rose.

"Our time is short," one faint voice said.
    "To-day we've done our best
On different sides. What matters now?
    To-morrow we're at rest.
Life lies behind. I might not care
    For only my own sake;
But far away are other hearts
    That this day's work will break.

"Among New Hampshire's snowy hills
    There pray for me, to-night,
A woman, and a little girl
    With hair like golden light."

And at the thought broke forth, at last,
    The cry of anguish wild
That would no longer be repressed,—
    "O God! my wife and child!"

"And," said the other dying man,
    "Across the Georgia plain
There watch and wait for me loved ones
    I'll never see again.
A little girl with dark bright eyes
    Each day waits at the door;
The father's step, the father's kiss,
    Will never meet her more.

"To-day we sought each other's lives;
    Death levels all that now,
For soon before God's mercy-seat
    Together shall we bow.
Forgive each other while we may;
    Life's but a weary game;
And right or wrong, the morning sun
    Will find us dead the same."

The dying lips the pardon breathe,
    The dying hands entwine;
The last ray dies, and over all
    The stars from heaven shine;
And the little girl with golden hair,
    And one with dark eyes bright,
On Hampshire's hills and Georgia plain,
    Were fatherless that night.

                              ELLEN H. FLAGG.

19. THE DAWNING FUTURE.

Closing stanza of patriotic poem, "The Patriot South," by the President of Tulane University, Louisiana.

Thus, in the march of time, and long procession
Of coming ages, year on year,
We mark the great Republic's proud career,
Like Philip's phalanx, manifold,
With bucklers linked, one front against aggression,
Till Freedom's perfect vision is enrolled,
And man, with eye unsealed, its glories shall behold.

WILLIAM PRESTON JOHNSON.

PART XI.

SCHOOL-ROOM ECHOES AND HINTS.

1. AMERICAN EDUCATION.

We have been accustomed to regard a free-school system as the chief corner-stone of the Republic, and popular education as the only safe and stable basis for popular liberty. So thought our fathers before us; and the principle may be found interwoven in a thousand forms into the very thread and texture of our political institutions.

Education, civil and religious, — the education of the sanctuary and the school-house, — was, we all know, from the first settlement of the American Colonies, a matter in regard to which all property was held in common, and every man was bound to contribute to the necessities of every other man; as much so as personal protection, public justice, or any other of the more obvious duties of government, or the rights of the governed.

Children should be educated as those by whom the destinies of the nation are one day to be wielded; and free schools should be cherished as places in which those destinies are even now to be woven. It has been recorded as a saying of Mahomet that "the ink of the scholar and the blood of the martyr are equal." But in this we must all agree, that nothing but the ink of the scholar can preserve what the blood of the martyr has purchased.

The experiment of free government is not one which can be tried once for all. Every generation must try it for itself. Our fathers tried it, and were gloriously successful. We are now engaged in the trial; and, thank God, we have not yet failed! But neither our success, nor that of our fathers, can afford anything but example and encouragement to those who are to try it next. As each new generation starts up to the responsibilities of manhood, there is, as it were, a new launch of Liberty, and its voyage begins afresh. The winds and the waves must be propitiated before the shore is left; but this propitiation consists, not in some cruel proceeding, like that prescribed by the heathen oracle to the Grecian fleet, in binding son or daughter upon the pile of sacrifice, but in a process not more certain to call down the blessing of Heaven upon the enterprise, than it is to promote the true happiness and welfare of those upon whom it is performed.

Sons and daughters devoted to education are the only sacrifice which God has prescribed to render the progress of free government safe and certain.

ROBERT CHARLES WINTHROP.

CONTENTMENT.

Not that which men do covet most is best,
  Nor that thing worst which men do most refuse;
But fittest is that all, contented, rest
With that they hold: each hath his fortune in his breast,
  It is the mind that maketh good or ill;
That maketh wretch or happy, rich or poor;
  For some that hath abundance at his will,
Hath not enough, but wants in greatest store;
And other, that hath little, asks no more;
  But in that little is both rich and wise.

EDMUND SPENSER (In "Fairy Queen").

2. THE SCHOOL-TEACHER.

The conqueror moves in a march. He stalks onward with the "pride, pomp, and circumstance" of war,—banners flying, shouts rending the air, guns thundering, and martial music pealing, to drown the shrieks of the wounded and the lamentations for the slain.

Not so the school-teacher. He meditates and purposes in secret the plans which are to bless mankind. He slowly gathers round him those who are to further their execution. He quietly, though firmly, advances in his humble path, laboring steadily, but calmly, till he has opened to the light all the recesses of ignorance, and torn up by the roots all the weeds of vice.

His is a progress not to be compared to anything like a march; but it leads to a far more brilliant triumph, and to laurels far more imperishable than the destroyer of his species, the scourge of the world, ever won. Such men, deserving the glorious title of Teachers of Mankind, I have found laboring conscientiously, though perhaps obscurely, in their blessed vocation, wherever I have gone. Heaven be thanked, their numbers everywhere abound, and are every day increasing!

Their calling is high and lofty. Their fame is the prosperity of nations. Their renown will fill the earth in after ages, in proportion as it sounds not far off in their own times. Each one of these great teachers of the world, possessing his soul in peace, performs his appointed course, awaits in patience the fulfilment of the promises; and, resting from his labors, bequeaths his memory to the generation whom his works have blessed, and sleeps under the humble but not inglorious epitaph commemorating "one in whom mankind lost a friend, and no man got rid of an enemy."

Henry (Lord) Brougham.

3. DESIRABLE OBJECTS OF ATTAINMENT.

Aim at the attainment of clear and accurate habits of thought. A man may think a great deal, and not think clearly; and it is quite possible to mistake muddiness for depth. There are men who appear very thoughtful; but there seems to be neither beginning, nor middle, nor end to what they say. All is a confused jumble. Writing carefully is a good plan for acquiring habits of clear and concerted thought, since a man is more likely to detect the disorder of his thoughts in writing than in talking.

Aim at independence of thought. There are some men who go in leading-strings all their days. They always follow in the path of others, with no good reason for their own opinions. Independence of mind is not presumptuous self-confidence, which is the associate of ignorance; but it is a modest yet firm exercise of judgment upon subjects which the mind understands, — the opposite of that slavish habit which makes one man the mere shadow of another.

Acquire habits of observation. We live in a world of wonders. A thousand objects appeal to a proper use of our eyes and our ears. Books teach much, but that practical knowledge, so useful in the progress of life, that tact in business, so desirable, can only be gained by observation. As a mode of study, it is the cheapest and most convenient of all. Its handmaid is curiosity; and we should never let false pride, lest we should display ignorance, prevent us from asking a question, when it can be answered. The learned John Locke, on being asked how he had contrived to accumulate a mine of knowledge so rich, deep, and extensive, answered that "he attributed what little he knew to the not being ashamed to ask for information, and to the rule he laid down of conversing with all descriptions of men on those topics chiefly that formed their own professions and pursuits."

Cultivate humility. It is the attribute of great and noble minds. Sir Isaac Newton spoke of himself, at the close of life, as "a child who had spent his time in gathering pebbles on the shore, while the ocean remained untraversed;" and Mozart, the great musician, just before he died, said, "Now I begin to see what might be done in music." These ascended to a high elevation on the mountain of knowledge; but this gave them a better idea of the loftiness of the summit. The more we know, the more we shall be convinced of our own ignorance. This is trite enough; but if the great apostles of science and philosophy confessed they knew so little, what ground of boasting can there be for the tyro in their schools? Humility — so beautiful and becoming, so allied to true intellectual greatness — is of itself favorable to mental improvement. It opens the mind to receive instruction with docility, and makes one willing to be taught and corrected. Cultivate humility!

JOHN STOUGHTON.

---

4. SELF-SACRIFICING AMBITION.

WE need a loftier ideal to nerve us to heroic lives. To know and feel our nothingness, without regretting it; to deem fame, riches, personal happiness, to be but shadows, of which human good is the substance; to welcome pain, privation, ignominy, so that the sphere of human knowledge, the empire of knowledge, be thereby extended, — such is the soul's temper which the heroes of the coming age should possess.

When the stateliest monuments of mighty conquerors shall have become shapeless and forgotten ruins, the humble graves of earth's Howards and Frys shall still be freshened by the tears of fondly admiring millions; and the proudest epitaph shall be the simple entreaty, —

"Write me as one who loved his fellowmen."

Say not that I thus condemn and would annihilate ambition. The love of approbation, of esteem, of true glory, is a noble incentive, and should be cherished to the end. But the ambition which points the way to fame over torn limbs and bleeding hearts, which rejoices in the Tartarean smoke of the battle-field and the desolating tramp of the war-horse, — that ambition is worthy only of "archangel ruined." To make one conqueror's reputation, at least one hundred thousand bounding, joyous, sentient beings must be transformed into writhing and hideous fragments; must perish untimely, by deaths of agony and horror, leaving half a million widows and orphans to bewail their loss in destitution and anguish. This is too mighty, too awful a price to be paid for the fame of any hero, from Nimrod to Wellington.

True fame demands no such sacrifice of others. It requires us to be reckless of the outward well-being of but one. It exacts no hecatomb of victims for each triumphant pile; for the more who covet and seek it, the easier and more abundant is the success of all. With souls of celestial temper, each human life might be a triumph which angels would lean from the skies, delighted to witness and admire.

HORACE GREELEY.

SOUL CULTURE.

DELIGHTFUL task! to rear the tender thought,
To teach the young idea how to shoot;
To pour the fresh instruction o'er the mind,
To breathe the enlivening spirit, and to fix
The generous purpose in the glowing breast!

JAMES THOMSON.

5. THE PUBLIC SCHOOL TEACHER IN THE REPUBLIC.

Upon every teacher in the public schools of the United States, whether man or woman, the State has laid a dual responsibility : —

1. A duty of immediate, but relatively of secondary, importance, namely, to teach the children of the people those elementary branches of knowledge which shall fit them for self-support, a useful and an honest life, and thus subserve their material interests; and

2. Far above and beyond this plain and simple function, that grave responsibility, peculiar to the office of the American teacher alone, out of which has been evolved during the present century the institution of the American Free Public School, namely, the imperative duty of preparing the children committed to their care to become not only self-supporting and intelligent citizens, but citizens thoroughly loyal to the Republic : noble types of American citizenship, fitted to be governors of men: sovereigns worthy of their birthright as free men, "distinctly American in character and purpose." This is a duty which calls for far higher qualities and attainments than that which seeks to promote the merely material interests of the pupil. It is a duty which has to do largely with the moral and spiritual nature of the child, which demands the possession of talents and an intellectual training of a high order, the wise exercise of which elevates the work of the teacher to the importance, rank, and dignity of a profession second to no other.

With all knowledge, so far as the first group of duties is concerned, teachers may be eminently disqualified to teach American boys and girls, in the rudest log schoolhouse, situated in the remotest corner of the Union, because they are ignorant of, or fail to appreciate, or do not heartily believe in, or are actually hostile to, American institutions and ideals, and are therefore incapable of putting themselves in touch with the spirit of the republic in which they live. Hence, neither by reason of their great learning, their scholarship, or their piety, alone; nor, indeed, by virtue of all these acquirements combined, are they fitted for the noblest work which the American teacher is called upon to perform, if they lack the one indispensable quality of unswerving loyalty to American principles and republican ideals. The questions, therefore, which the American parent is beginning to ask of teachers, of school committees, of superintendents, of commissioners and boards of education, and which are destined to become more urgent, more searching, and more imperative day by day, as these parents come to understand better the true functions of the public school and its relations to a loyal citizenship, are, to what extent are the teachers in our public schools animated by the noble spirit and the high purpose which characterized the fathers of the republic, and which qualifies them to raise up and patriotically train American youths?

First, and most essential of all, teachers should be enthusiastic lovers of their country, understanding well and believing in its characteristic institutions, familiar with its ideals, faithfully obeying its laws, thoroughly in touch with the spirit of the republic, presenting to their pupils in their personal character and daily conduct living examples of the high-minded, high-purposed, broad-cultured, large-hearted, and loyal American citizen.

As citizens, they should have a profound appreciation of the civil, educational, and religious liberties enjoyed by the people under our form of government, and be prepared to explain to others, not teachers, who have not had opportunities for study, precisely wherein these liberties differ from those accorded by other governments, in other lands, to their people. The great principle that "all men are created equal before the law" should not only be made the most vital element of their political faith, but should become an indispensable factor in the discipline, rulings, and daily government of the school. They should make themselves perfectly familiar with the complex yet harmonious relations which they as citizens bear to the several local governments, — village, town, county, and state, — and to that of the nation under which they live, and are protected in their persons, their property, and their civil and religious rights.

As teachers, they should be filled with a deep and abiding sense of the responsibility resting upon them of so shaping the future lives and so moulding the character of their pupils that in due time these pupils shall become worthy citizens of a country of which each one is an essential and integral part, each competent to do its share in guiding the future life and defending the honor of the republic.

A distinguished educator, in speaking of the public school system as the basis of social unity in a republic, has said : " As I estimate the various professions in their various moral advantages, the moral advantage of the teacher's profession lies in its patrotism, especially as related to the common school system. It has its fascinations in many other directions, but here is its pressing obligation ; here is its magnificent opportunity. To these teachers, therefore, is committed the task, not only of training their pupils to be self-supporting citizens, but citizens capable of controlling and guiding, by the wise exercise of a thoroughly trained mind and will, every intellectual power and moral force, every physical impulse, passion, and desire, so that all the powers of both mind and body shall contribute in their maximum degree to the making of a noble man or woman, a self-reliant, self-poised, self-governing citizen, a citizen distinctly and avowedly American, — one whose mental, moral, and spiritual training has been such as to teach not only how to die for, but the nobler purpose, — because more difficult, — how best to LIVE for one's country."

GEORGE T. BALCH. February 17, 1894.

---

6. SOULS, NOT STATIONS.

Who shall judge a man from manners?
  Who shall know him by his dress?
Paupers may be fit for princes,
  Princes fit for something less.
Crumpled shirts and dirty jacket
  May beclothe the golden ore
Of the deepest thoughts and feelings;
  Satin vests could do no more.

There are springs of crystal nectar
  Ever welling out of stone;
There are purple buds and golden,
  Hidden, crushed, and overgrown.
God, who counts by souls, not dresses,
  Loves and prospers you and me,
While He values thrones, the highest,
  But as pebbles in the sea.

Man upraised above his fellows,
  Oft forgets his fellows then;
Masters, rulers, lords, remember
  That your meanest hinds are men!
Men by labor, men by feeling,
  Men by thought, and men by fame,
Claiming equal rights to sunshine
  In a man's ennobling name.

There are foam-embroidered oceans,
    There are little weed-clad rills,
There are feeble inch-high saplings,
    There are cedars on the hills.
God, who counts by souls, not stations,
    Loves and prospers you and me;
For to Him all vain distinctions
    Are as pebbles in the sea.

Toiling hands alone are builders
    Of a nation's wealth and fame;
Titled laziness is pensioned,
    Fed, and fattened on the same;
By the sweat of other's foreheads
    Living only to rejoice,
While the poor man's outraged freedom
    Vainly lifteth up its voice.

Truth and justice are eternal,
    Born with loveliness and light;
Sunset's wrongs shall never prosper
    While there is a sunny right;
God, whose world-wide voice is singing
    Boundless love to you and me,
Sinks oppression, with its titles,
    As the pebbles in the sea.
                          Anon.

IMMORTALITY.

Oh, no! it is no flattering lure, no fancy weak or fond,
When Hope would bid us rest secure in better life beyond.
Nor loss, nor shame, nor grief, nor sin, her promise may
    gainsay;
The voice divine hath spoke within, and God did ne'er
    betray.
                          SARAH F. SMITH.

7. WHAT IS AMBITION?

What is ambition? 'T is a glorious cheat!
Angels of light walk not so dazzling
The shining walls of heaven. The unsearched mine
Hath not such gems. Earth's constellated thrones
Have not such pomp of purple and of gold.
It hath no features. In its face is set
A mirror, and the gazer sees his own.
It looks a god, but it is like himself!
It hath a mien of empery, and smiles
Majestically sweet, — but how like him!

. . . .

His kindred are forgotten or estranged;
Unhealthful fires burn constant in his eye;
His lip grows restless, and its smile is curled
Half into scorn, till the bright, fiery boy,
That was a daily blessing but to see,
His spirit was so bird-like and so pure,
Is frozen, in the very flush of youth,
Into a cold, care-fretted, heartless man.

But what is its reward? At best, a name!
Praise, when the ear has grown too dull to hear;
Gold, when the senses it should please are dead;
Wreaths, when the hair they cover has grown gray;
Fame, when the heart it should have thrilled is numb;
All things but love — when love is all we want.
And close behind comes Death, and ere we know
That e'en these unavailing gifts are ours,
He sends us, stripped and naked, to the grave!

Nathaniel Parker Willis.

8. THE ORATOR DESCRIBED.

IMAGINE to yourselves Demosthenes, addressing the most illustrious assembly in the world, upon a point whereon the fate of the most illustrious of nations depended.

How awful such a moment! How vast the subject! Is the man possessed of talents equal to the great occasion? Yes, superior! By the power of his eloquence, the augustness of the assembly is lost in the dignity of the orator; and the importance of the subject, for a while, is superseded by admiration of his talents.

With what strength of argument, with what powers of the fancy, with what emotions of the heart, does he assault and subjugate the whole man, and at once captivate his reason, his imagination, and his passions! To effect this, must be the utmost effort of the most improved state of human nature. Not a faculty that he possesses is here unemployed; not a faculty that he possesses but here is exerted to its utmost pitch. All his internal powers are at work. All his external, testify their energies. Within, the memory, the fancy, the judgment, the passions, are all busy. Without, every muscle, every nerve, is excited. Not a feature, not a limb, but speaks. The organs of the body, attuned to the exertions of the mind, through the kindred organs of the hearers, instantly vibrate those energies from soul to soul.

Notwithstanding the diversity of minds in such a multitude, by the lightning of eloquence they are melted into one mass; the whole assembly, actuated in one and the same way, become, as it were, but one man, and have but one voice. The universal cry is, "Let us march against Philip! Let us fight for our liberties! Let us conquer, or die!"

RICHARD BRINSLEY BUTLER SHERIDAN.

9. PROCRASTINATION.

Be wise to-day. 'T is madness to defer;
Next day the fatal precedent will plead;
Thus on, till wisdom is pushed out of life.

Procrastination is the thief of time:
Year after year it steals, till all are fled,
And to the mercy of a moment leaves
The vast concerns of an eternal scene.
. . . .

Of man's miraculous mistakes, this bears
The palm, — that all men are about to live,
Forever on the brink of being born.
All pay themselves the compliment to think
They one day shall not drivel; and their pride,
On this reversion, takes up ready praise,
At least, their own; their future selves applaud.
How excellent that life they ne'er will lead!
Time lodged in their own hands is Folly's vails;
That lodged in Fate's, to wisdom they consign:
The thing they can't, but purpose, they postpone.
'T is not in folly not to scorn a fool,
And scarce in human wisdom to do more.
All promise is poor dilatory man,
And that through every stage. When young, indeed,
In full content, we sometimes nobly rest
Un-anxious for ourselves; and only wish,
As duteous sons, our fathers were more wise.

At thirty, man suspects himself to be a fool;
Knows it at forty, and reforms his plan;
At fifty, chides his infamous delay,
Pushes his prudent purpose to resolve;

In all the magnanimity of thought,
Resolves, and re-resolves; then dies the same.
And why? Because he thinks himself immortal.
All men think all men mortal but themselves;
Themselves, when some alarming shock of fate
Strikes through their heart some sudden dread;
But their hearts wounded, like the wounded air,
Soon close: where passed the shaft, no trace is found.

EDWARD YOUNG.

10. A PETITION TO TIME.

Touch us gently, Time.
   Let us glide adown thy stream
Gently, as we sometimes glide
   Through a quiet dream.
Humble voyagers are we:
   Husband, wife, and children three
(One is lost, — an angel, fled
   To the azure overhead).

Touch us gently, Time.
   We've not proud or soaring wings;
Our ambition, our content,
   Lies in simple things.
Humble voyagers are we,
   O'er life's dim, unsounded sea,
Seeking only some calm clime:
   Touch us gently, gentle Time.

BRYAN WALLER PROCTER (Barry Cornwall).

11. TO-MORROW.

"To-morrow," didst thou say?
Methought I heard Horatio say, "To-morrow!"
Go to! I will not hear of it. "To-morrow?"
'T is a sharper, who stakes his penury
Against thy plenty; takes thy ready cash
And pays thee nought but wishes, hopes, and promises,—
The currency of idiots; injurious bankrupt,
That gulls the easy creditor.
      "To-morrow?"
It is a period nowhere to be found
In all the hoary registers of Time,—
Unless, perchance, in the fool's calendar.
Wisdom disclaims the word, nor holds society
With those who own it.
      No, my dear Horatio,
'T is Fancy's child, and Folly is its father;
Wrought of such stuff as dreams are, and as baseless
As the fantastic visions of the evening.

But soft, my friend, arrest the present moments,
For, be assured, they all are arrant tell-tales;
And though their flight be silent, and their paths
Trackless as the winged couriers of the air,
They post to heaven, and there record thy folly;
Because, though stationed on the important watch,
Thou, like a sleeping, faithless sentinel,
Didst let them pass unnoticed, unimproved.
And know for that thou slumberest on thy guard,
Thou shalt be made to answer at the bar
For every fugitive; and when thou thus
Shalt stand impleaded at the High Tribunal
Of hood-winked Justice, who shall tell thy audit?

Then stay the present instant, dear Horatio;
Imprint the marks of wisdom on its wings.

'T is of more worth than kingdoms; far more precious
Than all the crimson treasures of life's fount.
Oh, let it not elude thy grasp! but, like
The good old patriarch upon record,
Hold the fleet angel fast until he bless thee.

NATHANIEL COTTON.

---

12. THE GREAT GOOD MAN.

First Speaker.

How seldom, friend, a good man inherits
  Honor and wealth, with all his worth and pains.
It seems a story from the world of spirits
When any man obtains that which he merits, —
  Or any merits that which he obtains.

Second Speaker.

For shame, my friend; renounce that idle strain.
What wouldst thou have a good great man obtain?
Goodness and greatness are not means, but ends.
Hath he not always treasures, always friends,
The great good man? Three treasures, — love, and light,
  And calm thoughts, equable as infant's breath;
And three fast friends, more sure than day, or night, —
  Himself, his Maker, and the Angel Death.

SAMUEL TAYLOR COLERIDGE.

GOODNESS AND GREATNESS.

GOODNESS is the greatest of all the virtues and dignities of the mind, being the character of the Deity.

GREATNESS is gained by a winding stair, and the power to do good is the true and lawful end of aspiring.

LORD FRANCIS BACON.

13. TRUE ELOQUENCE.

When public bodies are to be addressed on momentous occasions, when great interests are at stake, and strong passions excited, nothing is valuable in speech, farther than it is connected with high intellectual and moral attainments.

Clearness, force, and earnestness are the qualities which produce conviction. True eloquence, indeed, does not consist in speech. It cannot be brought from far. Labor and learning may toil for it, but they will toil in vain. Words and phrases may be marshalled in every way, but they cannot compass it. It must exist in the man, in the subject, and in the occasion. Affected passion, intense expression, the pomp of declamation, all may aspire after it. They cannot reach it. It comes, if it come at all, like the outbreaking of a fountain from the earth, or the bursting forth of volcanic fires, with spontaneous, original, native force. The graces taught in the schools, the costly ornaments, and studied contrivances of speech, shock and disgust men when their own lives, and the lives of their wives and children, and their country, hang on the decision of the hour. Then, words have lost their power. Rhetoric is vain, and all elaborate oratory contemptible. Even genius itself then feels rebuked and subdued as in the presence of higher qualities. Then, patriotism is eloquent. Then, self-devotion is eloquent.

The clear conception, outrunning the deductions of logic, the high purpose, the firm resolve, the dauntless spirit, speaking on the tongue, beaming from the eye, informing every feature, and urging the whole man onward to his object, — this, this is eloquence, or rather it is something greater and higher than eloquence; it is action, noble, sublime, God-like action.

Daniel Webster.

14. THE CHRISTIAN ORATOR.

By the introduction of Christianity, a tribune was erected from which the most sublime truths were boldly announced to all the world; from which the purest lessons of morality were made familiar to the ignorant multitude, — a tribune so authoritative, so august, that, before it, emperors soiled with the blood of the people, were humbled; a tribune which singly and fearlessly has pleaded the cause of the poor against the rich, of the oppressed against the oppressor, and of man against himself.

There, all become ennobled and deified. The Christian orator can reveal to his hearers a destiny grander than glory, or more terrible than death. From the highest heavens he can draw down an eternal hope to the tomb, where Pericles could only bring tributary lamentations and tears. If, with the Roman orator, he commemorates the warrior fallen on the field of battle, he gives to the soul of the departed that immortality which Cicero dared promise only to his renown. He charges Deity itself with the acquittal of a country's gratitude.

That science of morals, that experience of mankind, those secrets of the passions, which were the constant study of the philosophers and orators of antiquity, ought to be his, also, to command. It is for him, more than it was for them, to know all the windings of the human heart, all the vicissitudes of the emotions, all the sensibilities of the human soul. And this, not with the view of exciting those violent affections, those popular animosities, those fierce kindlings of passion, those fires of vengeance and hate, in the outburst of which the triumph of ancient eloquence was attained, but to appease, to soften, to purify the soul.

Armed against all the passions, without the privilege of availing himself of any, he is obliged, as it were, to create a new passion, if by that name we may profane the profound, the sublime sentiment which can alone vanquish and replace all others in the heart, — an intelligent, religious enthusiasm. It is that which should impart to his elocution, to his thoughts, and to his words, the inspiration of a prophet rather than the art and manner of the orator.

Abel François Villemain.

15. A GOOD NAME.

It is ever to be kept in mind that a good name is in all cases the fruit of personal exertion. It is not inherited from parents; it is not created by external advantages: it is no necessary appendage of birth or wealth or talents or station, but the result of one's own endeavors, the fruit and reward of good principles, manifested in a course of virtuous and honorable action. The attainment of a good name, whatever be the external circumstances, is wholly within the young man's power. However humble his birth, or obscure his condition, he has only to fix his eye on the prize and press toward it, in a course of useful and virtuous conduct, and it is his. How many of our worthiest and best citizens have risen to honor and usefulness by dint of their own persevering exertions!

In the formation of character, personal exertion is the first, the second, and the third virtue. A good name will not come without its being sought. All the virtues of which it is composed are the result of untiring application and industry. Nothing can be more fatal to the acquirement of a good character than a treacherous confidence in external advantages. These, if not seconded by your own exertions, will drop you, mid-way; or perhaps you will not have started, while the diligent traveller will have won the race.

It is of the highest importance that you have a commanding object in view, and that your aim in life be elevated. It is an old proverb, that "he who aims at the sun, to be sure, will not reach it, but his arrow will fly higher than if he aimed at an object on the level with himself." Just so in the formation of character. Set your standard high, and you cannot fail to rise higher than if you aimed at some inferior excellence. Young men are not, in general, conscious of what they are capable of doing. They do not task their faculties, nor improve their powers, nor attempt, as they ought, to rise to superior excellence. The consequence is that their efforts are few and feeble; they are not waked up to anything great or distinguished, and therefore fail to acquire a character of decided worth.

You may be whatever you resolve to be! Resolution is omnipotent! Aim at excellence, and excellence will be attained. "I cannot do it," never accomplished anything; "I will try," has wrought wonders. A young man who sets out in life with a determination to excel, can hardly fail of his purpose. There is, in his case, a steadiness of aim, a concentration of feeling and effort, which bear him onward to his object with irresistible energy, and render success in whatever he undertakes, certain.

JOEL HAWES.

But he that filches from me my good name,
Robs me of something which not enriches him,
And makes me poor indeed.

SHAKESPEARE.

16. THE PHILOSOPHER'S SCALES.

"What were they?" you ask. You shall presently see:
These scales were not made to weigh sugar and tea;
Oh, no! for such wonderful properties had they,
That qualities, feelings, and thoughts they would weigh,
Together with articles small or immense,
From mountains or planets to atoms of sense.
Nought was there so bulky but there it could lay,
And nought so ethereal but there it would stay,
And nought so reluctant but in it must go;
All of which some examples more clearly will show.

The first thing he tried was the head of Voltaire,
Which retained all the wit that had ever been there;
As a weight, he threw in a torn scrap of leaf,
Containing the prayer of the penitent thief;
When the skull rose aloft with so sudden a spell
As to bound like a ball on the roof of the cell.

Next time he put in Alexander the Great,
With a garment that Dorcas had made, for a weight;
And though clad in armor from sandals to crown,
The hero rose up, and the garment went down.

A long row of almshouses, amply endowed
By a well-esteemed Pharisee, busy and proud,
Now loaded one scale, while the other was pressed
By those mites the poor widow dropped into the chest:
Up flew the endowment, not weighing an ounce;
And down, down, the farthing's worth came with a bounce.

By further experiments (no matter how),
He found that ten chariots weighed less than one plough;
A sword with gilt trappings rose up in the scale,
Though balanced by only a tenpenny nail;
A lord and a lady went up at full sail
When a bee chanced to drop on the opposite scale.

Ten doctors, ten lawyers, two courtiers, one earl,
Ten counsellors' wigs full of powder and curl,
All heaped in one balance, and swinging from thence,
Weighed less than one atom of candor and sense;
And not mountains of silver and gold would suffice
One pearl to outweigh,— 't was the "Pearl of Great Price"!

At last the whole world was howled in at the grate,
With the soul of a beggar to serve as a weight,
When the former sprang up, with so strong a rebuff
That it made a vast rent, and escaped at the roof;
While the scale with the soul in 't so mightily fell
That it jerked the philosopher out of his cell.

JANE TAYLOR.

17. THE HILL OF SCIENCE.

I WAS wandering in a beautiful and romantic country till curiosity began to give way to weariness, and sleep stole insensibly over me as I was indulging in agreeable reveries. In the middle of a vast, extended plain arose a mountain, higher than I had any conception of before. It was covered with a multitude of people, chiefly youth, many of whom pressed forward with the liveliest expressions of ardor in their countenances, though the way was in many places steep and difficult. Those who had just begun to climb the hill, thought themselves not far from the top; but new hills were continually rising to their view, and the summit of the highest seemed but the foot of another, till the mountain appeared to lose itself in the clouds. "All this," said a friendly instructor, who suddenly appeared, "is the Hill of Science. On the top is the Temple of Truth, whose head is above the clouds, and a veil of pure light covers her face. Observe the progress of her votaries. Be silent and attentive."

Then I viewed the multitudes who were climbing the steep ascent, among them, a youth of a lively look, a piercing eye, and somewhat fiery and irregular in all his motions. His name was Genius. He darted like an eagle up the mountain, and left his companions gazing after him with envy and admiration; but his progress was interrupted by a thousand caprices. When Pleasure warbled in the valley, he mingled in her train. When Pride beckoned toward the precipice, he ventured to the tottering edge. He delighted in devious paths; and made so many excursions from the road, that his feebler companions often outstripped him. I observed that the Muses beheld him with partiality; but Truth often frowned, and turned aside her face. While Genius was thus wasting his strength in eccentric flights, I saw a person of very different appearance, named Application. He crept along with a slow and unremitting pace, his eyes fixed on the top of the mountain, patiently removing every stone that obstructed his way. Indeed, there were few who ascended the hill with equal steadiness; for they were continually solicited by a numerous crowd of Appetites, Passions, and Pleasures, whose importunity they became less and less able to resist. The hill appeared more steep and rugged; their sight grew dim, and their feet tripped at every little obstruction. I saw with some surprise that the Muses, whose business was to cheer and encourage, would often sing in the bowers of Pleasure, and accompany those who were enticed away at the call of the Passions. But they forsook them when they lost sight of the hill, and led them away, without resistance, to the cells of Ignorance or the mansions of Misery. Among the innumerable seducers, to draw away the votaries of Truth from the path of Science, there was one, so gentle and languid in her attempts, that I should scarcely have taken notice of her, but for the numbers she had imperceptibly loaded with her chain. Indolence, for so she was called, contented herself with retarding their progress; and the purpose she could not force them to abandon, she persuaded them to delay. Of all the unhappy deserters from the path of Science, none seemed less able to return than the followers of Indolence. The captives of Appetite and Passion would often seize the moment when their tyrants were languid or asleep, to escape from their enchantment; but the dominion of Indolence was constant and unremitted, and seldom resisted until resistance was vain.

I turned my eyes toward the top of the mountain, where the air was always pure and exhilarating; and "Happy," said I, "are they who are permitted to ascend the mountain." Then a form of diviner features and benign radiance, standing by me said, "Happy are they whom Virtue conducts to the Mansions of Content. I am Virtue, and am found in the vale, and yet I illuminate the mountain. I cheer the cottager at his toil, and inspire the sage at his meditation. I mingle in the crowd of cities, and bless the hermit in his cell. I have a temple in every heart that owns my influence; and to him that wishes for me, I am ever present. Science may raise thee to eminence; but I alone can guide thee to felicity!"

While Virtue was thus speaking, I stretched out my arms towards her, with a vehemence that broke my slumber. The chill dews were falling around me, and the shadows of evening stretched over the landscape. I hastened homeward, and resigned the night to silence and meditation.

JOHN AIKEN.

18. THE SERPENT OF THE STILL.

They tell me of the Egyptian asp,
    The bite of which is death;
The victim yielding with a gasp
    His hot and hurried breath.
The Egyptian queen, says history,
    The reptile vile applied,
And in the arms of agony
    Victoriously died.

They tell me that in Italy
    There is a reptile dread,
The sting of which is misery,
    And dooms the victim dead.
But it is said that music's sound
    May soothe the poisoned part,—
Yea, heal the galling, ghastly wound,
    And save the sinking heart!

They tell me, too, of serpents vast
    That crawl on Afric's shore,
And swallow men. (Historians past
    Tell us of one of yore.)
But there is one, of a kind
    More fatal than the whole,
That stings the body and the mind,—
    Yea, it devours the soul!

'T is found almost o'er all the earth,
    Save Turkey's wide domains;
And there, if e'er it had a birth,
    'T is kept in mercy's chains.
'T is found in our own gardens gay,
    In our own flowery fields,
Devouring, every passing day,
    Its thousands at its meals!

Its poisonous venom withers youth,
  Blasts character and health;
All sink before it,— hope and truth,
  And comfort, joy, and wealth.
It is the author, too, of shame,
  And never fails to kill.
Reader, dost thou desire the name?
  "The Serpent of the Still!"
                    Milford Bard. JOHN LOFLAND.

---

19. COURAGE.

Courage! Nothing can withstand
Long, a wronged, undaunted land,
If the hearts within her be
True unto themselves and thee,
Thou freed giant, Liberty!

Courage! Nothing e'er withstood
Freedmen fighting for their good.
Armed with all their fathers' fame,
They will win and wear a name
That shall go to endless glory,
Like the gods of old in story,
Raised to heaven and heavenly worth
For the good they gave to earth.
  . . . . . .
Courage! Who will be a slave,
That hath strength to dig a grave,
And therein his fetters hide,
And lay a tyrant by his side?
Courage! Hope, howe'er he fly
For a time, can *never* die!
Courage, therefore, brother men!
Courage! To the fight again!
                    BRYAN WALLER PROCTER.

20. THE SANCTUARY WITHIN THE BREAST.

For man there still is left one sacred charter;
    One refuge still remains for human woes.
Victim of care, or persecution's martyr,
    Who seek'st a sure asylum from thy foes,
Learn that the holiest, safest, purest, best,
      Is man's own breast!

There is a solemn sanctuary, founded
    By God himself, not for transgressors meant;
But that the man oppressed, the spirit-wounded,
    And all beneath the world's injustice bent,
Might turn from outward wrong, turmoil, and din,
      To peace within.

Each bosom is a temple when its altar,
    The living heart, is unprofaned and pure.
Its verge is hallowed: none need fear or falter
    Who thither fly; it is an ark secure,
Winning, above a world o'erwhelmed with wrath,
      Its peaceful path.

O bower of bliss! O sanctuary holy!
    Terrestrial antepast of heavenly joy!
Never, oh, never may misdeed or folly
    My claim to thy beatitudes destroy!
Still may I keep this Paradise unlost,
      Where'er I'm tost!

HORACE SMITH.

Ye are the temple of the living God.

Bible

21. DEEDS OF KINDNESS.

Suppose the little cowslip
   Should hang its golden cup,
And say, "I'm such a tiny flower,
   I'd better not grow up;"
How many a weary traveller
   Would miss its fragrant smell!
How many a little child would grieve
   To lose it from the dell!

Suppose the glittering dew drop
   Upon the grass should say,
"What can a little dew-drop do?
   I'd better roll away;"
The blade on which it rested,
   Before the day was done,
Without a drop to moisten it,
   Would wither in the sun.

Suppose the little breezes,
   Upon a summer's day,
Should think themselves too slight to cool
   The traveller on his way;
Who would not miss the smallest
   And softest ones that blow,
And think they made a great mistake
   If they were talking so?

How many deeds of kindness
   A little child may do,
Although it has so little strength,
   And little wisdom, too!
It needs a loving spirit,
   Much more than strength, to prove
How many things a child may do
   For others, by its love.

EPES SARGENT

22. MILITARY TRAINING IN THE SCHOOLS.

EXTRACT from an Address delivered, by the Editor of "Beacon Lights of Patriotism," before the Boston High Schools upon presenting diplomas to the graduating classes, June 29, 1886, — placed among "School-Room Echoes and Hints," as a suggestion of the higher uses of military drill.

THIS diploma which I present to you, young gentlemen, in the name of the school authorities of Boston, has a higher import than as a simple memorial of certain military duty done. I do not emphasize the suggestion that you thereby become better prepared to serve the State and Nation in some future struggle for good order or national defence. Much less do I claim that conduct becoming an officer and a gentleman cannot become the law of life to all who consecrate their youthful time and talent to the behests of true manhood, without military exercise. There ever has been, and there ever will be, a spiritual exaltation of all worthy motives, when thoughtful preparation is made for a possible exposure of life to rescue suffering humanity, or serve one's country. But the occasion which crowns your duties and studies here with this official recognition, obtains emphasis from far higher considerations than those of mere physical development; from something broader and more vital to the commonwealth and nation than fitness for battle-issues, their sacrifices, and their laurels. They who value this special training only by the tests of the gymnasium, or by those equivalents which fix the standards of the field or camp, fail to grasp the true meaning of this special line of duty and study. Have there been numberless small details, tiresome routine, rigid and exacting formulæ? Have there been still positions, artificial attitudes, until even your eyes were controlled by the will of others? But there is law in all such details, until their realized expression has become harmony, the merging of details into system, — hence, *character.*

The world is full of men who recall school-days with sad regrets that they clung to narrow lines of study without a right conception of the value of all co-ordinate methods which educate for real life. The stern exactions of mathematics, the wealth of historic examples, the luxuries of classic lore and poesy, represent, indeed, jealous mistresses; but their wisest votaries have ever respected the loves of other swains, have respected the enthusiasms of other minds, until each has been refined, strengthened, and blessed thereby. It is just here that I offer a suggestion, and express my appreciation of the enhanced value which your education has acquired through this special factor, — some knowledge of the military art. The thousands who witnessed your annual parade were impressed by the ultimate unity toward which all true education ought to be directed, as they marked the unfolded elements of that successful parade. A single careless guide, or misplaced "camp-color," would have made your true alignments impossible. An error in "sizing" your ranks, would have destroyed symmetry, and that steady bearing which exhibited conscious power. A mis-step would have spoiled a wheeling, or some other critical movement. Loss of cadence in step, as in music, would have destroyed both force and harmony. Assertions of individual will, or indifference to any preparatory order, would have made the whole parade a farce. Absolute subordination to duty became a vital factor, as in every rightful endeavor. Every limb and muscle of every form, every spiritual servant of each individual will, must be in accord with the magnetic sway of the master-mind in charge, if the completed whole, the mighty regimental-unit, were to maintain its character. The law of self-restraint, of deference to authority; the inertia of compressed as well as perfected details, became exponents of the value of your experience as cadets of the public schools of your native city.

Trace back, at some wakeful hour hereafter, the experiences of your school-days here. Recall the tough places and the innocent jokes of the "awkward squad;" then the emulations, perhaps the jealousies, of successful competition; and then, the movements of unwilling subordination when your task was to obey, and pride resented the restraint! When life's real battles shall demand similar self-restraint, similar regard for authority, and perhaps a more complete abnegation of self, in the higher welfare of the State, you will see how you have earned, yes, have won, that which a diploma may emblem, but can never reward. Add to the well-trained mind and the disciplined body the crowning grace of soul-virtue, such as the Man of Nazareth expressed in life and precept, and you will be blessed in life, and receive the plaudit, "Well done," in the Great Hereafter.

23. AIM HIGH.

Extract from Address before the graduating class of the Peirce School of Business and Shorthand, Philadelphia, Penn., December 20th, 1893.

You are about to go into business. That is a very broad word in the dictionary, but narrowed in its present use. In the street it has only to do with transactions that can be represented in figures. Addition, subtraction, and division are its elements, and the successful man is he who works all his problems by addition, and leaves subtraction and division to his competitors.

But the word has a wider meaning. "Wist ye not that I must be about my Father's business?" This was spoken of mighty concerns; but not such as can be expressed in shekels or talents. The first qualification is character. A good character for integrity, for truthfulness, for fairness, is the strongest lifting power that any young man can carry into and through his business life. I do not mean to say that dishonesty and lying and trickery never lead to wealth. They do! The Psalmist found that out, and our observation is larger than his. But the natural and ordinary fruit of vice and fraud is failure, even by the money test. The criminal is not always revealed before the fact, or caught after it, but the pawnbroker gets the stolen jewels, and the thief becomes a fearsome fugitive. If you want to get the full use of your money, the comfort of it, then be careful that no tainted dollar gets into your till. There is more good in a moderate accumulation than in great riches, more time for good thoughts and good company, for wife and child and neighbors, and for God.

The highest places are peaks. Men are not made happy or prosperous in the mass, but singly. There is a duty to one's self, to one's family, as well as to society. You do not injure any man if, in the competitions of life, by fair methods, by greater skill or thrift, you go to the front. There is nothing more wholesome, more helpful to the striving, than the illustrations which every community affords of the triumphs of pluck and thrift over hard and discouraging conditions The presence of a man on the peak, who was but lately in the gorge, is conclusive evidence of a path, and it is much wiser to give our strength to climbing than to stone-throwing. He should send his "Hail, brother!" down, and we should send ours up. His elevation should not chill his human sympathy, nor excite our envy. He can be, he will be, if he is a true man, more helpful to us up there than down here.

Let fidelity be your watchword! However simple the task, let it be done with scrupulous faithfulness. However small the trust, let there be no default. Settle it now, as an inflexible purpose, that you will never, for a moment, use for your own purposes one cent of another's money in your keeping, without his consent, however desperate your need. The temptation to use for a little while, and then return, is full of subtilty and danger, and "many there be that go in thereat." A cheerful face and spirit has a large commercial estimation. The man who mumbles protests over his work will not survive the first reduction of the force.

To make one's self the most valuable man in the shop, the store, or office, is the best assurance of advancement. If you have a way to make in life, the place to begin is where you stand. If it happen to be rock excavation there, do not run forward to find a soft place. It is a waste of time! Life is not like a railroad that can be surveyed from end to end before construction begins. What is not within your reach, is clearly not this day's work for you. Aim high, but have regard to the range of your gun. And, above all, do not forget that the man whose plans take account of every hour of life, except the supreme hour, is unspeakably foolish!

Benjamin Harrison.

AIM AT PERFECTION.

Aim at perfection in everything, though in most things it is unattainable; however, they who aim at it, and persevere, will come much nearer to it than those whose laziness and despondency make them give it up as unattainable.

Lord Chesterfield.

24. CULTURE OF THE MORAL VIRTUES.

From Address, July 7, 1892, before National Teachers' Association at Saratoga, N. Y.

As we go to the Spartans to learn the possibilities of physical culture, and to the Athenians to learn the possibilities of æsthetic culture, so we go to the peoples who have exalted the moral virtues to learn the possibilities of ethical culture. History and biography present marvellous object-lessons in point. The savage is a savage from habit, for savagery is in the line of least resistance. The unthinking masses move round and round in the treadmill of custom, for this is easier than independent action. The Jew teaches fidelity. He is a Jew from conviction as well as duty. For many centuries it has cost much to be a Jew, but their history is a striking lesson of the virtue of fidelity to enlightened conviction. Fidelity grows into a fixed habit. Through all the centuries the profound belief in Jehovah, and in the Hebrew scriptures, has made the Jewish people a perpetual miracle.

The Scotch teach us integrity. Go to the homes, the schools, and the kirks of Scotland, and you find that integrity in things great and small is every way inculcated. They are a living object-lesson in the practical culture of the moral virtues.

The Quaker teaches us truthfulness. His word stands for more than the oaths of other men. Early and always, the Quaker child and youth learns to love truth, and speak and act truth.

The world's moral heroes teach us the moral virtues. We study the life of Jesus as the one perfect life. We study the lives of the best women and men, that we may discover how they grew into moral greatness; and herein sacred and classic literature must be counted at their highest value. A moral atmosphere conditions the growth of the moral virtues. A sturdy moral manhood is almost impossible in the midst of moral pestilence. Our first care should be to remove alluring temptations and degrading influences. Moral pest-houses are very necessary. The second care should be to throw around the child and youth all favoring influences. Helpful environments, helpful literature, helpful society, helpful work are of incalculable value. Our third care should be to incite high purposes and earnest work. The idle classes, rich and poor, are our moral lepers.

Moral ancestry tends to morality, and practical ethics may gain valuable lessons from the study of heredity. The little child realizes that it ought to obey its parents. This impulse to obey because it ought, is conscience. The child thus early gains the intuition of right, and begins to do moral acts. The greatest thing in education is the development of the habit of doing what we believe we ought to do. This is the education of conscience. The key-note in moral culture is love and duty. The millions pitch the tune of human conduct too low. Will it give me pleasure? Will it pay? Is it good policy? The consequent moral degradation is appalling. But duty is the key-note of every grand life. Conscience stands for duty, for it is our capability to feel duty-impulses. Find right, choose right, do right, enjoy right, are the immediate mandates of conscience. As the needle points to the pole, so conscience impels each one to do duty as he understands it. Here all vital, moral culture has its root. From infancy to age, the greatest thing in education is so to foster the ethical impulses that they shall become practically imperative in controlling human conduct. The noblest work of God is a man who, from principle and from habit, does what he deems is right. The highest work of the educator is the development of such men and women. JOSEPH BALDWIN.

25. PATRIOTIC WORDS FOR THE YOUNG.

Extracts furnished from Address delivered in honor of Washington's Birthday, 1894.

ALL our knowledge of facts is worthless unless boys and girls have the life which shall use them well. It is not purchased science which we want. It is passionate love of country, and the one hundred and thirty-seventh Psalm, a "Psalm of exile," shows the feeling which compelled Israel to return to Jerusalem, her home. To a people of faith like hers, the love of country is like the love of home and of God. The three indeed are one. The man who sang this song lived in the midst of the luxury of the capital of the world, but he had not learned to chatter in the accents of a broken dialect, nor the languid negation of an absentee.

Now, in the training of our children, whether in city or country, we want to teach them definitely, and at an early age, what their duties to the State are, and will be. A nation is not a heap of sand-grains. It is an organism all alive, in which each cell and germ feeds each other, and by each other is fed. And as every cell in an apple-tree belongs to an apple-tree, and every cell in an oak tree belongs to an oak, and as no cell can live alone, — not an hour, — so does every child of America belong to America, and America belongs to every child of hers. We are not attempting to describe, far less to measure, the strength of separate threads, all woven and twisted in the great webwork which we call America. But we are teaching them that that web has been woven by infinite love, that its history is history wrought out in God's purpose. And our boys and girls must, from the first, know that their life-blood gives the color, and their vigor, the strength, to the fabric. They are never to see their flag without a grateful smile. They are never to sing her songs, but as they sing hymns in worship. They are never to call their birth a poor accident of fortune. Always they are to thank God, as the first of His gifts, and the greatest, that they were born Americans. Or, if He have brought them hither in the shadow of His clouds by day, or in the blaze of His watchfires by night, from less favored lands, they are always to thank Him that America welcomed them with a mother's arms. You may call the organic tie mysterious. So is the attraction of gravitation. Nobody has ever explained either; but for all that, no man should doubt their power. Birth, blood, climate, language, history, the line of my ancestors, the color of the sunset, the shape of the snowdrifts, the old stain of blood on the pavement, or the memory of battle, — every outward circumstance and every sacred memory combine to make my life and the nation's life. Because God is, and reigns, my country is, and I am. His life, my life, and her life are one!

Our boys and girls are to be trained, not only to know this, but to feel it. They are to be Christian patriots. And then we are sure that they will be good citizens. We do not build on their learning, nor on their graces, nor their creed, — not, God knows! on their wealth. No! We ask them to love their home, because it is God's home; to serve the State, because it is God's kingdom; and this is the whole duty of man.

EDWARD EVERETT HALE.

PART XII.

THE FIFTH CENTURY OF AMERICAN CIVILIZATION BEGUN.

1492–1892.

---

1. A PROCLAMATION.

By the President of the United States.

WHEREAS, by Joint Resolution, approved June 20, 1892, it was Resolved by the Senate and House of Representatives of the United States of America, in Congress assembled, "That the President of the United States be authorized and directed to issue a Proclamation recommending to the people the observance of the discovery of America, on the twenty-first day of October, 1892, by public demonstrations, and by suitable exercises in their schools, and other places of assembly," —

Now, therefore, I, Benjamin Harrison, President of the United States of America, in pursuance of the aforesaid Joint Resolution, do hereby appoint Friday, October 21, 1892, the four hundredth anniversary of the Discovery of America by Columbus, as a general holiday for the people of the United States. On that day, let the people, so far as possible, cease from toil, and devote themselves to such exercises as may best express honor to the discoverer, and their appreciation of the great achievements of the four completed centuries of American life.

Columbus stood in his age as the pioneer of progress and achievement. The system of universal education is, in our age, the most prominent and salutary feature of the spirit of enlightenment, and it is peculiarly appropriate that the schools be made by the people the centre of the day's demonstration. Let the National Flag float over every school-house in the country, and the exercises be such as shall impress upon our youth the patriotic duties of American citizenship.

In the churches, and in other places of assembly of the people, let there be expressions of gratitude to Divine Providence for the devout faith of the discoverer, and for the divine care and guidance which has directed our history, and so abundantly blessed our people.

In testimony whereof, I have hereunto set my hand and caused the seal of the United States to be affixed.

Done at the City of Washington, this twenty-fourth day of July, in the year of our Lord, one thousand eight hundred and ninety-two, and of the Independence of the United States, the one hundred and seventeenth.

BENJAMIN HARRISON.

By the President.

JOHN W. FOSTER, *Secretary of State.*

2. WELCOME TO THE NATIONS.

Pursuant to the Proclamation of the President, the entire nation carried into effect the wishes of the American Congress, states and cities, schools and churches, uniting in one universal jubilee. Representatives from nearly all the governments of the world gathered at Chicago to witness the formal ceremonies of dedicating the proposed Park, and appropriate buildings, to a World's Fair, or Columbian Exposition. In the absence of President Harrison, during the fatal illness of his wife, the Vice-President, Levi P. Morton, delivered an Address of Welcome to the Nation's guests.

Extract from Address of Vice-President Morton.

DEEP indeed must be the sorrow which prohibits the President of the United States from being the central figure in these ceremonies. I am here in behalf of the government of the United States, in behalf of all the people, to bid All hail to Chicago! All hail to the Columbian Exposition!

I am not here to vaunt the wonderful story of this city's rise and advancement; of the matchless courage of her people, her second birth out of the most notable conflagration of modern times, nor of the eminent position she has conquered in commerce and manufactures, in science and the arts, or to dilate upon the marvellous growth and energy of the second commercial city of the Union. From the St. Lawrence to the Gulf, and from the peerless Cosmopolitan Capital by the Sea to the Golden Gate of California, there is no longer a rival city to Chicago, except to emulate her in promoting the success of this work. As we gaze upon these munificent erections, with their columns and arches, their entablatures and adornments, when we consider their beauty and rapidity of realization, they would seem to be evoked at a wizard's touch of Aladdin's lamp.

Columbus is not here in chains, nor are Columbian ideas in fetters. I see him, as in the great picture under the dome of the Capitol, with kneeling figures about him, betokening no longer the contrition of his followers, but the homage of mankind, with erect form and lofty mien, animating these children of a new world to higher hopes and holier purposes. Columbus lived in an age of great events. His character was complex, and his attainments are to be estimated by those of his contemporaries, and not by other standards.

Concerning ourselves, the statistics are familiar, and constitute a marvel. We are near the beginning of another century, and if no serious change occurs in our present growth, in the year 1935, in the lifetime of many men now in manhood, the English-speaking Republicans of America will number more than one hundred and eighty millions; and for these, John Bright, in a burst of impassioned eloquence, predicts one people, one language, one law, one faith, and, all over the wide continent, the home of Freedom, and a refuge for the oppressed of every race and clime. Like him, let us have faith in our future. To insure that future, the functions must be kept pure; public integrity must be preserved. While we reverence what Garibaldi and Victor Emanuel fought for, — the union of peoples, — we must secure, above all else, what Steuben and Koskiusco aided our fathers to establish, — liberty regulated by law.

If the time should ever come when men trifle with the public conscience, let me predict the patriotic action of the Republic in the language of Milton: —

"Methinks I see, in my mind, a noble and puissant nation, rousing herself like a strong man after sleep, and shaking his invincible locks; methinks I see her as an eagle mewing her mighty youth, and kindling her undazzled eyes at the full midday beams; purging and unscaling her long abused sight at the fountain itself of heavenly radiance, while the whole noise of timorous and flocking birds, with those also that love the twilight, flutter about, amazed at what she means."

3. DEDICATION OF COLUMBIAN EXPOSITION.

Extracts from Oration of Hon. HENRY WATTERSON, an orator of the day.

No twenty centuries can be compared with these four centuries, either in importance or interest, as no previous ceremonial can be compared with this, in its wide significance and reach, because, since the Advent of the Son of God, no event has had so great an influence upon human affairs as the discovery of this Western Hemisphere. Each of the centuries that have intervened marks many revolutions. The story of the least of the nations would fill a volume. In what I have to say, I shall confine myself to my own.

We have, in our own time, seen the Republic survive an irrepressible conflict, sown in the blood and the marrow of the social order. We have seen the Federal Union, not too strongly put together in the first place, come out of a war of sections stronger than when it went into it; its faith renewed, its credit rehabilitated, and its flag saluted with love and homage by sixty millions of God-fearing men and women, thoroughly reunited and homogeneous. The young manhood of the country may take this lesson from those of us who lived through times that did indeed try men's souls; when, pressed down from day to day by awful responsibilities and sacrifices, each night brought a terror with every thought of the morrow; and when, look wherever we would, there was light and hope nowhere that "God reigns and rules," and that this fair land is, and has always been, in His own keeping.

But there is no geography in American manhood. It needs but six weeks to change a Vermonter into a Texan.

When upon the battle-field or the frontier, Puritan and Cavalier were convertible terms, having in the beginning a common origin, and so diffused and diluted on American soil as no longer to possess a local habitation or a nativity, except in the national unit.

The men who planted the signals of American civilization upon that sacred rock by Plymouth Bay were Englishmen; and so were the men who struck the coast a little lower down, calling their haven of rest after the great Republican Commoner, and founding by Hampton Roads a race of heroes and statesmen, the mention of whose names brings a thrill to every heart.

The South claims Lincoln, the immortal, as its own. The North has no right to reject Stonewall Jackson, the one typical Puritan soldier of the war, for its own. Nor will it.

But we have come here, not so much to recall by-gone sorrows and glories, as to bask in the sunshine of present prosperity and happiness; to exchange patriotic greetings, and indulge good auguries; and, above all, to meet upon the threshold the stranger within our gates, not as a foreigner, but as a guest and friend for whom nothing we have is too good. From wheresoever he cometh, we welcome him with all our hearts. The son of the Rhine and the Garonne, our godmother, to whom we owe so much, he shall be our Lafayette, the son of the Rhine and the Moselle, he shall be our Goethe and our Wagner; the son of the Campagna and the Vesuvian Bay, he shall be our Michael Angelo and our Garibaldi; the son of Aragon and the Indies, he shall be our Christopher Columbus, fitly honored at last, throughout the world.

Our good cousin of England needs no words of special civility and courtesy from us. For him the latch-string is ever on the outer side, though whether it be or not, we are sure that he will enter and make himself at home.

A common language enables us to do full justice to one another, at the festive board, or in the arena of debate, warning both of us, in equal tones, against any further parley on the field of arms. All nations and all creeds are welcome here, — from the Bosphorus and the Black Sea, from Holland dike and Alpine crag, from Belgrade and Calcutta, and round to Chinese seas and the busy marts of Japan, the Isles of the Pacific and the far-away Capes of Africa; Armenian, Christian, and Jew. The American loves no country except his own, but, loving all manhood as his brother, bids you enter and fear not, bids you partake with us of these fruits of four hundred years of American government and development, and behold these trophies of one hundred years of American independence and freedom.

We are met this day to honor the memory of Christopher Columbus, to celebrate the four hundredth annual return of the year of his transcendent achievement; and, with fitting rites, to dedicate to America and the universe a correct exposition of the world's progress between the years 1492 and 1892.

---

4. THE SCHOOLS TAKE PART.

Extract from the same Oration as above.

AT this moment, in every part of the American Union, the children are taking up the wondrous tale of the discovery of America by Christopher Columbus; and from Boston to Galveston, from the little log school-house in the wilderness to the towering academy in the city or town, may be witnessed the unprecedented spectacle of a powerful nation captured by an army of Liliputians, of embryo men and women, of toppling boys and girls, and tiny elves, scarce big enough to lisp the numbers of the National Anthem, scarce strong enough to lift the miniature flags that make of arid street and autumn wood an emblematical garden, to gladden the sight and to glorify the Red, White, and Blue.

See "Our young barbarians all at play;" for, better than this, we have nothing to exhibit!

These, indeed, are our crown-jewels, the truest, though the inevitable off-spring of our civil development; the representatives of a manhood vitalized and invigorated by toil and care, of a womanhood elated and inspired by Liberty and Education.

God bless the children and their mothers! God bless our country's flag, and God be with us now and ever! God in the roof-trees' shade, and God in the highway! God in the wind and the waves! God in all our hearts!

HENRY WATTERSON.

5. DEDICATION EXERCISES.

Extracts from Oration of Hon. CHAUNCEY M. DEPEW, an orator of the day.

THIS day belongs, not to America, but to the world. The results of the day it celebrates are the heritage of the peoples of every race and clime. We celebrate the emancipation of man. The preparation was the work of almost countless centuries; the realization was the revelation of one. The Cross on Calvary was hope; the cross raised on San Salvador was opportunity. But for the first, Columbus never would have sailed; but for the second, there would have been no place for the planting, the nurture, and the expansion of civil and religious liberty. Ancient history is a dreary record of unstable civilizations. Each reached its zenith of material splendor, and perished. Their destruction involved a sum of misery and relapse which almost made their creation a curse rather than a blessing. Force was the factor in the government of the world when Christ was born, and force was the source and exercise of authority, both of Church and State, when Columbus sailed from Palos. The Wise Men travelled from the East towards the West under the guidance of the Star of Bethlehem. The spirit of the equality of all before God and the law, moved westward from Calvary with its revolutionary influence upon old institutions, to the Atlantic Ocean. Columbus carried it westward across the seas. The emigrants from England, Ireland, Scotland, and Wales, from Germany and Holland, from Sweden and Denmark, from France and Italy, from Spain and Portugal, under its guidance and inspiration, moved west, and west, building States and founding cities, until the Pacific limited their march. The exhibition which the Republic of the United States will here present, and to which, through its Chief Magistrate, it invites all nations, condenses and displays the flower and fruitage of this transcendent miracle.

The force, however, which made possible America, and its reflex influence upon Europe, was the open Bible by the family fireside. Civil and religious freedom are founded upon the individual and his independence, his worth, his rights, and his equal status and opportunity. The time had come for the emancipation of the mind and soul of humanity. The factors wanting for its fulfillment were the new world and its discoverer.

God always has in training some commanding genius for the control of great crises in the affairs of nations and peoples. Their number is less than the centuries, but their lives are the history of human progress. Though

Cæsar and Charlemagne, and Hildebrand and Luther, and William the Conqueror, and Oliver Cromwell, and all the epoch-makers prepared Europe for the event, and contributed to the result, the lights which illumine our firmament to-day are Columbus the discoverer, Washington the founder, and Lincoln the savior. The Puritan settled in New England, and the Cavalier in the South. They represented the opposition of spiritual and temporal life and opinions. The processes of liberty liberalized the one and elevated the other. Their union in a common cause gave the world a republic both stable and free. It possessed conservatism without bigotry, and liberty without license. It was nurtured by the toleration and patriotism which bound together in a common cause the Puritans of New England and the Catholics of Maryland, the Dutch Reformers of New York and the Huguenots of South Carolina, the Quakers and Lutherans of Pennsylvania and the Episcopalians, Methodists, Presbyterians, Baptists, and religionists of all and of opposite opinions in the other colonies. The men who wrote in the cabin of the Mayflower the first charter of freedom, a government of just and equal laws, were a little band of protestants against every form of injustice and tyranny. The leaven of their principles made possible the Declaration of Independence, liberated the slaves, and founded the free commonwealths which form the Republic of the United States. Jefferson's superb crystallization of the popular opinion, that "all men are created equal, that they are endowed by their Creator with certain inalienable rights, that among these are life, liberty, and the pursuit of happiness," had its force and effect in being the deliberate utterance of the people. It was Magna Charta and the Petition of Rights planted in the virgin soil of the American wilderness, and bearing richer and riper fruit.

After a century of successful trial, the system has passed the period of experiment, and its demonstrated permanency and power are revolutionizing the governments of the world. It has raised the largest armies of modern times for self-preservation, and, at the successful termination of the war, returned the soldiers to the pursuits of peace. It has so adjusted itself to the pride and patriotism of the defeated that they vie with the victors in their support of, and enthusiasm for, the old flag and our common country. Imported anarchists have preached their baleful doctrines, but have made no converts. Socialism finds disciples only among those who were its votaries before they were forced to fly from their native land, but it does not take root upon American soil. The citizen can worship God according to his belief and conscience, or he may neither reverence nor recognize the Almighty. And yet, religion has flourished, churches abound, the ministry is sustained, and millions of dollars are contributed annually for the evangelization of the world. The United States is a Christian country, and a living and practical Christianity is the characteristic of its people.

The spirit and object of this exhibition are peace and kinship. The grandeur and beauty of this spectacle are the eloquent witnesses of peace and progress. The Parthenon and the cathedral exhausted the genius of the ancient and the skill of the mediaeval architect in housing the statue or spirit of Diana. In their ruins or their antiquity, they are mute protests against the merciless enmity of nations, which forced art to flee to the altar for protection. The United States welcome the sister Republics of the Southern and Northern Continents, and the nations and peoples of Europe and Asia, of Africa and Australia, with the products of their lands, of their skill, and of their industry, to this city of yesterday, yet clothed with royal splendor as the Queen of the Great Lakes. The peace of the world permits and protects their efforts in utilizing their powers for man's temporal welfare. The result is this Park of Palaces. The originality and boldness of their conceptions, and the magnitude and harmony of their creations, are the contributions of America to the oldest of the arts, and the cordial bidding of America to the peoples of the earth to come and bring the fruitage of their age to the boundless opportunities of this unparalleled exhibition.

If interest in the affairs of this world are vouchsafed to those who have gone before, the spirit of Columbus hovers over us to-day. Only by celestial intelligence can it grasp the full significance of this spectacle and ceremonial.

From the first century to the fifteenth counts for little in the history of progress; but in the period between the fifteenth and twentieth is crowded the romance and reality of human development. Life has been prolonged and its enjoyment intensified. The powers of the air and the water, the resistless forces of the elements, which in the time of the discoverer were the visible terrors of the wrath of God, have been subdued to the service of man. Art and luxury which could be possessed and enjoyed only by the rich and noble, the works of genius which were read and understood only by the learned few, domestic comforts and surroundings beyond the reach of lord or bishop, now adorn and illumine the homes of our citizens. Serfs are sovereigns, and the people are kings. The trophies and splendors of their reign are commonwealths, rich in every attribute of great States, and united in a Republic whose power and prosperity and liberty and enlightenment are the wonder and admiration of the world.

Chauncey Mitchell Depew.

6. COLUMBUS THE DISCOVERER OF AMERICA.

From the same Oration.

NEITHER realism nor romance furnishes a more striking and picturesque figure than that of Christopher Columbus. The mystery about his origin heightens the charm of his story. That he came from among the toilers of his time is in harmony with the struggles of our period. Forty-four portraits of him have descended to us, and no two of them are the counterfeits of the same person. Each represents a character as distinct as its canvas. Strength and weakness, intellectuality and stupidity, high moral purpose and brutal ferocity, purity and licentiousness, the dreamer and the miser, the pirate and the Puritan, are the types from which we may select our hero. We dismiss the painter, and piercing, with the clarified vision of the dawn of the twentieth century, the veil of four hundred years, we construct our Columbus.

The perils of the sea, in his youth, upon the rich argosies of Genoa, or in the service of the licensed rovers, who made them their prey, had developed a skilful navigator and intrepid mariner. They had given him a glimpse of the possibilities of the unknown, beyond the highways of travel, which roused an unquenchable thirst for adventure and research. The study of the narratives of previous explorers, and diligent questionings of the daring spirits who had ventured far towards the fabled West, gradually evolved a theory, which became in his mind so fixed a fact that he could inspire others with his own passionate beliefs. The words, "That is a lie!" written by him on the margin of nearly every page of a volume of the travels of Marco Polo, which is still to be found in a Genoese library, illustrate the scepticism of his beginning, and the first vision of the New World, the fulfilment of his faith.

To secure the means to test the truth of his speculations, this poor and unknown dreamer must win the support of kings, and overcome the hostility of the Church. He never doubted his ability to do both, though he knew of no man living who was so great in power or lineage or learning that he could accomplish either. Unaided and alone, he succeeded in arousing the jealousies of sovereigns, and dividing the councils of ecclesiastics. "I will command your fleet and discover for you new realms, but only on condition that you confer on me hereditary nobility, the Admiralty of the Ocean and the Vice-Royalty, and one-tenth of the revenues of the New World," were the haughty terms to King John of Portugal. After ten years of disappointment and poverty, subsisting most of the time upon the charity of the enlightened monk of the convent of Rabida, who was his unfaltering friend, he stood before the throne of Ferdinand and Isabella, and, rising to imperial dignity in his rags, embodied the same royal conditions in his petition. The capture of Granada, the expulsion of Islam from Europe, and the triumph of the Cross, aroused the admiration and devotion of Christendom; but this proud beggar, holding in his grasp the potential promise and dominion of El Dorado and Cathay, divided with the Moslem surrender the attention of sovereigns and bishops. France and England indicated a desire to hear his theories and see his maps, while he was still a suppliant at the gates of the camp of Castile and Aragon, the sport of its courtiers, and the scoff of its confessors. His unshaken faith that Christopher Columbus was commissioned from Heaven, both by his name and by divine command, to carry "Christ across the sea" to new continents and pagan peoples, lifted him so far above the discouragements of an empty purse and a contemptuous court, that he was proof against the rebuffs of fortune or of friends. To conquer the prejudices of the clergy, to win the approval and financial support of the State, to venture upon that unknown ocean, which, according to the beliefs of the age, was peopled with demons and savage beasts of frightful shape, and from which there was no possibility of return, required the zeal of Peter the Hermit, the chivalric courage of the Cid, and the imagination of Dante. Columbus belonged to that high order of cranks who confidently walk "where angels fear to tread," and often become the benefactors of their country or their kind.

It was a happy omen of the position which woman was to hold in America, that the only person who comprehended the majestic scope of his plans, and the invincible quality of his genius, was the able and gracious queen of Castile. Isabella, alone of the dignitaries of that age, shares with Columbus the honors of the great achievement. She arrayed her kingdom and her private fortune behind the enthusiasm of this mystic mariner, and posterity pays homage to her wisdom and her faith.

The overthrow of the Mahommedan power in Spain would have been a forgotten scene, in one of the innumerable acts in the grand drama of history, had not Isabella conferred immortality upon herself, her husband, and their dual crown by her recognition of Columbus. The devout spirit of the queen and the high purpose of the explorer inspired the voyage, subdued the mutinous crew, and prevailed over the raging storms. They covered with the divine radiance of religion and humanity, the degrading search for gold, and the horrors of its quest, which filled the first century of the conquest with every form of lust and greed.

The mighty soul of the great admiral was undaunted by the ingratitude of princes and the hostility of the people, by imprisonment and neglect. He died as he was securing the means and preparing a campaign for the rescue of the Holy Sepulchre at Jerusalem from the infidel. He did not know, what time has revealed, that while the mission of the crusades of Bouillon and Richard of the Lion Heart was a bloody and fruitless romance, the discovery of America was the salvation of the world. The one was the symbol, the other the spirit; the one death, the other life. The tomb of the Saviour was a narrow and empty vault, precious only for its memories of the supreme tragedy of the centuries; but the new continent was to be the home and temple of the living God.

All hail, Columbus, discoverer, dreamer, hero, and apostle! We, here, of every race and country, recognize the horizon which bounded his vision and the infinite scope of his genius. The voice of gratitude and praise for all the blessings which have been showered upon mankind by his adventure is limited to no language, but is uttered in every tongue. Neither marble nor brass can fitly form his statue. Continents are his monument, and unnumbered millions, present and to come, who enjoy in their liberties and their happiness the fruits of his faith, will reverently guard and preserve from century to century his name and fame.

7. THE COLUMBIAN EXPOSITION OPENED.

Address by the President of the United States, May 1st, A. D. 1893.

I AM here to join my fellow-citizens in the congratulations which befit this occasion.

Surrounded by the stupendous results of American enterprise and activity, and in view of these magnificent evidences of American skill and intelligence, we need not fear that these congratulations will be exaggerated.

The enthusiasm with which we contemplate our work, intensifies the warmth of the greeting we extend to those who come from foreign lands to illustrate with us the growth and progress of human endeavor in the direction of a higher civilization.

We who believe that popular education and the stimulation of the best impulses of our citizens lead the way to a realization of the national destiny which our faith promises, gladly welcome the opportunity here afforded us, to see the results accomplished by efforts which have been exerted longer than ours in the field of main improvement; while in appreciative return, we exhibit the unparalleled advancement and accomplishment of a young nation, and present the triumphs of a vigorous, self-reliant, and independent people.

We have built these splendid edifices; but we have also built this magnificent fabric of popular government, whose grand proportions are seen throughout the world We have made and have gathered together objects of use and beauty, the product of American skill and invention; we have also made men who rule themselves.

It is an exalted mission in which we and our friends from other lands are engaged, as we co-operate in the inauguration of an enterprise devoted to human development; and in the undertaking we have entered upon, we exemplify in the noblest sense the brotherhood of nations.

Let us hold fast to the meaning that underlies this ceremony, and let us not lose the impressiveness of the moment. As, by a touch, the machinery that gives life to this vast exposition is now set in motion, so at the same instant let our hopes and aspirations awaken force which in all time to come shall influence the welfare, dignity, and the freedom of the world.

GROVER CLEVELAND.

CONTRIBUTING NATIONS.

The aggregate sum of six millions of dollars was appropriated by the governments of the following nations to secure their proper representation at the World's Columbian Exposition: —

Argentine,
Austria,
Belgium,
Bolivia,
Brazil,
British Guiana,
British Honduras,
Barbadoes,
Columbia,
Costa Rica,
Canada,
Cape Colony,
Ceylon,
Cuba,
Denmark,
Danish West Indies,
Dutch Guiana,
Dutch West Indies,
Ecuador,
France,
Germany,
Great Britain,
Greece,
Guatemala,
Hawaii,
Honduras,
Hayti,
India,
Japan,
Jamaica,
Leeward Islands,
Liberia,
Mexico,
Morocco,
Netherlands,
Nicaragua,
Norway,
New South Wales,
Orange Free State,
Paraguay,
Peru,
Russia,
Salvador,
San Domingo,
Spain,
Sweden,
Trinidad.

8. THE CONGRESS OF NATIONS.

No feature of the World's Columbian Exposition was more striking and representative of human necessities, aspirations, and possibilities than that one Congress, familarly styled "The Parliament of Religions." One orator, already cited, thus voiced its lesson, " Sublime the thought, to have the proclamation go out from the great Exposition that God reigns, and that man is his servant; that all progress begins and ends with Him who is the Alpha and Omega of all things." The following, from the Chicago " Inter-Ocean " was designed to develop the thought. The occasion was more conspicuously memorable for concerted prayer of the representatives of all religions, each striking the New Liberty Bell, as its prayer was uttered. The Old Liberty Bell, transported from Independence Hall, Philadelphia, added interest to the dedication of the new, by comparison of size and voice.

PROLOGUE.

"Of one blood," the Father "all nations, made,"
Whatever their race, their nation, or grade,
And breathed of Himself that spirit of life,
With warmth in its charge, with health ever rife,
Which bids its quick currents with infinite force
Flow back in its tide to the Heavenly source,
Whenever the soul, from its taints set free,
Asserts its proud right to full liberty.

The struggles of ages, their passions and hates;
The ruins of empires, of peoples and States;
The greed of the few enforced by the sword;
The sweep of the many, — a desperate horde;
The battle for self; the license of lust
Which laid generations low in the dust, —
Had mocked the swift ages with devilish glee
And robbed, in the name of fair liberty.

The essence divine, its fervor and glow,
Still pulsed in all hearts with feverish flow.
At altars and fanes and numberless shrines,
Regardless of sect, regardless of climes,

The soul sought relief from taintings within, —
Some cleansing of blood from inflowing sin, —
And ever aspired how best to be free
In the freedom of sinless liberty.

1. THE EXPOSITION OPEN.

COLUMBIA winged a welcome
  For all the sons of earth,
To the abundant feast she spread,
  From her abounding wealth;
Her mighty inland mart, the place,
  By flowing inland sea,
Where marble mansions filled the space, —
  To every nation free.

Art, Science, Industry, and Arms
  Were called to there compete;
Beauty and grandeur lent their charms,
  In concert chaste and mete; —
That thus, from nations far and near,
  Alike as guest and brother,
Whate'er their name, their race, or sphere,
  Might fellowship together.

Each potent force in Nature's hold,
  Released at bid of man,
Was marshalled by his courage bold
  To dignify the plan.
Land, wave, and overhanging sky,
  By keen electric skill,
Were made their subtle powers to ply,
  The wondrous best to fill.

Material schemes their part fulfilled,
  And zeal had nought to crave;
Material wealth was freely spilled —
  "No limit," but the grave.

While yet the assembled throngs
   Held breath, in silence bound,
Through concert as to one desire,
   For sights, — this life beyond.

II. THE PARLIAMENT OF RELIGIONS.

Thus the mighty mart of the mighty West
   Where Columbia's feast was spread,
Brought not alone material wealth, for test.
   But treasures of the heart and head.
Religion's plea and deepest human need
   Outbalanced all material good,
And from all climes and for each varied creed,
   Some earnest waiting sponsor stood.

As when the earthquake rocks the solid earth
   And finite skill proves faint and vain,
While anxious hearts, dispelling thirst for mirth,
   Invoke the great Creator's name,
So doth the mighty concourse wait
   As one by one in turn appears,
To cast his transit on that future state
   That has no stint by counted years.

As rays from all encompassed bounds combine
   Beneath the glist'ning convex lens;
As Magi once pursued the "Promised Star,"
   And earnest hope with action blends, —
So at this Parliament, devout, supreme,
   Gathered with zeal from everywhere,
One voice, one cry ascends, and this the theme,
   "To prayer!" for aid, "To prayer! To prayer!"

III. THE NEW LIBERTY BELL.

Those guests from many climes had often heard
   How Liberty this land possessed,
And that the tongue of Independence Bell
   Would never tire, could never rest;
Yet, lest its lesser size, these later years,
   Should fail to reach all human kind,
A larger bell was cast, dispelling fear, —
   The tale to ever keep in mind.

As stripes in "starry banner" count thirteen,
   Those first-born States to honor well,
That many "thousand weight" was fitly seen
   To rightly gauge in size the bell;
And lest no bronze could fill the standard sought,
   All relics prized, of arms or art,
With eager zest and will were quickly brought,
   As tributes from the people's heart.

And now this sacred bell hath sounded clear,
   "Strike, strike at will, ye people, all!"
And, "Winds, oh, quickly reach the Father's ear,
   With humblest prayer and faintest call.
Sound deep within each anxious, waiting soul
   That hence shall homeward quickly go,
And cheer its onward way to Freedom's goal,
   Where streams of mercy ever flow."

Then let each soul, with faith, in earnest vow
   For peace, fraternity, and right,
That all the earth, with joy, may humbly bow,
   And pledge to Liberty their plight.
So shall each stroke on vocal, mellow bell
   Give tone to life and strength to prayer;
The accents reach the skies where angels dwell,
   And God, who dwelleth everywhere.

IV. THE ECHO.

As stricken wave, its motion, never lost,
  Is felt on farthest shore;
As new-born star its light forever speeds,
  Though Time shall be no more;
As thought, while body rests, out-reaches space,
  To grasp its destiny;
So shall thy strokes, O bell, be carried on,
  And ring eternally.

H. B. C.

---

9. OUR FUTURE.

From Address delivered at the opening of the World's Auxiliary Congress, at the Columbian Exposition, October 21, 1892, by Bishop Ireland. "This organization" is stated, as follows, "to embrace international conventions or Congresses of workers and scholars of the whole world, along all lines of human progress in the various departments of civilized life, crowning the work of all other departments with the fragrance of heaven, in the department of religion."

The history of humanity is a history of progress. A narrow survey of the scene will not always bring out this important truth. There are, in the tide of progress, backward currents and tortuous windings. We must consider the general movement, of which the trend ceases not to be toward higher planes:—

"Forward, then; but still remember how the course of time
  will swerve,
Crook, and turn upon itself in many a backward streaming curve."

Disguised in a rhythm of rise and decline, of ebb and flow, of growth and decay, the progress of humanity continues, and the hopes of the workers in the cause of humanity obtain their rewards:—

"Through the ages one increasing purpose runs,
  And the thoughts of men are widening with the progress
    of the suns."

The future. What will it be? Material progress, no doubt, will continue onward, with ever increasing velocity. The wildest dreams, scarcely, I believe, foreshadow the realities. Nothing need be unexpected. Much will depend upon the intelligence and zeal of those whom position and talent have made the leaders of thought and action. Seldom in all history did such deep responsibilities rest upon their fellows as there do to-day. Scarcely ever was humanity pregnant with such momentous possibilities; scarcely ever were similar opportunities offered to do great things. There will be no rosebush without thorns; no day without the nearness of evening shade; no life without the menace of death. There will be inequalities among men, and passions will disturb the peace of souls; but I do believe there will be more mercy in the world, more justice, more righteousness. There will be more respect for manhood, more liberty for the individual. The brotherhood of man will be more widely recognized, and its lessons more faithfully practised. Brute force will more and more yield before reason; mind will more and more assert itself over matter and over passion.

In the course of history, God selected, now one nation, and now another, to be the guide and exemplar of humanity's progress. At the opening of the Christian Era, mighty Rome led the vanguard. Iberia rose up, the mistress of the times when America was to be born into the family of civilized peoples. The great era, the like of which has not been seen, is now dawning upon the horizon. Which will be Providence's chosen nation, to guide now the destinies of mankind?

The noble nation is before my soul's vision. Giant in stature, comely in every feature, buoyant in the freshness of morning youth, matronly in prudent stepping, the etherial breezes of liberty waving with loving touch her tresses, she is, no one seeing her doubts, the queen, the conqueror, the mistress, the teacher of the coming ages. To her keeping the Creator has intrusted a great continent, whose shores two oceans lave, rich in all nature's gifts, embosoming useful and precious minerals, fertile in soil, salubrious in air, beauteous in vesture. For long centuries had He held in reserve this region of His predilection, awaiting a propitious moment in humanity's evolutions to bestow it upon man, when man was ready to receive it. Her children have come from all countries, bearing with them the ripest fruit of thought, labor, and experience. Adding thereto, high inspirations and generous impulses, they have built up a new world of humanity. This world embraces the hopes, the ambitions, the dreamings of humanity's priests and seers. To its daring in the face of progress, to its offerings at the shrine of Liberty, there seems to be no limit; and yet, prosperity, order, peace, spread over its vast area their sheltering wings.

The Nation of the future. Need I name it? Your hearts quiver, loving it:—

> "My country 't is of thee,
> Sweet land of Liberty,
> Of thee I sing."

We commemorate the discovery of America four hundred years ago. Behold the crowning gift to humanity from Columbus, whose caravels plowed ocean's uncertain billows in search of a great land, and from the all-ruling Providence, whose wisdom and mercy inspired and guided the immortal Genoese mariner!—the United States of America.

JOHN IRELAND.

10. DISCOVERY DAY.

Immortal morn, all hail!
That saw Columbus sail
   By Faith alone!
The skies before him bowed,
Back rolled the ocean proud,
And every lifting cloud
   With glory shone.

Fair science then was born.
On that celestial morn,
   Faith dared the sea;
Triumphant o'er foes
Then Truth immortal rose,
New heavens to disclose,
   And earth to free.

Strong Freedom then came forth,
To liberate the earth
   And crown the right;
So walked the pilot bold
Upon the sea of gold,
And darkness backward rolled,
   And there was light.

Sweep, sweep across the seas!
Ye rolling jubilees,
   Grand chorus raise.
The world adoring stands,
And, with uplifted hands,
Offers from all her lands,
   To God the praise.

Ye hosts of Faith, sing on!
The victories ye have won
   Shall time increase;

>And, like the choral strain
>That fell on Bethlehem's plain,
>Inspire the perfect reign
>Of Love and Peace.
>
>HEZEKIAH BUTTERWORTH.

11. THE FUTURE OF THE UNITED STATES.

WHAT is to be the destiny of this Republic? The Old World has already revealed to us, in its unsealed books, the beginning and the end of all its own marvellous struggles in the cause of Liberty. Greece, lovely Greece, "the land of scholars and the nurse of arms," where sister Republics in fair possessions chanted the praises of Liberty, fell not when the mighty were upon her. Her sons were united at Thermopylæ and Marathon, and the tide of her triumph rolled back upon the Hellespont. She was conquered by her own factions. She fell by the hands of her own people, by her own corruptions and dissensions.

And Rome, where and what is she? Where are the Republics of modern times, which clustered round immortal Italy? We stand the experiment of government by the people. We are in the vigor of youth. The Atlantic rolls between us and any formidable foe. Within our own territory we have the choice of many products, and many means of independence. The government is mild. The press is free. Religion is free. Knowledge reaches, or may reach, every home.

Already has the age caught the spirit of our institutions. It has ascended the Andes, and snuffed the breezes of both oceans. It has infused itself into the life-blood of Europe, and warmed the sunny plains of France, and the lowlands of Holland. It has touched the philosophy of Germany and the North; and, moving south, has opened to Greece the lessons of her better days.

I call upon you, fathers, by the shades of your ancestors, by all you are or hope to be, Resist every object of disunion, every encroachment upon your liberties, every attempt to fetter your consciences, to smother your public schools, or extinguish your system of public instruction!

I call upon you, mothers, by the love of your offspring, Teach them, as they climb upon your knees, or lean upon your bosoms, the blessings of liberty. Swear them at the altar, as with their baptismal vows, to be true to their country, and never to forget or forsake her.

I call upon you, young men, to remember whose sons you are, — whose inheritance you possess. Life can never be too short which brings nothing but disgrace and oppression. Death never comes too soon, if necessary in defence of the liberties of your country.

I call upon you, old men, for your counsels, and your prayers, and your benedictions. May not your gray hairs go down in sorrow to the grave with the recollection that you have lived in vain. May not your last sun sink in the west upon a nation of slaves.

No! I read in the destiny of my country far better hopes, far brighter visions. May he who, at the distance of another century, shall stand here to celebrate this day, still look upon a free, happy and virtuous people! May he, with all the enthusiasm of truth, exclaim that here is still his country!

JOSEPH STORY.

12. AMERICAN DESTINY.

GEORGE BERKELEY, Bishop of Cloyne, Ireland, visited America in 1728, to found a college for educating the North American Indians. On his return he thus forecast the destiny of America.

THE Muse, disgusted at an age and clime
    Barren of every glorious theme,
In distant lands now waits a better time,
    Producing subjects worthy fame.

In happy climes, where from the genial sun
    And virgin earth such scenes ensue,
The force of Art by Nature seems outdone,
    And fancied beauties by the true;

In happy climes, the seat of innocence,
    Where Nature guides and Virtue rules,
Where men shall not impose, for truth and sense,
    The pedantry of courts and schools,

There shall be sung another golden age,—
    The rise of empire and the arts;
The good and great inspiring epic rage;
    The wisest heads and noblest hearts;

Not such as Europe breeds in her decay:
    Such as she bred when fresh and young,
When heavenly flame did animate her clay,
    By future poets shall be sung.

Westward the star of empire takes its way:
    The first four acts already past,
A fifth shall close the drama with the day;
    Time's noblest offspring is the last.

13. OUR HISTORY.

What has our country done to repay the world for the benefits we have received from others?

Is it nothing for the universal good of mankind to have carried into successful operation a system of self-government uniting personal liberty, freedom of opinion, and equality of rights with national power and dignity such as never before existed, only in the Eutopian dreams of philanthropists? Is it nothing, in moral science, to have anticipated, in sober reality, numerous plans of reform in civil and criminal jurisprudence, which are but now received as plausible theories by the politicians of Europe? Is it nothing to have been able to call forth on every emergency, either in peace or war, a body of talents always equal to the difficulty? Is it nothing to have improved the sciences, enriched human knowledge, and augmented the power and the comforts of civilized man, by miracles of mechanical invention? Is it nothing to have given to the world examples of disinterested patriotism, of political wisdom, of public virtue; of learning, eloquence, and valor, never exerted save for some praise-worthy end?

No, Land of Liberty! Thy children have no cause to blush for thee. What though the arts have reared few monuments among us, and scarce a trace of the Muse's footstep is to be found in the paths of our forests, or along the banks of our rivers, — yet our soil has been consecrated by the blood of heroes and by great and holy deeds of peace. Its wide extent has become one vast temple, sanctified by the prayers and blessings of the persecuted of every sect, and the wretched of all nations.

Land of Refuge! Land of Benedictions! Those prayers still arise, and they still are heard, " May peace be within thy walls, and plenteousness in thy palaces. May there be no decay, no leading into captivity, no complaining in thy streets. May truth flourish out of the earth, and righteousness look down from Heaven."

JULIAN CROMMELIN VERPLANCK.

---

14. THE FUTURE OF OUR LANGUAGE.

THE products of the whole world are, or soon may be, found within our confederated limits. God is bringing hither the most vigorous scions from all European stocks, to make of them all a new man,—not a Saxon, German, Gaul, or Helvetian, but an American. Here they will unite as one brotherhood, will have one law, will share one interest.

Spread over the vast region from the frigid to the torrid zone, from the Eastern to the Western ocean, every variety of climate, choice of pursuit, and modification of temperament, the ballot-box fusing together all rivalries, they shall have one national will. What is wanting in one race will be supplied by the characteristic energies of the others; and what is excessive in either, will be checked by the counter action of the rest. Nay, though for a time the newly-come, may retain their foreign vernacular, our tongue, so rich in ennobling literature, will be the tongue of the nation and the accent of its majesty. Eternal God, who seest the end from the beginning, Thou alone canst tell the ultimate grandeur of this people.

Such is the sphere, present and future, in which God calls us to work for Him, for our country, and for mankind. The language in which we utter truth will be spoken on this continent, a century hence, by thirty times more millions than those dwelling on the island of its origin. The openings for trade on the Pacific coast, and a railroad across the Isthmus, will bring the commerce of the world under the control of our race.

The empire of our language will follow that of our commerce; and the empire of our institutions, that of our language. The man who writes successfully for America will yet speak for the world!

GEORGE W. BETHUNE.

---

15. PROGRESS IS CONSTANT.

LET us be of good cheer. Humanity has ever advanced, urged by the instincts and necessities implanted by God. Whatever is good, whatever is just, whatever is humane, must prevail. In the recognition of this law there are motives to beneficent activity which shall endure to the last syllable of time.

Let the young embrace it. They shall find in it an ever living spring. Let the old cherish it still. They shall derive from it fresh encouragement. It shall give to all, old and young, a new appreciation of their existence, a new sentiment of their force, a new revelation of their destiny.

Be it then our duty and our encouragement to live and labor, ever mindful of the future; but let us not forget the past. All ages have lived and labored for us. From one has come art, from another jurisprudence, from another the mariner's compass, from another the printing-press; from all have proceeded lessons of truth and virtue. The earliest and most distant times are not without a present influence on our daily lives. The mighty stream of progress, though fed by many tributary waters and hidden springs, derives something of its force from the early currents which leap and sparkle in the distant mountain recesses, among rapids, and beneath the shade of primeval forest.

Nor should we be too impatient to witness the fulfilment of our aspirations. The daily increasing rapidity of discovery and the daily multiplying efforts of beneficence, in later years out-stripping the imaginations of the most sanguine, furnish well-grounded assurance that the advance of man will be with a constantly accelerating speed. The extending intercourse among the nations of the earth, and among all the children of the human family, gives new promise of the complete diffusion of truth, penetrating the most distant places, chasing away the darkness of night, and exposing the hideous form of slavery, of war, of wrong, which must be hated as soon as they are clearly seen.

Learn to reconcile order with change. This is a wise conservatism. This is a wise reform. Rightly understand these terms, and who would not be conservative? Who would not be a Reformer, — a conservative of all that is good, a reformer of all that is evil; a conservative of knowledge, a reformer of ignorance; a conservative of truths and principles whose seat is in the bosom of God, a reformer of laws and institutions which are but the imperfect work of man?

Blending these two characters in one, let us seek to be, at the same time, Reforming Conservatives and Conservative Reformers.

CHARLES SUMNER.

16. AMERICA THE CHILD OF DESTINY.

I may be an enthusiast, but I cannot but give utterance to the conceptions of my own mind. When I look upon the special developments of European civilization, and see on the southern shore of that continent an humble individual, amidst untold difficulties and repeated defeats, pursuing the mysterious suggestions which the mighty deep poured unceasingly upon his troubled spirit, till at last, with great and irrepressible energy of soul, he discovered that there lay, in the far western ocean, a continent open for the infusion of those elementary principles of liberty which were dwarfed in European soil, — I have conceived that the hand of Destiny was there!

When I saw the emigration of the Pilgrims from the chalky shores of England, in the night fleeing from their native home; when father, mother, brother, wife, sister, lover, were all lost by those melancholy wanderers "stilling the mighty hunger of the heart," and landing amidst cold and poverty and death, upon the rude rocks of Plymouth, — I have ventured to think the Will of Deity was there!

When I have remembered the Revolution of 1776, — the seven years of war; three millions in arms against the most powerful nation in history, and vindicating their independence, — I have thought that their sufferings and death were not in vain!

When I have gone and seen the deserted hearthstones, looked in upon the battle-field, upon the dying and dead, heard the agonizing cry, "Water, for the sake of God! Water!" seen the dissolution of this being, pale lips pressing in death the yet loved image of wife, sister, lover, — I will not deem all these in vain!

Like the Roman who looked back upon the glory of his ancestors, in woe exclaiming, —

"Great Scipio's ghost complains that we are slow,
And Pompey's shade walks unavenged among us,"

the great dead hover about me. Lawrence speaks, "Don't give up the ship!" and Henry, "Give me Liberty or give me death!" and Adams, "Survive or perish, I am for the Declaration!" and Allen, "In the name of the living God, I come!"

Come, then, thou Eternal! who dwellest not in temples made with hands, but who, in the city's crowd or by the fair forest stream, revealest thyself to the earnest seeker after the true and the right, inspire my heart; give me undying courage to pursue the promptings of my spirit; and, whether I shall be called in the shades of life to look upon as sweet and loved faces as now, or, shut in by sorrow and night, horrid visions shall gloom upon me in my dying hour — O my Country, mayst thou yet be free!

CASSIUS MARCELLUS CLAY.

17. THE PACIFIC SHORE.

From Swett's "Common School Readings," H. H. Bancroft & Co., San Francisco, California.

LONG years ago, a little band
  Of Pilgrims, from a distant shore,
Found a wild home in that cold land
  Where the Atlantic surges roar.
They were strong, iron-hearted men, —
  Oppression's stern, unbending foes;
And in each rugged mountain glen
  The village church and school-house rose.

Those Pilgrim sires have passed away,
  But still they live in deathless fame;
And Pilgrim mothers of that day
  Are crowned with an immortal name.
They have departed, but have left
  A glorious legacy behind,
Of which we cannot be bereft,—
  The freedom of the human mind.

We find a new and pleasant home,
  From want, and war, and danger free,
Spanned with warm skies and crystal dome,
  Laved by Pacific's calmer sea.
The church and school-house, side by side,
  Were nurseries of New England's men;
And may they be our boast and pride,
  Adorning every golden glen.

Great God, thy kind and bounteous care
  Hath cast our lot in goodly lands,
With summer skies and valleys fair,
  And rivers paved with golden sands.
God of our fathers, crown and bless
  This golden land of Pacific's shore,
With plenty, peace, and happiness,
  And liberty, forevermore !

                                      ANON.

18. THE TWENTIETH CENTURY.

FROM Address delivered by President Gates of Amherst College, while at Rutger's College, New Jersey, to students upon completion of a course of college study. (Contributed.)

WHAT is the age in which you are called to act ?

You belong, by God's appointing, to the twentieth century,—that century whose vast titanic forces, the thundering machinery of this, our age of steam, but half foretells; while the flashing light and subtle force of electricity, which we are only beginning to draw from its exhaustless reservoirs, gives us lightning-like glimpses of the vast potentialities and the intensified activities of the unknown coming age, in which you shall be actors. For you are to be American citizens; and in the next century, America is to give form and color to the life of the world.

When the eighteenth century drew to a close, all eyes were bent upon France. A desperate struggle with the king was followed in swift succession by the terrible scenes of the French Revolution, and the wars of Napoleon, with their world-wide transforming issues. France was the vortex of the seething whirlpool in that period of transition and transformation, out of which has come the nineteenth century, with the abolition of human slavery, with the ballot placed in every man's hands. The nation which is to give color and form to the life of the twentieth century was hardly yet full-born when the nineteenth century opened. From May until September, 1787, the Convention in Philadelphia was engaged in those earnest debates from which emerged the Constitution of the United States, which Gladstone calls "the most wonderful work ever struck off at one time by the mind and purpose of men." The nation which was then feeling its way through the dark dawning of our history, stands, to-day, among the mightiest of earthly powers. Thoughtful men, the world over, are convinced that the closing decade of this century, like that of the last, will be a transition period, ushering in great social and economic changes in Europe and throughout the world. In all such changes toward more popular forms of government, America must be, as she is, to-day, the world's example.

We believe in God's government of the world. We

believe that the mighty evolution of government "of the people, by the people, for the people," is of God's own evoking. At such a time, called to be citizens in such a nation, you do well to ask earnestly, "What are the strong sweeping tendencies of the age? What is their true significance for me?"

The nineteenth century, as it draws to a close, seems to sound out as a keynote to the twentieth century, "Now that all men govern, it is decreed that all men must be laborers too! If all are to govern, all must serve! Fitness for kingship is only proved by fitness to serve!" This is the emphasized utterance of our times. The rich man who uses his wealth is a true laborer for the common welfare. But he must vitalize it, animate it, if he would prove the wealth is really and properly his. The rich man who does not aim to do anything for the world with his money, is but an able-bodied pauper. God's law holds everywhere of property and of personal power of every kind: "Use it, or lose it."

This doctrine will always meet with a protest; but protest to *whom?* To God? His answer is clear: "If any will not work, neither shall he eat." Will they address their protest to their fellow-men? The solid phalanx of laborers, the world's honestly-busied millions, with ballots in their hands, answer the protest thus: "Under God's Providence, we, the working majority, make the laws. Work has not made us wiser than the laws of God, and we say, too, If any will not work, neither shall he eat."

Get work, young men! You will be in harmony with the keynote of your century. But know well that no plan can be devised by which men can be made good and happy in the mass. A century of constant legislation has not made happiness universal. This is not due to bad laws in society, or to bad laws in nature, but directly to men's wilful desires and passions. Society will be purified, institutions will be made and kept better, only as men are made better, one by one. Be it your highest duty and noblest service of your fellow-man, then, while earnestly doing your appointed work, to win all men whom you can influence, by example and by invitation, one by one, to a saving knowledge of the Living God.

With us, in the form of government which Providence has given us, and in which we believe, "The people are king." And the loyal prayer and hope of our hearts is, "May God save the king!"

---

19. PATRIOT SONS OF PATRIOT SIRES.

THE BOYS OF TO-DAY, THE MEN OF THE FUTURE.

Written for "Beacon Lights of Patriotism," by Rev. Samuel Francis Smith, author of "America," which was written in 1832.

> The small life, coiled within the seed,—
>   A promise hid away,—
> But dimly heralds what shall be
>   When comes the perfect day;
> But sun and rain and frost and heat
>   Enrich the fertile fields,
> And the small life of earlier years
>   A waving harvest yields.
>
> The corn that slumbers in the hill —
>   A disk of golden grain —
> Stands up at last, a rustling host,
>   And covers all the plain.

Who knows to what the infant germ
    In coming seasons leads,
Or how the golden grain expands,
    And mighty armies feeds?

The acorn in its little cup,
    High on the breezy hill,
Waits for the fulness of the times,
    Its mission to fulfil,
And year by year grows grand and strong.
    What shall the future be?
A noble forest on the land,
    Or navy on the sea?

The bright-eyed boys who crowd our schools,
    The knights of book and pen,
Weary of childish games and moods,
    Will soon be stalwart men,—
The leaders in the race of life,
    The men to win applause;
The great minds born to rule the State,
    The wise, to make the laws.

Teach them to guard with jealous care
    The land that gave them birth,
As patriot sons of patriot sires,—
    The dearest spot of earth.
Teach them the sacred trust to keep
    Like true men, pure and brave;
And o'er them, through the ages, bid
    Freedom's fair banner wave.

MEMORIAL OBSERVANCES.

The various centennial celebrations since 1876 have given fresh prominence to Memorial Days in American history. The founders of New England, of New York, of Maryland, of the Carolinas, and of Georgia, are no longer the sole representatives of a Forefathers' Day. The Western States, and the Pacific States as well, begin to honor the quarter and the half century of their local histories.

"Discovery Day" is to have a place in future recognition, since the commencement of the fifth century of the civilization of America. Arbor Day, Labor Day, and others supplement the holidays which Independence Day inaugurated. It is proper that our children should thus honor memorable names, events, and dates throughout the land; and, as never before, all sections have a common interest in the memories of all sections.

Washington's Birthday, more than any other, occurs at a season when all schools are in session; and a programme of alternate selections from this volume, not necessarily occupying more than an hour and a quarter of time, has been outlined, as a suggestive guide to such observance.

ORDER OF EXERCISES.

(A Picture of Washington rests upon an Easel, or within reach.)

Opening Tableau. — Thirteen young ladies bearing scarf, flag, shield, or belt, each having the name of one of the original colonies, escort their teacher, who carries a wand or flag, and the insignia "Columbia" upon brow, breast, or belt, to the stage or platform, where they occupy seats in the order of their colonial charters, from right to left. The audience rise and stand during singing.

I. MUSIC.
  Hail Columbia . . . .   *Hopkinson.*

II. RECITATION.
  ⎰ Seventy-Six . . . . . . *Bryant*   107
  ⎜ Lexington . . . . *Weems* .   213
 or ⎨ Bunker Hill . . . . . . *Pierpont.*   216
  ⎜ Alamance . . . . *Whiting* . .   217
  ⎱ Valley Forge . . . . . . *Brown* .   217

III. DECLAMATION.
  ⎰ Washington's Training . . . *Upham* . . .   123
  ⎜ Carolina and Mecklenberg . . . *Delke* . . .   109
 or ⎨ The First Congress . . . . *Marcy* . . .   112
  ⎜ The Lesson of the Revolution . . *Sparks* . . .   115
  ⎱ The American Constitution . . *Legare* . . .   119

IV. RECITATION.

or
{
Washington as a Leader . . *Pierpont* . . . 122
The True Cost of Liberty . . *Giles* 138
Our Nationality . . . . . *King* 255
Our Country . . . . . . *Sargent* . . . 255
Patriots and Martyrs . . . . *Anon.* 166
}

V. MUSIC.

or
{
Columbia, Gem of the Ocean (Red, White, and Blue).
E Pluribus Unum.
Keller's American Hymn.
}

VI. DECLAMATION.

or
{
The Unselfishness of Washington *Paine* . . . 125
True Liberty . . . . *Robertson* . . . 263
True Nobility . . . . *Swain* 276
True Glory . . . . *Milton* . . . 197
Patriotism . . . . *Meagher* . . . 231
}

VII. RECITATION.

or
{
Washington as a Guide for Youth . *Dwight* . . . 126
Our History . . . . *Verplanck* . . . 390
Our Future . . . . *Ireland* . . . 283
Our Destiny . . . . *C. M. Clay* . . 394
Fatherland . . . . *Fallersleben* . . 92
}

VIII. MUSIC.

or
{
Hail to the Chief.
To Thee, O Country 222
Our Martyred Dead 188
}

IX. DECLAMATION.

or
{
Washington as a Soldier . . *No. Am. Review* . 129
Courage . . . . *Proctor* . . . 349
Our Flag is There . . . . . *Am. Naval Officer* 180
The Flower of Liberty . . . *Holmes* . . . 163
The National Ensign . . . . *Winthrop* . . . 225
}

CLOSING TABLEAU. — Representatives of the colonies leave the stage and pass to the rear of the audience, where they are joined by representatives of the added States. These, in pairs, promenade the aisles, where practicable, and ascend the stage responsive to Columbia's call of the States, forming a crescent before Columbia, the right and left joining the left and right of those who represent the original States. Columbia, as they approach, waves her wand or banner and recites Mrs. Sigourney's poem, —

"Stars in my Country's Sky! Are Ye all There?"

Each, in order of admission, responds, "Here am I," and the audience, rising, unites in singing, —

"The Star-Spangled Banner."

X. RECITATION.
  Washington's Resignation of his Commission 135
  The Mt. Vernon Tribute . . . . *Day* 133

A selected pupil advances and places a wreath about the head of Washington, while all recite, in unison, —

  Crown our Washington . . *Butterworth* . 125

XI. RESPONSE OF REPRESENTATIVES OF THE STATES
  Onward, Flag of Glory, flying . . . *Phelps* . . . 404
  Banner Land of Human Progress . *Crane* . . . 404

XII. MUSIC.
  America. Sung by all, standing.

CROWNING WASHINGTON.

The original scene of "Crowning Washington," referred to on page 125, and very generally adopted, provides for the recitation of a special obligation to be faithful to flag, God, and country.

The late Colonel George T. Balch, of New York, whose contribution on page 329 was received but a few days before his death, also provided a solemn obligation, to be repeated by all school-children in unison.

In each case all pupils saluted, as the tribute was paid to the name of Washington.

The following stanzas, referred to in the foregoing program, are appropriately added in this connection.

STARS IN MY COUNTRY'S SKY! ARE YE ALL THERE?

I.
Are ye all there? Are ye all there,
 Stars in my country's sky?
Are ye all there? Are ye all there,
 In your shining homes on high?
"Count us! Count us," was their
  answer,
 As they dazzled on my view,
In glorious perihelion,
 Amid their field of blue.

II.
I cannot count you rightly;
 There's a cloud with sable rim;
I cannot make your number out,
 For my eyes with tears are dim!
O bright and blessed angel,
 On white wing floating by,
Help me to count and not to miss
 One star in my country's sky!

III.
Then the angel touched my eyelids,
 And touched the frowning cloud;
And its sable rim departed,
 And it fled with murky shroud.
There was no missing Pleiad
 'Mid all that sister race;
The Southern Cross gleamed radiant
  forth,
And the Pole-Star kept its place!

IV.
Then I knew it was the angel
 Who woke the hymning strain
That at our Redeemer's birth
 Pealed out o'er Bethlehem's plain;
And still its heavenly key-tone
 My listening country held,
For all her constellated stars
 The diapason swelled.

Also, the closing stanza of "The New Song of Freedom," written for the "Patriotic Reader" by Sylvanus Dryden Phelps.

"Onward! flag of glory flying,
  Grandest earthly banner, thou;
Higher rise, to fame undying,
  Borne aloft by Freedom now!
Thine, O Stars and Stripes, the story
Of a nation's wondrous birth,
Symbols of its brightening glory,
Won from field and conflict gory,
  Symbol of its power and worth!"

Also, the closing stanzas of "Columbia to the Front," written for "Columbian Selections" by Oliver Crane.

"Banner-land of human progress,
  Hopes of man are in thy trust;
Float aloft thy fateful standards,
  Let them never trail in dust.
Be Columbia's fair escutcheon
  Never stained by sanctioned crime;
Be her name in highest honor
  Held by all of every clime."

" Ever 'Onward' be advancing,
  Hold the right and spurn the wrong;
Take the front, and, ne'er retreating,
  Make thine arm for justice strong.
Strong for Freedom's holy conquests,
  Strong to lift the trodden down.
So, undimmed shall be thy glory,
  And eternal thy renown."

SCHOOL FLAG HONORS.

The care of the School Flag, its hoisting and lowering, should be assigned to meritorious pupils, and suitable salutes be given by all present when it is hoisted or lowered.

When proper to have the flag at half-mast, it should first be raised to mast-head, and dropped to place. It should also be returned to mast-head before being hauled down, when the mourning tribute comes to an end.

[From the "Youth's Companion" Program. By permission.]

SYMPOSIUM OF PATRIOTIC SONGS.

FOR USE IN MEMORIAL OBSERVANCES.

COLUMBIA, THE LAND OF THE BRAVE.

Shaw.

O Columbia, the gem of the ocean,
    The home of the brave and the free,
The shrine of each patriot's devotion,
    A world offers homage to thee.
Thy mandates make heroes assemble,
    When Liberty's form stands in view,
Thy banners make tyranny tremble,
    When borne by the Red, White, and Blue.

When war winged its wide desolation,
    And threatened the land to deform,
The ark then of Freedom's foundation,
    Columbia, rode safe through the storm,
With the garlands of victory around her,
    When so proudly she bore her brave crew,
With her flag proudly floating before her,
    The boast of the Red, White, and Blue.

Chorus.—When borne by the Red, White, and Blue,
    When borne by the Red, White, and Blue,
    Thy banners make tyranny tremble,
    When borne by the Red, White, and Blue.

HAIL, COLUMBIA, HAPPY LAND!

Hopkinson.

Hail, Columbia, happy land!
Hail, ye heroes, heaven-born band,
Who fought and bled in Freedom's cause,
Who fought and bled in Freedom's cause,
And, when the storm of war was gone,
Enjoyed the peace your valor won:
Let Independence be your boast;
Ever mindful what it cost,
Ever grateful for the prize,
Let its altars reach the skies.

Immortal patriots! rise once more!
Defend your rights, defend your shore;
Let no rude foe, with impious hands,
Let no rude foe, with impious hands,
Invade the shrine where sacred lies,
Of toil and blood the well-earned prize;
While offering peace, sincere and just,
In Heaven we place a manly trust,
That truth and justice may prevail,
And every scheme of bondage fail.

Chorus. — Firm, united, let us be,
　　　　Rallying round our liberty,
　　　　As a band of brothers joined,
　　　　Peace and safety we shall find.

THE STAR-SPANGLED BANNER.

Key.

Oh, say, can you see, by the dawn's early light,
　What so proudly we hailed at the twilight's last gleaming?
Whose broad stripes and bright stars, through the perilous fight,
　O'er the ramparts we watched, were so gallantly streaming!
And the rockets' red glare, the bombs bursting in air,
Gave proof through the night that our flag was still there:
Oh, say, does that star-spangled banner yet wave
O'er the land of the free and the home of the brave?

Oh, thus be it ever, when freeman shall stand
　Between their loved home and the war's desolation!
Blest with victory and peace, may the Heaven-rescued land
　Praise the Power that hath made and preserved us a nation!
Then conquer we must, for our cause it is just;
And this be our motto, "In God is our trust;"
And the star-spangled banner in triumph shall wave
O'er the land of the free and the home of the brave.

E PLURIBUS UNUM.

Cutter.

Though many and bright are the stars that appear
　In that flag by our country unfurled,
And the stripes that are swelling in majesty there,
　Like a rainbow adorning the world,
Their light is unsullied as those in the sky
　By a deed that our fathers have done,
And they 're linked in as true and as holy a tie
　By their motto of "Many in One."

Then up with our flag! — let it stream on the air;
　Though our fathers are cold in their graves,
They had hands that could strike, they had souls that could dare,
　And their sons were not born to be slaves.
Up, up with that banner! where'er it may call,
　Our millions shall rally around,
And a nation of freemen that moment shall fall
　When its stars shall be trailed on the ground.

GOD SAVE THE STATE.

Brooks (Air: "Italian Hymn").

God save our native land!
Firm may she ever stand,
   Through storm and night!
When the wild tempests rave,
Ruler of wind and wave,
Do Thou our country save
   By Thy great might.

For her our prayer shall rise
To God above the skies;
   On Him we wait:
Thou who art ever nigh,
Guarding with watchful eye,
To Thee aloud we cry,
   God save the State!

KELLER'S AMERICAN HYMN.

Keller.

Speed our Republic, O Father on high;
   Lead us in pathways of justice and right;
Rulers as well as the ruled, "One and all,"
   Girdle with virtue, the armor of night.

Foremost in battle for Freedom to stand,
   We rush to arms when aroused by its call;
Still, as of yore, when George Washington led,
   Thunders our war-cry, "We conquer or fall!"

Faithful and honest to friend and to foe, —
   Willing to die in humanity's cause, —
Thus we defy all tyrannical power,
   While we contend for our Union and laws.

Rise up, proud eagle, rise up to the clouds;
   Spread thy broad wings o'er this fair western world.
Fling from thy beak our dear banner of old, —
   Show that it still is for Freedom unfurled.

   Hail, three times hail, to our country and flag!

(Repeat last two lines as chorus.)

Hail, three times hail, to our country and flag!
Rulers as well as the ruled, "One and all,"
Girdle with virtue, the armor of night,
Hail, three times hail, to our country and flag!

"RING! RING! OF LIBERTY AND PEACE!"

CARRINGTON.

Air: "No. IV., Holtzman's Short Masses," Meesburg, 1776; adopted by Rouget de Lisle for his "Marseilles Hymn;" and as appropriate for American national sentiment.

(Written, in harmony with the suggestion that the bells throughout the land be rung at the same hour, on the Centennial Anniversary of the Inauguration of President Washington, April 30, 1889, and that the custom be observed at his recurring birthdays and each Independence Day, thereafter.)

YE sons of this grand land of Liberty,
   Ring! ring! throughout the welkin, ring!
Your homes, your shrines, your blessings, many: —
   Recount their wealth, their praises sing!
   Recount their wealth, their praises sing!
Ring bells, in every tower and steeple!
   With throbbing heart and steady hand,
   Proclaim, at once, throughout the land,
We are a free and happy people!

   Chorus. — Ring! ring! the mandate, sound!
       Let discord wholly cease!
     Ring! ring! the gladness all around!
       Of Liberty and Peace!
     Ring! ring! the mandate, sound!
       Let discord wholly cease!
     Ring on! Ring loud! the mandate, sound
       Of Liberty and Peace!

Columbia! call the past before thee!
   Ring! ring! with each repeated peal,
The notes of gladness, thrift, and glory!
   Proclaim your will, — the nation's weal!
   Proclaim your will, — the nation's weal!
Bind every wound that still is bleeding;
   Soothe every heart that anguish feels;
   Each stroke, new hope for man reveals, —
Ring! while yet at the altar kneeling!

Chorus.

To Washington, who gave us Freedom,
   Ring! ring! By stroke on every bell,
Tell all the earth, of faith and wisdom,
   That built the State so strong and well,
   That built the State so strong and well.
From lakes, to gulf and seas, we gather;
   No barrier shall divide our land;
   But pressing onward, hand in hand,
The sons shall bless their Nation's Father.

Chorus.

ALPHABETICAL INDEX OF TITLES.

		PAGE
Abraham Lincoln	Newman	317
Abraham seeking a Country	Editor	17
Address of Caradoc the Bard	Bulwer	234
Address of General Wolfe before Quebec		233
Adherbal before the Roman Senate	Sallust	74
Again Brethren and Equals	Patterson	306
Age of Work (The)	Kennedy	264
A Good Name	Hawes	342
Aim at Perfection (Apothegm)	Chesterfield	356
Aim high	Harrison	354
All-sufficient Strength (Apothegm)	Racine	295
Alcoholic and Tobacco Habit (The)	Dow	298
A Mecca for the Blue and the Gray. (Gettysburg)	Gordon	302
America, an Aggregate of Nations (Apothegm)	Tupper	108
America, Fairest of Freedom's Daughters	Rankin	159
America, the Child of Destiny	C. M. Clay	394
American Census (The), 1790 to 1890	Official	120
American Constitution (The)	Hamilton	116
American Constitution, no Experiment	Legare	119
American Constitution Tested	J. Adams	118
American Destiny	Berkeley	389
American Education	Winthrop	323
American Nationality	Choate	141
American Republic (The) a Christian State	Gibbons	160
A Nation's Strength	Psalm xxxiii.	47
Ancient Landmarks (Apothegm)	Solomon	97
A People Delivered	Geikie	21
A Preventive "No" (Apothegm)	Solomon	285
A Republic Defined	Lamartine	156
A Sketch of Moses	Hastings	29
A Star in the West	Cook	125
As thy Day, thy Strength shall be	Carrington	295
At the Old Home again	Bryant	97
Banner Land of Human Progress	Crane	404
Bannockburn	Burns	199
Battle-Field (The)	Bryant	181
Battle of Alamance (The)	Whiting	206
Battle of Bunker Hill (The)	Pierpont	216
Battle of Lexington (The)	Weems	214
Battle of Linden (The)	Campbell	212
Battle of Waterloo (The)	Byron	213
Be just and fear not	Shakespeare	248
Belligerent Non-combatants	Sherman	308
Benefits of the Civil War	Busbee	310
Better than Gold	Smart	286
Bivouac of the Dead	O'Hara	184
Boadicea and her last Struggle	Cowper	235
Bonaparte to his Army (1796)	Translation	242
Brotherly Love illustrated. (Jonathan and David)	Bible	92
Burial of the Deliverer (The)	Alexander	30
Burial of Sir John Moore (The)	Wolfe	210
Burlesque Challenge to America	Lemon, in "Punch"	249

		PAGE
Cæsar's Death justified . . . . Cassius		67
Carolina and Mecklenburg . . . . Delke		109
Carthage in Peril . . . . Hannibal		62
Christianity as a Political Force . . . . Dix		146
Columbian Exposition opened . . . . Cleveland		377
Columbian Exposition proclaimed . . . . . . Harrison		361
Columbian Oration . . . . Depew		368
Columbian Oration . . . . Watterson		365
Columbia the Land of the Brave . . . . Shaw		405
Columbia to the Front . . . . Crane		404
Columbus the Discoverer . . . . Depew		373
Contentment (Apothegm: from "Faerie Queen") . Spenser		324
Contributing Nations at Columbian Exposition . . Official		378
Courage . . . . Procter		349
Critical Conditions of Labor . . . . Harrison		268
Crown our Washington . . . . Butterworth		134
Culture of the Moral Virtues . . . . Baldwin		357
David, the Patriot King . . . . Geikie		36
"Dead on the Field of Honor" . . . . Chamberlain		246
Death of Osceola . . . . Street		207
Death or Liberty . . . . Weld		251
Death the Peacemaker. The Blue and the Gray . Flagg		320
Decoration Day . . . . Longfellow		316
Decoration Day Eve . . . . Smith		313
Decoration Day Ode . . . . Phelps		314
Deeds of Kindness . . . . Sargent		351
Degeneracy of Athens . . . . Demosthenes		69
Desirable Objects of Attainment . . . . Stoughton		326
Dirge for the Soldier . . . . Boker		192
Discovery Day . . . . Butterworth		386
Don't give too much for the Whistle . . . . . Franklin		277
England's Relations to America . . . . Macintosh		84
E Pluribus Unum . . . . Cutler		407
Erin and the Days of Old . . . . Moore		80
Eve of Decoration Day . . . . Smith		313
Fabricius refuses Bribes . . . . Pliny		53
Fall of the Indian Heroes . . . . Miller		204
Fatherland . . . . Arndt		89
Fatherland (My) . . . . Fallersleben		104
Fatherland (The) . . . . Lowell		91
Father Land and Mother Tongue . . . . Lover		93
First American Congress, noticed . . . . Marcy		112
First American Congress, remembered (Apothegm) . Lee		113
First Civil Code ever enacted . . . . Bible		25
First Constitution ever promulgated . . . . . Moses		24
Flower of Liberty (The) . . . . Holmes		164
Fourth of July (The) . . . . Webster		110
Freedom . . . . Lowell		245
Future of our Language (The) . . . . Bethune		391
Grattan's Appeal for Ireland . . . . Grattan		244
General Washington's Resignation, Dec. 23, 1783		135
Getting the right Start . . . . Holland		257
Gettysburg. A Mecca for the Blue and the Gray . Gordon		302
God save the State . . . . Brooks		407
Goodness and Greatness (Apothegm) . . . . . Bacon		339
Gospel Code Announced . . . . New Testament . . .		28
Gustavus Augustus, King of Sweden, to his Soldiers . Lefevre		238
Hail Columbia, Happy Land . . . . Hopkinson		406
Hannibal pleads for Peace . . . . Livy		64
Haste not, Rest not . . . . Goethe		262
Hebrew Codes (The) Developed . . . . Editor		28
High Tide at Gettysburg . . . . Thompson		219
Hill of Science (The) . . . . Aiken		345
Home . . . . Barton		104

ALPHABETICAL INDEX OF TITLES. 411

		PAGE
Home, Sweet Home	*Payne*	106
Horatius at the Bridge	*Macaulay*	49
House (The) where I was born	*Hood*	96
How to Have just what we Like	*H. Smith*	291
How to take it (Apothegm)	*Racine*	294
How we take it	*Miller*	293
Idleness a Crime	*Carrington*	151
If I were a Voice	*Mackay*	286
Immortal Memories	*Sheridan*	309
Immortality (Apothegm)	*S. F. Smith*	353
Independence Day	*Blaine*	108
Individual Purity the Hope of the State	*Sprague*	141
Jerusalem avenged	*Byron*	46
Jonathan's Love for David	1 *Samuel xviii.* 1	92
Joan of Arc's Farewell to Home	*Schiller*	201
Joshua, the Patriot General	*Geikie*	32
Keller's American Hymn	*Keller*	406
Labor Hours have Limits	*Macaulay*	274
Land of my Birth (The)	*Cook*	94
Laus Deo	*Whittier*	170
Law (The) of Labor (Apothegm)	*Crisis Thoughts*	275
Law (The) of Virtue (Apothegm)	*Cicero*	59
Leonidas	*Croly*	203
Lesson of the American Revolution (The)	*Sparks*	115
Let there be Light	*Mann*	237
Liberty of the Press	*Baker*	151
Liberty (The Cost of)	*Giles*	138
Liberty (The Torch of)	*Moore*	157
Look not upon the Wine when it is red	*Willis*	297
Love of Country	*Scott*	106
Marathon by Starlight	*Montgomery*	200
Merit before Birth	*Curtius*	72
Might makes Right	*Nat. Preceptor*	197
Mighty Word " No " (The)	*Cuyler*	283
Military Training in the School	*Editor*	352
Mourning Hero's Vision (The)	*Kossuth*	189
Mt. Vernon, Home of Washington	*Day*	133
My Fatherland	*Fallersleben*	104
National Ensign (The)	*Winthrop*	225
National Injustice	*Parker*	155
New Home-Country occupied, B. C. 1451-1443	*Geikie*	32
New England	*Percival*	82
New England and Virginia	*Winthrop*	85
Nineteenth Century (The) ends Slavery	*Lamar*	305
No Conflict now	*Devens*	303
No Excellence without Labor	*Wirt*	272
No Man knoweth his (Moses) Sepulchre	*Bryant*	31
No Peace without Liberty	*Kossuth*	139
No Slave beneath the Flag	*Taylor*	169
Not to myself alone	*Webb*	282
Old England	*Eliot*	79
Old Home (The) and the New	*Bleakie*	102
Old (The) Oaken Bucket	*Woodworth*	100
Once at Battle Eve	*Kraut*	222
Onward, Flag of Glory	*Phelps*	404
Our Banner Unrent: its Stars Unobscured	*Ross*	307
Our Country	*Peabody*	165
Our Country	*Sargent*	255
Our Flag is there		180
Our Future	*Ireland*	383
Our Future	*Story*	387
Our Gardener's Burial	*London Spectator*	102

ALPHABETICAL INDEX OF TITLES.

		Page
Our Heritage	Lowell	171
Our Heroes	Andrew	312
Our History	Verplanck	390
Our Martyred Dead	Trafton	188
Our Nationality	King	143
Our Own the Best (Apothegm)	Racine	94
Our Relations with England	Everett	81
Patriot's (The) Aspiration (Apothegm)	S. Adams	117
Patriot's Cry (The) (Paraphrase)	Psalm cxxxvii	48
Patriot Dead (The)	S. F. Smith	300
Patriot King in Mourning (The)	Willis	38
Patriot President (The)	London Punch	174
Patriot Prince (The)	Carrington	175
Patriot Sons of Patriot Sires	S. F. Smith	399
Patriotic Song	Kinkel	168
Patriotic Words for the Young	Hale	359
Patriotism	Meagher	231
Patriots and Martyrs	Holbrook	105
Petition to Time	Procter	337
Pilgrims of New England	Choate	86
Plea of the Pocomtuc Chief	Everett	241
Poverty of the Soul (Apothegm)	Montesquieu	154
President Lincoln at Gettysburg, Nov. 19, 1864		299
Press On	Benjamin	253
Prince Adherbal before the Roman Senate	Sallust	74
Principles of the American Revolution	Quincy	114
Proclamation of the Columbian Exposition	Harrison	361
Procrastination	Young	336
Progress is Constant	Sumner	392
Regulus before the Roman Senate	Sargent	56
Representative Government trustworthy	Æmilius	51
Reverence for Law	Hopkinson	147
Ring, Ring the Bells	Carrington	408
Review of the Dead	Stockard	186
Road (The) to Happiness open	Pope	280
Rocks of my Country	Hemans	95
Roman Liberty in Peril	Publius Scipio	60
Roman Senate (The) and American Congress compared	Kossuth	173
Ruth and Naomi	Peabody	35
Sanctuary (The) within the Breast	H. Smith	350
Saul and Jonathan lamented	Bible	40
Schools (The) take Part in Columbian Celebration	Watterson	367
Scipio declines Hannibal's Overtures for Peace		65
Scorn to be Slaves	Warren	229
Seeking a Country	Editor	17
Self-respect (Apothegm)	Cato	61
Self-sacrificing Ambition	Greeley	327
Separate as Billows, One as the Sea	Stephens	304
Separation from Traitors	Cicero	58
Serpent (The) of the Still	Lofland	348
Seventy-six	Bryant	107
Sincerity and Truth (Apothegm)	Montaigne	145
Solomon, the Wise King	Editor	41
Song of the Union	Cummings	179
Soul Culture (Apothegm)	Thomson	328
Souls, not Stations	Anonymous	332
Stars in my Country's Sky	Sigourney	403
Storming of Monterey	Hoffman	218
Success in Life	Childs	265
Supremacy of Conscience	Storrs	259
The Age of Work	Kennedy	264
The Alcoholic and the Tobacco Habit	Dow	298
The American Census, 1790 to 1890	Official	120
The American Constitution	Hamilton	116
The American Constitution no Experiment	Legare	119

ALPHABETICAL INDEX OF TITLES. 413

Title	Author	Page
The American Constitution tested	Adams	118
The Battle-Field	Bryant	181
The Battle of Bunker Hill	Pierpont	216
The Battle of Lexington	Weems	214
The Battle of Linden	Campbell	212
The Battle of Waterloo	Byron	213
The Battle of Alamance	Whiting	206
The Bended Bow	Hemans	226
The Bivouac of the Dead	O'Hara	184
The Boston Massacre	Hancock	227
The Boy of Ratisbon	Browning	209
The Brave at Home	Read	193
The Burial of Sir John Moore	Wolfe	210
The Burial of the Deliverer	Alexander	30
The Christian Orator	Villemain	341
The Columbian Exposition opened	Pres. Cleveland	377
The Columbian Exposition proclaimed	Pres. Harrison	361
The Congress of Nations	Editor	379
The Cost of Liberty	Giles	138
The Critical Conditions of Labor	Harrison	268
The Dawning Future	Johnson	322
The Death of Osceola	Street	207
The Defiant Seminole Chief	Patten	240
The Degeneracy of Athens	Demosthenes	69
The Despoiler doomed	Isaiah	43
The Dying Trumpeter	Mosen	206
The Eve of Decoration Day	Smith	313
The Exiles in Egypt	Editor	19
The Fatherland	Lowell	91
The First American Congress	Maxcy	112
The First Civil Code	Bible	25
The First Congress (Apothegm)	Lee	113
The First Constitution	Moses	24
The Flower of Liberty	Holmes	163
The Fourth of July	Webster	110
The Future of our Language	Bethune	394
The Gospel Code Announced	New Testament	28
The Great American Republic a Christian State	Gibbons	160
The Great Good Man	Coleridge	339
The Great Question settled	Curtis	301
The Hebrew Capital despoiled	Heber	42
The Hebrew Codes developed	New Test'nt Records	26
The Hebrew Minstrel's Lament	N. E. Magazine	45
The Hill of Science	Aiken	345
The Honored Dead	Beecher	182
The House where I was born	Hood	96
The Ideal Citizen	Habberton	148
The Land of my Birth	Cook	94
The Law of Labor	Crisis Thoughts	275
The Law of Virtue	Cicero	59
The Lesson of the Revolution	Sparks	115
The March of Freedom	Parker	232
The Mighty Word "No"	Cuyler	283
The Mourning Hero's Vision	Kossuth	189
The National Ensign	Winthrop	225
The New Country occupied	Geikie	32
The New Liberty Bell	Carrington	382
The New Song of Freedom	Phelps	404
The Nineteenth Century ends Slavery	Lamar	305
The Noise of Arms (Apothegm)	Montaigne	193
The Old Home and the New	Blenkie	102
The Old Oaken Bucket	Woodworth	100
The Orator described	Sheridan	335
The Pacific Shore	Anonymous	395
The Parliament of Religions	Carrington	381
The Patriot Dead	Smith	300
The Patriot King in Mourning	Willis	38
The Patriot President	London Punch	174
The Patriot Prince	Carrington	175

ALPHABETICAL INDEX OF TITLES.

		Page
The Patriot's Aspiration (Apothegm)	S. Adams	117
The Patriot's Cry (Paraphrase)	Psalm cxxxvii	48
The People Triumphant	Everett	140
The Philosopher's Scales	Taylor	344
The Pilgrims of New England	Choate	85
The Principles of the Revolution	Quincy	114
The Public School Teacher in the Republic	Balch	329
The Puritan	Macaulay	88
The Reign of Peace	Thornton	198
The Review of the Dead	Stockard	186
The Richest Prince	Korner	167
The Road to Happiness open	Pope	280
The Roman Senate and the American Congress	Kossuth	173
The Sanctuary within the Breast	H. Smith	350
The Schools take Part	Watterson	367
The Scourge of War	Burleigh	194
The School-teacher	Brougham	325
The Serpent of the Still	Loyland	348
The Soldier's Widow	Willis	191
The Star-spangled Banner	Key	406
The Storming of Monterey	Hoffman	218
The Supremacy of Conscience	Storrs	259
The Three W's, — Watch, Work, Wait	N. Y. Churchman	290
The Torch of Liberty	Moore	157
The True Aspiration of Youth	Montgomery	260
The True Grandeur of Nations	Sumner	137
The Twentieth Century	Gates	396
The Unselfishness of Washington	Paine	123
The Wail of Jugurtha	Wolfe	76
The Warrior's Wreath	Anonymous	198
The World would be Better for it	Cobb	288
The Worth of Fame	Baillie	289
The Young American	Everett	256
To-morrow	Cotton	338
To thee, O Country	Eichberg	224
To whom Honor be due	From the German	261
True Aspiration of Youth (The)	Montgomery	260
True Eloquence	Webster	340
True Glory	Milton	195
True Liberty	Robertson	263
True Liberty (Apothegm)	Bruyère	158
True Nobility	Swain	276
Tubal Cain	Mackay	178
Unselfishness of Washington	Paine	123
Valley Forge	Brown	217
Vindication of Virginius	Kellogg	54
Virtue uncorrupted by Fortune	Quintus Curtius	71
Wail (The) of Jugurtha	Wolfe	76
Warren's supposed Address at Bunker Hill	Pierpont	230
Washington, a Model for Youth	Dwight	126
Washington as a Leader	Pierpont	127
Washington as a Soldier	Carrington	129
Washington's Resignation, Dec. 23, 1783		135
Washington's Training	Upham	112
Washington, Unselfishness of	Paine	123
Wedding (The Norwegian March of Grieg (in verse)	Johnson	98
Welcome to the Nations	Morton	363
We were Boys together	Morris	92
What might be Done	Anonymous	292
What is Ambition?	Willis	334
Whittling typical of Young America	Pierpont	279
Wisdom and Wealth	Khnemnitzer	287
Woodman, spare that Tree	Morris	101
Ye are the Temple of the Living God	Bible	350

BIBLIOGRAPHY AND ACKNOWLEDGMENTS.

A SPECIAL VOLUME, designed to inculcate patriotic sentiment, would be incomplete without recognition of earlier American effort, in similar endeavor.

Prior to 1860, and before sectional sentiment had disturbed national unity, choice Biblical, classical, and colonial selections appeared in all school reading-books. Then followed illustrated series, with less space for the teachings of the fathers. Old gems of British literature were dropped as "old style." And yet the lexicographer, Webster, the geographer, Onley, and the grammarian, Lindley Murray, crowned their other service to the young, by culling all literature, for use in reading, recitation, and declamation.

The following named volumes are among those which have been utilized in the present compilation.

"American Selections," 1796, Noah Webster; "The Columbian Orator," 1797; and the "American Preceptor," 1799, Caleb Bingham; "The Speaker," 1803, William Enfield; "The English Reader," 1807, 1823, 1831, Lindley Murray; "The American Reader," 1810, Asa Lyman; "The American Orator," 1811, 1813, Increase Cooke; "The Historical Reader," 1825, J. L. Blake; "The Classical Reader," 1826, Greenwood & Emerson; "Porter's Analysis," 1828, Ebenezer Porter; "Studies in Poetry and Prose," 1830, George B. Cheever; "The National Reader," 1829, 1833, 1834, John Pierpont; "The Popular Reader," 1834, Jason Onley; "The First Class Reader," 1834, B. D. Emerson; "The United States Speaker," 1835, John E. Lovell; "The National Preceptor," 1835, Ansel Phelps; "The Rhetorical Reader," 1835, Ebenezer Porter; "The School Reader Series," 1836, Charles W. Sanders; "The American Elocutionist," 1844, William Russell; "The American Common School Reader," 1844, Goldsbury & Russell; "McGuffey's Rhetorical Guide," 1844, (The Eclectic Series); "The Elementary School Reader," 1846, Samuel J. Randall; "Town's Readers," Salem Town; "The Southern Speaker and Reader," William R. Babcock; "The Mandeville Series," 1849, Henry Mandeville; "Webb's Normal Readers," J. Russell Webb; "Parker's School Readers" (a series), 1851, Richard J. Parker; "The National Speaker," 1851, Henry B. Megathlin; "The American Orator" (with 567 autographs of eminent orators), 1852, L. C. Munn; "Book of Eloquence," 1852, Charles Dudley Warner; "Sargent's Standard Speaker," 1852, Epes Sargent; "Sargent's Standard Series," 1854, Epes Sargent; "The American School Reader,"

1855, Asa Fitz; "The American Comprehensive Reader," 1856, William D. Swan; "The Progressive Readers" (a series), 1856, Town & Holbrook; "The National Readers" (a series), 1857, Parker & Watson; "The North American Reader," 1858, David D. Tower; "The Progressive Speaker," 1858, Oliver Ellsworth; "Willson's Readers" (chiefly scientific), 1859, Marcius Willson.

Shortly after 1860, conservative compilers began to restore valuable old selections. Thus, 1865, "Hillard's Readers" (Taintor Brothers, Merrill & Co., New York); in 1865, "The American Speaker," John D. Philbrick (Thompson, Brown & Co., Boston); and in 1869, J. Madison Webb's "Independent Series" (A. S. Barnes & Co., New York), preserved much of the old patriotic literature. In 1866, R. R. Raymond's "Patriotic Speaker" appeared as one of the "Northend Series," published by W. S. P. Hopkins, of New York.

Many book publishers of to-day still represent old publishing houses. D. Appleton & Co., A. S. Barnes & Co., and Harper Bros., of New York; and J. B. Lippincott Co., and E. H. Butler & Co. (the latter acquiring the business of Cowperthwaite & Co.), of Philadelphia, have been related to similar work for nearly half a century. In Boston, Phillips, Sampson & Co., Robert S. Davis & Co., and Taggart & Thompson, are succeeded by Leach, Shewell & Sanborn, and Thompson, Brown & Co. In 1868, Ginn Bros. began business, succeeded, in 1874, by Ginn & Heath, and in 1885, by Ginn & Co.; and in the same year, D. C. Heath & Co. were established. In New York, Mark H. Newman & Co., Ivison & Phinney, and Sheldon, Lamport & Blakeman, disappeared, but Ivison, Lamport & Blakeman, and Sheldon & Co. carried on school-book work. In Philadelphia, Charles De Silver's Sons perpetuated "Sargent's Readers." In Cincinnati, William B. Smith & Co., and Hinkle, Wilson & Co. survived in Van Antwerp, Bragg & Co. In California, A. L. Bancroft & Co. became H. H. Bancroft & Co., and The Bancroft Co.; and in North Carolina, Alfred Williams & Co. brought out the "North Carolina Speaker." Other publishers engaged in similar work. The American Book Co., in 1888, merged the interests of many of the large houses in one common interest.

In 1885, Edgar O. Silver, previously with D. Appleton & Co. of New York, began business in Boston. Silver, Rogers & Co. succeeded, and in 1888 the house was organized under the present style of Silver, Burdett & Co.

To all these houses the compiler of this "Patriotic Series" is indebted for favors extended. Special recognition is due to James A. Potts & Co. (publishers of Geikie's "Hours with the Bible"); Fords, Howard & Hurlburt (publishers of Beecher's works, and Bryant's "Library of Poetry and Song"); and to Houghton & Mifflin, of Boston, who, by special arrangement, are represented in the writings of Whittier, Longfellow, Holmes, and Lowell.

As a general rule, selections which can be found in the "Patriotic Reader" (Human Liberty Developed), 1888, and "Columbian Selections," 1892, are not reproduced in this volume.

To statesmen, scholars, educators, and writers who have contributed original matter, or submitted matter to be edited for this volume, and to those who have in advance endorsed the plan of the present work, grateful thanks are extended.

HENRY B. CARRINGTON.

Hyde Park, Mass., March 2, 1894.

BIOGRAPHICAL INDEX OF AUTHORS.

[Abbreviations are explained by the first use of a term, as Harvard College, or University, afterwards, Harv. Coll., or Univ. Literary titles are omitted; but in parentheses, *where educated*. The term "soldier" means military service, but only higher grades are specified. The usual abbreviations for countries are given, and "b." for *born*; "d." for *died*.]

Adams, John, orator, diplomatist; Signer of Dec. Am. Ind.; 2d Pres. U. S.; b. Braintree, Mass., 1735; (Harv. Coll., 1755); d. July 4, 1826. "American Constitution tested," p. 118.

Adams, Samuel, orator; Signer of Dec. Am. Ind.; Gov. Mass.; b. Boston, 1722; (Harv. Coll. 1740); d. 1808. Apothegm, "The Patriot's Aspiration," p. 117.

Aiken, John, Brit. poet, author, writer; b. Leicester, Eng., 1747; d. 1822. "The Hill of Science," p. 345.

Alexander, Mrs. Cecil Frances (*née* HUMPHREY), Eng. poetess; b. Strabane, Ireland, 1830. "The Burial of Moses," p. 30.

Andrew, John Albion, lawyer, statesman; Gov. Mass.; b. Windham, Maine, 1818; (Bowdoin Coll. 1837); d. 1867. "Our Heroes," p. 312.

Arndt, Ernst Moritz, Germ. poet and writer; b. Prussian Island of Rugen, 1769; (Prof. at Griefswalde and Univ. of Bon.); d. 1860. "Fatherland," p. 89.

Bacon, Lord Francis, philosopher and writer; b. London, 1561; d. 1626. "Goodness and Greatness," p. 359.

Baillie, Joanna, Eng. poetess; b. near Glasgow, Scotland, 1762; d. 1851. "The Worth of Fame," p. 289.

Baker, Colonel Edward Dickinson, soldier, orator; U. S. Sen., Oregon; killed in battle at Ball's Bluff, 1861. "The Liberty of the Press," p. 151.

Balch, Colonel George T., soldier, writer, educator; (U S. Mil. Acad.); b. Me., 1831; d. 1894. "The Public School-teacher in a Republic," p. 329.

Baldwin, Joseph, teacher, educator, author; Pres. School of Pedagogy, Univ. of Texas; b. Newcastle, Penn. 1827; (Bethany Coll., West Va., 1852). "Culture of the Moral Virtues," p. 357.

Bard, Milford. See Lofland, John. "The Serpent of the Still," p. 348.

Barton, Bernard, known as the "Quaker Poet;" b. London, Eng., 1784; d. 1849. "Home, dear Home," p. 104.

Beecher, Henry Ward, Congregational minister, journalist, lecturer, author; b. Litchfield, Conn., 1813; (Amherst Coll., 1834); d. 1887. "The Honored Dead," p. 182.

Benjamin, Park, poet, journalist, traveller; b. Demerara, Guiana, 1809; (Trinity Coll., Hartford, Conn.); d. 1864. "Press On," p. 253.

Berkley, George, Eng. bishop, scholar, traveller, missionary; b. Kilcrin, Ireland, 1684; (Trinity Coll., Dublin); d 1753. "American Destiny," p. 389.

Bethune, George W., Dutch Reformed minister, scholar, poet; b. New York City, 1805; (Dickenson Coll., Penn., 1828); d. 1862. "The Future of our Language," p. 381.

Blaine, James Gillespie, journalist, statesman; U. S. Sen., Me.; b. Washington Co., Penn., 1830; d. 1892. "Independence Day," p. 108.

Bleakie, Robert, Am. manufacturer; b. Rutherglen, Scotland, 1833. "The Old Home and the New," p. 103.

Boker, George H., poet, diplomatist; b. Phil., Penn., 1823 (Princeton Coll., N. J., 1842). "Dirge for the Soldier," p. 192.

Bonaparte, Napoleon, soldier, emperor of France; b. Ajaccio, Corsica, 1769; d. at St. Helena, 1821, prisoner of war to Great Britain. "Address to the Army of Italy, 1796," p. 242.

Brooks, Charles Timothy, Unit. min., poet; b. Salem, Mass., 1813; d. 1883. "God save the State," p. 407.

Brougham, Lord Henry, British peer, author, statesman; b. Edinburgh, Scotland, 1779; (Edinburgh Univ.); d. 1868. "The School Teacher," p. 325.

Brown, Henry Armitt, lawyer, orator; b. Phil., Penn., 1844; (Yale Coll., now Yale Univ., 1865); d. 1878. "Valley Forge," p. 207.

Browning, Robert, Eng. poet; b. near London, 1812; (Univ. of London). "The Boy of Ratisbon," p. 209.

Bruce, Robert, king of Scots; b. 1274; won the battle of Bannockburn, June 24, 1314; d. 1329.

Bruyère (Brü-e' yair', or Brü' yair'), French moralist and scholar; b. at Dourdan, Normandy, 1646; d. 1696. "True Liberty" (apothegm), p. 158.

Bryant, William Cullen, journalist, poet, scholar; b. Cunningham, Mass., 1794; (Williams Coll., Mass., 1813); d. 1878. "No Man knoweth his Sepulchre," p. 30. "At the Old Home Again," p. 97. "Seventy-Six," p. 107. "The Battle Field," p. 181.

Bulwer, Edward George (Baron Lytton), novelist, poet; b. Heyden Hall, Norfolk Co., England, 1803; (Cambridge Univ., 1823); d. 1873. "Address of Caradoc the Bard," p. 234.

Burleigh, William Henry, mechanic, journalist, poet; b. Woodstock, Conn., 1812; d. 1871. "The Scourge of War," p. 191.

Burns, Robert, Scotch poet; b. Ayr, Scotland, 1786; d. 1858. "Bannockburn," p. 199.

Busbee, Charles Manly, lawyer, orator; b. Raleigh, N. C., 1845; (Hampden Sydney Coll., Va., and Univ. N. C.); "Benefits of the Civil War," p. 310.

Butterworth, Hezekiah, poet, journalist, traveller; Asst. Ed. "Youth's Companion" since 1871; b. Warren, R. I., 1839. "Crown Washington," p. 136. "Discovery Day," p. 386.

Byron, George Gordon Noel (Baron), Brit. poet; b. London, 1788; (Cambridge Univ., Eng.); d. 1824. "Jerusalem avenged," p. 46. "The Battle of Waterloo," p. 213.

Campbell, Thomas, Scotch poet; b. Glasgow, Scotland, 1777; (Glasgow Univ.). "The Battle of Linden," p. 212.

Carrington, General Henry Beebee, teacher, lawyer, soldier, author; b. Wallingford, Conn., March 2, 1824; (Yale Coll., Conn., 1845). "Washington as a soldier," p. 129. "Idleness a Crime," p. 151. "The Patriot Prince," p. 175. "Watch, Work, Wait," p. 290. "As thy Day, thy Strength," p. 295. "The Congress of Nations," p. 379. "Military Training in Schools," p. 352. "The Law of Labor," p. 275. "Ring! ring the Bells!" p. 408. Editorial matter and Notes.

Carrington, Robert Chase, student; b. Crawfordsville, Indiana, Jan. 28, 1872; (Phillips Acad., Exeter, N. H.). Preparation of Vocabulary, p. 425.

Cassius, Caius Longinus, Roman soldier, patriot, statesman; d. by suicide b. c. 42. "Cæsar's Death justified," p. 67.

Cato, Marcus Portius, Roman patriot and philosopher; b. 95 b. c.; d. 46 b. c. "Self Respect" (apothegm), p. 6. "The Law of Virtue" (apothegm), p 59.

Chamberlain, General Joshua L., lawyer, soldier, educator; Gov. S. C., Pres. Bowdoin Coll., Me., 1871-1883; b. Brewer, Me., 1828; (Bowdoin Coll., Me., 1852). "Dead on the Field of Honor," p. 246.

Chesterfield, Earl Philip Dormer Stanhope, courtier, orator, and wit; (Cambridge Univ., Eng.); d. 1773. "Aim at Perfection" (apothegm), p. 356.

Childs, George Washington, journalist, publisher, philanthropist; b. Baltimore, Md., 1829; d. 1894. "Success in Life" (contributed), p. 265.

Choate, Rufus, lawyer, scholar, orator, statesman; U. S. Sen. Mass.; b. Ipswich, now Essex, Mass., 1799; (Dartmouth Coll., N. H., 1819); d. 1858. "The Pilgrims of New England," p. 86. "American Nationality," p. 141.

Cicero, Marcus Tullius, Roman orator, statesman; b. 106 b. c.; d. 48 b. c. "Separation from Traitors," p. 58.

Clay, Cassius Marcellus, lawyer, orator; b. Madison Co., Ky., 1810. "America the Child of Destiny," p. 394.

Cleveland, Stephen Grover (using the name Grover, only, in office), lawyer, politician; Gov. N. Y.; 22d and 24th Pres. U. S.; b. Caldwell, N. J., 1837. "The Columbian Exposition opened," p. 377.

Cobb, Mark Huntington, teacher, early advocate of political reform, writer, journalist, and poet; b. on Beech Hill, Colebrook, Litchfield Co., Conn., 1828; Cashier U. S. Mint, Phil., Penn. "The World would be better for it," p. 288.

Coleridge, Samuel Taylor, poet, critic; b. at Ottery, St. Mary, in Devonshire, England, 1772; (Jesus' Coll., Cambridge); d. 1834. "The Great Good Man," p. 339.

Cook, Eliza, Eng. poetess; b. near London, 1817. "The Land of my Birth," p. 94. "A Star in the West," p. 125.

Cotton, Nathaniel, Eng. physician, poet; b. 1707; d. 1788 (specially honored by Cowper). "To-morrow," p. 399.

Cowper, William, Eng. poet; b. Hertfordshire, Eng., 1731; d. 1800. "Queen Boadicea and her last Struggle," p. 235.

Crane, Oliver, Presb. min., Orientalist, author, poet; b. West Bloomfield, N. J., 1822; (Yale Coll., 1845). "Columbia to the Front" (extract), p. 404.

Croly, George, rector of Eng. Church, author, orator, poet; b. Dublin, Ireland, 1780; d. 1860. "Leonidas," p. 203.

Cummings, Jeremiah W., Rom. Cath. priest, author, scholar, poet; built and officiated in St. Stephen's Church, N. Y., from its erection, 1856, until his death; b. Washington, D. C., 1823; (Coll. Propaganda, Rome). "Song of the Union," p. 179.

Curtis, George William, journalist, scholar, author; b. Providence, R. I., 1824; d. 1892. "The Great Question settled," p. 301.

Cutter, George Washington, poet; b. Ky. 1814; d. 1865. "E Pluribus Unum," p. 406.

Cuyler, Theodore Ledyard, Presb. min.; author, temperance advocate; b. Aurora, N. Y., 1822; (Coll. of N. J., 1841. "The Mighty Word 'No,'" p. 283.

Day, Rev. William, as designated on back of picture at Mt. Vernon. "Washington," p. 133.

Delke, James A., teacher for more than fifty years; Prof. Belles Lettres, Union Univ., Tenn.; Prof. Chowan Bapt. Fem. Inst., N. C.; scholar and poet; b. in Virginia; (Univ. of N. C.); d. 1893. "Carolina and Mecklenburg," p. 109.

Demosthenes, greatest of Grecian orators, patriot and statesman; b. near Athens, Greece, 385-385; d. 322 B.C. "The Degeneracy of Athens," p. 139.

Depew, Chauncey Mitchell, lawyer, orator, scholar; b. Peekskill. N. Y., 1834; (Yale Coll., 1856). "Columbian Oration at World's Exposition," p. 358. "Columbus the Discoverer," p. 373.

Devens, General Charles, lawyer, soldier, jurist; b. Charlestown. Mass., 1820; d. 1892. "No Conflict now," p. 303.

Dix, General John A., lawyer, soldier, statesman; U. S. Sen. N. Y.; b. Boscawen, N. Y., 1798; d. 1879. "Christianity as a political Force," p. 146.

Dow, General Neal, temperance reformer, soldier, philanthropist; b. Portland, Me., 1804; contributes paper, "The Alcoholic and Tobacco Habit," p. 298.

Dwight, Timothy. Cong. min., theologian, author; Pres. Yale Coll.; b. Northampton, Mass., 1752; (Yale Coll., 1769); d. 1817. "Washington a Model for Youth," p. 126.

Eichberg, Phillipine, (afterwards Mrs. J. B. King); b. Geneva, Switzerland. "To thee, O Country" (written at the age of fifteen), p. 222.

Elliott, Ebenezer, poet, the "Corn-Law Rhymer;" b. near Rotherham, Eng., 1781; d. 1849. "Old England," p. 79.

Emilius (Æmilius) Paulus, Roman general, killed at the battle of Cannæ, 216 B.C. "Representative Government trustworthy," p. 51.

Everett, Alexander Hill, scholar, diplomatist; b. Boston, Mass., 1793; (Harv. Coll., 1806); d. 1847. "The Young American," p. 258.

Everett, Edward, orator, statesman; U. S. Sen. Mass.; b. Dorchester, Mass., 1792; (Harv. Coll., 1811); d. 1865. "Our Relations with England," p. 81. "The People triumphant," p. 138. "Plea for the Pocumtoc Chief," p. 241.

Fabricius, Caius Luscius, Roman general and statesman, of great purity of life; ambassador to King Pyrrhus, B.C. 280. "Refuses Bribes," p. 53.

Fallersleben, poet and linguist (see HOFFMANN). "Fatherland," p. 92.

Flagg, Ellen H., née **Brown,** poetess; b. Providence, R. I., 1842; d. 1884. "Death the Peacemaker," p. 320.

Franklin, Benjamin, printer, patriot, diplomatist, statesman, discoverer in physics, essayist, and proverbialist; b. Boston, Mass., 1706; d. 1790. "Don't give too much for the Whistle," p. 277.

Gates, Merrill Edward, educator, scholar, writer; Pres. Rutgers Coll., N. J.; Pres. Amherst Coll., Mass.; b. Warsaw, N. Y., 1848; (Rochester Univ., N. Y.). "The Twentieth Century," p. 396.

Geikie, Cunningham, Presb. min., author, Biblical scholar; b. Edinburgh, Scotland, 1826; (Univ. Edinburgh). "A People delivered," p. 21. "Joshua the Patriot General," p. 32. "David the Patriot King," p. 36.

Gibbons, James, (Cardinal) Rom. Cath. Church; b. Baltimore, Md., 1834; (Baltimore Coll. and St. Mary's Sem.). "The American Republic a Christian State," p. 159.

Giles, Henry, Unitarian min., writer; b. Wexford Co., Ireland, 1809; came to America, 1840; d. 1882. "The Cost of Liberty," p. 138.

Goethe, John Wolfgang, scholar and poet; b. at Frankfort-on-the-Main, 1749; (Strasburg Univ., 1770); d. 1832. Extract from "Haste not, Rest not," p. 262.

Gordon, General John Brown, lawyer, soldier, statesman; Gov. Ga.; U. S. Sen. Ga.; b. Upson Co., Ga., 1832. "Gettysburg: a Mecca for the Blue and the Gray," p. 302.

Grattan, Henry, Irish orator, statesman, and patriot; b. Dublin, Ireland, 1750; (Trinity Coll., Dublin, Ireland); d. 1820. "A Plea for Ireland," p. 214.

Greeley, Horace, printer, journalist, politician; b. Amherst, N. H., 1811; d. 1872. "Self-sacrificing Ambition," p. 327.

Habberton, John, soldier, journalist, author; b. Brooklyn, N. Y., 1842. "The Ideal Citizen," p. 118.

Hale, Edward Everett, Unitarian min., journalist, lecturer, author; b. Boston, Mass., 1822; (Harv. Coll., 1839). "Patriotic Words for the Young," p. 359.

Hamilton, Colonel Alexander, soldier, financier, statesman, patriot; b. West Indies, 1757; d. 1804. "The American Constitution," p. 116.

Hancock, John, statesman, patriot, orator; Pres. Continental Congress; signer of Dec. Am. Ind., 1776; Gov. Mass.; b. Quincy, Mass., 1737; (Harv. Coll., 1754); d. 1793. "The Boston Massacre," p. 227.

Hannibal, Carthaginian general; b. 247 B.C.; d. 183 B.C. "Address to his Soldiers in Italy," p. 62. "Appeals to Scipio for Peace," p. 64.

Harrison, General Benjamin, lawyer, soldier, statesman; U. S. Sen., Indiana; 23d Pres. U. S.; b. South Bend, O., Aug. 20, 1833; (Miami Univ., O., 1852). "Proclamation of World's Exposition," p. 36. "The Critical Conditions of Labor," p. 268. "Aim High," p. 354.

Hastings, Horace Lorenzo, evangelist, journalist, hymnologist, Biblical scholar, and author; b. Blanford, Mass., 1831. "A Sketch of Moses," p. 29.

Hawes, Joel, Cong. min., writer, theologian; b. Medway, Mass., 1799; d. 1867. "A good Name," p. 343.

Heber, Reginald, Eng. bishop and poet; b. Cheshire, Eng., 1783; (Oxford Univ., 1803); d. 1826. "The Hebrew Capital despoiled," p. 41.

Hemans, Felicia Dorothea (née BROWNE), Eng. poetess; b. Liverpool, Eng., 1784; d. 1835. "Rocks of my Country," p. 95. "The Bended Bow," p. 226.

Hoffman, Charles Fenno, novelist, poet, journalist; b. N. Y. City, 1806; (Columbia Coll., N. Y.); died 1884. "The Storming of Monterey," p. 218.

Hoffmann, August Heinrich (also called HOFFMANN VON FALLERSLEBEN), poet and linguist; b. Fallersleben, Hanover, 1798; (Göttingen and Bonn); d. 1874. "My Fatherland," p. 92.

Holland, Josiah Gilbert ("Timothy Titcomb"), journalist, author; b. Belchertown, Mass., 1819; d. 1881. "Getting the right Start," p. 257.

Holmes, Oliver Wendell, versatile poet and wit, scholar, author; Prof. Anatomy and Physiology, Harv. Coll.; b. Cambridge, Mass., 1809; (Harv. Coll., 1829). "The Flower of Liberty," p. 164.

Hood, Thomas, Eng. author and humorist; b. London, Eng., 1798; d. 1845. "The House where I was born," p. 96.

Hopkinson, Joseph, jurist; b. Phil., Penn., 1770; (Univ. Penn.); d. 1842. "Reverence for Law," p. 147. "Hail, Columbia, Happy Land," p. 405.

Houdon (oo don), **Jean Antoine,** eminent sculptor; b. at Versailles, France, 1741; d. 1828; executed bust of Washington, now in the Richmond capitol, Va. This statue has its type in the St. Memin crayon, owned by J. C. Brevoort, New York, from which H. B. Hall & Sons made their celebrated engraving of Washington. See frontispiece.

Ireland, John, Rom. Cath. bishop, orator, temperance advocate; b. Burnchurch, near Filtrin, Ireland, 1838; emigrated to St. Paul, Minn., while a boy; (Grande Seminary, Hyères, France); chaplain 5th Minn. Reg. "Our Future," p. 383.

Johnson, Colonel Charles Wesley, printer, soldier, elocutionist, musician; Secy. Minn. Senate 7 years; Clerk U. S. Sen., 1883-1893; b. Belleville, St. Clair Co., Ill., March 17, 1843. "The Norwegian Wedding March of Greig," in verse, p. 98.

Johnson, William Preston, educator, scholar; Pres. La. State Univ. and A. and M. Coll., Baton Rouge, La., 1880; since 1883, Pres. Tulane Univ., La.; b. Louisville, Ky., 1831; (Yale Coll., 1852). "Our Dawning Future," p. 322.

Keller, Matthias, musician; b. Würtemberg, Germany, 1813; d. Boston, 1875. "Keller's American Hymn," p. 407.

Kennedy, John Pendleton, popular writer, scholar, statesman; b. Baltimore, Md., 1795; Sec. Navy, 1852; d. 1870. "The Age of Work," p. 264.

Kellogg, Elijah, Cong. min., lecturer, poet, author; b. Portland, Me., 1813; (Bowd. Coll., Me., 1840). "Vindication of Virginius," p. 54.

Key, Francis Scott, lawyer, jurist, poet; b. Frederick Co., Md., 1779; d. 1843. "The Star-spangled Banner," p. 406.

Khnemnitzer (IVAN IVANOVITCH), Russian fabulist and poet; b. St. Petersburg, Russia, 1744; d. 1784. "Wisdom and Wealth," p. 287.

King, Thomas Starr, Unit. min., lecturer, author; b. N. Y., 1824; d. 1864. "Our Nationality," p. 143.

Kinkel, John Gottfried, theologian, poet; b. Obercassel, Germany, 1815; (Univ. Bonn). "Patriotic Song," p. 168.

Korner, Andreas Justinus, scholar, poet; b. Ludwigsburg, Germany, 1786; (Univ. Tübingen); d. 1862. "The richest Prince," p. 167.

Kossuth, Louis, patriot, orator, statesman; Gov. Hungary in revolution of 1848; b. Monok, Hungary, 1802; visited the United States, 1851; d. in exile, 1894. "No Peace without Liberty," p. 139. "The mourning Hero's Vision," p. 189. "The Roman Senate and American Congress," p. 173.

Krout, Mary Hannah, teacher, journalist, poet; in 1894, of ed. staff of Chicago

"Inter-Ocean;" correspondent from foreign parts; b. Crawfordsville, Ind., "The Battle Eve," p. 222.

Lamar, Lucius Quintus Cincinnatus, lawyer, statesman, jurist; U. S. Sen., Miss.; b. Putnam Co., Ga., 1825; (Emory Coll., Ga., 1845); d. 1892. "The Nineteenth Century ends Slavery," p. 305.

Lamartine, Alphonse de, French orator, historian, poet; b. at Mâcon, on the Saône, 1792; (College of Illey, 1809); d. 1869. "A Republic defined," p. 156.

Lee, Richard Henry, patriot, orator, statesman; signer Dec. Am. Ind.; b. Westmoreland Co., Va., 1732; Pres. Am. Cong., 1784; U. S. Sen., Va.; (educated in Eng.); d. 1794. "The First Congress" (apothegm), p. 113.

Lefevre, Pierre François, French dramatist and poet; b. Paris, 1741; d. 1813. "Gustavus Vasa to his Soldiers," p. 258.

Legare, Hugh Swinton, lawyer, statesman, scholar; b. Charleston, S. C., 1797; (South Car. Coll., 1815); d. 1843. "The American Constitution no Experiment," p. 119.

Lincoln, Abraham, lawyer, politician, statesman; 16th Pres. U. S.; b. Hardin Co., Ky., 1809; assassinated April 14, and died April 15, 1865. "Address at Gettysburg, Nov. 19, 1863," p. 299.

Lofland, John (*alias* MILFORD BARD), poet, journalist; subject of a tribute by Whittier; published "The Harp of Delaware," 1828; b. at Milford, Del., 1798; (Milford Acad.); d. 1849. "The Serpent of the Still," p. 348.

Lover, Samuel, Irish novelist, humorist, painter, poet; b. Dublin, Ireland, 1797; d. 1868. "Father Land and Mother Tongue," p. 93.

Livy, Titus, Roman historian; b. Patavium, Italy, 39 B. C.; d. 17 A. D. "Address of Hannibal to his Army," p. 62. "Scipio's Reply to Hannibal," p. 65.

Longfellow, Henry Wadsworth, poet and scholar; b. Portland, Me., 1807; (Bowd. Coll., 1825); d. 1882. "Decoration Day." p. 316.

Lowell, James Russell, poet, critic, scholar, diplomatist; b. Cambridge, Mass., 1819; (Harv. Coll., 1838); d. 1892. "The Fatherland," p. 91. "Our Heritage," p. 171. "Freedom," p. 245.

Macaulay, Thomas Babington (Baron), Eng. writer, journalist, statesman, historian; b. Leicester, Eng., 1800; (Trinity Coll., Cambridge, 1822); d. 1859. "Horatius at the Bridge," p. 49. "Labor Hours have Limits," p. 274.

Mackay, Charles, Scottish poet; b. Perth, Scotland, 1814. "Old Tubal Cain," p. 178. "If I were a Voice," p. 236.

Mackintosh, Sir James, author, orator, statesman; b. near Inverness, Scotland, 1765; (King's Coll., Aberdeen, 1788); d. 1832. "England's Relations to America," p. 84.

Mann, Horace, lawyer, educator, scholar, pioneer in the American common-school system; Pres. Antioch Coll., Ohio; b. at Franklin, Norfolk Co., Mass., 1796; (Brown Univ., R. I., 1819); d. 1859. "Let there be Light," p. 236.

Marius, Caius, an eminent Roman general, of low birth, but became eminent; b. near Arpinum, Italy, 157 B. C.; d. 86 B. C. "Merit before Birth," p. 73.

Maxcy, Jonathan, eminent Baptist divine; Pres. Union Coll., N. Y.; Pres. South Carolina Coll.; b. Attleborough, Mass., 1768; (Prof. Brown Univ., 1791); d. 1820. "The First American Congress," p. 112.

Meagher, General Thomas Francis, soldier, patriot; b. at Waterford, Ireland, 1823; gallant in the Am. Civil War; d. 1867. "Patriotism," p. 231.

Milford Bard. (See John Lofland.)

Miller, Cincinnatus Heine (JOAQUIN), poet; b. Cincinnati, Ohio, 1842. "Fall of the Indian Heroes," p. 204.

Miller, Theodore de Clermont, physician, N. Y. City; author of "Is there Room among the Angels?" "The Old Willow Chair," etc.; b. Hampton, Vt., 1841; (Fair Haven High School, Vt.; Normal Coll., Greenwich, N. Y.; Med. Univ., Burlington, Vt.). "How we Take It," p. 293.

Milton, John, patriot, author, among greatest of poets; b. London, Eng., 1608; d. 1764. "True Glory," p. 195.

Montgomery, James, poet; b. Ayrshire, Scotland, 1771; d. 1864. "The True Aspiration of Youth," p. 260.

Montgomery, General Richard, soldier, patriot, poet; b. at Swords, near Filtrin, Ireland, 1736; (Trin. Coll., Dublin); killed in battle before Quebec, 1775. "Marathon by Starlight," p. 200.

Montaigne, Michel Eyquem (ā′kon′) **de**, French philosopher and essayist; b. in Perigord, France, 1533; d. 1592. Apothegm, "Sincerity and Truth," p. 145. "The Noise of Arms," p. 193.

Montesquieu, Charles de Secondat de, moralist and political essayist, author of "Spirit of Laws;" b. near Bordeaux, France, 1689; d. 1755. "Poverty of the Soul" (apothegm), p. 154.

Moore, Thomas, Irish poet; b. at Dublin, Ireland, 1779; (Trin. Coll., Dublin, and Middle Temple, London; visited the United States, 1804; d. 1852. "The Torch of Liberty," p. 157.

Morris, George P., poet, journalist; b. 1802, at Phil., Penn., 1864. "We were Boys Together," p. 92. "Woodman, spare that Tree," p. 101.

Morton, Levi Parsons, banker, diplomatist; Vice Pres. U. S.; b. Shoreham, Vt., 1824. "Welcome to the Nations," p. 363.

Mosen, Julius, scholar and poet; b. in Saxony, 1803; (Univ. Marieny); d. 1867. "The Dying Trumpeter," p. 206.

Newman, John Philip, journalist, author, orator, lecturer; Meth. Episc. bishop; b. 1826; (Cazenovia Sem., N. Y., 1849). "Abraham Lincoln," p. 517 (contributed).

O'Hara, Theodore, poet, soldier; b. Kentucky, 1820; d. 1867. "The Bivouac of the Dead," p. 184.

Parbodie, William Jewett, poet; b. Providence, R. I., 1812; d. 1870. "Our Country," p. 165.

Paine, Robert Treat, writer, poet; b. Taunton, Mass., 1773; (Harv. Coll., 1792); d. 1849. "The Unselfishness of Washington," p. 123.

Parker, Theodore, Unit. min., scholar; b. Lexington, Mass., 1810; (Harv. Coll.); d. 1860. "National Injustice," p. 155. "The March of Freedom," p. 230.

Patten, Colonel George W., soldier, military writer, poet; b. Newport, R. I., 1808; (Brown Univ., R. I., and U. S. Mil. Acad.); d. 1882. Called the "Poet Laureate of the Army." "The Seminole's Lament," p. 240.

Patterson, James Willis, orator, educator; U. S. Sen., N. H.; b. Henniker, N. H., 1823; (Dartmouth Coll., 1840); d. 1893. "Again Brethren and Equals," p. 396.

Payne, John Howard, actor, poet; b. N. Y., 1792; d. 1852. "Home, Sweet Home," p. 106.

Peabody, William B. O., Unit. min., poet, author; b. Exeter, N. H., 1799; (Harv. Coll., 1816); d. 1847. "Ruth and Naomi," p. 35.

Peale (pēl), Charles Wilson, naturalist and painter; pupil of West, in England; b. Charlestown, Md., 1744; d. 1827; painted a portrait of Washington. See frontispiece.

Percival, James Oates, eminent poet, medical scientist, and scholar; b. Berlin, Conn., 1795; (Yale Coll., 1815); d. 1856. "New England," p. 82.

Phelps, S. Dryden, Bapt. min., poet; b. Suffield, Conn., 1816; (Brown Univ., 1844). "Decoration Day Ode," p. 314. "The New Song of Freedom," p. 404.

Pierpont, John, Univ. min., poet; b. Litchfield, Conn., 1785; (Yale Coll., 1804); d. 1866. "Washington as a Leader," p. 127; "Battle of Bunker Hill," p. 230; "Whittling Typical of Young America," p. 279.

Pope, Alexander, Eng. poet and critic; b. London, 1688; d. 1744. "The Road to Happiness Open," p. 280.

Proctor, Bryan Waller (*alias* BARRY CORNWALL), Eng. poet; b. 1790; d. 1874. "A Petition to Time," p. 337. "Courage," p. 359.

Quintius Curtius, Roman historian. Birth and death not known. "Virtue Uncorrupted by Fortune," p. 71.

Quincy, Josiah, patriot, orator, political essayist; b. Mass., 1744; d. 1775. "The Principles of the Revolution," p. 114.

Racine, Jean, French dramatic poet; b. Ferte Milon, France, 1639; (Coll. of Beauvais); d. 1699. "Our Own the Best" (apothegm), p. 94. "How to take it" (apothegm), p. 294.

Rankin, Jeremiah Eames, writer, poet; b. Thornton, N. H., 1828; (Middlebury Coll., Vt., 1849). "America, Fairest of Freedom's Daughters," p. 159.

Read, Thomas Buchanan, artist, poet; b. Chester, Penn., 1822; d. 1872. "The Brave at Home," p. 136.

Robertson, Frederick William, Eng. min., original thinker; b.1816, London, Eng.; (Oxford Univ., 1836); d. 1853. "True Liberty," p. 263.

Ross, General Lawrence Sullivan, lawyer, soldier; of Va. and Ky. parentage; b. at Bentonsport, Iowa, 1838; (Wesleyan Univ., Alabama). "Our Banner Unrent: its Stars Unobscured," p. 307.

Sallust, Caius Crispus, Roman historian; b. 86 B. C.; d. 36 B. C. "Adherbal before the Roman Senate," p. 74.

Sargent, Epes, journalist, scholar, writer; b. Gloucester, Mass., 1812; d. 1880. "Regulus before the Roman Senate," p. 56. "Our Country," p. 255. "Deeds of Kindness," p. 351. By permission of executors.

Schiller, Johann Christoph Friedrich von, dramatic poet; b. Marbach, Germany, 1759; d. 1805. "Joan's Farewell to Home," p. 301.

Scipio, Africanus (Scipio the Greater), Roman general of eminence, who subdued Carthage, 203 B. C. "Rejects Hannibal's Plea for Peace," p. 45.

Scipio, Publius Cornelius, a Roman general, killed in battle, 211 B. C. "Address to his Soldiers, threatened by Hannibal, in front of Rome," p. 60.

Scott, Sir Walter, novelist, poet; b. Edinburgh, Scotland, 1771; d. 1832. "Love of Country," p. 106.

Shakespeare, William, the greatest dramatic poet; b. at Stratford-on-Avon, 1564; d. 1616. "Be just, and fear not," p. 248. "A Good Name," p. 343.

Shaw, David T. "Columbia, Land of the Free" ("The Red, White, and Blue"), p. 405.

Sheridan, General George Augustus, soldier, lecturer, politician; b. Millbury, Mass., 1840. "Immortal Memories," p. 309.

Sheridan, Richard Brinsley, orator and dramatist; b. Dublin, Ireland, 1751; d. 1816. "The Orator described," p. 335.

Sherman, General William Tecumseh, soldier; b. Lancaster, Ohio, 1820; (U. S. Mil. Academy, 1840); d. 1892. "Belligerent Non-combatants," p. 308.

Sigourney, Lydia (*née* HUNTLEY), poetess, author; b. Norwich, Conn., 1781; d. 1865. "Stars in my Country's Sky, are ye all there?" p. 403.

Smart, Alexander, Scotch poet; b. in Scotland; in 1860 published "Songs of Labor and Domestic Life." "Better than Gold," p. 286.

Smith, Horace, Eng. humorist and writer; b. London, 1780; d. 1849. "How to have just what we like," p. 291. "The Sanctuary within the Breast," p. 350.

Smith, Samuel Francis, Bapt. min., journalist, hymnologist, and poet; b. Boston, Mass., 1808; (Harv. Coll., 1829). "The Patriot Dead," p. 300. "Eve of Decoration Day," p. 313. "Patriot Sons of Patriot Sires," p. 399.

Smith, Sarah F., English poetess. "Immortality" (apothegm), p. 333.

Sparks, Jared, biographer, historian; b. Wilmington, Conn., 1789; (Harv. Coll., 1815); d. 1866. "The Lessons of the Revolution," p. 115.

Spenser, Edmund, Eng. poet; b. London, about 1553; (Pembroke Hall, Cambridge); d. 1599, in great destitution. (Apothegm) "Contentment," p. 324.

Sprague, Charles, merchant, banker, poet; b. Boston, Mass., 1791; d. 1875. "Individual Purity the Hope of the State," p. 144.

Stephens, Alexander Hamilton, politician, legislator, statesman; b. Taliferro Co., Ga., 1812; d. 1883. "Separate as Billows, but one as the Sea," p. 304.

Stockard, Henry Jerome, educator, philologist; b. Chatham Co., N. C., 1858; (Graham Coll. and Univ. N. C.); Prof. Eng. Lit., Univ. N. C. "The Review of the Dead," p. 186.

Story, Joseph, legal author, jurist, statesman; b. Marblehead, Mass., 1779; (Harv. Coll., 1798); d. 1845. "The Future of the United States," p. 387.

Storrs, Richard Salter, Cong. divine, orator, scholar, author; b. Braintree, Mass., 1821. "The Supremacy of Conscience," p. 259.

Stoughton, John, English divine; author of ecclesiastical literature; b. Norwich, Eng., 1807; (Highbury Coll. and Univ. Coll., London); d. 1834. "Desirable Objects of Attainment," p. 326.

Street, Alfred Billings, writer and poet; b. Poughkeepsie, N. Y., 1811; d. 1881. "The Death of Osceola," p. 307.

Stuart, Gilbert Charles, American painter, studied in England under West and Sir Joshua Reynolds; b. Narragansett, R. I., 1756; d. 1828; painted portrait of Washington, 1792. See frontispiece.

Sumner, Charles, lawyer, orator, statesman; U. S. Sen., Mass.; b. Boston, Mass., 1811; (Harv. Coll., 1830); d. 1874. "The True Grandeur of Nations," p. 137. "Progress is constant," p. 392.

Swain, Charles, Eng. writer, engraver, and author, known as "the Manchester poet;" b. Manchester, Eng., 1803; d. 1874. "True Nobility," p. 276.

Swett, John, teacher; Supt. Pub. Ins., Cal.; Supt. Schools, San Francisco. Credited to "Common School Readings"; "What might be done" (anon.), p. 292. "The Pacific Shore," p. 395.

Taylor, George Lansing, Meth. Episc. min., lecturer; b. Skeneatles, N. Y., 1835; (Columbia College, N. Y., 1861). "No Slave beneath the Flag," p. 169.

Taylor, Jane, Eng. writer and poet; b. London, 1783; d. 1824. "The Philosopher's Scales," p. 34.

Thompson, William H., lawyer, soldier journalist, and poet; known as the "champion archer of America;" b. Calhoun, Ga., 1848; (Ga. Mil. Institute). "High Tide at Gettysburg," p. 249.

Thomson, James, Scottish poet; b. 1834; for a while a soldier; d. 1882. "Soul Culture" (apothegm), p. 328.

Thornton, Eliza, poetess; b. Northampton, N. H., 1795; d. 1854. "The Reign of Peace," p. 198.

Trafton, Mark, Meth. Episc. min., temperance advocate, poet; b. Bangor, Me., 1810. "Our Martyred Dead," p. 188.

Trumbull, Colonel John, American painter and soldier; studied in London under West; aid-de-camp of Washington; b. Lebanon, Conn., 1756; d. 1813; painted a portrait of Washington, as well as the most famous battle-scene pictures of the Revolutionary War. See frontispiece.

Tupper, Martin Farquhar, Eng. poet, novelist; b. London, 1810. "America an Aggregate of Nations," p. 108.

Tuttle, Joseph Farrand, Presb. min., journalist, scholar; Pres. and Pres. Emeritus of Wabash Coll., Indiana; b. Bloomfield, N. J., 1818; (Marietta Coll., Ohio, 1841); contributes "Death or Liberty," by Theodore D. Wehl, p. 251.

Upham, Charles Wentworth, Unit. min., writer; b. St. Johns, New Brunswick, 1802; at Salem, Mass., 1824; d. 1875. "Washington's Training," p. 121.

Upham, James Bailey, versatile writer, journalist, associated with "Youth's Companion" since 1872; originated the system of placing the national flag in all schools; b. Newhampton, N. H., 1845. p. 134.

Verplanck, Gulian Crommelin, essayist, scholar; b. N. Y., 1786; d. 1870. "Our History," p. 390.

Villemaine, Abel François, writer, eminent critic, orator; French Minister of State; b. Paris, 1790; (Coll. Louis le Grand); d. 1870. "The Christian Orator," p. 341.

Warren, General Joseph, physician, patriot, soldier, orator; b. Roxbury, Mass., 1741; (Harv. Coll., 1759); Pres. Provincial Cong., 1774; killed at Bunker Hill, June 17, 1775. "Scorn to be Slaves," p. 229.

Washington, General George, "Father of his Country" and first President of the United States; b. Westmoreland Co., Va., Feb. 22, 1732; d. Dec. 14, 1799. "Resignation of his Commission," p. 154.

Watterson, Henry, journalist, versatile writer, politician; b. Washington, D. C., 1840. "Dedication Oration at Columbian Exposition," p. 365. "The Schools take Part," p. 367.

Webb, J. Russell, journalist, writer, educator; b. Brownsville, Jefferson Co., N. Y., 1824; (N. Y. State Normal School). "Not to Myself alone." p. 283, credited to his volume for schools.

Webster, Daniel, lawyer, orator, politician, statesman; U. S. Sen. Mass.; b. Salisbury, N. H., 1782; (Dartmouth Coll., N. H., 1801). "The Fourth of July," p. 110. "True Eloquence defined," p. 340.

Weems, Mason L., Prot. Episc. min., Virginia, biographical author; d. 1825. "The Battle of Lexington," p. 214.

Weld, Theodore Dwight, early reformer, anti-slavery orator; b. Hampton, Conn., 1803; (Hamilton Coll., N. Y., Lane Seminary, and Oberlin Coll., Ohio). "Love of Liberty illustrated," p. 251.

Whiting, Seymour W., banker at Raleigh, N. C.; b. New England; d. 1854. "Battle of Alamance described," p. 206.

Whittier, John Greenleaf, philanthropist and poet; member of the Society of Friends; b. Haverhill, Mass., 1808; d. 1892. "Laus Deo," p. 170.

Willis, Nathaniel Parker, journalist, poet, versatile writer; b. Portland, Me., 1807. "The Patriot King in Mourning," p. 38. "The Soldier's Widow," p. 191. "Look not upon the Wine," p. 297. "What is Ambition?" p. 331.

Winthrop, Robert Charles, scholar, historian, orator, philanthropist, and statesman; Speaker U. S. House of Representatives; U. S. Sen. Mass.; Pres. Mass. Hist. Soc.; Pres. Peabody Trustees; Pres. Mass. Bible Soc.; b. Boston, Mass., 1809; (Harv. Coll., 1826). "New England and Virginia," p. 85. "The National Ensign," p. 220. "American Education," p. 323.

Wirt, William, lawyer, author, statesman; b. Bladensburg, Md., 1772; d. 1834. "No Excellence without Labor," p. 282.

Wolfe, Charles, Irish clergyman and poet; b. Dublin, Ireland, 1791; (Dublin Univ.); d. 1823. "The Burial of Sir John Moore," p. 210. "The Wail of Jugurtha," p. 75.

Wolfe, General James, British soldier; b. Kent, England, 1726; killed on the Heights of Abraham, near Quebec, 1759. "Address to his Troops," p. 233.

Woodworth, Samuel, journalist, poet; b. Scituate, Mass., 1785; d. 1842. "The Old Oaken Bucket," p. 100.

Young, Edward, philosopher, scholar, physician; b. Somersetshire, Eng., 1773; (London Univ. and Edinburgh Univ.); d. 1829. "Procrastination," p. 336.

VOCABULARY AND PRONUNCIATION

OF

PROPER NAMES AND SPECIAL WORDS.

Key to the Pronunciation of Words. — Webster's International Dictionary, 1894, is the authority for this key, as also for the accentuation and syllabication of the words in this vocabulary.

ā as in āle.	i as in ice.	o͞o as in fo͞od.
ă " senăte.	ĭ " Idea.	o͝o " fo͝ot.
â " câre.	ĭ " ĭll.	ou " out.
ă " ăm.	ō " ōld.	oi " oil.
ä " ärm.	ȯ " obey.	ai " chair.
à " àsk.	ô " ôrb.	g " go.
a " final.	ŏ " ŏdd.	ng " sing.
ạ " ạll.	ū " ūse.	ŋ " iŋk.
ē " ēve.	ŭ " ŭnite.	th " then.
ė " ėvent.	ṳ " rṳde.	th " thin.
ĕ " ĕnd.	ụ " fụll.	n " bon.
ẽ " fẽrn.	ŭ " ŭp.	ñ as ny in cañon.
ê " thêre.	û " ûrn.	w same as v.
e " recent.	ȳ " pitȳ.	zh as z in azure.

a̤, e̤, i̤, o̤, ṳ, obscure sound similar to that of short u.

Patriotic literature and its associated sentiment calls into use the largest possible range of the words of the English language. Many of these have poetic, or political forms, not in common use. A brief statement of those which are of special value to right understanding of the text, and of allusions which require explanation, is therefore appended. (Prepared by R. CHASE CARRINGTON.)

a-base'ment (ȧ-bās'ment), *being humbled, or brought low.*
a-bashed' (ȧ băsh't), *made ashamed.*
a-bat'ed (ȧ bāt'ĕd), *lessened, or destroyed.*
Ab da lon'i mus (Ab dä lŏn' ĭ mŭs), *a poor gardener made king of Sidon, by Alexander the Great.*
a-blaze' (ȧ-blāz'), *on fire, or in a blaze.*
Ăb' nė gā' tion (-shŭn), *denial; hence, dropping one's own choice.*
A'-bram (A' bram), *afterwards called Abraham, "Father of Nations," a pioneer Hebrew patriarch who sought a new country for his home, about the year, 1996 B. C.*
Ăb' sȧ lom, *rebel son of King David, met with a violent death, about 1023 B. C.*
ab-hor'red (ăb hŏrd'), *greatly hated.*
a-bom'i na ble (ȧ bŏm'ĭ-nȧ-b'l), *detestable.*
ab-rupt'ly (ăb rŭpt' lĭ), *suddenly.*
ab'so lute (ăb'sō-lūt), *complete, unlimited.*
ab-solve' (ăb-sŏlv'), *to loosen, or free from obligation.*

ac-com'pa-ni-ment (ăk kŭm'pȧ nĭ ment), *something that goes with a principal thing.*
ac-com'plish (ăk-kŏm'plĭsh), *to do.*
ac-com'plish ed (ăk kŏm'plĭsht), *finished.*
ac-cred'it ed (ăk krĕd'ĭt ĕd), *recognized.*
ac-cu'mu-la ted (ăk-kū'mụ lāt ĕd), *collected, brought together.*
ac cursed' (ăk kûrst'), *detestable, worthy of being cursed.*
a-chiev ed' (ȧ chēvd'), *performed, or acquired.*
ac-knowl'edge (ăk nŏl'ĕj), *admit as true.*
ac'ȯ-nite (ăk'ȯ nīt), *a poisonous plant, used in poetry for poison generally.*
ac-quir'ed (ăk kwīrd'), *gained, or obtained.*
ac'tu-a ted (ăk tū ā'tĕd), *incited to action.*
a-cute'ness (ȧ kūt'nĕs), *sharpness, also, depth of feeling.*
Ăd ăm (" created "), *the first man.*
ȧ-dăpt'ĕd, *suited, or fitted to.*
ad'e-quate (ăd'ē kwāt), *fully sufficient.*

Ad hēr'bal, *a prince of Numidia, son of Micipsa, put to death by his foster-brother Jugurtha.*
ad-here' (ăd hēr'), *to join to, to be devoted to.*
ăd-jŭst'ment, *regulation, settlement.*
ad min'is-tra'tion (ăd mĭn'ĭs tra'shŭn), *management; hence, the executive department of a government.*
à-dŏpt'ĕd, *taken as one's own.*
ăd-vĕn'tŭre (-tŭr), *an act of risk, a bold act.*
ăf-fĭn'ĭ-tỹ, *relationship, resemblance.*
af-fright' (ăf frīt'), *to cause fear.*
à-frĕsh', *anew, once again.*
à-frown' (à froun'), *to look ugly, to frown.*
air'ĭ-lỹ (âr'ĭ lỹ), *light as air.*
Āl'a mănce, N. C., *the place where the first armed resistance to British authority was made, May 7, 1771. See p. 206.*
Āl'bĭ ŏn, *ancient name of England, still used in poetry.*
al'che-mist (ăl'ke mĭst), *one who sought to convert other metals into gold.*
Ăl ĕx ăn'der, *King of Macedon, 356-324 B. C.*
Ăl gi dŭs' (Ăl jĭ'dŭs), *a mountain of Italy consecrated to Diana.*
Ăl-lē'vĭ-ā tion (-shŭn), *lessening of burdens or sorrow.*
Ăl-lī'ănce (Ăns), *mutual aid under agreement.*
al lies' (Ăl līz'), *parties bound to mutual aid.*
al-loy' (Ăl loi'), *admixture of anything which lessens the value.*
al-lure'ments (ăl lūr'ments), *temptations, motives to action.*
à-lŏft', *high in the air, or upon a ship's mast.*
al'tar (ăl'tẽr), *a high place for sacrifice; hence a sacred place, as on our country's altar, the family altar.*
al'ter-ca tion (ăl tẽr kā'shŭn), *hot words of dispute.*
Ăl-tẽr'nā-tive (tĭv), *a choice of two.*
Ăm'ă lĕk, *A son of Esau, and his descendants, bitter foes of Gideon, Saul, and David.*
a-massed' (à-măst'), *collected in a heap, or in quantity.*
Ăm-bas'sa-dor (see embassador).
Ăm'ĭ-tỹ, *harmony, friendship.*
an'arch-ist (ăn'ärk-ĭ t), *one opposed to law.*
an'ces-tors (ăn'sĕs tẽrs), *persons from whom our parents are derived.*
an'guish ed (ăŋ'gwĭsht), *extremely pained, distressed, or tortured.*
an'i mate (ăn'ĭ māt), *to give life, to quicken.*
ăn'ĭ mŏs'ĭ-tỹ, *hatred prompting revenge.*
an'nals (ăn nalz), *a series of events in order, without historical comment.*
ăn-nĭ'hĭ-lāt ĕd, *destroyed.*
à-noint', *to smear with oil as a sign of consecration, and therefore to consecrate.*
an-tag'o nism (ăn tăg'ŏ nĭz'm), *opposition of action, contention.*
ăn'te-past, *a foretaste.*
an tic'i pate (ăn tĭs'ĭ pāt), *to foresee, and also to do beforehand.*

an-ti̇̄'nĭ-ty (ăn tĭk'wẽ tỹ), *ancient time.*
ăp'à-thỹ, *want of feeling, void of passion or sensibility.*
ap'pa-rĭ'tion (ăp'pă rĭsh'ŭn), *a mere appearance, without reality, usually spoken of as a ghost.*
ap-pease' (ăp pēz'), *to quiet, to pacify.*
ap-pend'age (ăp pĕnd'āj), *something attached to a greater or more important thing, though not necessary to it.*
ăp-pli'ance (-ans), *the thing applied, or employed.*
ăp-prō'prĭ-ā'tion (-shŭn), *assignment to a special use or purpose.*
ăpt'est' (out of use), *most fit.*
Ăr'ăb, *a desert wanderer, native of Arabia.*
Ăr'à-bỹ, *the country of Arabia.*
är'bĭ-tẽrs (tẽrz), *persons selected to decide a controversy.*
är'bĭ-trā rỹ, *ruled by the will, despotic.*
Arch-an'gĕl (ärk ăn jĕl), *an angel of the highest order.*
ar'du-ous (är'dū ŭs), *difficult, laborious.*
ăr'ĭd, *dry, parched with heat.*
ar-ray' (ăr rā'), *to place in order of battle, to adorn with dress.*
ar-tif'-ĭ cer (är tĭf'ĭ sẽr), *a skillful designer, or mechanic.*
ar'tĭ fĭ'cial (är tĭ fĭsh'al), *not natural.*
Ăs'kĕ lŏn', *a walled city of the Philistines, on the Mediterranean coast, first captured by the Hebrews, about 1426 B. C.*
Ăs syr i a (ăs sĭr'ĭ a), *an ancient empire, with Babylon and Nineveh its chief cities, conquered by Cyrus the Mede, about 568 B. C.*
à-tound'ing, *tending to astonish.*
à sŭn'der, *divided, or separated, into parts.*
à trō'cious (à trō'shŭs), *very cruel, or criminal.*
Ăt tūn ed' (ăt tūnd'), *set in harmony.*
an'di-tor (a'dĭ tẽr), *listener.*
Auer'stält (ow ẽre stĕt), *scene of a disastrous Prussian defeat, 1814.*
aug-ment'er (ag mĕnt'er), *one that augments or increases.*
au'gust (a gŭst'), *majestic, inspiring awe.*
Au rō'ra (a rō'rá), *the goddess of morning; the dawn.*
aus-ter'ĭ ty (as tẽr'ĭ tỹ), *severity of manners or life.*
aux-il'iary (agz ĭl'yà rỹ), *aiding, helping.*
av'a-rice (ăv'á rĭs), *greediness or extreme desire to become rich.*
a venge' (à-vĕnj'), *to inflict punishment for injury.*
a-ver'sion (à vẽr'shŭn), *hatred or dislike.*
à-wards', *judgments, final decisions.*
aw ed' (awd'), *struck with awe, influenced by fear or reverence.*
awk'ward (ăk'wẽrd), *clumsy, bungling.*
ax'-man (ăks man), *wood-chopper.*

Bā'bĕl, *meaning confusion, a noted tower at Babylon, built about 2218 B. C., described in the eleventh chapter of Genesis.*
Băb ỹ lon', *the chief city of Chaldea, captured by Cyrus the Persian king, about 563 B. C.*

SPECIAL VOCABULARY. 427

back'slid'er (băk slī'd ẽr), *one who abandons the faith and practice of a religion professed.*
bag'a-telle (băg'a tĕl'), *a trifle, a thing of no importance.*
bāle'ful, *destructive or deadly.*
băn, *curse, prohibition.*
bănd'ĕd, *bound with a band, hence united together.*
bănk'rŭpt, *broken in business, unable to pay just debts.*
Băn'nŏck bŭrn, *famous in Scottish history as the scene of a great battle between Robert Bruce and King Edward of England.*
bärd, *a poet of the ancient Celts.*
bar'rack (băr'răk), *house in a fort or town, for soldiers.*
Băr-sur-Aube (bär' sür ōb'), *a town in France famous for a battle in which Prince William of Prussia (afterwards Emperor) was wounded, but greatly distinguished himself.*
bär'tẽr, *to trade one commodity for another.*
bā'sĭs, *foundation or support.*
bas'tion (băs'chŭn), *projection of a fortress.*
băt'tẽr ed (băt tẽrd), *bruised, shattered.*
bat'tle-cloud (băt t'l kloud), *signs of coming battle.*
bat'tle-ment (băt t'l' ment), *a wall raised on a building with openings.*
bau'ble (ba̤'b'l), *a trifling piece of finery.*
Bă vā'rī a, *a kingdom of the German Empire.*
bay (bā), *a prize garland made of laurel.*
bea'con (bē'k'n), *a signal erected to warn of danger.*
beak'er (bēk'ẽr), *a drinking cup, formerly passed around to guests.*
bē'a-tif'ic (bē ȧ tĭf'ĭk), *blessed, able to make blessed, used only of a state after death.*
beau'i-de'al (bō'-ĭ-dē'ăl), *a faultless image or conception of the mind.*
beech'en (bēch''n), *made of beechwood.*
Bē-ēr'shē bă, *the most southern town in the land of Canaan and famous in Hebrew history.*
bē-fĕll', *happened, referring generally to some ill or misfortune.*
bē-gŏt', *generated, as, a father begot a son.*
be-guile' (bē-gīl'), *to delude, to deceive.*
bē-hōld'ĭng, *looking on, seeing.*
be-lea'guer ed (bē lē'gẽrd), *besieged, blockaded.*
bĕl'frȳ, *that part of a steeple or tower in which a bell is hung.*
Bĕl'gĭ ŭm, *in Europe. Its capital, Brussels.*
Bĕl-shăz'zăr, *king of Babylon, slain at the capture of the city by Cyrus, about 540 B. C.*
be-mock'ing (bē mŏk'ĭng), *sneering at, treating with derision.*
ben'e-dic'tions (bĕn'ē dĭk'shŭns), *uttered blessings, or expressions of gratitude.*

ben'e-fac'tion (bĕn ē făk'shŭn), *a benefit conferred, a gift.*
bē-nĕf'ĭ-cent (-sĕnt), *doing good, doing acts of charity.*
be-nign' (bē nīn'), *kindly, gracious.*
Bĕn'thăm, Jĕr'e̤my, *a celebrated English reformer, died 1848.*
be-numb'ed (bē-nŭmd)', *without sensation, as from cold.*
be-queath'ed (bē kwēth'd), *given by will.*
be'som (bē'zŭm), *a sweep or broom, used figuratively.*
be-siege' (bē sēj'), *to beset or surround a place for its capture.*
Bĕth'pē'ōr, *a city of Moab near Mt. Nebo.*
be-tide' (bē tīd'), *to happen to, to occur.*
be-troth'ed (bē-trŏtht'), *engaged to be married.*
bick'er-ings (bĭk'ẽr ĭngz), *petty quarrels.*
big'ot (bĭg ŭt), *one obstinately and unreasonably wedded to a particular creed or opinion.*
birth'right (bẽrth'rĭt), *what comes to one by birth, as child or as citizen.*
biv'ouac (bĭv'wăk), *an encampment without tents or covering.*
blănd', *soft, mild, gentle.*
blăn'dĭsh-ments, *soft words or actions.*
blares' (blârz), *sounds loudly, like the blare of a trumpet.*
blăst, *to strike, to injure, to destroy.*
blĕnch, *to shrink, to start back.*
blĕnd'ing, *mingling, harmonizing.*
block-ade' (blŏk ād'), *a shutting up from escape, or all access from without.*
bond'age (bŏnd ăj), *slavery or subjection.*
bonds'men (bŏndz'men'), *slaves, or those bound to serve without wages.*
bōōn, *a gift or favor granted.*
Brăd'dŏck (dŏk), *a British general, defeated by the Indians, 1755.*
braid'ed (brād'ĕd), *woven or entwined together.*
brănd, *a burning piece of wood, and hence a mark burned in.*
bray'ed (brād), *pounded or ground as in a mortar.*
bra'zen (brā'z'n), *made of, or pertaining to, brass.*
breast'ing (brĕst ing), *meeting with the breast; opposing in front, as breasting the waves.*
bribe (brīb), *to hire for bad purposes, as, to corrupt a judge.*
bril' lian-cy (brĭl'yan sȳ), *great brightness.*
brĭm'ming, *full to the top or brim.*
bris'tling (brĭs'slĭng), *standing up erect like bristles.*
bŭf' fȧ lō (so called), *the wild ox, or bison, of North America.*
bŭf'fĕt-ing, *striking with the hands, a succession of blows.*
bul' bul, *the bird known as the nightingale.*
bŭlk' ȳ, *large, of great size*
Bull (bull), *name of a constellation of stars.*
bur'nish ed (bũr'nĭsht), *polished, made bright.*
bus'tle (bŭs's'l), *great stir, noise, or agitation.*

SPECIAL VOCABULARY.

ca-bal′ler (kà băl′ lẽr), *one who plots with others to effect a common object.*
cab′i net (kăb′ ĭ nĕt), *the private (cabinet) advisers of a ruler.*
ca′ dence (kā′ dĕns), *a measure in music; hence, a military step.*
caĭ′ tiff (kā′ tĭf), *a mean rascal, a slave.*
Caĭ′us Licĭn′ ĭ ŭs (kā′yŭs), *a Roman Tribune.*
Caĭ′us Mar′ ĭ ŭs (kā′yŭs), *a Roman general who conquered Jugurtha.*
ca-jole′ (kå jōl′), *to coax, to delude by flattery.*
cal′en der (kăl′ ĕn dẽr), *a register of the year, or of facts, in order.*
cam paign′ (kăm pān′), *a period of military service in the field.*
Ca′na an (kā′ nan), *name given to the land occupied by the descendants of Canaan, Noah's grandson, and acquired by the family of Abraham, according to promise.*
can′ cel ed (kăn′sĕld), *crossed out, annulled.*
can′ di date (kăn′ dĭ dāte), *one who seeks some office or position.*
can′ o py (kăn′ ȯ pȳ), *a covering over the head; hence, the sky is called a canopy.*
ca′ per (kā′ pẽr), *to dance, or skip about.*
ca price′ (kȧ prēs′), *a whim, or fancy.*
Car′mel (kär′mĕl), *a famous mountain of Palestine.*
car′nage (kär′nåj), *great destruction of men, slaughter.*
Car′ thage (kär′ thĭj), *a city of Africa, the chief rival of Rome.*
Cas til′ ian (kăs tĭl′ yan), *pertaining to Castile in Spain; and, figuratively, courtly, — as, Castilian dignity.*
Cat′a line (kăt′ ȧ lĭn), *a Roman traitor denounced by Cicero, p. 58.*
ce les′ tial (sẽ lĕs′ chal), *heavenly.*
cen′sure (sĕn′shụr), *to find fault with and condemn as wrong.*
cer′e mo nies (sĕr′ ė mô nĭz), *special forms observed in religion, or upon public occasions.*
cer e mo′ni ous (sĕr ė mō′nĭ ŭs), *formal, very precise.*
ce ru′le an (sẽ rụ′ lė an), *sky-colored, blue.*
chafe (chāf), *to fret against, to excite.*
Chal de′ a (kăl dē′a), *an ancient country watered by the rivers Tigris and Euphrates, of which Babylon and Nineveh were the principal cities.*
chalk′y (chạk′ȳ), *resembling chalk, white with chalk.*
chal′ lenge (chăl′ lĕnj), *to call to a contest.*
chăn′nĕl, *that through which anything passes; as, the channels of prosperity.*
chănt′ed, *sung after the manner of a chant.*
chăp′ lĕt, *a garland or wreath to be worn on the head.*
char′ac ter (kăr′ ăk tẽr), *distinctive qualities, as a whole, of a person or thing.*
charms (chärmz), *qualities that attract.*
char′ ter, *a written grant of lands, rights, or privileges.*

chas′ ten ing (chā′ s'n ĭng), *disciplining, purifying.*
check′ ed (chĕkt), *stopped or restrained.*
chem′ ist (kĕm′ ĭst), *one versed in chemistry.*
chem′ is try (kĕm′ ĭs trȳ), *a science relating to the elements and properties of material bodies or substances.*
chi can′ er y (shė kān′ ẽr ȳ), *trickery.*
chief′ tain (chēf′ tĭn), *a chief or leader.*
chimes (chīmz), *a set of bells tuned to each other; the music made by the bells.*
Christ ian′ i ty (krĭs chăn′ ĭ tȳ), *the religion of Christ.*
cir′cuit (sẽr′ kĭt), *any space or extent measured by traveling round.*
cir′cum stan′ces (sẽr′ kŭm stăns′ĕz), *the facts which surround a person; his worldly estate.*
clad (klăd), *clothed.*
clam′or ed (klăm′ ẽrd), *cried aloud with much noise and confusion.*
clar′ i o net′ (klăr′ ĭ ȯ nĕt′), *a wind instrument with a single reed.*
clas′sic (klăs′sĭk), *of the first rank, after the best model or authority.*
clat′ ter ing (klăt′ tẽr ĭng), *making a rattling noise.*
click (klĭk), *a slight, sharp noise.*
clo′ven (klō′v'n), *divided or parted.*
clutch′ ed (klŭcht), *seized or grasped.*
coat′ of mail (kōt′ of māl), *a defensive garment of metal links.*
co-e′val (kọ ē′ val), *of the same age.*
co′ex ten′ sive (kō ĕks tĕn′sĭv), *of equal extent.*
co he′sive (kọ hē′ sĭv), *that has the power of sticking or cohering.*
coils (koilz), *winds itself; often used with about or around.*
co in′ci dent (kọ ĭn′ sĭ dent), *happening together, concurrent.*
col′ league (kŏl′ lēg), *an associate in the same office or duty.*
co lo′ni al (kọ lō′ nĭ al), *pertaining to a colony.*
co los′sal (kọ lŏs′sal), *very large, huge.*
Cȯ lŭm′ bĭ ȧ (kọ-), *name derived from that of Columbus the discoverer of America, and familiarly applied to the United States.*
Co mi′ ti un (kọ mĭsh′ ė ụm), *an assembly hall of the old Roman people.*
cŏm mem′o rāte (kŏm-), *to honor by special ceremonies some name or event.*
com min′gle (kŏm mĭn′ g'l), *to mingle or mix together.*
Com′ mon wealth (kŏm mŭn wĕlth), *a free state, or a government of the people.*
cŏm mū′ nĭ tȳ (kŏm-), *a society of people having common rights and privileges, or common interests.*
com′pass (kŭm′pas), *an instrument for determining directions on the earth's surface.*
com peers′ (kŏm pērz′), *equals.*
com pen sa′ tion (kŏm pĕn sā′ shŭn), *an equivalent for services, loss, or suffering.*
com pe ti′ tion (kŏm pė tĭsh′ ŭn), *rivalry.*

com pet' i tor (kŏm pĕt' ĭ tẽr), *a rival.*
com plain' kŏn plān), *to find fault.*
com plai'sant (kŏm plă'zănt), *pleasing in manners, civil, courteous.*
com'plex (kŏm'plĕks), *made up of several parts, complicated.*
com pose' (kŏm pōz'), *to form by uniting two or more parts; to invent and put together; to calm, to quiet, to settle.*
com pre hen'sion (kŏm prē hĕn'shŭn), *capacity of knowing; having full knowledge of a subject.*
com press'ed (kŏm prĕst') *pressed or forced into smaller space.*
con'cave (kŏn' kăv), *hollow, arched, or rounded; as, the sky.*
con cen'ter ed (kŏn sĕn'tẽrd), *concentrated.*
con cep'tion (kŏn sĕp' shŭn), *one's idea of a subject or thing.*
con cern'ed (kŏn sẽrnd'), *interested, engaged, anxious.*
con cert'ed (kŏn sẽrt'ĕd), *agreed upon, or planned and acted accordingly.*
con clu'sive (kŏn klū'sĭv), *final, decisive.*
con di'tion (kŏn dĭsh' ŭn), *state, circumstances.*
con' dor (kŏn' dŏr), *a large bird found in the Andes of South America.*
con fed'er ate (kŏn fĕd' ẽr āt), *united in a league; bound together by an agreement.*
con for ma'tion (kŏn' fŏr mā' shŭn), *agreement, arrangement.*
con fus'ed (kŏn fūzd'), *mixed, disordered.*
con grat' u late (kŏn grăt' ū lāt), *to wish joy to another.*
con' jur er (kŭn' jūr ẽr), *one who practices magic arts.*
con' quest (kŏn' kwĕst), *a complete victory, and also, that which is conquered.*
con'science (kŏn'shens), *one's inner sense or perception of right or wrong, applying to one's own actions.*
con se cra'tion (kŏn sē krā'shŭn), *the setting apart to a sacred use.*
con se cra'ted (kŏn sē krāt'ĕd), *separated from a common to a sacred use.*
con'ser va'tion (kŏn'sẽr vā' shŭn), *the act of preserving from change or loss.*
con serv'a tism (kŏn sẽrv' ă tĭz'm), *reluctance to change old customs.*
con serv'a tive (kŏn sẽrv ă tĭv), *one who aims to preserve from radical change.*
con sign'ed (kŏn sīnd'), *delivered; committed for keeping or management.*
con sist'ent (kŏn sĭs' tent), *fixed, firm; not contradictory, agreeing with.*
con'stan cy (kŏn'stăn sȳ), *fixedness; firmness of mind, lasting affection.*
cŏn'stĕl lā' ted (kŏn-), *grouped, as stars in a constellation; united in one splendor. Constellations of stars, and special stars, referred to on page 233, — "Orion," "The Greater and Lesser Bear," "The Bull," "The Twins," "The Crab," "The Maid," "The Scales." Referred to by Horace Mann, page 238, — "Orion," "The Pleiades," and "Sirius."*

con stit'u ent (kŏn stĭt' ū ent), *necessary, as a part; also a term applied to those who elect a representative to office.*
cŏn sŭm' māte (kŏn-), *complete, perfect; to the utmost degree or extent.*
con sum ma'tion (kŏn'sŭm mā'shŭn), *completion, end.*
con ta'gious (kŏn tā' jŭs), *that may be communicated one to another; catching.*
con temn' (kŏn tĕm'), *to despise, scorn.*
cŏn tĕm' pō rā rȳ (kŏn-), *living or being at the same time.*
Cŏn tĭ nĕnt'al Cŏn' gress (kŏn-), *the American Congress before the colonies became states.*
con tin'u al ly (kŏn tĭn' ū al lȳ), *without stopping, unceasing, repeatedly.*
con' tra band (kŏn' trā bănd), *forbidden by law or treaty.*
con tra ven'ed (kŏn tră vēnd'), *opposed, obstructed.*
con triv'ance (kŏn trĭv'ans), *the thing invented; also, a plan or scheme.*
cŏn'trŏ vẽr' sȳ (kŏn-), *dispute, opposition.*
con va les'cent (kŏn vă lĕs'sent), *renewal of health after sickness.*
con ver'san cy (kŏn vẽr'san sȳ), *familiarity.*
con vert' i ble (kŏn vẽrt' ĭ b'l), *that may be converted or changed.*
con vul'sive ly (kŏn vŭl'sĭv lȳ), *with a violent shaking or agitation.*
co-op'er a'tion (kō-ŏp' ẽr ā' shŭn), *working together to the same end.*
co-ŏr'di nate (-nāt), *equal, running together.*
cor re spond'ence (kŏr rē spŏnd' ens), *relation, fitness; intercourse by letter.*
cor rup'tion (kŏr rŭp'shŭn), *destruction of natural form; impurity; bribery.*
cour'te sy (kŭr'tē sȳ), *politeness of manners; civility.*
Crab krăb), *the name of a group, or constellation, of stars.*
craft (krăft), *cunning, art, skill.*
crag'gi est (krăg'gĭ est), *rugged, rocky.*
crash (krăsh), *the loud sound, as of many things fallen and breaking.*
crĕ dū' lĭ tȳ (krē-), *disposition to believe upon slight or no evidence.*
cred'u lous (krĕd' ū lŭs), *apt to believe on slight evidence; easily deceived.*
creed (krēd), *a system of belief.*
crept (krĕpt), *crawled, as a serpent.*
cres'cent (krĕs'sent), *the figure of the new moon; the design of the Turkish flag; figuratively the Turkish power.*
crest'ed (krĕst'ĕd), *adorned with a crest or plume.*
crip'ple (krĭp' p'l), *to lame, to disable.*
crit'ic al (krĭt' ĭ kal), *decisive; important, as regards the consequences.*
croak'er (krōk'ẽr), *a grumbler; one who forebodes evil.*
Croe'sus (krē'sŭs), *a rich king of Lydia, born 590 B. C., subdued by Cyrus.*
Crŏm'wĕll, Ŏl' ĭ vẽr (krŏm-), *a most extraordinary man, Lord Protector during*

the life of the English Commonwealth; b. Huntingdon, Eng., 1599; d. 1658.

crook'ed (krŏŏk'ĕd), *bent, curved; morally perverse, or wandering from duty.*

cru'ci ble (krụ'sĭ b'l), *a vessel used for melting ores, metals, etc.*

cru'ci fy (krụ'sĭ fī), *to put to death by nailing to a cross.*

cruse (krụs), *a small cup or vessel.*

cũl'mĭ nā tĭng (kŭl-), *reaching the meridian, as, the sun; and hence, reaching its highest point.*

curb'ed (kûrb-), *reined in, checked.*

cur'ren cy (kŭr'rĕn sў), *that which continually passes from hand to hand, as coin or banknotes.*

Cym'ri an (kĭm'rĭ on), *pertaining to the ancient Welsh.*

cy'pher (sī'fẽr), *in Arithmetic, a character (formed thus, 0,) which expresses nothing; hence, a man of no account.*

cy'press (sī'prĕs), *an evergreen tree; an emblem of mourning.*

Cy prus (sī'prŭs), *an island in the Mediterranean Sea.*

Cyrus (the Great) (Sī'rŭs), *founder of the Persian Empires, and noted in Biblical as well as other ancient history; described in the Books of Daniel, Ezra, and Isaiah; conquered Babylon; died about 529 B. C. See p. 16.*

damp'en ed (dămp'nd), *moistened, chilled; weakened, discouraged.*

Dan'i el (dăn'yĕl), *a learned Hebrew prophet, afterwards Prime Minister to the king of Babylon.*

därts, *shoots like a dart.*

dăs'tard (-tẽrd), *a coward, a sneak.*

daunt'less (dänt'lĕs), *bold, fearless.*

daz'ed (dāzd), *dazzled, overpowered with light.*

dead'li er (dĕd'lĭ ẽr), *more deadly.*

de base'ment (dē bās'ment), *degradation; reduction of purity, quality, or value.*

Deb'o rah (dĕb'ō rāh), *a noted Hebrew judge, leader, and prophetess; flourished about 1285, B. C.*

dec'a logue (dĕk'ȧ lŏg), *the ten commandments given to Moses on Mount Sinai.*

de cay' (dē kā'), *corruption, decline.*

de cem'vir (dē sĕm'vẽr), *one of the ten magistrates in ancient Rome.*

de cis'ion (dē sĭzh'ŭn), *firmness; final judgment; determination.*

deck (dĕk), *to array, to adorn, to dress.*

dec'la ra'tion (dĕk'lȧ rā'shŭn), *a positive statement, a proclamation.*

dec'o ra'tion (dĕk'ō rā'shŭn), *ornament; hence, badge of honor or merit.*

de co'rum (dē kō'rŭm), *propriety of speech or behavior; opposed to rudeness.*

de creed' (dē krēd'), *determined, ordered.*

de cree' (dē krē'), *an order, rule, or law.*

def'er ence (dĕf'ẽr ens), *deferring to, regard for, submission of opinion to that of another; hence, respect.*

de fer'ring (dē fẽr'ĭng), *postponing.*

de fi'ance (-ans), *contempt of opposition or danger; a daring.*

de fi'ed (dē fīd'), *challenged, set at naught, dared all risk.*

de file', *to make unclean or impure.*

de gen'er a cy (dē jĕn'ẽr ȧ sў), *a growing worse or inferior.*

de grad'ed (dē grād'ĕd), *reduced in rank.*

deign (dān), *to condescend, to grant or allow.*

Dē'ĭtў, *God, the Supreme Being; also used of the heathen gods or goddesses.*

de lib'er āte ly, *not hastily or rashly.*

de lĭr'ĭ ŭm, *a wandering of the mind, unnatural excitement.*

de lūd'ĕd, *deceived, misled.*

de lu'sion (dē lū'zhŭn), *deception, false idea or fancy.*

delve (dĕlv), *to dig, as with a spade.*

dem'a gogue (dĕm'ȧ gŏg), *a leader who pleases the people for selfish purposes.*

dem ō crat'ic (-krăt'ĭk), *popular, pertaining to a government by the people.*

dem o li'tion (dĕm ō lĭsh'ŭn), *the act of pulling down, destruction.*

Dē mŏs'the nēs, *the most celebrated Grecian orator.*

de nun'ci a'tion (dē nŭn'sĭ ā'shŭn), *a public accusation or arraignment.*

de press'ing, *pressing down, wearing, enfeebling.*

de priv'ed (dē prīvd'), *stripped of, bereft, divested.*

de scend'ant (dē sĕnd'ant), *any person proceeding from an ancestor, near or remote.*

de sid'ẽ rā'tȧ, *a Latin term for things specially desired, or needed.*

de spite'ful ly, *hatefully, maliciously.*

de spoil'ed (dē spoild'), *stripped, robbed.*

dĕs'pŏt, *a ruler with absolute power; hence, a tyrant.*

dĕs'tĭ nў, *state or condition predetermined, future fate.*

dē tĕst'ȧ ble (-b'l), *extremely hateful.*

de thron'ed (dē thrŏnd'), *removed or driven from a throne.*

de tract'er (dē trăkt'ẽr), *one who attempts to lessen the worth or reputation of another.*

de'vi ous (dē'vĭ ŭs), *out of the common way or track; wandering, roving.*

di'a dĕm, *the badge of royalty worn on the head; a crown.*

di'a lĕct (-lĕkt), *a branch or corruption of a parent language; speech, or manner of speaking.*

dic ta'tor (dĭk tā'tẽr), *one who dictates or orders; one vested with absolute power.*

dif fuse' (dĭf fūze'), *to spread abroad.*

dĭg'nĭ tĭes (-tĭz), *high honors or positions in a state.*

dĭl'ȧ tō'rў, *slow or tardy; making delay.*

dĭl'i gent ly (dĭl'ĭ jent lў), *with steady application and care, with industry.*

dĭm'ĭ nū'tion (-shŭn), *a lessening, a making smaller.*

dĭm'lĕss, *that cannot be dimmed, or made less bright.*

SPECIAL VOCABULARY. 431

din, *noise ; a loud sound long continued.*
dire' ful, *dreadful, terrible.*
dirge (dērj), *a song expressing sorrow and mourning.*
dis as' trous (dĭz ăs' trŭs), *working loss or injury.*
dis cern' (dĭz zĕrn'), *to discover; to see, to discriminate.*
dis cre' tion (dĭs krĕsh' ŭn), *prudence, or discernment and judgment.*
dis fig ure ment (dĭs fĭg ūr ment), *change of form to the worse.*
dis gŭst', *distaste ; hence, aversion.*
dis par'age ment (dĭs păr'ăj ment), *injury by comparison with something inferior ; reproach, disgrace.*
dis pel' led (dĭs pĕld'), *driven away, scattered.*
dis pens'er (dĭs pĕn'sẽr), *one who dispenses or distributes.*
dis perse' (dĭs pẽrs'), *to scatter, to separate.*
dis sĕm' ble (-b'l), *to hide under a false appearance, to disguise.*
dis sĕm' Ĭ nā' tion (-shŭn), *the act of scattering and propagating, like seed.*
dis sĕn'sion (-shŭn), *contention, strife, discord.*
dĭs'sĬ pā tĕd, *scattered, wasted, loose ; hence, devoted to pleasure and vice.*
dĭs'sō lūte, *given to vice and dissipation.*
dis solve' (dĭz zŏlv'), *to liquefy, to melt ; to break up, to destroy.*
dĭs tĕm' pẽr, *disease.*
dis tinct' (dĭs tĭŋkt'), *separated by a visible mark ; separate.*
dis tract'ed (dĭs trăkt' ĕd), *deranged, perplexed.*
dis trŭst', *doubt, want of confidence or faith.*
dĭt' tў, *a song, a sonnet.*
di' vers (dī' vẽrz), *different, several.*
dĭ vẽr'sĬ tў, *difference, variety, unlikeness.*
dĬ vīne' lў, *in a godlike manner, in the supreme degree.*
doom'ed (dōōmd), *condemned, fated.*
Dor'cas (dôr' kas), *a benevolent seamstress in the days of Saint Peter,* A. D. 38.
drăg'on (ŭn), *a winged serpent of old time romance.*
drain'ed (drānd), *emptied of water or other liquid ; exhausted.*
drench'ed (drĕncht), *soaked, thoroughly wet.*
driv'el (drĭv' 'l), *to be weak or foolish, to dote.*
drōōp'ing, *sinking, languishing, failing.*
Dru'id, *a priest or minister of religion among the ancient Celtic nations.*
dun'geon (dŭn'jŭn), *a dark prison cell.*
dūr'a ble (-b'l), *lasting.*
dŭsk'ў, *partially dark or obscure.*
dwarf'ed (dwȧrft), *hindered from growth to natural size.*
dў'nas tў, *a system of government, generally of some race or family.*

Ē' bal, *an historic mountain of Palestine.*
ebb'ed (ĕbd), *flowed back ; as, the tide.*
Eb'er hard, *"the bearded," first duke of Würtemberg, called the father of his country ; born* 1415, *died* 1496.
Ē' bers (ā bĕrs), *George, a learned German writer, and eminent traveller in Egypt and Palestine, born* 1837.
ĕb' ŏn, *like ebony; black.*
ec cen' tric (ĕk sĕn' trĭk), *odd, peculiar ; irregular.*
e clips'ing (ĕ klĭps'-), *darkening, obscuring; and hence, surpassing.*
ĕc'sta sў (ĕk-), *excessive joy, rapture.*
Ē' den, *the place in which God placed Adam and Eve.*
ĕd' Ĭ fĭce (-fĭs), *a building, a structure.*
ef face' (ĕf fās'), *to blot out, to erase.*
ĕf fŭl' gence (-jĕns), *a flood of light ; lustre, brightness.*
ē lăb' ō rāte, *wrought with labor, studied.*
ĕl' ẽ ments, *forces of Nature ; the first principles or original parts of anything.*
Ĕl' Ĭ ŏt. See Locke.
e lix' ir-vī' tæ (ĕ lĭks' ẽr), *"elixir of life," a fabulous drink supposed to perpetuate life.*
e lude' (ĕ lūd'), *to escape, to evade by artifice.*
e mā' ci ā' ted (ĕ mā' shĬ ā' tĕd), *reduced by loss of flesh ; thin, lean.*
ĕm'a nate (-nāt), *to proceed from a source.*
e man' ci pa'tion (ĕ măn'sĬ pā'shŭn), *deliverance from bondage or subjection.*
e mas'cu late (ĕ măs' kŭ lāt), *to weaken, to make effeminate.*
em balm'ed (ĕm bämd'-), *preserved from decay.*
ĕm băs'sa dor (-dẽr), *a representative of the highest rank from one government sent to another.*
embat'tled (ĕm băt' t'ld), *arrayed in order of battle ; furnished with battlements.*
ĕm' blĕm, *a sign, a symbol.*
ĕm bōld' ĕn (-'n), *to make bold.*
ĕm' ẽr ald, *a precious stone of a green color.*
e merg'en cy (ĕ mẽr' jĕn sў), *any event or occasion demanding prompt action ; pressing necessity.*
ĕm Ĭ grā'tion (-shŭn), *removal from one country to another with a view to settling there.*
ĕm'Ĭ nence (-nens), *a high place ; hence, elevation, or distinction.*
ĕm' ŭ lā' tion (-shŭn), *rivalry to excel.*
en act' ment (ĕn ăkt' ment, *the passing of a bill into a law.*
en am' el ed (ĕn ăm' ĕld), *overlaid or adorned with enamel.*
en co' mi ast' ic (ĕn kō' mĬ ăs' tĭk), *bestowing praise ; commending.*
en coun'ter (ĕn koun'tẽr), *a sudden meeting of persons ; hence, a conflict in battle.*
en croach' ment (ĕn krōch' ment), *a gradual entering or trespass upon the rights or property of others.*
en dow'ed (ĕn doud'), *enriched with any gift or faculty.*
ē nẽr' vā tĕd, *weakened, enfeebled.*
en fee'bled (ĕn fē' bl'd), *weakened, deprived of strength.*

SPECIAL VOCABULARY

en gross'ed (ĕn grōst'), *fully occupied.*
en hanc'ed (ĕn hănst'), *increased in value.*
en join'ed (ĕn joind'), *ordered, directed.*
en thrall'ed (ĕn thrạl'd'), *enslaved, reduced to servitude.*
en tic'ed (ĕn tīst'), *persuaded, allured to evil.*
en trench' ment, *see intrenchment.*
E pām I nŏn' das, *a famous Theban general who defeated the Spartans at Leuctra,* B. C. 371.
ep'ic (ĕp'ĭk), *narrative, a narrative poem.*
E pī' rŭs, *western Greece, or the modern Albania.*
ep'i taph (ĕp'ĭ tăf), *an inscription in honor of the dead.*
E' qui (ē'kwī), *Roman knights.*
e' quine (ē'kwīn), *pertaining to the horse, of the horse kind.*
eq' ui page (ĕk' wĭ pāj), *the furniture of a military man; and also, a carriage of state, a vehicle.*
e quiv' a lent (ē kwĭv'á lent), *equal to, that which is equal with something else.*
ē' ra, *a fixed point of time; a succession of years proceeding from a fixed point of time.*
Ē' rin, *Ireland.*
er rat'ic (ĕr răt'ĭk), *wandering, irregular, uncertain.*
ĕrr'ing, *wandering from the right way, sinning.*
er u di' tion (ĕr ụ dĭsh' ŭn), *earning.*
Ē' rȳx, *a mountain in Sicily named from a rival of Hercules, who was killed there.*
es pous'al (ĕs pouz' ạl), *betrothal, adoption.*
es' sence (ĕs' sens), *the very substance of a thing.*
es sen'tial (ĕs sĕn' shạl), *absolutely necessary.*
es trang'ed (ĕs trănjd'), *alienated.*
e thē' re al (-ạl), *consisting of ether or spirit, heavenly.*
eu'lo gy (ū' lō jȳ), *praise, encomium.*
Eu phra' tes (ū frā' tēz), *a river of Mesopotamia.*
Eve, *the mother of mankind, consort of Adam.*
e' ven tide (ē' v'n tīd), *early evening.*
ov' er glā'de, *swampy land covered with heavy brush.*
ex act' er (ĕgs ăkt' ĕr), *one who exacts or demands much.*
ĕx ăs'pĕr āte (ĕgs-), *to anger to a high degree.*
ex e cra'tion (ĕks ē krā' shŭn), *a curse pronounced, utter detestation expressed.*
ex emp' tion (ĕgs ĕmp' shŭn), *freedom or immunity from service, immunity.*
ex hil' a ra'ting (ĕgs ĭl' à rā' tĭng), *enlivening.*
ex' i gen' cy (ĕks' ĭ jen'sȳ), *an emergency.*
ex'ile (ĕks' īle), *one banished from one's country.*
ĕx pănd'ĕd (ĕks-), *extended, enlarged.*
ĕx pē' dĭ ĕnt (ĕks-), *a means to an end, means employed in an emergency.*

ĕx pīre' (ĕks-), *to breathe out, to die.*
ĕx pō' nĕnt (ĕks-), *an index or representative.*
ex pos'ed (ĕks pōzd'), *laid open, uncovered.*
ĕx pound' (ĕks-), *to explain, to interpret.*
ĕx tĕn' sīve lȳ (ĕks-), *widely, largely.*
ex tern' al (ĕks tĕrn' ạl), *outward, visible.*
ex trav'a gant (ĕks trăv' à gaunt), *excessive, wasteful.*
ex treme' ly (ĕks trēm' lȳ), *to the utmost point.*
ex ult' (ĕgs ŭlt'), *to rejoice in triumph.*

Fā' bĭ ŭs, Quin' tĭ ŭs Măx' ĭ mŭs, *a Roman general famous for careful plans, and hence surnamed "the Delayer;" hence, also, the origin of Washington's "Fabian policy."*
fa cil' i ties (fà sĭl' ĭ tĭz), *the means by which any act is rendered easy, advantages.*
fac' tor (făk' tĕr), *an essential part, or agent.*
fac'ul ty (făk' ŭl tȳ) *the power of doing anything, ability.*
fal' chion (fạl' chŭn), *poetic name given to a sword.*
făl' lā cy (-sȳ), *deception, mistake.*
fa mil' iar ize (fà mĭl' yĕr ĭz), *to make well known.*
fa năt'ic al (-ĭ kal), *wild and biased in opinion; possessed by a kind of frenzy.*
fan' cy (făn' sȳ), *notion, image, thought.*
farce (färs), *an empty show.*
fāt' ĕd, *destined, doomed.*
fath' om (făth' ŭm), *a measure of length of six feet.*
fath'om, *to sound or try the depth.*
fa tigue' (fà tēg'), *weariness, exhaustion.*
fawn' (fạn), *to flatter servilely, to court meanly.*
fe ro' cious (fē rō' shŭs), *fierce, savage.*
fĕs' tĕr ing, *rankling, corrupting with sores.*
fĕs' tĭ val (-vạl), *a public festive gathering.*
fĕt' tĕr, *to chain or bind.*
feud (fūd), *a deadly quarrel.*
fī' ăt, *a decree, a command.*
field' mar' shal (fēld' mär' shal), *a military officer of high rank.*
fiend (fēnd), *a bitter foe of good, a devil.*
fig' ure head (fĭg' ūr hĕd'), *the figure on the prow of a ship.*
filch, *to steal slyly, to pilfer.*
fiord (fyŏrd, i or y syllable), *a frith or arm of the sea (sometimes fjord).*
fir' ma ment (fĕr' má ment), *the region of the air, the sky.*
flănk' ing, *guarding or attacking on the flank.*
flăt' tĕr ȳ, *false praise.*
flur' ri ed (flŭr' rĭd), *agitated.*
foe' man (fō-), *an enemy.*
fōld' ĕd, *doubled, laid in plaits.*
foot' ing, *standing, as on one's feet; basis of action.*
for bear' ance (fŏr bâr' ans), *the exercise of patience, lenity.*
fore cast' (fōr kăst'), *to foresee, foretell.*

SPECIAL VOCABULARY.

fŏr lôrn', *solitary, wretched.*
fôr' mĭ da ble (-b'l), *exciting dread.*
fôr' mŭ læ (plural of formula), *set forms.*
fôr' tĭ fĭ cā' tion (-kā' shŭn), *defensive works, a fort.*
fôr' trĕss, *an extensive fort.*
for' tune (fôr' tŭn), *chance, luck; wealth.*
fos' ter ed (fŏs' tĕrd), *nourished.*
found' er ed (-dĕrd), *sunk; as, a ship in the sea.*
Frănk, *a member of an early German tribe that founded the monarchy of France.*
fraud' u lent ly (frąd' ů lent lĭ), *by fraud.*
fray (frā), *an encounter or skirmish.*
fren' zied (frĕn' zĭd), *affected with madness or rage.*
frĕt' tĕd, *vexed.*
front' let (frŭnt' lĕt), *a band worn on the forehead.*
fru i' tion (fru ĭsh' ŭn), *use accompanied with pleasure; realized plans.*
func' tion a ries (fŭŋk' shŭn â rĭz), *persons holding official place.*
fus' ing (fūz' ĭng), *melting.*

gal' ax y (găl' ăks y̆), *a cluster, as of stars.*
gall' ing (gąl' ĭng), *fretting, vexing.*
gär' land (-land), *a wreath of flowers to be worn on the head.*
gar' ni ture (gär' nĭ tŭr), *ornaments of dress or equipment.*
Găth, *an ancient Philistine city on the coast of Palestine.*
gau' dy (gąd' y̆), *showy, beyond good taste.*
gauge (gāj), *a measure, a standard.*
Gaul (gąl), *a name of ancient France; also, an inhabitant of Gaul.*
Gā' zȧ, *an ancient walled city of the Philistines in Palestine.*
gen' ius (jĕn' yŭs), *special intellectual powers.*
ge' ni us (jē' nĭ ŭs), *a good or evil spirit, or demon.*
Gĕrā' zĭm, *a city of the Philistines in Palestine.*
Gĭd' ĕ ŏn, *a Hebrew general, about 1245 B. C.*
gĭg' gle (-g'l), *a silly audible laugh.*
Gĭl bō' ȧ, *a mountain in Palestine where Saul fell in battle.*
gim' crack (jĭm' krăk), *a toy, a pretty thing.*
gird (gĕrd), *to put on, as a belt or girdle.*
gla' cier (glā' shẽr), *a slow-moving river or field of ice.*
glaz' ed (glāzd), *made smooth and shining like glass.*
glebe (glēb), *turf, soil.*
glide (glīd), *to move smoothly.*
glimpse (glĭms), *a short, quick view.*
gllut' ĕd, *gleamed, glittered.*
goad' ed (gōd' ĕd), *pushed on by a goad, roused, incited.*
goal (gōl), *the end, or final purpose.*
gŏb' lĕt, *a drinking-cup with no handle.*
gŏd' lĕss, *impious, ungodly.*
Gȯ mŏr' rah, *a city of Palestine destroyed by fire from Heaven.*

gŏn dȯ lier' (-lēr), *a man who rows a gondola.*
gore (gōr), *blood, thick or clotted blood.*
gorge (gȯrj), *a narrow passage, a defile between mountains.*
gorg' ed (gȯrjd), *glutted, stuffed with food.*
grad' u al (grăd' ů al), *proceeding by steps or degrees.*
graft' ĕd, *inserted on another stock.*
gran' a ries (grȧ' na rĭz), *storehouses for grain.*
gran' deur (grăn' ŭr), *greatness, splendor of appearance*
graph' ic al ly (ġ ăf' ĭ kal lỷ), *with good delineation.*
grōp' ĭng, *feeling the way, as in darkness.*
grŭb' bĭng, *digging up by the roots.*
guar' an tee' (găr' ăn tē'), *to warrant, to make sure.*
guin' ea (gĭn' ė), *a gold coin of England worth about $5.00.*
gull (gŭl), *a kind of sea-fowl.*
gŭr' gling, *flowing in a broken, noisy current.*
gŭsh, *to pour forth freely, as a fluid.*
gyves (jīvz), *fetters, shackles.*

hăb ĭ tā' tion (-shŭn), *place of abode.*
hȧ bĭt' ŭ al (-al), *according to habit.*
hail' ed (hāld), *called to from a distance, accosted.*
hal le lu' iah (hăl lū' ya), *a term of praise.*
hal' low (hăl' lō), *to consecrate.*
Hăm, *son of Noah, ancestor of the African and Ethiopian races.*
Hămp' dĕn, Jŏhn, *an eminent English patriot, b. 1594; d. 1643.*
hăng' ĭng gär' dens (-d'ns), *the artificial gardens of ancient Babylon.*
Hăn' nĭ bal, *a Carthaginian general. See p. 62.*
har' bin ger (här' bĭn jẽr), *that which goes before telling of something else to come, a forerunner.*
härd' ĭ lỷ, *with great boldness, stoutly.*
har' ness (här' nĕs), *the military dress or armor of a man or horse.*
haugh' ty (hą' tỷ), *proud and disdainful.*
haunt (hąnt), *a place to which one frequently resorts.*
haz' ard (-ẽrd), *to chance, to risk, to peril.*
heath' er (hĕth' ẽr), *a low shrub growing in Scotland.*
Hĕl' ĭ cŏn (-kŏn), *a mountain in Greece, home of the Muses.*
Hĕl' lĕs pŏnt, *a narrow strait upon which Constantinople is situated.*
hĕl' mĕt, *defensive armor for the head.*
Hĕl vē' tian (-shŭn), *pertaining to the Swiss.*
hem' or rhage (hĕm' ȯr rȧj), *a discharge from the blood-vessels.*
Hĕn' ry (-rĭ), Pat' rick (păt' rĭk), *a celebrated patriot and orator; opposed the British Stamp Act, 1765; delegate to Am. Congress, 1774; advocated armed resistance to Great Britain, 1775; Governor, Virginia. See p. 113.*

28

He phes'ti on (hē fēs'tĭ ŏn), *a Macedonian honored by Alexander the Great.*
he red'I ta ry, *descending from an ancestor; as, to a child or heir.*
her'it age (hĕr'ĭt āj), *an inherited possession.*
Hi emp'sal, *a Numidian prince assassinated by Jugurtha.*
hire'ling, *one who is hired, a mercenary.*
hoard'ed (hōrd'ĕd), *laid up or stored; as, money.*
Hō'fer, Andreas, *a celebrated Tyrolese patriot; b. 1767; was betrayed and shot by the French at Mantua, 1810.* See p. 232.
hom'age (hŏm'āj), *reverence, respect.*
Ho rā'tio (-shō), *a fictitious person.*
horde (hōrd), *a company of wandering people without fixed homes.*
Hō'reb, *a mountain in Arabia famous in Bible history.*
ho ri'zon (hō rī'zŭn), *the line of seeming contact of earth and sky.*
ho san'na (hō zăn'nä), *an exclamation of praise to God.*
hos'tage (hŏs'tāj), *one delivered to an enemy as a pledge for the performance of promised acts.*
hov'er (hŭv'ĕr), *to hang over, as on wings.*
How'ard, John, *English philanthropist, b. 1726, d. 1790.*
hu mil'I ty, *humbleness of mind.*
Hŭn, *one of a warlike nomadic tribe of Northern Asia.*
Hŭn'ga ry, *a portion of the Austrian Empire, once an independent nation.*
hurl'ed (hŭrld), *thrown with violence.*
hush'ed (hŭsht), *silenced, calmed.*
Hy ge'ia (hī jē'yä), *fabled goddess of health.*
hy poc'ri sy (hĭ pŏk'rĭ sȳ), *deceitful appearance, false pretense.*

Ĭ bē'rus, *a river in Spain once separating possessions of Rome and Carthage.*
I cil'I us, *a Roman Tribune espoused to Virginia.*
Id'I ŏt, *a natural fool.*
ĭ dŏl'á try, *the worship of anything not God.*
ĭg nō'ble (-b'l), *base, not honorable.*
Ĭg'no min y, *shame, dishonor.*
ĭl lū'mĭ nāte, *to throw light upon, to supply with light.*
im ag'ĭ na ry (ĭm ăj-), *visionary, not real.*
im brue (ĭm brū'), *to wet, to soak, to saturate.*
im men'sĭ ty, *vastness.*
im mŏr'tăl ize, *to render immortal.*
im mū'nĭ ty, *freedom from obligation, a special privilege.*
im mū'ta ble (-b'l), *unchangeable.*
im pair' (ĭm pâr'), *to weaken, to lessen.*
im pĕnd'ing, *hanging over, threatening.*
im pĕn'e tra bly, *solidly, not to be penetrated.*
im pĕr cep'ti ble (-sĕp tĭ b'l), *very fine, not visible to the senses.*

im pĕt'ū ŏs'ĭ ty, *a great rushing, or violence.*
im'pĭ ous (-ŭs), *profane, irreverent.*
im plead'ed (ĭm plēd'ĕd), *sued at law.*
im pŏl'I tic (-tĭk), *not wise, ill adapted.*
im pose' (ĭm pōz'), *to lay on; as, an obligation or burden.*
im pre ca'tion (ĭm prē kā'shŭn), *a curse.*
im prŏmp'tū, *off-hand, without previous study.*
in cal'cu la ble (ĭn kăl'ku lå b'l), *beyond calculation.*
in can ta'tion (ĭn kăn tā'shŭn), *the act of enchanting, a song of enchantment.*
in cen'tive (ĭn sĕn'tĭv), *motive or spur to action.*
in'ci dent (ĭn'sĭ dent), *happening, an event.*
in cite'ment (ĭn sīt'ment), *motive, incentive.*
in con sĭd'er āte (ĭn kŏn-), *thoughtless.*
in con sist'en cy (ĭn kŏn sĭs'ten sȳ), *self-contradiction.*
in cum'bent (ĭn kŭm'bent), *lying or resting upon; as, a duty or obligation.*
in dĕm'nĭ ty (-tĭ), *to make good against loss.*
in er'tia (ĭn ĕr'shĭ ä), *inherent or acquired force.*
in ĕv'ĭ ta ble (-b'l), *unavoidable.*
in fec'tion (ĭn fĕk'shŭn), *communication of like qualities.*
in fĕst', *to trouble greatly, to harass.*
in flex'i ble (ĭn flĕks'ĭ b'l), *unalterable.*
in iq'ui ty (ĭn ĭk'wĭ tȳ), *wickedness.*
in'no cence (ĭn'nō sens), *freedom from sin; simplicity, purity.*
In ŏr'dĭ nāte, *excessive.*
in scrib'ed (ĭn skrībd'), *written on, engraved, drawn within.*
In sĭn ū ā'tion (-shŭn), *hint or allusion of a mean sort.*
Ĭn'so lent (-lent), *overbearing in manner.*
In sōōth', *a poetical expression like in truth or in fact.*
In spĭ rā'tion (-shŭn), *a highly exciting influence, moral or spiritual.*
In sta bĭl'ĭ ty, *want of stability or of firmness in purpose, changeableness.*
in'stinct (ĭn'stĭŋkt), *natural impulse.*
In stĭ tū'tion (-shŭn), *that which is founded or established by authority, and intended as permanent.*
In tĕg'rĭ ty, *uprightness.*
In ten'sive ly, *by increased degree or force.*
In tĕrn'al (-al), *interior, domestic as opposed to foreign.*
In tŏl'er a ble (-b'l), *unendurable.*
In trĕnch'ment (-ment), *a ditch with earthen parapet for defence.*
In tre pĭd'ĭ ty, *fearlessness, boldness.*
in trin'si cal (ĭn trĭn'sĭ kal), *essential.*
in twin'ed (ĭn twīnd'), *twined or twisted together.*
In ŭn'dā ted, *overflowed, deluged.*
In vād'er, *one who enters with hostile intent.*
In vi'ō la bly, *without profanation, breach, or failure.*

In volve', *to envelop, to entangle.*
ire (ir), *extreme anger, wrath.*
Ir rā'dī āte, *to emit rays, to shine.*
ir re sist' i bly (ir rē zĭst' ĭ bly̆), *with a power that cannot be overcome.*
ir re spect' ive (ĭr rē spĕk' tĭv), *not having regard to.*
I' ser ō' zĕr), *a river in Bavaria.* See p. 212.
is' o late (ĭ' sō lāt), *to place by itself.*
Is' ra el ite (ĭz' rā ĕl it), *a descendant of Jacob, a Jew.*

jack' al (jăk' al), *a wild animal which preys upon the dead.*
Ja' cob (jā' kŭb), (*the supplanter*) *son of the Hebrew patriarch Isaac.*
jeal' ous (jĕl' ŭs), *suspicious of rivals.*
Je hō' văh, *Hebrew name of the Supreme Being.*
Jē' na, *a town in Saxe Weimar, Germany, famous for the battle of Jena, 1806.* See p. 177.
jeop' ard y (jĕp' ĕrd y̆), *exposure to injury, peril.*
Jĕph' tha (-tha), *a Hebrew judge and warrior.*
jerk'ed (jẽrkt), *twitched suddenly.*
Jŏn' a thăn, *son of King Saul.* See p. 40.
Jôr' dan (-dẽn), *the most notable river in Palestine.*
Jō' sĕph, *son of Jacob and prime minister of Egypt.* See p. 19.
Jŏsh' ū ă, *successor to Moses.* See p. 32.
jū' bī lee (-lē), *a season of public joy and festivity.*
Jū' dah, *eldest son of Jacob, and founder of the Hebrew royal line ending with Christ.*
ju di' cial (jū dĭsh' al), *pertaining to a court of justice.*
ju di' cious (jū dĭ;h' ŭs), *according to good judgment.*
Jū' no, *a celebrated goddess among the ancients.*
jū ris pru' dence (-lens), *the science of law.*
jŭst ĭ fī' a ble (-b'l), *that may be vindicated on principle, defensible.*

Kā' dĕsh, *a famous halting-place of the Hebrews before they entered Canaan.* See p. 32.
Kham sin' (kăm sēn'), *a wind of the Sahara desert. Egypt.*
kins'man (kĭnz' man), *one related by blood.*
knave (nāv), *a dishonest person, a rogue.*
knell (nĕl), *the sound of a funeral bell.*
knit (nĭt), *to unite or interweave.*
knoll (nōl), *a small round hill.*

lā bō' rĭ ous (-ŭs), *requiring labor, toilsome.*
lā bûr' nŭm, *a small tree, native of the Alps.*
lack' ey (lăk' y̆), *an attending servant, a footman.*
La Fay ette', or La fay ette' de (dẹh lä fā yĕt'), *Marquis Gilbert Motier, soldier,*
statesman, patriot; b. Chavagnah, France, 1757; as friend of Washington, illustrious in arms and counsels, 1777-1781; the guest of America, 1824; d. 1834. See p. 131.
lăg' gard (-gerd), *one who lags or loiters.*
lair (lâr), *the den of a wild beast.*
lā mĕnt' ing, *bewailing, bemoaning.*
lan'guid (lăn' gwĭd), *indisposed to effort.*
lar' gess (lär' jĕs), *bounty distributed among the people.*
lā' tent (-tent), *hidden, secret.*
laud' a tō ry̆ (lad'-), *containing praise, tending to praise.*
launch (lanch), *to set afloat, as, a ship on the water; to start.*
lau' rels (la' rĕls), *honors, fame.*
lä' vä, *melted rock ejected from a volcano.*
league (lēg), *a union of two or more parties for mutual interest.*
Lĕb' ă nŏn, *a mountain of Palestine.*
lĕg' ă cy (-sy̆), *a gift by will.*
leg' end (lĕj' ĕnd), *a wonderful story from the past, a myth, a fable.*
leg' is la tive (lĕj' ĭs lā tĭv), *law making.*
lē gĭt' ĭ māte (lē jĭt'-), *according to law, genuine.*
lei' sure (lē' zhûr), *spare time.*
li bā' tion (-shŭn), *a liquor poured out as an offering to deity.*
li cen' tious (lĭ sĕn' shŭs), *wanton, impure.*
lĭn' den (-dĕn), *the lime-tree.*
lĭn' ĕ ă ment (-ment), *feature, outline; as, of the face.*
liq' uid (lĭk' wĭd), *a fluid; hence, flowing.*
lĭt' ter, *to scatter loosely; shreds, fragments, and the like.*
loathe (lōth), *to detest, to abhor.*
loath' some (lōth' sŭm), *disgusting.*
Locke (lŏk'), John, *eminent English philosopher and philanthropist; b. 1632, d. 1704* (*noticed on page 79*). *The following, eminent for patriotism, are also cited on the same page:* Cromwell, Oliver, *b. 1599, d. 1658;* Eliot, Sir John, *b. 1590, d. 1632* (*in the Tower of London*); Hampden, John, *b. 1594, d. 1634 killed in the battle of Edgefield*); Knox, John, *b. 1505, d. 1572;* Milton, John, *b. 1608, d. 1674;* Pym, John, *b. 1584, d. 1643;* Russell, Lord William, *b. 1639, d. 1683* (*beheaded*); Sydney (Sidney), Algernon, *b. 1622, d. 1683* (*beheaded*); Vane, Sir Henry, *b. 1612, d. 1662* (*beheaded*); Watts, Isaac, *b. 1674, d. 1748.*
Lŏn gī' nŭs, *a famous Greek critic, secretary of Queen Zenobia of Palmyra.* See p. 236.
lore (lōr), *learning, knowledge of letters.*
Lough Neagh (lŏk nā), *a famous lake in Ireland.* See p. 81.
low' er ing (lou' ẽr ĭng), *appearing dark or threatening.*
lū' mĭ nā ry̆, *any body that gives light, but chiefly one of the celestial orbs.*
lure (lūr), *to entice, to attract.*
lū' rĭd, *ghastly, livid.*
lus' cious (lŭsh' ŭs), *delicious.*
lus' trous (lŭs' trŭs), *bright, shining.*

lus′ ty, *stout, robust, vigorous.*
lux′u ry (lŭk′ shu ry̆), *high living in the gratification of acquired tastes.*
lyre (lir), *a kind of harp.*

Mac′ ca bees (măk′ kȧ bēz), *distinguished Hebrews of the centuries preceding the advent of Christ.* See p. 37.
Măc ĕ dō′ nĭ ȧ, *an empire founded B. C. 814, made famous by Philip and Alexander the Great.*
mag′ a zine′ (măg′ ȧ zēn′), *war supplies, the storehouse for supplies; also, a pamphlet periodically published, containing various writings.*
ma gi′ cian (mȧ jĭsh′ an), *one skilled in magic, an enchanter.*
Măg′ nȧ Char′ ta (kär′ tȧ), *the Bill of Rights forced from King John of England by his patriotic barons.* See pp. 120, 161.
măg nȧ nĭm′ ĭ ty̆, *generosity expressed in action.*
măg nĕt′ ĭc (-ĭk), *having attractive properties.*
măg nĭf′ ĭ cent (-sent), *splendid.*
Ma gyr (maj′ ẽr), *the Hungarian stock of which Kossuth was intensely proud.*
main tain′ed (mān tānd′), *upheld.*
mȧ jĕs′ tic (-tĭk), *grand, stately.*
Mal′ a chi (măl′ȧ ki), *the last Hebrew prophet.*
măn′ ĭ fĕst ly̆, *plainly, clearly.*
măn′ tling, *covering, cloaking.*
Măr′ ȧ thŏn, *ten miles from Athens, where Miltiades routed the Persians,* B. C. 490. See p. 200.
mar′ gin (mär′ jĭn), *small strip or border.*
märk, *to draw a visible line, to note closely.*
mar′red (märd), *defaced, impaired.*
märt, *a market.*
mar′ tial (mär′ shal), *warlike, military.*
mar′ tyr (mär′ tẽr), *one who suffers death for a cause.*
mär′ vĕl, *to wonder.*
mär′ vĕl lous (mär′ vĕl ŭs), *wonderful*
mȧ tẽr′ nĭ ty̆, *motherhood.*
mȧ tū′ rĭ ty̆, *ripeness, completeness.*
max′ im (măks′ ĭm), *a principle accepted as true.*
May′ flow er (mā′ flou ẽr), *the name of the ship that brought the Pilgrims to New England.* See p. 87.
maze (māz), *perplexity, a labyrinth.*
mead (mēd), *a meadow.*
mea′ ger (mē′ gẽr), *scant, poor, thin.*
mean′ est (mēn′ ĕst), *basest.*
me chan′ ic al (mē kăn′ ĭ kal), *acting as machinery; hence, from force of habit.*
Meck′ len burg (mĕk′ lĕn bûrg), *a town in North Carolina famous for its early declaration of independence of British rule.* See p. 109.
Mede (mēd), *a native of Media, Asia.*
Mŏ dē′ bȧ, Battle of. See p. 36.
me di oc′ ra cy (mē dĭ ŏk′ rȧ sy̆), *the rule of men of average or ordinary ability.*
med ĭ tā′ tion (-shŭn), *deliberate thought.*

meed (mēd), *reward, recompense.*
mĕm′ ō rȧ ble (-b′l), *worthy of remembrance.*
mĕn′ tal (-tal), *relating to the mind.*
merg′ ing (merj-), *blending as one.*
Mĕs′ ō pō tā′ mĭ′ ȧ, *the country watered by the Euphrates and the Tigris rivers.*
mete (mēt), *to measure.*
mē′ tĕ or (-ẽr), *a luminous body darting through the atmosphere.*
mē trŏp′ ō lĭs, *the chief or principal city.*
Mĭ cĭp′ sȧ, *king of Numidia, in Africa,* B. C. 119. See p. 74.
Mĭ′ dĭ ăn, *an inhabitant of Arabia.*
mien (mēn), *appearance, carriage.*
mĭl lĕn′ nĭ al (-al), *pertaining to the Millennium, or a thousand years.*
min′ ion (mĭn′ yŭn), *a servile follower of a prince.*
mĭs nō′ mẽr, *a misnaming.*
mĭs′ sile (mĭs′ sĭl), *something thrown; as, a dart or arrow.*
mite (mit), *a small coin; hence, anything small.*
Mō′ ăb, *a son of Lot.*
mŏd′ ĕl, *a pattern to be imitated.*
mō lĕst′, *to disturb.*
mon′ arch y (mŏn′ ärk y̆), *a government by one person, a kingdom.*
mŏn′ stẽr, *a deformed or unnatural creature.*
mōōd, *a condition of mind.*
Mos′ lem (mŏz′ lĕm), *a Mohammedan.*
mould (mōld), *to shape.*
mould′ er ing (mōld′ ẽr ĭng), *turning to dust.*
Mō′ zärt, Wolf gang, *a celebrated German musician,* b. 1756, d. 1791.
munch′ ing, *chewing eagerly, by great mouthfuls.*
mū′ ral (-ral), *pertaining to a wall.*
mū′ ral crown (kroun), *among the ancient Romans, a gold crown bestowed upon him who first mounted the wall of a besieged place and there lodged a standard.*
mûrk′ y̆, *dark, gloomy.*
Muse′ like (mūz′ līk), *like a Muse, poetic.*
mu si′ cian (mū zĭsh′ an), *one proficient in music.*
mŭs′ tẽr, *to enroll; as, to muster soldiers.*
mute (mūt), *dumb, silent.*
mū′ tĭ lā′ tĕd, *deprived of a limb or an essential part.*
mū′ tĭ nous (-nŭs), *disposed to defy authority.*
mu′tu al (mū′ tū al), *reciprocal.*
myr′ i ad (mĭr′ ĭ ad), *a great number.*
mys te′ ri ous (mĭs tē′ rĭ ŭs), *strange, not understood.*

na′ tion ăl′ ĭ ty (năsh ŭn-), *national character.*
naught (nat), *nothing.*
Năz′ ȧ rēne′, *a native of Nazareth.*
Nē′ bō, *a mountain where Moses was buried.* See p. 30.
nec′ ĕs sȧ ry̆ (nĕs-), *indispensable.*
nec′ tar (nĕk′ tẽr), *the drink of the gods; and hence, any sweet drink.*

SPECIAL VOCABULARY. 437

ne go'ti ate (nĕ gō' shĭ āt), *to hold intercourse with another respecting some proposed transaction.*
neigh (nā), *to whinny as a horse.*
neu trăl' ĭ ty (nū-), *the state of taking no part on either side.*
New ton, Isaac (nū' tŏn ī' zăk), *an English philosopher, b. 1642, d. 1727.* See p. 81.
nice (nīs), *discriminating, delicate, exact.*
nĭg' gard (-gẽrd), *miserly, mean.*
night' bead (nīt' bĕd), *dew-drop.*
Nĭn'ĕ vĕh, *joint capital with Babylon of Assyria.*
Nō' ăh, *saved the race from the deluge, about* B. C. 2350.
nŏd' dĭng, *moving the head up and down.*
nŏ măd' ic (-ĭk), *pastoral, wandering for pasturage.*
Nŭ mĭd' ĭ a (-a), *in Africa, the country of Micipsa.* See p. 74.
nur' ture (nûr' tûr), *to nourish, to care for, to train.*

ŏb' lĭ gȧ tō rȳ, *binding in law or conscience.*
ŏb lĭv' ĭ on (-ĭ ŏn), *state of being forgotten.*
ob scure (ŏb skūr'), *not plain, indistinct.*
ŏb' stȧ cle (k'l), *an obstruction.*
ŏb' vĭ ous (-ŭs), *plain, easily seen.*
of fĭ' ci ate (ŏf fĭsh' ĭ āt), *to act in the duties of an office.*
off' spring (ŏf'-), *a child, a descendant.*
ō' men, *a sign of some future event.*
ŏm nĭp' ō tent (-tent), *almighty.*
ŏn' sĕt, *an attack or assault.*
ŏr' a cle (-k'l), *an answer, by one inspired, to inquiries as to some future event.*
or daiu' ed (ôr dând'), *appointed, decreed.*
or' i flamme (ŏr' ĭ flăm), *the royal standard of France.*
o rĭg' i nal (ō rĭj' ĭ nȧl), *first, the first copy.*
Ō rī' ŏn, *a constellation in the northern sky.*
ŏr' nȧ ments (-ments), *decorations.*
Ō'tĭs, Jāmes, *a celebrated American orator of the Revolutionary period, b. Barnstable, Mass., 1725; d. 1783.*
ō' vẽrt, *open to view, apparent.*
ō' vẽr thrown' (-thrōn'), *defeated, ruined.*
ō' vẽr tures (-tūrz), *proposals made; as, overtures of peace.*

pa cif' ic (pȧ sĭf' ĭk), *conciliatory, peaceful.*
pag' eant (păj' ent), *a splendid show or parade.*
Păl' grāve, *a princely title.* See p. 168.
pall (pȧl), *a mantle for the dead.*
păl mĕt' tō, *the Southern palm.*
păm' per ed (-pẽrd), *fed to the full, glutted.*
pan a ce' a (păn ȧ sē' ȧ), *a cure-all, a solace for affliction.*
pan' e gyr ist (păn' ē jĭr ĭst), *one who bestows praise, or eulogizes.*
pa py' rus (pȧ pī' rŭs), *an Egyptian plant from which the ancients made their paper; hence, an old manuscript.*
păr' ȧ mount, *superior to all others.*
părch' ment (-ment), *a sheepskin prepared for writing upon.*

Pā' rĭ an (-an), *pertaining to Paros, an island famous for its marble.*
Păr nas' sian (-năsh' an), *pertaining to Mount Parnassus, in Greece.*
păr' rĭ cide (-sĭd), *one who murders a parent.*
pas' tor al (păs' tẽr al), *pertaining to shepherd life.*
pā' thŏs, *tender emotion expressed.*
pā' trĭ arch (-ärk), *the ruling head of a family, peculiar to the early Jews.*
pā' trĭ ŏt ĭsm (-ĭz'm), *love of country.*
pā' trŏn, *one who countenances and supports a person or a work.*
Paul' ŭs Ēmĭl' ĭ ŭs (păl-), *a Roman general, died* B. C. 168. See p. 51.
peal (pēl), *a loud sound; as, of a bell or of thunder.*
peas' ant (pĕz' ant), *a rustic, a countryman.*
pe cul' iar (pē kūl' yẽr), *odd, particular.*
pĕd' ant ry (-ant rȳ), *boastful display of learning.*
peer (pēr), *an equal.*
pĕlf, *ill-gotten gain.*
pĕn' ū rȳ, *extreme poverty.*
Pe' quod (pē' kwŏd), *name of an early Indian tribe of New England.*
perch' ed (pẽrcht), *placed on a perch, as a bird.*
pẽrĕn' nĭ ăl, *unceasing, never failing.*
pẽr fĭd' ĭ ous (-ŭs), *false to a trust.*
pẽr' fĭ dȳ, *violation of faith.*
Pẽr' ĭ cles (-klēz), *a distinguished Athenian who died about* B. C. 429.
pẽr' jur ed (pẽr' jûrd), *forsworn.*
per' ma nent (pẽr' mȧ nent), *fixed, durable.*
pẽr pĕt' ū al (-al), *never ceasing, endless.*
pẽr pĕt' ū ate (-āt), *to make perpetual.*
pẽr plex' (-plĕks), *to embarrass, to puzzle.*
pẽr vẽrt', *to corrupt.*
pĕt' rĕl, *a sea-fowl.*
pha' lanx (fā' lănks), *a Grecian military formation, in solid square.*
phan' ta sy (făn' tȧ sȳ), *a fancy of the imagination.*
Pha' ra oh (fā' rō), *name of the rulers of Egypt in the early ages.*
Phil' ip (fĭl' ĭp), *king of Macedon, father of Alexander the Great; died* B. C. 336.
Phil is' tines (fĭ lĭs' tĭns), *a warlike people in the early Hebrew times.*
phrase (frāz), *a short sentence or expression.*
phys' ic al (fĭz' ĭ kal), *pertaining to the body, or to material things.*
pil' lage (pĭl' lāj), *to plunder.*
pīl' lar ed (-lẽrd), *supported by pillars.*
Pĭl' lars (-lẽrz) of Her' cu les (hẽr' kŭ lēz), *name given the opposing bluffs at the entrance of the Mediterranean Sea.*
pine (pīn), *to languish, to waste away with longing.*
pin' ion (pĭn' yŭn), *to confine, to shackle.*
pin' ion (pĭn' yŭn), *a wing.*
pĭs' ton (-tŭn), *a short solid cylinder which exactly fits the cavity of a pump, and works up and down in it, used on engines, etc.*
pĭt' tance (-tans), *a small amount.*

plăn' ĕt, *a heavenly body which revolves around the sun.*
pla teau' (plă tō'), *a level, elevated tract of land.*
pleas' ant ry (plĕz-), *gayety, lively talk.*
pledge (plĕj), *a security for the performance of an act.*
Ple' ia des (plē' ya dēz), *seven stars in the constellation of Taurus.*
plŭmp, *of full form, fat.*
plŭn' der, *stolen property, booty.*
pō' e sy, *poetry.*
pō' lar (-ler), *pertaining to the poles of the earth.*
pol i ti' cian (pŏl ĭ tĭsh' an), *one versed in politics and policy.*
pŏmp, *great show or parade.*
Pom' pey (pŏm' pĭ), *a distinguished Roman, died* B. C. 48. See p. 68.
por' cu pine (pôr' kū pĭn), *a small animal furnished with quills which it can erect at pleasure in self-defence.*
pore (pōr), *a minute opening in the skin.*
por tĕnd' ed, *foreshadowed, prophesied.*
pŏst, *a military station.*
pō' tent (-tent), *powerful.*
pounce (pouns), *to fall suddenly upon and seize with the claws, as the hawk.*
prae' tor (prē' tŏr), *an ancient Roman judge.*
prai' rie (prā' rĭ), *a tract of land, mostly level, covered with tall, coarse grass.*
prec' i pice (prĕs' ĭ pĭs), *a steep, perpendicular descent.*
pre cip' i tate (-sĭp' ĭ tāt), *to press with eagerness.*
pre cise' ly (-sīs' lĭ), *exactly.*
pre-ĕm' i nent (-nent), *eminent above others.*
preen (prēn), *to trim or dress with the beak, as the feathers.*
pref' ace (prĕf' ăs), *preliminary remarks.*
pre fer' ment (-ment), *advancement.*
prĕg' nant (-nant), *fruitful, teeming with future results.*
prej' u dice (prĕd' jū dĭs), *a bias for one as against another.*
prĕl' ate (-lāt), *a bishop of the church.*
pre' ma ture (-tūr), *too soon.*
prĕm' I ses (-ĕz), *in logic, the first propositions from which a conclusion is drawn; a building and grounds.*
pre rŏg' a tive (-tĭv), *an exclusive privilege or right.*
pre sump' tive (prē zŭmp' tĭv), *grounded upon probable evidence, arrogant.*
pre vail' (prē vāl'), *to succeed.*
prey (prā), *that which is seized, or may be seized by violence, to be devoured.*
prin' ci ples (prĭn' sĭ p'lz), *admitted truths.*
pris' oner (prĭz' 'n er), *one deprived of liberty.*
pri vā' tion (-shŭn), *absence of what is necessary for ordinary comfort.*
proc' ess (prŏs' ĕs), *method of action.*
proc' la ma' tion (prŏk' la mā' shŭn), *a public, official declaration.*
pro cur' ed (prō kūrd'), *obtained.*
pro di' gious (prō dĭj' ŭs), *huge, wonderful.*

pro fane' (prō fān'), *irreverent, secular.*
prog' e ny (prŏj' ĕ nĭ), *children, lineage.*
prone (prōn), *inclined.*
prŏp a găn' dĭst, *one who promotes a system of principles.*
pro pi' tious (prō pĭsh' ŭs), *favorable.*
prŏs' trate (-trāt), *lying at length, completely down.*
prō tēst', *to declare against.*
Prŏv' I dence (-dens), *Divine Superintendence.*
prŏv' ince (-Ins), *a country belonging to a kingdom or state.*
prow' ess (prou' ĕs), *bravery, valor.*
prowl (proul), *to rove around for prey or plunder.*
prun' ed (prŭnd), *trimmed.*
Pu' nic (pū' nĭk) War, *between Rome and Carthage,* 264 B. C.
purg' ed (pûrjd), *purified, cleansed.*
Pū' rĭ tan (-tan), *a religious dissenter in the time of Queen Elizabeth of England, and later.*
Pȳm, Jōhn, *eminent English statesman,* b. 1584 ; d. 1643. See p. 79.

quail (kwāl), *to fail in spirit.*
quaint (kwānt), *odd, fanciful.*
quench (kwĕnch), *to extinguish; as, to quench a fire.*
quick' en ing (kwĭk' 'n Ing), *animating.*
quiv' er (kwĭv' ẽr), *to tremble.*

răb' Id, *mad, raging mad.*
rack (răk), *an ancient instrument of torture.*
rā' dĭ ance (-ans), *brightness.*
răk' Ing, *scraping; as, with a rake.*
răl' ly ing, *assembling, restoring to order.*
răm' părts, *fortifications.*
rănk, *grade or position.*
rănk' ly, *with vigorous growth.*
rap' ine (răp' ĭn), *the act of plundering, spoliation.*
răpt, *enveloped, infolded.*
răp' tūr ous (-ŭs), *ecstatic, transporting; as, rapturous joy.*
rare (râr), *uncommon.*
ra' tion al (răsh' ŭn al), *reasonable.*
Rat' is bon (răt' ĭz bŏn), *a town in Bavaria, Germany, famous in Napoleon's battle history.* See p. 209.
rav' age (răv' ăj), *to despoil or lay waste.*
rave (rāv), *to wander in mind.*
ra' ven (rā' v'n), *a black bird of the crow species.*
rav' en ous (răv' 'n ŭs), *devouring with eagerness, eager for prey.*
rav' ish ed (răv' Isht), *delighted beyond expression.*
realm (rĕlm), *region, country, domain.*
rear' ed (rērd), *lifted up, brought up, educated.*
re buff' (-bŭf), *a sudden check.*
re cip' ro cal (rē sĭp' rō kal), *mutual, giving and receiving.*
reck (rĕk), *to regard, to mind, to care.*
rec' om pense (rĕk' ŏm pens), *compensation, reward.*

Red' Branch, *an ancient order among the Irish.* See p. 80.
re deem'ed (rē dēmd'), *ransomed; hence, reformed.*
re doubt' (rē dout'), *a kind of fortification.*
reek'ing (rēk'ĭng), *steaming, emitting vapor.*
reel'ing (rēl'ĭng), *staggering.*
re förm'er, *one who effects a reformation.*
ref'uge (rĕf'ūj), *a protecting shelter.*
re gen'er a ted (rē jĕn'ẽr ā tĕd), *born again, renewed.*
reg'is ter (rĕj'ĭs tẽr), *an accurate record.*
Reg'u lŭs, *a Roman general and patriot tortured to death by the Carthaginians* B. C. 251. See p. 56.
re hearse' (rē hẽrs'), *to recite, to repeat.*
reign (rān), *rule, to rule.*
re ject'ed (rē jĕk'tĕd), *cast off, thrown away.*
re lease' (rē lēs'), *to set free.*
re lig'ious (rē lĭj'ŭs), *pertaining to religion, godly.*
re lin'quish, (rē lĭŋ'kwĭsh), *to leave, to give up.*
rem'nant (-nant), *that which is left.*
re morse'less (rē môrs'lĕs), *cruel without remorse.*
re mote' (rē mōt'), *distant.*
ren'dez vous (rĕn'dē vōō), *an appointed place of meeting.*
rend'ing, *tearing apart by force.*
re pĕll'ĭng, *resisting successfully.*
Reph'i dim (rĕf'ĭ dĭm), *a place famed for a victory of the Hebrews over King Amalek.* See p. 33.
re plĕn'ĭsh ĭng, *supplying what has been wasted or spent.*
rĕp rē sent'a tive (-zĕnt'a tĭv), *one who acts for, and in the place of, others.*
re press', *to put down, to subdue.*
re pŭg'nant (-nant), (followed by to) *opposed, contrary.*
re puls'ed (rē pŭlst'), *repelled, driven back.*
re sem'ble (rē zĕm'b'l), *to bear the likeness of.*
re sourc'es (rē sōrs'ĕz), *reserve supplies.*
re splĕn'dent (-dent), *bright with luster.*
re spŏn'sĭ bĭl'ĭ tẙ, *the state of being accountable or answerable.*
rĕs to rā'tion (-shŭn) *replacing to a former condition.*
re strict'ed (re strĭkt'ĕd), *limited, restrained.*
res ur rec'tion (rĕz ŭr rĕk'shŭn), *return of the dead from the grave.*
re tärd'ĭng, *delaying, making to go slow.*
re tôrt', *a severe reply.*
re trĕnch', *to lessen, to curtail, to live at less expense.*
rĕt rĭ bū'tion (-shŭn) *fitting reward or punishment.*
re turn'ed (rē tûrnd'), *sent back, restored.*
rĕv ē lā'tion (-shŭn), *the disclosure of what had been unknown.*
re veng'ed (rē vĕnjd'), *spitefully punished in return for an injury.*
rĕv'ẽr ence (-ens), *respect coupled with fear, veneration.*
re vers'ed (rē vẽrst'), *turned back, overthrown, completely changed.*
rē vī v'al (-al), *return of activity.*
rē vŏlt, *a casting off of allegiance to one's government.*
Rhine'land (rin'lănd), *the borders of the river Rhine.*
rife (rīf), *prevailing, abounding.*
right (rīt), *just claim or privilege.*
rig'id (rĭj'ĭd), *stiff; hence, exact.*
ri'val ry (-val ry), *competition, a strife to obtain an object another is pursuing.*
roam (rōm), *to wander.*
rob'ed (rōbd), *dressed in a robe; hence, with elegance.*
rō mān'tic (-tĭk), *wild, fanciful, unusual.*
roof'-tree (-trē), *a sheltering tree.*
ro'se ate (rō'zē āt), *resembling a rose in color or fragrance, blooming.*
rous'ed (rouzd), *suddenly awakened to action.*
rou tine' (rōō tēn'), *a fixed way.*
ruf'fian (rŭf'yan), *a brutal fellow.*
rŭg'ged, *rough, uneven, hard.*
rŭsh'ing, *hurrying violently.*
Rus'sell (rŭs'el), William, *a distinguished English patriot; born* 1639, *beheaded* 1683.
rus'tic (rŭs'tĭk), *rural, unpolished.*
ruth'less (-lĕs), *pitiless, without mercy.*

Sā'bä, *an island of the West Indies.* See p. 98.
Sa'bines (sā'bīnz), *an ancient tribe merged with the Romans by forced marriages.*
sā'bẽr, *a sword for mounted men.*
sā'ble (-b'l), *black.*
sack'cloth (săk'klŏth), *rough cloth worn in mourning.*
sack'ed (săkt), *pillaged.*
sac'ra ments (săk'ra ments), *religious ordinances.*
sa'cred (sā'krĕd), *holy, consecrated.*
sa gā'cious (-shŭs), *wise, or acute in thought and action.*
sage (sāj), *a wise man.*
Sa gŭn'tŭm, *a city in Spain famous for the contests between Scipio and Hannibal.* See p. 63.
Sā'lem, *a fond Hebrew epithet for Jerusalem.* See p. 45, 48.
săl'ly, *a rush of besieged troops upon the besiegers.*
săl'ū tā rẙ, *beneficial, wholesome.*
sanc'ti fied (săŋk'tĭ fīd), *made holy.*
sanc'tion (săŋk'shŭn), *approval.*
sanc'tū ā rẙ (săŋk-, *a holy place for divine worship.*
săn'dal (-dal), *a kind of shoe protecting the sole of the foot.*
san'guine (săŋ'gwĭn), *ardent, confident.*
sap'phire (săf'ĩr), *a precious stone of a blue color.*
Sär dĭn'ĭ a (-a), *an Italian state taken by the Romans from the Carthaginians.* See p. 63.
sā'trap, *a Persian governor.*
sa'tyr (sā'tẽr), *a mythological monster, part man and part goat.*

Saul (sal), *the first Hebrew king, 1095-1056, B. C.* See p. 40.
sā' vor (-vēr), *taste, flavor, odor.*
sā' vor, *to have the appearance of.*
Sax' on (săks' ŭn), *an English element derived from the German invasion.*
scab' bard (skăb' bērd), *a sword sheath.*
scale (skāl), *to climb, to surmount.*
scales (skālz), *balances for determining weights.*
scalp (skălp), *the skin on the top of the head.*
scant' i ly (skănt' ĭ lў), *sparingly.*
scathe (skāth), *to injure, to waste.*
scep' ter (sĕp' tēr), *an official emblem of authority.*
sci en tif' ic (si ĕn tĭf' ĭk), *according to the rules of science.*
sci' on (sī' ŭn), *a young shoot; hence, son or child.*
Scip' i o (sĭp' ĭ ō), *a Roman general victorious over Hannibal.* See p. 65.
scoop'ed (skōōpt), *taken out or up, as with a scoop.*
scope (skōp), *space, range of action or ability.*
scorn (skôrn), *to despise, to disdain.*
scourge (skûrj), *a harsh whip; hence, to whip, to punish.*
scowl (skoul), *a wrinkling of the brows in displeasure.*
scru' pu lous (skru'pŭ lŭs), *very particular or exact.*
scru' ti ny (skru' tĭ nў), *close search or inquiry.*
sculp' tor (skŭlp' tēr), *one who carves images in stone or wood.*
se ces' sion (sĕ sĕsh' ŭn), *the act of withdrawing from fellowship.*
se clud' ed (sĕ klŭd' ĕ l), *retired, separated from others.*
sect (sĕkt), *a body of persons holding a special religious belief.*
sec' u lar (sĕk' ū lēr), *worldly, not spiritual.*
se du' cer (sĕ dū' sēr), *one that entices another from virtue.*
seer (sēr), *a prophet, one who foresees future events.*
seeth' ing (sēth' ĭng), *boiling.*
self' a base' ment (-ment), *humiliation from a sense of shame.*
sen' sĭ bĭl' ĭ tў, *delicacy of feeling.*
sen' tient (sĕn' shent), *having power to think.*
sep' ul cher (sĕp' ŭl kēr), *a grave, a tomb.*
se rēne' (-rēn'), *calm, unruffled.*
serf, *one whose service belongs to a certain estate.*
se' ries (sē' rēz), *a succession of similar things.*
ser' ried (sĕr' rĭd), *compact, dense.*
serv' ile (-ĭl), *slavish.*
serv' ĭ tude (-tūd), *bondage, slavery.*
ses' sion (sĕsh' ŭn), *the time or term of sitting of a body.*
sev' er ed (sĕv' ērd), *parted by force, cut off.*
shaft, *an arrow or spear.*

shal' low (shăl' lō), *not deep.*
shape' less (shāp' lĕs), *without regular form.*
Shăr' on (-ŭn), *a beautiful valley in Palestine famous for its roses.*
shat' ter ed (shăt' tērd), *broken in pieces, disordered.*
sheathe (shēth), *to put in a sheath.*
shel' ter ed (shĕl' tērd), *protected, covered.*
Shi' loh (shi' lō), *site of the Hebrew tabernacle for more than 300 years; also, a title of the promised Messiah.* See p. 45.
shred, *a fragment, a piece.*
shrewd (shrud), *keen, discerning, artful.*
shrine, *a tomb or altar, a sacred place.*
shrĭnk, *to recoil, to draw back.*
shriv' el ed (shrĭv' l'd), *shrunk, drawn up into wrinkles.*
shroud, *covering for the dead.*
shŭt' tle (-t'l), *an instrument carrying swiftly the thread in the act of weaving.*
sic' kle (sĭk' k'l), *a reaping-hook for cutting grain or grass.*
Si' don, *once the seaport of Damascus, and very wealthy.* See p. 71.
sĭg nĭf' ĭ cant (-kant), *bearing a meaning.*
sin' ews (sĭn' ūz), *tendons that give strength.*
sire (sīr), *father, ancestor.*
Sĭr' ĭ us, *the "dog star."* See p. 237.
sĭ z' ĭng, *arranging by size; as, a company of soldiers.* See p. 352.
slack' en (slăk' 'n), *to relax, to loosen.*
slaugh' ter (slạ' tēr), *to kill, to butcher.*
slōth, *sluggishness, laziness.*
smite (smīt), *to strike, to blast, to destroy.*
snare (snâr), *a trap.*
soar (sōr), *to rise on wings.*
sō brī' ē tў, *soberness, seriousness.*
so ci' e ty (sō sī' ē tў), *company, fellowship.*
Sŏc' ra tes (sŏk' ra tēs), *the most celebrated philosopher of Athens; forced to take poison,* B. C. 400.
Sŏd' om, *a city of Palestine destroyed by fire from heaven* B. C. 1898. See p. 43.
so' lace (sŏl' ăs), *that which comforts or soothes.*
so lic' it ed (sō lĭs' ĭt ĕd), *earnestly asked or requested.*
sŏl' ĭ tā rў, *lonely, single.*
solve (sŏlv), *to explain.*
sŏm' ber, *gloomy, dark.*
so nō' rous (-rŭs), *sounding clear.*
sôr' dĭd, *stingy, mean.*
sov' er eign ty (sŭv' ēr ĭn tў), *supremacy.*
span'ned (spănd), *measured; as, with the hand.*
Spär' ta (-ta), *a famous Greek state.* See p. 69.
spe' cies (spē' shēz), *sort or kind.*
spe cif' ic (spē sĭf' ĭk), *definite, particular.*
spec' i men (spĕs' ĭ men), *a sample representing the whole.*
spec' ta cle (spĕk' tă k'l), *a show or sight.*
spell (spĕl), *a charm.*
spells (spĕlz), *seasons of attack; as, of sickness.*
spĕnt, *exhausted.*
sphere (sfēr), *range of action or influence.*

Spice Isles (spīs īlz), *islands in the East India Seas, famous for spices.* See p. 98.
splen' dor (-dẽr), *great brightness and display.*
spoil' ed (spoild), *rendered useless, ruined.*
spŏn tā' ne ous (-ŭs), *proceeding from natural impulse.*
sports' man (-man), *a hunter, one who takes pleasure in hunting.*
spray (sprā), *a kind of mist where water flies in small particles.*
spŭrn, *to reject with scorn.*
squad' ron (skwŏd' rŭn), *a body of cavalry, or fleet of ships.*
stag' es (stāj' ĕs), *scenes, or successive periods or degrees.*
stăg' ger Ing (reeling, walking unsteadily.*
stake (stāk), *a mark or limit.*
stake, *a bet or wager.*
stalk (stak), *to walk with stiff and haughty step.*
stamp' ed (stămpt), *strongly marked.*
stănd' ard (-ẽrd), *a rule or guide, a nation's banner.*
stär'-span' gled (spăng' g'ld), *spangled or covered with stars.*
sta' tion (stā' shŭn), *position or post assigned.*
stat' ure (stăt' ŭr), *natural height.*
stăt' utes (-ŭts), *the enacted laws of a state.*
staunch (stănch), *steady, strong.*
stead' fast ly (stĕd' fàst lỹ), *firmly, constantly.*
stealth' y (stĕlth' ỹ), *unperceived, unnoticed.*
steep' ing (stēp' ing), *soaking, imbuing.*
stĕm, *to make progress against, to check.*
stē' rē ō typ ed (-tīpt), *formed in a fixed, unchangeable manner.*
stẽrn, *severe, harsh.*
stī' fling, *suffocating.*
stir' ring (stẽr' ring), *putting in motion.*
stocks (stŏks), *a machine for confining one's limbs.*
stō' ic (-ĭk), *one who takes life's incidents without feeling.*
strain (strān), *a violent effort; a part of a tune.*
strănd, *the sea-shore.*
stra te' gic al (stra tē' jĭ kal), *pertaining to strategy, or military science.*
strĕss, *force, importance.*
stretch' ed (strĕ ht), *drawn out in length.*
strick' en (strĭk' 'n), *struck down, worn out, as with age.*
stroke (strōk), *a blow.*
stroke, *to rub gently.*
struc' ture (strŭk' tŭr), *a building of some size.*
stŭbb' born (-bẽrn), *obstinate, unyielding.*
stū pĭd' ĭ tỹ, *mental dullness.*
sŭb du' ed -dūd), *conquered.*
sŭb jū gā' tion (-shŭn), *the act of subduing another.*
sŭb lime' (-līm'), *grand and lofty.*
sŭb ŏr' dĭ nate (-năt), *inferior in importance.*
sŭb sĭst', *to live.*

sŭb' stance (-stans), *the essential part of anything.*
sŭb stăn' tial (-shal), *real, solid.*
sŭb' stĭ tū tĕd, *put in the place of another.*
sub' tile (sŭt' t'l), *fine, artful, cunning.*
sŭb vẽr' sion (-shŭn), *overthrow.*
sŭc' cor (sŭk' kẽr), *aid, deliverance from distress.*
sŭf' fer ance (-ans), *endurance, toleration.*
suf fice' (sŭf fīz'), *to be enough, to content.*
suf fi' cient ly (-fĭsh' ent lỹ), *enough.*
sŭf' frage (sŭf' fràj), *a vote, a voice in an election.*
sŭl' trỹ, *very hot and oppressive.*
sŭm' ma rỹ, *an abridged account.*
sŭmp' tū ous (-ŭs), *costly, splendid.*
sŭn' dered (-dẽrd), *divided, parted.*
sū pẽr fĭ' cĭ tỹ, *excess.*
sū pẽr năt' ū ral (-ral), *miraculous.*
sū pẽr nū' mer à rỹ, *more than needed.*
sū pẽr sede' (-sēd), *to take the place of.*
sū pẽr stī' tion (-stĭsh' ŭn), *absurd religious belief.*
sŭp' ple ment (-ment), *an additional part.*
sŭp' plĭ ant (-ant), *a humble petitioner.*
sŭp plĭ ca' tion (-kā' shŭn), *entreaty, prayer.*
sŭp press' (-prĕs'), *to subdue, to stifle.*
sū preme' (-prēm'), *above all others.*
surge (sŭrj), *to swell and roll, as waves.*
sŭr mount' ĕd, *overcome.*
sŭr vīv' ing, *outliving.*
sus pect' (sŭs pĕkt'), *to mistrust.*
swains (swānz), *rustic lovers.*
sweep (swēp), *to brush along, to pass with pomp.*
swĕll, *to increase, to grow larger.*
swīng' ing, *vibrating.*
swōop, *to pounce upon and seize.*
sym' bol (sĭm' bŏl), *a sign or emblem.*
sym' me try (sĭm' me trỹ), *harmony of proportion.*

tăb' er na cle (-k'l), *a tent in which the Jews worshipped, and hence a place of worship.*
tac' it (tăs' ĭt), *silent, implied but not expressed.*
tac' tic al (tăk' tĭ kal), *pertaining to military science.*
taint' ings (tānt' ings), *stains, spots.*
tal' is man (tăl' ĭz man), *something that produces marvellous effects.*
Tar' quin (tär' kwĭn), *name of a royal family of ancient Rome.*
tăt tōō', *a drum-beat or trumpet call, the soldier's call to retire at night.*
taunts (tant), *derides, mocks, jeers.*
taw' ny (tă' nỹ), *of a yellowish-dark color.*
teem' ing (tēm' ing), *being full, fruitful.*
Tĕll, Wĭl' liam, *a famous Swiss patriot.* See p. 232.
tĕm' pẽr à ment (-ment), *the peculiar mental and physical character of an individual.*
tĕm' pẽr ate (-āt), *moderate, not excessive.*
tem' pẽr ed (tĕm' pẽrd), *brought to a proper temper or humor.*
tĕm' p˘ à rỹ, *for the time being only.*

tĕn' dẽr nĕss, *sensibility of the softer feelings.*
tĕn' e ment (-ment), *dwelling, abode.*
tẽr' mī nal (-nal), *forming the end or extremity.*
tẽr mī nā' tion (-shŭn), *the end.*
tex' ture (tĕks' tūr), *the interwoven threads, as of a garment.*
Thẽr mŏp' ў lae (-lē), *a pass in Greece where, B. C. 480, 300 Spartans withstood the vast army of Xerxes.*
thor' ough ness (thŭr' ō nĕ s), *completeness.*
thrall (thrạl), *a slave.*
threnes (thrēnz), *dirges, grief-songs.*
thrĕsh' ōld, *the door-sill, entrance.*
thrĭft, *frugality, good husbandry.*
thrĭll' ing, *intensely exciting.*
throng' ed (thrŏngd), *crowded.*
thŭd, *a dull sound.*
ties tīz), *bonds or obligations.*
tinc' tur ed (tĭnk' tūrd), *tinged as with something foreign.*
tŏl' ẽr ate (-āt), *to suffer to be or to be done.*
tŏm' a hawk (-hạk), *a war hatchet used by American Indians.*
tongue (tŭng), *language, from tongue, the organ of speech.*
tŏr' ment, *extreme pain, anguish.*
tŏr nā' dō, *a whirling tempest.*
tŏr' rent (-rent), *a rushing stream.*
tŏr' rid, *very hot, as the Torrid Zone.*
tor' tu ous (tŏr' tū ŭs), *winding, twisting.*
tor' ture (tŏr' tūr), *extreme pain, agony.*
toss' ed (tŏst), *thrown with a jerk.*
tŏt' tẽr ing, *shaking as if to fall, threatening to fall.*
touch' stone (tŭch' stōn), *any test by which the qualities of a thing are tried.*
tow' er ing (tou' ẽr ing), *rising aloft.*
tra' ces (trā' sĕz), *marks or tracks left by anything in passing.*
trade (trād), *barter, the business of exchanges.*
tra dī' tion a ry (-dĭsh' ŭn ā rў), *transmitted from age to age by word of mouth.*
tra duc' ed (trā dūst'), *misrepresented, defamed.*
trail' ed (trāld), *dragged behind.*
trai' tor (trā' tẽr), *one who is untrue to his country.*
trăm' pled (-p'ld), *trod on, trodden under foot.*
tran' quil (trăŋ' kwĭl), *calm, undisturbed.*
trăn scend' ent (-sĕnd' ent), *surpassing others.*
trăns fõr mā' tion (-shŭn), *change of form.*
trăns mĭt', *to pass from one to another.*
trăns mū tā' tion (-shŭn), *change of nature or substance.*
trăns' ports, *raptures, ecstasies.*
treach' er ous (trĕch' ẽr ŭs), *faithless, traitorous.*
trea' ty (trē' tў), *an agreement formally made between nations.*
tre mĕn' dous (-dŭs), *astonishing by its force or extent.*
trĕm' ū lous (-lŭs), *trembling, quavering.*
tress' es (trĕs' ĕz), *ringlets or locks of hair.*
tri bū' nal (-nal), *a court of justice.*

trĭb' une (trĭb' ūn), *a Roman officer.*
trite (trīt), *worn out, common.*
tri um' phant (trī ŭm' fant), *victorious.*
trīv' ī al (-al), *trifling.*
tro' phies (trō' fĭz), *memorials of victory.*
trough (trŏf), *a hollow wooden vessel, the hollow of the waves.*
troupe (trōōp), *a company, generally of actors or musicians.*
truce (trŭs), *a temporary cessation of hostilities.*
trŭst, *confidence, reliance.*
Tū' bal Cain (kān), *the first skilled worker in brass and iron.* See p. 178.
type (tīp), *a pattern or emblem.*
ty' rant (tī' rant), *a despot, an oppressor.*

ū nā nĭm' ĭ tў, *agreement in opinion.*
ū nắn' ĭ mous (-mŭs), *being of one mind.*
un a vail' ing (ŭn a vāl' ing), *ineffectual.*
ŭn bī' ased (bī' ạst), *impartial.*
ŭn chain' ed (-chānd'), *unbound.*
ŭn con dī' tion al ly (-kŏn dĭsh' ŭn al lў), *without conditions.*
ŭn con fin' ed (-kŏn fīnd'), *free from restraint.*
ŭn con' quer ed (-kŏn' kẽrd), *unsubdued.*
ŭn con strain' ed (kŏn strānd'), *free from constraint.*
ŭn couth' (-kōōth'), *odd, not refined.*
ŭn daunt' ed (-dạnt' ĕd), *not disheartened.*
ŭn de nī' a ble (-b'l), *that cannot be denied.*
ŭn drain' ed (-drānd'), *not freed from water, unexhausted.*
ŭn ẽrr' ing, *without error.*
ŭn ex ẽrt' ĕd (ŭn ĕgz-), *not put forth, not called into action.*
ŭn flĭnch' ing, *not shrinking.*
ŭn fōld' ing, *revealing, making known.*
ŭn gall' ed (ŭn gald'), *unchafed.*
ŭn grudg' ing (-grŭj' ing), *freely giving.*
u nique' (ū nēk'), *odd, singular.*
u' nĭ son (ū' nĭ sŭn). *harmony, agreement.*
ŭn re mĭt' ting, *continued, incessant.*
ŭn rī' val ed (-rī' vald), *without a rival.*
un scath' ed (ŭn skāthd'), *uninjured.*
ŭn sul' li ed (-sŭl' lĭd), *not tarnished.*
ŭn trăm' mel ed (-mĕld), *not confined, not shackled.*
ŭn veer' ing (-vẽr' ing), *unchanging.*
ŭrn, *a kind of vase largest in the middle.*
u surp' er (ū zŭrp' ẽr), *one who seizes the power or property of another without right.*

val' iant (văl' yant), *brave in action.*
van' quish ed (văn' kwĭsht), *conquered.*
vă.' sal (-sal), *a bondsman.*
vaunt' ing (vănt' ing), *boasting, bragging.*
vē' lĕ mence (-mens), *great force, ardor.*
vĕn' ẽr a ble (-b'l), *worthy of veneration.*
vĕn' om (-ŭm), *poison.*
vẽr' dant (-dant), *green, fresh.*
vẽr' ĭ ĕst, *to the highest degree.*
Vẽr' non (-nŭn), Mount. See p. 133.
Ver sailles' (vẽr sālz'), *a once royal suburb of Paris.* See p. 176.
ves' pers (vĕs' pẽrz), *religious evening service.*

vest' ment (-ment), *garment, a covering.*
vet' er an (-an), *one old in service.*
vi' bra ted, *quivered, moved to and fro.*
vice (vis), *sin, depravity.*
vi' cious (vĭsh' ŭs), *ugly in spirit.*
vi cis' si tude (vĭ sĭs' sĭ tūd), *change, revolution; as, in human affairs.*
vil' lain (vĭl' lĭn), *a scoundrel.*
vine' clad (vīn' klăd), *covered with vines.*
vĭn' dĭ cate (-kāt), *to justify and defend.*
vir' tu ous (vẽr' tū ŭs), *morally good.*
vis' age (vĭz' ȧj), *the face, the countenance.*
vis' ion (vĭzh' ŭn), *something imagined, though not real.*
vi' tal (-tal), *necessary to life, highly important.*
vo ca' tion (vō kā' shŭn), *occupation.*
vŏl' ley (-lў), *a discharge from many small arms at once.*
Vol taire de (dĕh vŏl tēr'), François Marie Aronet, *a celebrated French author and infidel, b. 1694, d. 1778.*
vŏl' ŭn tā' rĭ lў, *of one's own choice.*
vo lup' tu ous (vō lŭp' tū ŭs), *given to sensual pleasures.*
vō' tā ries (-rīz), *those devoted to some particular worship or pursuit.*
vouch safe' (-sāf'), *to condescend, to grant.*
voy' age (voi' ȧj), *a journey by sea.*
vul' gar (vŭl' gẽr), *common, low, unrefined.*

wail' ing (wāl' ĭng), *lamenting with groans.*
Wallace (wŏl' lss), Sir William, *a Scotch hero, deliverer of his country; b. at Ellerslie, Scotland, 1270, executed by King Edward I., 1305.*
waste (wāst), *loss, useless expense.*
watch' fire (wŏch' fīr), *a fire used by a watch or a guard.*
wax' ed (wăkst), *increased, grown larger.*
weal (wēl), *welfare, well-being.*
well' ing (wĕl' ĭng), *issuing forth, as water from the earth, flowing.*
wĭl' dẽr nĕss, *a waste of uninhabited land or desert.*
wĭth' ẽr ĭng, *causing to shrink or fade.*
won' drous (wŭn' drŭs), *marvellous.*
wrest (rĕst), *to snatch by force.*
writhes (rīths), *twists so as to distort.*

yearn' ing (yẽrn' ĭng), *longing with intense desire.*

zeal (zēl), *ardor in the pursuit of anything.*
Zi' on (-ŭn), *a sacred name for Jerusalem, the Hebrew capital.* See p. 48.
zone (zōn), *a term used by military writers, meaning a belt or field of operations.*

www.ingramcontent.com/pod-product-compliance
Lightning Source LLC
Chambersburg PA
CBHW020524300426
44111CB00008B/538